Just Boris

Just Boris

The Irresistible Rise of a Political Celebrity

Sonia Purnell

Aurum

First published 2011 by
Aurum Press Limited
7 Greenland Street
London NW1 0ND
www.aurumpress.co.uk

A catalogue record for this book is available from the British Library.

ISBN 978 1 84513 665 9
Ebook ISBN 978 1 84513 741 0

1 3 5 7 9 10 8 6 4 2
2011 2013 2015 2014 2012

Typeset in Dante MT Std by SX Composing DTP, Rayleigh, Essex

Printed and bound in Great Britain by MPG Books, Bodwin, Cornwall

To the memory of my father
David Purnell, 1918–2010

Contents

Acknowledgements

To all those listed in the interviewee and contributor section at the end of this book, I offer my sincere thanks. To those who prefer to remain anonymous for understandable reasons, I am also very grateful for your invaluable contribution. Only with the co-operation of a multitude of people from all walks of life was this book possible. So many of you also made it an enjoyable exercise.

There were others who ensured the book jumped many hurdles, and without whose assistance, guidance, good humour, encouragement and support *Just Boris* would still be only an idea. The story starts with Francis Elliott, Robert and Rebecca Bomford, and continues with major roles played by my superbly determined agent Heather Holden Brown and wonderfully wise editor at Aurum, Sam Harrison. Jane Donovan copy-edited with immense rigour and added greatly to my efforts in the process, while Mark Swan came up with a striking and smart concept for the cover. Rob Dinsdale of HHB and Graham Coster, Barbara Phelan, Liz Somers and Melissa Smith of Aurum have all also contributed a great deal.

Thanks must also go to my mother Jean for putting me up and putting up with me while I did much of the writing; my niece Charlotte Lang, who helped with research early on, and Edward Randell, who did the same later (for both of whom great futures surely beckon); I am indebted to them both.

Many friends gave me much-needed support and encouragement, and I am grateful to all of them. Special mention must go, however, to Marcus Scriven, Alison Ramsey, Horace McDonald, Andy Corrigan, Jane Dyball, Ali Walsh, Alison Squire, Linda Valentine, Sue Purnell, Zeb Dare and Tanya Hughes. Mira Bar Hillel, Geoff Meade, George Jones, Mark Law, Gaby Hinsliff and many of the staff, past and present, of the *Evening Standard* were also generous with their time and thoughts. Heartfelt thanks also go to Michael Crick for his unparalleled feel for the political universe and the people who travel in it, as well as his sagacious advice on the art of biography-writing. Tom Fairbrother of Oxford University is without match in his infectious enthusiasm for spotting intriguing political connections and coincidences, and I am flattered by his unwavering interest and support. Paul Goodman shared many of his unusually astute observations with me. I was also the last person to interview the late, great Anthony Howard before he died – it was a privilege and I feel a real sadness that there will be no more such conversations. Many great names from journalism have lent their knowledge, expertise and insight to this book without wanting to be named. I am touched by how freely they gave their time and how figures from both domestic and EU politics have also been so generous. Many people close to the Johnson and Wheeler families too have been hugely forthcoming while wishing to remain anonymous.

Nor would this book be possible without help of all sorts from Guto Harri, Boris's communications chief, Penny Hatfield, the archivist at Eton, the staff at the Oxford Union, Edda Tasiemka and her team at the Tasiemka Library, Charles Grant at the Centre for European Reform, Catherine Temma, Lesley Smith, Lloyd Evans, Frances Goodhart and James Hanning. I am also grateful to Sir John Major for his swift and friendly replies to my questions and substantial contributions from Nick Boles MP and Stuart Reid. My thanks too to Lord Howard, who proved such excellent company, Dan Colson for a very entertaining lunch and Jasper Griffin for an inspiring one. There are so many others who helped with leads, thoughts, messages of encouragement, introductions and hot meals, not to mention emergency childcare; that very much includes Lewis.

But I must reserve the biggest thanks for those who have endured my frequent and sustained absences and my devotion to the book, almost always at their expense. They have never once complained. Book-writing is by nature a selfish business and I consequently owe more than I can say to my family, Jon, Laurie and Joey, for their patience, understanding and love.

London
July 2011

‘In our private business we are not suspicious of one another, nor angry with our neighbour if he does what he likes; we do not put on sour looks at him which, though harmless, are not pleasant. While we are thus unconstrained in our private business, a spirit of reverence pervades our public acts; we are prevented from doing wrong by respect for the authorities and for the laws, having a particular regard to those which are ordained for the protection of the injured as well as those unwritten laws which bring upon the transgressor of them the reprobation of the general sentiment.’

Pericles

Introduction

Just Boris – the only politician known so readily by his first name. Except, of course, it isn't his first name (which is Alexander) and his family, including his wife Marina, call him Al. Two generations back, the family name was different, too – not Johnson, but Kemal. Boris, the archetypal upper-class English eccentric, is actually descended down the male line from blond-haired Turks.

We may feel we know the public Boris, but so much about this multi-layered character is not quite as it seems. Even his trademark hair owes more to nurture then nature. When presented with the Brylcreem Best Celebrity Hairstyle prize in 2008, he couldn't help but boast: 'It's impossible to imitate, as it is a product of random and competing forces of nature!' His famous dishevelled look is actually, however, the product of a brisk, artful re-arrangement with his fingers (just before the cameras roll) rather than any naturally occurring disorder.

Call him Boris (his second name) or Al, much is known but little truly understood about this highly evasive figure. He is notoriously difficult to read, harder still to predict, yet beloved by millions and recognised by all. Through sheer force of personality and sleight of hand, Boris is pure box office – drawing adoring crowds like a David Beckham photocall, only perhaps with a higher class of banter and a far deeper timbre. He is set to be a dominant figure in all our lives for the next decade and beyond. The most unconventional, yet compelling politician of the post-Blair era, he is a man who wants to be our prime minister – and could yet succeed in his aim. But just who is Boris?

Like his hair, he is the one-off product of dozens of 'random and competing forces.' A comic turn, yes, but also the result of a heartbreaking childhood, he is a hugely ambitious figure, yet one who occasionally surrenders to a sort of professional death wish. A manic self-promoter, he also longs to be alone. He is a man of the people but also a politician, one who seems to change views more frequently than clothes, suggesting an ideological emptiness beneath the staunch Tory exterior.

When asked in a serious interview if he had any convictions, Boris quipped straight back, 'Only one – for speeding, but a very long time ago.' Life with him is laced with fun and jokes, but while the bumbling is now in retreat it has not yet been replaced by clarity and consistency. Take the environment. He was once noted for scorning the global warming agenda, with caustic rants about 'the cult of climate change.' Since then, he has flipped sides so many times that petrol-heads and eco-warriors take turns to denounce him as a traitor. Famously, he returned fire with the amusing retort: 'If the climate can change, I don't see why my mind can't!'

Like so many other Borissian handbrake turns, this was a cleverly executed move but it all leaves his audience uncertain as to where Boris's heart truly lies. Can he really be trusted to follow something through, or will principle always give way to the main chance? But then his flaws, his contradictions, his 'flexibility', his refusal to be consigned to any particular 'box' also seem to be Just Boris's most popular qualities. While few if any of us know what he really thinks about anything, the key to his all-conquering appeal is that he is considered so authentic.

For Boris is an original – the opposite of stereotype, the exception to the rule. Overweight and goosey-fleshed, he's the antithesis of an airbrushed male pin-up. He resembles a 'human laundry basket' and has a habit of forgetting to shower. Yet women adore him – even otherwise sensible ones ask him to sign their underwear or their bared breasts. And he laps up the attention. Even on his mayoral victory night, he made a beeline for the most attractive woman at the celebratory party and once tried to take one of his mistresses on a family holiday. But while women support, nurture and organise him – and quite often much more besides – he is neither faithful nor respectful to them and on occasion, offensive. His philandering is infamous, yet he scoops up the female vote. It all forms part of his self-avowed policy on cake: that is 'both having it and eating it.' And yet beneath all the determined optimism, there is a hint of something far more vulnerable, more troubled, more isolated. Who else in public life has such an obsessive desire to do it all alone?

Perhaps the answer to his character lies in his background. One side of Boris is an outrageous Right-wing toff, famous for peppering his plummy vowels with obscure Latin tags. A man who claims to have been sacked by the BBC for being too posh, he attended an upmarket boarding prep school before Eton and at Oxford joined the notoriously elitist Bullingdon Club. Yet now he's an all-conquering TV superstar in the age of 'anti-politicians' with mass-appeal as well as undeniable sex-appeal. Taxi drivers hail him cheerily as 'Bozza' and Manchester United fans chant his name to taunt their Merseyside opponents. His eye-rolling appearances on the BBC's *Have I Got News For You* are judged to be pop culture classics and he has been hailed as 'party Viagra' by *Tatler.* He is a superlative vote-catcher in an age when, for most people, politics has become one big yawn or an outrage. For all his establishment upbringing, in Boris there is the appeal of the outsider.

During Boris's early days at Westminster Michael Portillo – himself once a rising star – told the young Turk he had to make the choice between comedy and politics. Boris does not see why he should choose. Joking, to him, is a political device for reaching the widest possible audience – one that has proved enormously successful. 'Humour is a utensil that you can use to sugar the pill and to get important points across,' he told the *Wall Street Journal* during the 2008 London mayoral campaign. It also disarms his opponents. Joking has saved Boris from sounding too Right-wing, too ambitious or too tough. He knows it is 'essential' for someone of his background and self-regard not to 'appear too gritty or thrusting.'[1] It is all part of the light and shade that compose his character. Few get to see these underlying contrasts behind the public persona but as his number two in the Brussels bureau of the *Daily* and *Sunday Telegraph* in the early-1990s, I was fortunate enough to witness him on those extremely rare moments when he briefly lowers his guard. The EU story we were reporting was dominating the domestic news agenda and often we worked late into the night under intense pressure. During that formative time in his life, it was already clear I was dealing with a force of nature, someone unlike anyone else I had encountered or was likely to again. I have never forgotten the experience.

In a noisy corridor at a party in Brussels late in 1992, his soon-to-be wife Marina tracked me down to ask what I really thought of Boris. No doubt she realised that I must have an insight into this extraordinary man, as no one else had worked at such close quarters with him before. Emboldened by the intimacy of a large, jolly crowd, I delivered a verdict rather more candid than careful, but one I still hold to this day: 'I think he is the most ruthless, ambitious person I have ever met.' In the half-light she looked rather shocked – it was not then the prevailing view. Most thought of him as a charming, if shambolic hack defined by a love of classical civilisations and a problem with detail. But working with him so closely, I had observed that under a well-cultivated veneer of disorganisation lay not so much a streak of aspiration as a torrent of almost frightening focus and drive.

My judgment has been more than borne out by Boris's seemingly irresistible rise from mere newspaper scribe to political titan. I have watched his progress for the past two decades and it has not been achieved through bumbling or wearing his heart on his sleeve. As early as 2002, I invited readers of the *Independent on Sunday* to imagine him standing victorious on the steps of Downing Street with 'his smiling, highly presentable wife and four scrubbed-up kids fresh from his election triumph. As he lifts his arm to wave to the jubilant crowds waiting in the sunshine, the shreds of his ripped jacket pocket flap gently in the early summer breeze.'

This was probably the first time that it was suggested in print that Boris might be a future prime minister. Indeed it was considered a slightly outlandish prediction by those who had not encountered him up close, though not so now. The fact is that Boris stands out from the crowd like no other public figure of his generation. There may be a touch of the Marmite factor about him – many either love or loathe him. But a man who confesses to holding a 'Messiah complex'[2] about his own abilities to win over a crowd or get things done deserves a closer look. Just what drives this person who has already scored so highly in the lottery of life?

The Boris brand has sold well and made him a wealthy man. He owns two Georgian properties, one listed, together worth millions of pounds; he and his wife Marina have between them pulled in many hundreds of thousands of pounds a year throughout most of their almost two-decade long marriage. Publishers, TV companies, newspapers and events managers searching for an after-dinner speaker are prepared to pay well over the odds for a sprinkling of Johnson fairy dust. Yet one of the more consistent facets of Boris's personality is the pursuit of money, a trait that often gives an impression quite the opposite of jovial generosity. It is a puzzling preoccupation considering his obvious earning power and the evident combined wealth of the greater Johnson dynasty, who together own highly valuable houses or large tracts of land in London's Islington, Regent's Park and Notting Hill, as well as Oxfordshire, Somerset and Greece. 'The thing about the Johnsons is we don't have any money,' Boris's sister Rachel is apt to say when asked why her family are always in such a hurry. 'We have to earn our keep.'[3] Someone else described the psyche as akin to 'tramp dread' – the feeling that if you stop making money for an instant, you will end up sleeping in a cardboard box. However, the ceaseless drive to inflate the collective Johnsonian bank balance is sometimes hard to understand. Boris frequently tells colleagues how he frets about money and how he was angry with his father for selling his old Primrose Hill home 'on the cheap' for £4 million in July 2007. All the riches, the power and the glory are never quite enough, it seems.

What else is clear is that Boris is merely the (current) leading light of Britain's most powerful media and political dynasty. The Johnsons, who seek to dominate our national landscape, not only include sister Rachel and MP brother Jo but also father Stanley.

Collectively, they make merciless enemies and harbour long-held grudges. Rachel describes this as their 'Sicilian' side: cross them or criticise them – or worse still, mock them – at your peril. Accustomed to near-universal praise and affection, they ruthlessly close ranks against detractors.

In early 2010 Rachel, who assiduously maintains her links with Oxford University, nominated writer and critic Roger Lewis for the prestigious chair of poetry. He was a worthy contender and Rachel offered to recruit the Johnson 'block vote.' 'But then she came back and said that Boris had gone ballistic about the idea,' recalls Lewis. It seemed the Mayor had taken offence at a *Daily Telegraph* review that Lewis had written *four* years previously of an earlier biography of Boris by Andrew Gimson. Boris was, it appears, still seething.

Rachel emailed Lewis:

> 'I asked Boris today and he erupted rather and said you'd written ungraciously about his children's names in a newspaper and refused to sign, declaring that he would do anything in his power to prevent you from claiming the poetry chair. Can you clear this up pls?'

Rachel came back later:

> 'I think I have traced it back to your Gimson review . . . just read it online. You're toast, I'm afraid. He is very Sicilian when it comes to these little matters of his moral fitness for office and those who debate it publicly.'

In fact, Lewis had not written 'ungraciously' about Boris's children's names in the piece but he had questioned how Boris could risk hurting them by his persistent infidelity to Marina. After all, as a child Boris had been greatly affected by his own father Stanley's philandering, his mother's depression and their eventual divorce. Lewis's answer to his own question was that Boris is 'totally wrapped up in himself. As with Stanley, "abstinence and chastity count for nothing with Boris". In due course, Cassia Peaches, Lara Lettice, Milo and Theodore Apollo might like to tell their father what they think of that philosophy.'[4]

To the point and uncomfortable, perhaps, but the overall tone of the piece was jokey – even indulgent – rather than hostile to Boris or his family.

Eventually, Lewis came a distant and unexpected fifth in the poetry chair vote to Geoffrey Hill, although it is of course impossible to say what role, if any, Boris's eruption played in that. 'I'd always thought that he was the nice and funny person you see in public,' says Lewis, 'but I guess you don't get to be as famous as that by being nice to everyone. He won't put up with being teased himself whereas he's happy to dish it out. I thought as a public figure he was fair game for mockery but I was taken aback by his vindictive and rather petty streak. It was as if a sleepy old beloved labrador had turned round and bitten someone.'

For good measure, at the time of the appearance of Lewis's *Telegraph* article in 2006, the commissioning editor Sam Leith received an email from Boris (then MP for Henley and shadow higher education minister). It stated simply: 'Fuck off and die.'

While Boris avoids full-on public confrontation, he saves battles such as these for behind closed doors but those who have known him for years are aware that he makes a bad enemy and is now in a position of power. The wife of one of his Bullingdon Club cohorts at Oxford said that her husband would 'not speak about Boris, even off the record as he is frightened of what he might do back. A lot of people are.'

There are frequently collateral casualties with the great Boris blunderbuss, the smaller characters who fall under his wheels. But maybe few enough for that not to matter, and anyway, 'he makes us laugh, doesn't he?' And yet despite this coldly ruthless pursuit of his own advancement, Boris will on occasion take the opportunity to show kindness. For those he wants to keep onside, he has an instinctive feel for the gesture to a powerful person's child, the handwritten note for a favour granted, or sympathetic word to a grieving schoolmate's mother that prevents him from making the enemies that his actions might otherwise create.

In that, as in so much else, he resembles one of his political heroes, Benjamin Disraeli, who was also considered witty, alluring and clever, but for a long time more an amusing character than a serious player. Like Boris, 'Dizzy' disdained the male clubbiness of the House of Commons, preferring the company of women and, as a serious bon viveur, was on occasion touched by sexual scandal. Disraeli, who once declared: 'I love fame, I love reputation,' also loved the pursuit of pleasure in contrast to his great foe and rival, the pious and tormented Liberal leader, William Ewart Gladstone. Like Boris, Disraeli knew how to command affection through artful flamboyance and humour, and is consequently credited with bringing the Conservative party into the age of mass politics. Like Boris, he also enjoyed a mystique and evasiveness, but dropped followers intriguing clues about his real self in his novels. Above all, he was known for lack of political fixity, having changed sides in the key debate of his time, the Corn Laws. Thereafter he was forever tarred with both the inconsistency and loose cannon brushes. Furthermore, as a Jew in nineteenth-century Britain, he was much more of an outsider than Boris but none of that stopped him from completing the journey to Downing Street and being remembered as one of the towering greats of British politics.

Boris also likes to invoke Winston Churchill when he talks about his own multi-faceted career – noting the great war-leader similarly combined his beloved journalism with politics. Although he might have added that Churchill – another man with a great zest for life – struggled at times to be taken seriously after a patchy early career, having twice changed sides in the House of Commons. Indeed, although considered undoubtedly brilliant, Churchill was only grudgingly offered the premiership in 1940. But, as Boris has privately told sympathetic Tories, in the manner of Churchill, he also considers it his destiny to lead his country.

The fascinating question is: does Boris have, as they did, what it takes to go all the way? Are these grand comparisons absurd or insightful?

When I embarked on this book, I wanted to answer these and many other questions about Boris, the real Boris, to unpick the man from the artfully created myth. Not from the point of view of one drawn herself from the political elite, or the same caste or tribe as Boris – or even the same sex. Nor do I, like some of those who have indulged him, wish to be him either. I don't want to find excuses for his behaviour – as so many commentators have – but reasons. It is said to be the question he most dreads being answered, but it is time we knew: just what makes Boris tick?

Judging by the enthusiastic and generous support I have encountered from the many people I have spoken to during my research, I am not the only one who wants to know. Whether we be rival politicians, newspaper editors, spin doctors, enthusiastic supporters, bitter opponents, Left-leaning teachers, fashionistas, cabbies, couch potatoes or conscientious voters, we all love talking about Boris, speculating about his motives and pondering his future. We want to know and understand him more. Virtually every meeting or discussion I had, with nearly 200 contributors across Britain, America and Australia, overran its allotted time. Trains have been missed, appointments delayed, families at home kept waiting because people never tire of talking and asking about Boris. His appeal reaches way beyond Westminster into the heart of the nation and overseas.

Like my interviewees, I want to find out whether Boris is the cleverest man in the world – as he is said to believe – or merely one of the most cunning. Could he be, as he seems to believe, our saviour in times of political upheaval – a refreshing, break-the-mould leader? Or is this unlikely sex-god merely a calculated conceit, like his famous pre-ruffled hair?

Chapter One
'Peter Pan and Wendy'
Childhood, 1964–1977

For a boy about to be saddled with such a comically florid name, the birth of Alexander Boris de Pfeffel Johnson in the early afternoon of 19 June 1964 was a far from grand affair. His mother Charlotte, a 22-year-old student, endured the final stages of labour alone in a low-rent hospital known as 'the Clinic' on New York's Upper East Side. Her husband Stanley, 23, had been persuaded to attend only one of her antenatal classes and was not entirely sold on the idea that 'real men bothered' with what he later described as the 'horrific details'.[1]

So, when Stanley chose to 'step outside'[2] the hospital near the East River on East 70th Street in search of a hearty lunch, his timing may not have been entirely coincidental. In any case, the pizza he enjoyed on Second Avenue must have been quite substantial. By the time he returned, the baby had entered the world and was safely wrapped in swaddling clothes and placed in a long row of other arrivals in the nursery. His heels had been carefully dipped in black ink to make footprints, a rudimentary form of post-partum identity check to avoid mix-ups in a busy public maternity ward.

The 'lusty' newborn, weighing in at 9lb 1oz, already sported the whip of platinum hair that would help make him a national phenomenon but there was little else to indicate these were the first hours of the most famous member of what has become Britain's leading – and certainly its blondest – political and media clan. Or indeed, that the little scrap of humanity would later become the first

Conservative Mayor of London with a bigger personal mandate than almost any other elected office holder in Europe.

Both Boris's parents are English, but Stanley considered it vital to secure dual US/British citizenship for their son and registered him with the US authorities, as well as the British Consulate. For all his English eccentricities and mannerisms, by birth Boris is pure 'Noo York' and, in nationality terms at least, half-American.

Stanley was in the US on a Harkness Fellowship to study the then newfangled subject of creative writing at the State University of Iowa. Some of his fellow new graduates were perhaps surprised that he had won such a prestigious and generous prize as he had garnered only a second-class degree from Exeter College, Oxford. Charlotte, a bohemian soul from a family of liberal intellectuals, had accompanied her husband back in the autumn of 1963, but when she became pregnant with Boris, Stanley abandoned his studies. He had, in any case, grown disillusioned: his poetry – which had scooped the prestigious Newdigate Prize, back in Oxford – had not won the applause he had expected in Iowa and so he decided to change tack, and town, to a rather more Johnsonian economics degree at New York's Columbia University. But first, he wanted to get some travelling under his belt and so the couple headed for Mexico, initially by car and then Greyhound bus.

By this time Charlotte was suffering from morning sickness, exacerbated by the altitude in Mexico City. She was dreading the 20-hour slog by bus back to the border and then on to New York, but fortune shone on the Johnsons, as it so often does: in Mexico, they met up with a kindly Russian émigré whose daughter happened to be the girlfriend of one of Stanley's Exeter College friends. Boris Litwin showered the young couple with baby gifts and provided them with two air tickets, saving Charlotte much discomfort. In return, she gratefully promised that if the baby were a boy, he would take their benefactor's name.

Stanley could surely have made the gesture himself by buying the tickets, but as those who have known him for decades can testify, he does not believe in unnecessary comfort nor, indeed, in sickness – the Clinic where Boris was born, for instance, was frequented by poor

New Yorkers unable to afford full medical fees. It was by no means upmarket and, in a lot of locals' eyes, not even that respectable but it is not the Johnsonian way to waste money, however elevated their social aspirations. Stanley rarely admits to illness himself, nor notices it in others. The same is true of Boris, who is also, in adulthood, seldom known to be ill. As one observer has remarked: 'I'd never put him in charge of hospitals.'[3]

Naturally, while lying in hospital as a newborn, Boris would have had no idea how lucky his father had been, or would go on to be. The Harkness Fellowship – and the gift of air tickets – were just two examples of a serendipitous series of events in which freebies, jobs, holidays, houses, prizes and sponsorships have rained on Stanley, ensuring relative wealth even at university, and certainly thereafter. Such impossible good luck as he has experienced has had an effect on his mindset, which does not really register hardship or struggle. 'I do reject this idea that life is, in any way, an effort,' Stanley insists. 'I have, on the whole, found things to be a piece of cake.'[4] In turn, his redoubtable mother, Irène, thought his double crown demonstrated that he had simply been 'born lucky.'[5]

Boris's new home, financed by the Fellowship, was one such piece of luck. A bohemian 60ft-long single-room loft apartment, it was opposite the Chelsea Hotel, the crash pad beloved of rock stars such as Bob Dylan, Iggy Pop and Jimi Hendrix, on West 23rd Street. The bathroom was screened off by abstract paintings, the bath perched on stilts and there was a large yellow piano adorned with a 'vive la fun' logo. Above a lively neon-lit café called the Star Bar (where the Beatles' 'She Loves You' blared out on the jukebox until 4 a.m.), it was entertaining though hardly suitable for a newborn. The appearance of an intruder (who, one hot Manhattan night, had climbed in through a window left open) would be particularly alarming for any new mother, but Stanley, typically, treated the whole episode as one tremendous joke.[6]

After a few months, the couple decided to return to Britain so Charlotte could finish off the English degree she had interrupted to accompany her husband to America. Stanley says only now does he appreciate 'what a tremendous sacrifice'[7] she made in leaving Oxford mid-course. It was the first time that Boris – or rather 'Al' as he was, and still is, known to his family – would move house but he would do so a total of 32 times over the next 14 years.[8] As a whole, throughout his childhood he lived in five cities, five London boroughs, one Somerset village (in at least two different houses), three US states, three countries and two continents. During that time he attended three primary schools in two countries, one prep school and one public school.

Before they left North America in September 1964, Boris and his parents embarked on his first grand tour: of New Hampshire, Vermont and Canada. Not that he had much chancc to take it all in – he slept through most of it in a carrycot placed in Stanley's Chevrolet Bel Air Automatic (which came with the Harkness Fellowship). That summer, the new father proudly wrote to his own parents: 'I must say, Alexander Boris is fantastically well behaved and I catch myself completely forgetting he exists. He sleeps in the back of the car as we travel hundreds of miles, and sometimes we don't even stop while C. feeds him.'[9]

Charlotte also remembers Boris as being an 'incredibly good baby'[10] who rarely cried. In the new home, a modern flat in Summertown, Oxford, he would amuse himself with a saucepan or cardboard box while she continued with her studies. And just as well because she was already seven months pregnant with her second child (Rachel) when she took her Finals in the summer of 1965. At the time, she was bemused when in apparent denial of her marital status and patently obvious condition, her Oxford college, Lady Margaret Hall, continued to address her as Miss Fawcett, her maiden name. She went on to secure a respectable second-class degree.

Boris's self-containment may be due in part to quite severe deafness until he was about eight, leading to a series of operations to insert grommets. No doubt feeling detached from the world because of his poor hearing during those early years, it was some time before he became the rumbustious character he appears today. 'Glue Ear' can give rise to prolonged and painful infections, and Boris occasionally makes reference to how illness confined him to bed as a child. Even now, he attributes 'evasiveness' in his character to not being able to hear what people were saying when he was very young and therefore fearing he might say the wrong thing himself.[11] He was indeed a subdued, reflective small child and it was not until his teens when he could hear perfectly well that his present character emerged. Old friends of the Johnson family still marvel at his adult persona, barely recognisable from the young Boris they knew 40 years previously.

'As a child he was a quiet, studious chap, who worked very hard,' recalls Oliver Tickell, who knew Boris from family skiing holidays in Courchevel. 'He was rather modest about his ambitions then, or at least showing them. The flamboyant personality, big impression and self-projection came later.' 'He was very quiet, always with his nose in a book,' confirms Brian Johnson (no relation, but one of Stanley's closest friends), 'but he already had a sardonic sense of humour.' Photos during this period regularly show Boris as a serious, even solemn young boy, not the cheeky little rogue one might expect.

The transformation can probably be timed to his Eton years when he chose to morph from 'Al' (or Alex) into the more distinctive Boris. Even in adulthood, though, there are moments when he appears to retreat into an inner Al, far away from the commotion and distractions of life around him. Sometimes only a forceful and repeated direct question can pull him back from this private world, his re-entry into reality accompanied by much eye-rolling, hair-ruffling and frequent 'aaarhs' and 'grrrrs'. This detachment can be a somewhat disarming trait in such a physically large man with an even bigger personality, but it's a characteristic he shares with others who have suffered hearing difficulties and subsequently created their own internal worlds.

Boris's placid nature was doubtless a blessing for his mother, though, as she led a taxing, itinerant life. Stanley and Charlotte left Oxford in July 1965, this time moving to Crouch End in north London, while he struggled to launch a career that would put food on the table for his new family. He had tried his hand unsuccessfully at teaching and studying for a Masters in Agricultural Economics before apparently being recruited as a spy and offered, according to his own account, 'the most intensive training in clandestine techniques known to man.'[12]

Finally, in October 1965, Stanley was offered a plausible job – at the World Bank. He was due to start four months later in Washington DC, but the couple decided not to stay put until it was time to emigrate. Instead they decamped to a rented cottage high up on the snowy slopes of Exmoor for a long, hard winter with two small children and a wood-burner for heat. It suited Stanley as he could use the time to write his first novel, *Gold Drain*. Such a remote, rustic life was a far cry from Charlotte's urbane London upbringing in a large house in Cavendish Avenue, St John's Wood. It was also one of several episodes in Boris's early years where he and his sister Rachel led a rather isolated existence, rarely seeing anyone outside the family.

When the time came for Stanley to take up his contract at the World Bank, in February 1966, cases were packed for the fourth time in 20 months in preparation for the move back to the land of Boris's birth. Such a nomadic lifestyle was not only testing for the children, however: with a busy husband rarely at home, Charlotte was forced to cope with the practicalities of shipping around two youngsters under the age of two, mostly on her own. Throughout their marriage, it was not uncommon for Stanley to be away for up to six months at a time: Charlotte once claimed he was absent for a whole year writing one of his books, although he himself disputes this.

Only after camping out in the Dupont Plaza Hotel in Washington DC for a month and staying at other temporary accommodation did the family finally acquire their first real home for the price of $25,000. A white clapboard house on Morrison Street, just off Connecticut Avenue in the northwest of the city, it came complete with a garden, front and back, where the children could play (Boris says his earliest memory is his beloved Washington tree-house). For the Johnsons, life seemed to be settling down at last. Charlotte was helped by a string of young au pairs – even though, mysteriously, they tended not to stay very long – and was finding happiness in her burgeoning painting career. By now, she also had three children, having given birth to Leo in London on home leave in September 1967. 'They were quite a handful,' she admits.[13]

Soon the family had made a large circle of friends, many of them members of the British press corps. Perhaps best known were Charles

Wheeler, the distinguished BBC correspondent, and his Indian wife, Dip. It was at this very early stage in his life that Boris met their younger daughter, Marina.

But in April 1968, Stanley brought this golden, more rooted existence to an abrupt end. As an April Fool's joke he submitted what appeared to be a serious application to his employers at the World Bank for a $100 million loan to build three new pyramids and a sphinx to promote tourism in Egypt. Alas, the former US Defence Secretary Robert McNamara, who headed up the loan committee, was not amused. Stanley was forced to seek alternative employment, which with his ever-present serendipity he quickly found. But the new job – as project director to a national policy panel on population control chaired by the philanthropist John D. Rockefeller III – meant moving his family back to New York.

With three small children, Charlotte was packing up again just two years after landing in Washington and only four years after leaving New York the last time. Moreover, she had been keen to make any future upheaval a return to England as she was badly shaken by the growing turmoil in the US. The assassination of Martin Luther King in April 1968 had been followed by that of Robert Kennedy, the late President Kennedy's brother, two months later; there had also been increasingly violent riots over race and the Vietnam War. With an enormous sense of longing for her young family to be safe back at home in England, Charlotte told Stanley she had, 'had enough. Why don't we go back to England?'[14]

In June, however, the Johnsons duly moved north to New York, although Stanley did promise his long-suffering wife that they would all be heading back to England within a year. In the meantime, they rented a house on Harbor Island, Norwalk, Connecticut, with its own jetty looking out over Long Island Sound. Although helped by Vreni, a Swiss au pair, Charlotte was once again left alone for long periods of time with the children while Stanley travelled a total of 35,000 miles with his glamorous new job. After 12 months, and with the panel's report on population complete – which resulted in the formation of the United Nations Population Agency and acclaim from President Nixon – Stanley was at last able to keep his promise about returning to England. In the summer of 1969, the Johnsons packed up their belongings yet again and headed for JFK airport for a flight 'home'.

But where *was* home? For now it was to be Nethercote, the Exmoor river valley where Stanley's parents lived and where he and Charlotte had bought a cottage while still in the United States. As the eldest, Boris was given a small box-room of his own, where his early doodles ('Boo to grown-ups!' among them) may still be seen pinned to the wall. His aunt Birdie – a shy figure compared to her brother and his brood, as well as one of the few Johnson brunettes – still lives in the cottage today.

The main farmhouse, West Nethercote, was where Stanley's parents, Johnny and Irène, had lived since 1951, when they bought the farm for £4,500 with financial assistance from her wealthy father. A ramshackle series of buildings, with no proper bathrooms or electric power, it was a real-life version of *Cold Comfort Farm*. It also came with 250 acres of hill land, much of it rough grazing. Irène's father (also Stanley) had paid for his namesake grandson's school fees too as the farm was struggling and money was tight. When the younger Stanley later won a scholarship to Sherborne, a traditional public school in Dorset, the £150 saved was not given to the boy, as his grandfather suggested, but invested in three much-needed new cows.

The young Stanley's home life was shaped by Johnny's drinking, his sudden explosions of temper; also a lack of cash. Irène, meanwhile, was both an incurable optimist with a strong sense of humour and a font of uncomplaining support and tolerance in the face of adversity. Fortitude and loyalty, it seems, are requisite in Johnson women if they want to stay the course. Boris has undoubtedly inherited his grandfather's temper in moments of frustration or pressure but not his bibulous habits or opinion of politicians. 'All scoundrels,' was Johnny's decisive view.[15]

When Stanley and Charlotte first returned from America, his sister Hilary and her family inhabited the middle house, East Nethercote. The overall effect was of a rather ramshackle Johnson family compound, hemmed in by the steep sides of the valley and down a couple of miles of bumpy track. Irène regarded the place as something of a prison. It does seem rather cut off and basic – no doubt Charlotte, with her troop of small children and a frequently absent husband, often felt isolated here. Sometimes damp, often cold, even now Nethercote is an acquired taste (a 'bad case of self-conscious Londoners and over-done rustic,' complains one visitor). Back then, the ever-changing cast of au pairs accompanying Johnsonian family life would complain of bats in the bedrooms (they would swoop about at night, even get tangled up in their hair). Boris's grandmother would advise the young women to sleep with saucepans over their heads but this counsel was rarely sufficient to encourage them to stay.

One day when Boris was still very young, a hunt came chasing a stag beside the river below Nethercote and the creature was brought to bay by the hounds. After it had been shot, its heart was cut out by the hunters and given to one of his little brothers. 'We've got the heart! We've got the heart!' he excitedly chanted, carrying the still-beating organ up to the house. 'So, we cooked it up with a bit of flour,' Boris recalls, 'and the German au pair girl left the next day.'[16] Within a few months, Hilary, her husband, Peter Heanly, and their four sons emigrated to Australia, where they have lived ever since. (The boys have grown up true Aussies and in another departure seem to have been by-passed by the Johnson blond gene as they are all dark-haired.)

Despite, or perhaps because of Nethercote's testing geography, Stanley adores the place and has now bought the valley in which it sits to add to the sense of fiefdom. Even when they were living abroad, he took his children back to Nethercote every summer holiday and today still spends much of his time there. He exults in hurtling down the narrow, winding Somerset lanes, free from the restrictions of urban life. 'He and his car were well-known to the police,' reveals a close family friend. 'He used to revel in the number of times he had been stopped and let off – it was a badge of pride in a Johnson japes' kind of way.'

However Nethercote is emphatically not the classic country seat. Despite appearances, on a mathematical calculation Stanley is only three-eighths English. His father (half-Turkish and a quarter Swiss) scraped together every penny he had to buy the place because it represented the first chance to put down roots in his adopted country, as well as being a safe haven from the bloodshed and bitter disappointment that had hitherto blighted his family. Johnny was desperately trying to put behind him events that have shaped today's Johnsons, and arguably Boris, in particular. Embedded within the Johnsonian psyche is a surprising sense of insecurity: there is a very real, if well-disguised fear of being 'rumbled' and a concern that financial ruin, no matter how healthy the bank balances, is never far away. Deep down, the family still worry that all they have achieved might be taken from them. So, why is this?

Stanley's grandfather Ali Kemal was an Anglophile Turkish polemicist in the dying years of the Ottoman Empire, before and just after the First World War. Ali's father – Boris's great-great-grandfather – was from the blond-haired Turkish village of Kalfat in Anatolia and his mother was a fair blue-eyed Circassian whom, at least according to Johnson family legend, was of slave origin. The story goes that Hanife Fered bought her freedom by becoming Ali's father's second wife. Between them, these two ancestors are responsible for Boris's astonishing white-blond hair.

In a lifetime of trouble with the authorities, the devoutly Muslim Ali – who could recite the Koran off by heart from the age of six – was first arrested, aged 19, in 1888 for setting up a students' society. Following this, he spent many years in exile. Returning after the First World War, he left journalism for politics and aligned himself with the British and other victorious allies against the Nationalist movement then emerging under the leadership of Kemal Atatürk. Appointed interior minister in the Sultan's last government in May 1919, he was, as one contemporaneous commentator put it, 'the puppet of a puppet.'[17] Ali effectively outlawed Atatürk by instructing government outposts not to provide him with supplies or support. The subsequent row led to Ali's resignation, although he continued his opposition in print.

But he had chosen his enemies unwisely: Atatürk led the Nationalists to power in 1922, became father of modern Turkey and wasted no time in eliminating his enemies. Ali was then kidnapped by a Nationalist gang during his morning shave at Istanbul's elite Cercle d'Orient club, denounced as a traitor and attacked with sticks, stones and knives before finally being hanged and, allegedly, his body parts stuffed into a tree. For Boris, this untimely end to a proud man's life – recounted to all Johnsons from an early age – has proved a powerful lesson as to the dangers of full-frontal confrontation and inflexible principles. Generally, he avoids open defiance, preferring subtler, yet still effective ways of undermining enemies and rivals. From family history, he knows how 'sticking to your guns' can lead to disaster. Even his greatest fans concede that unlike his great-grandfather, he is unencumbered by ideological fixity, a characteristic that has thus far served him well: Boris prefers being liked to being consistent.

Back in 1909, Ali's half-English, half-Swiss first wife Winifred had given birth to their son Osman (Stanley's father) in Bournemouth because it was believed she would be safer there than in Turkey. Shortly after childbirth, she died of puerperal fever without having the chance to bid farewell to her husband. Following her death, Ali did not return to collect his son and so little Osman and his elder sister Celma were brought up by their English grandmother, Margaret Brun, and eventually took her maiden name (Johnson). Stanley believes that Osman had no recollection of meeting his father. Certainly, Ali was not much of a parent, paying little towards his children's upkeep and then leaving them in hardship after his death.

For the next 70 years, Osman effectively suppressed his Turkish roots. Early on in his life, his grandmother dropped the obviously Turkish name and he became Wilfred (his middle name) Johnson in honour of his mother. Bitter at being abandoned, Wilfred forbade any mention of Ali Kemal – but he was still an unspoken background presence throughout Boris's childhood. Boris's mother Charlotte once raised the subject with her parents-in-law, but was quickly hushed; she never tried again.

Wilfred, Boris's grandfather, became increasingly enchanted with the idea of Englishness and the ensuing security, and soon decided he wanted to blend in even more by becoming known as 'Johnny'. From Osman to Johnny in two jumps, he thus completed the progression from son of a Turkish Man of Letters to English public schoolboy (Boris was to continue the Johnsonian habit of elective changes of name and identity to suit circumstances in his own life). A taciturn man of little outward emotion, Johnny kept his Turkish ancestry extremely quiet, not least because the Turks had fought on the 'wrong' side in the war. Perhaps more importantly, casual racism, particularly among his peers at school, was then the norm. As Stanley puts it: 'Turks were basically wogs so if you were the son of a Turk, you were the son of a wog.'[18] When all maintenance ceased upon the death of Ali, Johnny had to leave school at 13 and ended up working on a farm in the Nile Delta belonging to a Swiss uncle. Here, with great good fortune, he met Boris's grandmother Irène Williams and married her in 1936. The match was to change his life and prospects.

Half-English, half-French Irène could (and often did) claim a little grandeur. She was born in 1907 in the grand Pavillion du Barry in Versailles belonging to Baron Hubert de Pfeffel, father of her rather stern-looking mother, Marie-Louise. In 2008 the BBC programme *Who Do You Think You Are*? established Irène was the great granddaughter of an actress and her German lover, one Prince Paul von Württemberg, a direct descendant of George II. This royal connection makes Boris an eighth cousin of Prime Minister David Cameron.

Known to Boris as 'Granny Butter', Irène may have been unaware of her royal German blood because of the illegitimacy but she certainly used to amuse her grandchildren with frequent claims to an aristocratic French lineage. At the time, this seemed somewhat implausible, even comic, as Boris and his siblings knew her as someone who worked hard with little fuss or glamour, often laboriously skimming cream off milk, which is presumably how she earned her family nickname. Clearly, Irène yearned for more and viewed rustic Nethercote as something of a prison. Her royal antecedence now proven, Boris no longer laughs at her pretensions. Instead he casts his mind back to the savage contrast between her affluent, early life and the 'extreme struggle against the elements on Exmoor where everything was covered in lichen. We were wrong to snigger.'[19]

Certainly, Irène was anxious for the tongue-twisting de Pfeffel (silent 'P') to remain in the family, which is why Boris still bears this as his third name today, and she urged her son Stanley (born August 1940 in Cornwall and one of two boys and two girls) to explore the possibility of claiming a French barony through her ancestry. After all, she had grown up with chauffeurs, housekeepers and a smart red Daimler called Poppy and it was her family money that helped keep the Johnsons afloat and ensured Stanley was educated as an English gentleman with a classical syllabus largely composed of Latin and Greek (Science did not feature, while Maths was a definite weak point – a foretaste of Boris's own academic inclinations).

Perhaps Irène recognised Stanley, though not the eldest son, was the most likely (and certainly the most driven) to restore her family to its rightful place in society. Those who have known him for most of his adult life remark how it has been his single-handed (and single-minded) ambition to create a new political and journalistic dynasty. He does not talk about his siblings. Indeed, former political commentator Anthony Howard (whose widow is godmother to Leo) once remarked: 'I've known Stanley for 50 years, but I didn't know that his brothers and sisters even existed – he must be a total egotist.'

Having been toughened up by his hard-knocks, 1950s public-school education, Stanley frowns on public displays of emotion and expects his children to show equal resilience. He admits to being unemotional and his manner can make him seem cold, retreating 'turtle-like' as one observer put it, when any kind of emotional topic is raised. He recalls his first night away at boarding school at the age of eight, listening with evident disgust to the 'snivelling' of a boy in the next bed – 'Well, I'm sure I missed my mummy too, but that didn't seem to me to be the point.'[20] And he also refers to the victim of prefects' repeated beatings as 'some poor snivelling sod.'[21]

For Stanley, a joke is the easy answer to any sensitive situation, however inappropriate. Some years ago at a New Year's Day lunch he bumped into a contemporary from his old Devonian prep school he hadn't seen in decades. The former school pal revealed how being abused sexually by the co-headmaster almost destroyed his life. In his autobiography Stanley tells how he decided it was best to respond with a flippant quip. '"He never made a pass at me!" I protested.' Unsurprisingly, the joke fell flat, his childhood friend retorting: '"Then you were one of the lucky ones"'.[22] It is unlikely Boris would have misread the situation so badly.

Stanley is not renowned for his tact – as he once observed: 'Human relationships remain a mystery to me.'[23] However, like all the Johnsons, he can also be charming and has got better at holding an audience over the years. The former foreign secretary Douglas Hurd describes him as 'good value' and 'impossible to dislike.' But as with his son, the act serves to conceal a steely, highly competitive core evident from his earliest time at school. Like many public schoolboys, Stanley seems to look back on his days in full-time education with unlimited affection and pride. A chunk of his memoirs, *Stanley I Presume?*, is taken up with recitations of school and university triumphs, prizes won, scholarships bagged, high marks scored, rugby tackles delivered. As he himself admits, in one of those appealing Johnsonian moments of self-knowledge, after all the glory at Sherborne, 'it took me quite some time to recover from a swollen head.'[24] In perhaps his first sweet taste of stardom, he was also head boy. 'Whenever I walked through the school, 660 boys stood to attention and took their hands out of their pockets,' he recalls.[25]

In stark contrast to his peripatetic adulthood as a boy Stanley led a restricted life, rarely straying off the farm apart from journeys to and from two private boarding schools, where he mixed with boys usually much wealthier than himself and of a certain class. Indeed, he claims that he had never even encountered a grammar school boy before he went up to Oxford in October 1959 at the age of 19 and found himself sharing a set of rooms with one. He appears to have been bewildered by the exoticism of his roommate's background: 'Mike told me how his father had once sought work during the Depression,' he recalls with amazement before adding, rather sweetly: 'I'm surprised Mike put up with me.'[26] Fortunately, the fascination seems to have been mutual. Stanley's physical and social isolation as a child may well explain the way he brought up his own family, though.

He had gone up to Oxford on a Stapledon Scholarship in Classics despite the fact that in one paper he wrote a short story, whereas he had actually been asked to write an essay. That he not only got away with it but was celebrated for doing so is pure Johnsonia – an illuminating insight into the family philosophy that somehow they are exempt from the restrictions applied to others. 'What on earth had possessed me, except possibly some kind of adolescent arrogance that had led me to think it was alright to break the rules as long as you did so in style?' Stanley asks rhetorically.[27]

As part of a life-plan he set himself three goals for his time in Oxford: 1) to win a Blue by playing rugby for the University; 2) to become President of the Union and 3) to bag a first in Greats, the Oxford name for Classics. None of these greater goals fell into his lap as he might have expected. He managed captain of the college rugby team, but never membership of the University XV. In the Union, he got no further than the Library Committee. Surprisingly, given the Johnsonian adulation of the ancient world, Stanley gave up the four-year slog of Classics – and had, in any case, notched up only a second in the first set of exams (known at Oxford as 'Mods') before he switched to English. 'Deep down, I knew I had taken the easy way out,' he says.[28]

But success and glory eventually arrived in the shape of the University's top poetry prize, the Newdigate – once won by Oscar Wilde. With this came other trophies. On 27 June 1962 he met the tawny-haired Charlotte Fawcett at the Encaenia, an Oxford ceremony, where he had been invited to read an extract from his winning work, 'May Morning'. Stanley, whose love life at Oxford by his own admission took a while to get going, could not have failed to notice the Newdigate Prize bestowed not just academic stardust but also a certain sexual glamour (this is a lesson in prizes begetting prizes that has also served Boris well). After a while, Charlotte – who wore a rabbit-fur waistcoat – invited Stanley to her room at Lady Margaret Hall for tea. Eight months later, in summer 1963, they were married in the Register Office in Marylebone Road, London (Stanley was just 22). As a honeymoon, they went potato picking on a friend's farm in Kent.

Boris's brains certainly did not come from Stanley alone. On Charlotte's side, he draws on an inheritance from a family who can justifiably claim to be genuine intellectuals, as well as leading lights in the Women's Suffrage Movement. Known to be unassuming, even shy, and imbued with an impeccable left-wing pedigree, the Fawcetts have long taken a lead in championing human rights, such as for unmarried mothers and their children. At the same time they have fought against judicial corporal punishment and racism. Charlotte's brother Edmund – Boris's uncle – started his career with the publishers New Left Books before joining the *Economist*, where his elegant prose meant that his Leftist views were tolerated. According to Rachel Johnson, Charlotte was the only Labour voter in the Exmoor village of Winsford, the nearest to Nethercote. In her youth she went on CND marches and anti-apartheid rallies, and before Stanley (a staunch Conservative since school), dated left-wing boyfriends. Unsurprisingly, her parents were somewhat shocked when she married a Tory with traditional shire-ish views. And although Boris has followed his father's party loyalties, it is also clear that he has absorbed much of the Fawcett liberal agenda, including a genuine abhorrence of racial discrimination.

Charlotte's father, Sir James Fawcett, served as bursar at All Souls College, Oxford in the 1960s but was previously a prominent barrister and member of the European Commission of Human Rights, where he did much to promote the cause of equal citizenship, and the first legal counsel to the International Monetary Fund. Her mother Beatrice was a Catholic convert of partly Jewish extraction. First to translate Thomas Mann, she was the daughter of a distinguished American palaeographer, Professor Elias Lowe. The distinguished Fawcett Society, which campaigns for women's equality, is named after a nineteenth-century forebear, Millicent Garrett Fawcett (her daughter – Philippa Fawcett – gave her name to the teacher training college where future London Mayor Ken Livingstone would study in 1970). A leading suffragist, Millicent was married to the Radical MP Henry Fawcett, appointed Postmaster General by Gladstone in 1880.

Charlotte's parents were also connected to many of the great liberal intellectuals of their generation. They were close friends, for instance, with the campaigners Lord and Lady Longford, whose novelist daughter Rachel Billington is godmother to Boris, Charlotte's closest friend and yet another Left-ish member of his extensive kith and kin.

Although Charlotte is much less frequently mentioned than Stanley, family friends acknowledge her enormous input into the children's development. They insist it is her warmth, creativity and wit that in large part account for Boris's subtleties and psychological insights, qualities that have marked him out from the crowd, as well as his own father. 'She is the genius,' remarks the writer and doctor James Le Fanu, a family friend married to Rachel's publisher. 'Boris is not the carbon copy of Stanley that many people believe, there is a great deal of his mother in him. She is the more interesting character, the ironist – like Boris.'

It is true that so much of Stanley's early life has contributed to the Boris the world knows today that many describe him as a 'chip off the old block' and it is possible, though not certain that Stanley invented the ever-popular Johnson bumbling old buffer schtick. Even if he did, he has never perfected it with the panache and Fawcett subtlety of Boris. Probably the more accurate assessment of father and son is that Stanley is the early factory prototype to Boris's refined, and more advanced, road model. As Douglas Hurd, who knows them both, puts it: 'Stanley and Boris are quite similar, but Boris has a sharper edge – both in his intelligence and his ambition.' Boris has learned, perhaps through Charlotte, how to conceal his ruthlessness – using bumbling, self-deprecation or humour, as needed. He is funnier, and more discerning than his father. Perhaps Charlotte rounded off some of his squarer edges by reminding her exceptional brood: 'It's nice to be important, but it's more important to be nice.'

Raised a Roman Catholic, she did not enjoy her own strict convent education, but is said to be both a moral and a spiritual person, if not overtly religious. When she had a knee operation, she came round from the anaesthetic to see a vision of her late mother standing over her at the side of the bed. 'She saw her clearly and talked about it afterwards in a matter-of-fact way,' says Le Fanu. 'It's just one way she's very special.'

When Stanley returned to Nethercote with Charlotte and the kids in 1969, his single-minded social and intellectual ambitions for their children were already clear. From an early age, the family atmosphere was decidedly highbrow and literary: children's arts programme *Vision On*, story slot *Jackanory* and *Blue Peter* were the only TV programmes permitted. The Johnsons were BBC, rather than ITV children, and Irène expected Rachel to read out leaders from *The Times* from the age of four. Always, the need to achieve was thrust home.

Later, on trips up to London to stay with her parents in Cavendish Avenue, Charlotte would educate her eldest three. Each child had an exercise book and would be taught a variety of different subjects. It was here that Boris displayed an early talent for painting, which he still enjoys today. (He loves painting cows. Indeed, he once vowed to do to the cow what Stubbs did for the horse, but confesses to being artistically challenged by the animal's 'odd, square bum.'[29]). Inside Cavendish Avenue was a cosy, yet inspiring education and one few children are privileged enough to enjoy; sadly, it could not last. Charlotte cherished it as much as her pupils, describing those days as 'one of the happiest times.'[30]

With his father's dynastic hopes resting on him, Boris soon scooped up academic prizes like rosettes at a gymkhana but he himself admits probably the single most galvanising event of his life – and the incident to install the formidable driving ambition we know today – was when Rachel, his younger sister by 15 months, learned to read before him. To this day, he can still feel the agony of her triumph. And the siblings acknowledge how much they spur each other on. 'At my 40th, he made a speech saying something like unless I had been born a year after him, he would never have done anything because by nature he is quite slug-like and contented,' says Rachel.[31] 'The pushiness, the forwardness, the cheekiness, Rachel just wanted to get on,' recalls her long-term boyfriend at Oxford, Sebastian Shakespeare. 'And always, always, she is competitive with Boris.'

With Stanley, the emphasis during those early years was placed on encouraging such competitive activity, whether it be running, jumping, eating the hottest mince pies at Christmas or possessing the blondest hair. If Boris, as the eldest, did not secure his rightful place by winning, he would erupt in anger. He once took his frustration out on a wall after losing a point to Rachel at table tennis, kicking it and breaking a toe in the process. To this day, he will invest an almost indecent ruthlessness into what is supposed to be an enjoyable game of what he calls 'whiff whaff' and frequently seeks to assert his superiority over employees or visitors by thrashing them in games of ping-pong over the Mayoral desk at City Hall. Of course this was a boy whose earliest recorded ambition was to be 'world king.'[32] His ferocious passion for supremacy in any contest has never waned, but appreciating the dangers of appearing over-ambitious in a self-deprecating country like Britain, he has become better at concealing it.

'Boris has always been very competitive, but that's what they teach you when you go to a very good school – to be the best,' explains Stanley. 'The children were competitive with each other – good, healthy sibling rivalry is what I would call it.'[33] Others might deem this ceaseless struggle for domination, which makes the Johnsons not exactly relaxing company, more of a blood sport. Coming second would never do, it was emphatically *not* about merely taking part. 'There were always high expectations of all the kids,' explains a close friend. 'They are a family where you definitely felt there was a culture, not put into words maybe, but an awareness of themselves as interesting people going to do big things.' Indeed, like a bunch of hyper-active boy scouts, the Johnsons are inveterate badge wearers, prize-baggers and point scorers. Sebastian Shakespeare recalls visiting Nethercote in the holidays: 'Mealtimes usually meant Stanley holding forth and him and Boris powering against each other. It was alpha males constantly sparring, with everyone else looking on. The other younger siblings would join in only occasionally from the sidelines – the hierarchy was clear.'

This rivalry sometimes gave rise to 'really violent fighting', which once saw younger brother Leo accidentally shooting Boris in the stomach with an air gun. Leo was supposed to have been shooting tin cans but had seen: '. . . a richer target nearby. Fortunately [Boris] survived [although] since it happened, he has always been very wary of me,' he says.[34] The incident is treated with the same hilarity as other Johnsonian 'antics', even though Boris had to be rushed to hospital for emergency treatment. Later, he even came to blows with Rachel after an argument over the identity of the lead singer of the Clash got out of hand.

But to interpret such behaviour as a sign of hostility between Boris and his siblings is to misunderstand the Johnsons. There is tension, yes, but little division among them. Constantly moving house meant it was nigh on impossible to form meaningful relationships with anyone else their own age, had they been urged to do so. In fact, seeking playmates outside the family who might not strive for such peaks of achievement was not encouraged. Throughout much of their childhood, bar the odd holiday with another suitably high-flying family, they were largely left to amuse themselves for they did not talk to other children. 'I remember Al had one friend, Carl, and he once went to Carl's house but I think that was it,' Rachel remembers. 'We never, ever, went to play with other children. We didn't need friends.'[35] Location and local chums could not provide a sense of being rooted and so close family filled the gap, which serves to explain two key facets of Boris's life. The first is the extraordinary clannishness of the Johnsons, very much an 'all for one, one for all' institution. Cross one of them and the others will close ranks. Marrying into the clan, like hitching up with a Royal, is not for the faint-hearted. Only the strongest and most independent survive, as Boris's first wife Allegra might testify.

Second, Boris has a habit of keeping other men, even those keen to become close friends, at arm's length. Neither a clubbable man, nor one who has bosom pals, he largely prefers female company. Only rarely in his life has he let down his guard. Men who have, for years, seen him socially say he is impossible to get to know: no real intimacy is ever shared, no male bonding reinforced over a pint. Offers of a companionable trip to the pub are frequently rejected with, 'I'm just off for a run, dear boy' – alone, naturally.

Despite Stanley's love of Nethercote, he did not stay there long after the family's return from America: ambition would not allow it. The autumn of 1969 saw more packing cases and a move to London, to an upmarket address in Maida Vale: 41 Blomfield Road, close to Paddington Station. They rented the house from friends of Charlotte's parents, thanks to another stroke of good fortune in the shape of a generous Ford Foundation grant for Stanley to do post-graduate research at the London School of Economics. He admits, however, that he 'didn't do as much studying as I should have done.'[36]

Politics, and the Conservative party in particular, now seized his attention. Stanley claims Douglas Hurd was instrumental in setting him up as the party's first-ever desk officer for the environment, although Hurd claims no such recollection. However Stanley secured it, the position was one of a portfolio of jobs held at the time – a multiple employment pattern, replicated later of course by Boris and Rachel. As part of the Conservative Research Department, Stanley came across a number of influential contacts, including current chairman of the BBC Trust Chris Patten, who recalls him as 'absurd, but harmless.'[37] Stanley did not stay long though. Wrongly expecting the Tories to lose the 1970 election, he instead embarked on yet another extended globetrotting mission with the aim of researching a new book. Boris and his siblings moved back to Nethercote with Charlotte, where they attended Winsford Village School, a white building next to the church. Once again, she was left to cope alone. On his return, however, Stanley decided it was time to buy a 'permanent' base in town and the result was a 'neat modern' house in Princess Road, just off Primrose Hill, London NW1 and near to London Zoo.

The children downed pencils in Somerset and enrolled at Primrose Hill Primary School, a late-Victorian board school, bang next-door. It was the same establishment attended by the future Labour leader Ed Miliband (who, being five years his junior, says he has no recollection of Boris) and his elder brother David (a year younger and so doubtless aware of Boris as a playground presence, but unwilling to discuss his memories). Astonishingly, Boris has managed to attend the same schools as both major party leaders in place in 2011. It is also remarkable that one state primary should have produced three prominent politicians in such a short space of time.

Primrose Hill also saw the start of a frustrating lifetime of musical endeavour, a rare activity in which Boris has been forced to accept almost abject failure. Soon Rachel was producing identifiable tunes from her descant recorder but her brother's output was annoyingly confined to shrill peeps and a quantity of warm spit. After dismissing the recorder as 'girly' at the age of 11, in an effort to 'express my musical personality,' as he puts it, he tackled the trombone.[38] His considerable wind power went in one end, but out of the other came only parps and what he refers to as a 'soft, windy afflatus.' There followed an embarrassing eviction from a rock band – 'on the not unreasonable grounds that I was the only would-be bass guitarist in history who could not play the opening bars of "Smoke on the Water."' Finally, at 17 he took up the piano and fell at the first fence, failing his Grade 1 despite 'months of brow-beading effort.'[39] It is not often that he is obliged to run up the white flag, but the musical challenge does seem to have defeated him.

In November 1972, the Johnson tribe (now numbering four with the addition of another brother, Jo, in late 1971) moved 500 yards away to 174 Regents Park Road. A substantial residence with a decent-sized garden in an elegant street, it marked a considerable rise in the Johnsons' social and financial standing. A delighted Charlotte was finally able to spread her wings and give each child his or her own bedroom, with rooms to spare. Stanley's career was beginning to bear financial fruit – boosted by an unexpected $10,000 cheque from Mr Rockefeller, with unintended irony, for 'continuing good work' on population control. As Stanley himself puts it, he has been 'dogged' by good luck all his life.

For once, he had wisely turned down another position in the US – although he initially accepted before recoiling from the prospect of subjecting Charlotte to yet another trans-Atlantic domestic wrench. But only a few weeks after moving to Regents Park Road, the young family were in any case uprooted once again, this time to a location that would help define Boris's life and provide him with some of his clearest, if not fondest, childhood memories. They were leaving their new home for another country, but this time it was not the US (and at least somewhat closer to home).

Stanley had tired of the 'ribbing' received from some in the population control sector. Now widely known as the father of a brood of four, it was clearly time to seek out new pastures where his own birth control techniques, or lack of them, would attract less comment. Of course, by the time he finished siring children, Stanley had raised his tally to six.

As usual on Planet Johnson, something turned up. This time it was a job in the environment sub-directorate at the European Commission in Brussels, something of a pioneering role as Stanley was one of the first British officials to be appointed following Britain's accession to the European Community in January 1973. While Charlotte was clearly not enthused, Stanley took her silence to indicate assent, or at least, in his words, an amber rather than red light. In April 1973, la famille Johnson set off across the Channel to Brussels. The Belgian and European capital, cowering below what often feel like the greyest skies in Europe, has a peculiar hold on Boris and his family. Such is the poor quality of light in this corner of Belgium that the late Roy Jenkins, when president of the Commission, regularly railed at what he deemed the 'Brabant gloom.' In those days, the bi-lingual city (French/Flemish) lacked the romance and glamour of Paris or the arty edginess of Amsterdam. Ranks of stolid bourgeois, early twentieth-century houses were deliberately left scruffy to avoid attracting the attentions of the ever-vigilant Belgian taxman and the modern European Community buildings near the Rond Point Schuman were indeed exercises in slap-sided ugliness.

Despite the weather and the drabness, not to mention the fact that it became the setting for a great deal of childhood pain and loneliness, the Johnsons seem curiously drawn to Brussels, returning time and again for work or study. For Boris, this was to be where he was first really singled out academically, where his mother suffered a nervous breakdown and his parents split up; where he made his name in journalism, where he lived with both his wives, divorced one and his first child was born. On his first visit, the family would stay for six formative years (the longest he himself had lived anywhere).

Home was initially a rented home in the leafy suburb of Uccle, although this was soon exchanged for a larger house the Johnsons bought nearby. For the grown-ups (working ones, anyway), Brussels' life was dazzlingly Continental. Lunch was sacrosanct and began at 12.45, and no one scheduled afternoon meetings until 3.15. A fine Belgian lunch was washed down with equally fine wine, everyone conversed in French and no one worked that hard, especially in the afternoon.

Meanwhile, Boris spent two years at school in Brussels, learning to be a 'good European' and rapidly becoming fluent in accent-less French. Although as an adult he has frequently played down his gift for foreign languages – adopting when it suits the classic 'Brit abroad' assault on French vowels and syntax – he is virtually bi-lingual and proficient in three more languages.

Whilst at school in Belgium he was able to revive his friendship with the quiet, but forthright Marina Wheeler, whose parents were also in Brussels, having moved over from Washington. It is fair to say she was not much impressed by the clever young blond and his increasingly flamboyant attempts to attract her attention. Indeed, he was 'generally to be avoided,' she decided.

While Stanley enjoyed his new job and social life enormously, life was less fun for Charlotte and the children. Brussels in those days was a dull, stuffy place with little to offer those not involved in the stimulating business of European integration. For children especially, it lacked excitement. The environmentalist Oliver Tickell recalls: 'My father [Sir Crispin Tickell, chef de cabinet to Roy Jenkins when commission president from 1977] and Stanley made friends in Brussels, but we knew the Johnson children less as we as a family deliberately chose not to spend too much time there. It was then a desperately dull place and we avoided it.'

Rachel has even bleaker memories, detached as they were from the comparative liveliness of central Brussels by the gloomy shadows of the Bois de la Cambre. She has told friends how the Johnson children, 'had to be close to survive. Brussels was a very strange place in the early days, with people feeling they were away from home and so maybe the ordinary rules didn't apply. People didn't work that hard like they do now, so they had other distractions, but that meant that stuck out on the outskirts of town where we were, it had the feel of that Hollywood movie *Ice Storm* [set in a New York commuter suburb, also cut off by woods]. There was the same bleakness, the disconnection'. She has described it as a time when 'our parents were breaking up – and breaking down. It was very hard, and Boris and I became very close as a way of dealing with it.'

Though now financially comfortable, for the Johnsons home life had become desperate. These were troubled and tortuous times, particularly for Boris as the eldest and his confidante, Rachel. As a result, they formed an unusually close bond, one that persists to this day. Stanley embarked on a series of affairs and after years of coping with his long absences, the constant moves and his infidelity, Charlotte was in a state of collapse. There were many names in the frame, including the wife of the editor of a major British newspaper. 'She is a very, very nice woman, but the number of people he had affairs with, Charlotte found it very hard to put up with,' recalled Anthony Howard. She told friends that her husband was 'one amazing womaniser.'[40] Even her growing reputation as a painter, with an exhibition in a gallery in the smart Sablon district of central Brussels, failed to rescue her from despair.

In 1974, a year after moving to Brussels when her youngest child Jo was not yet three and Boris just 10, Charlotte had a nervous breakdown. She was admitted to the Maudsley Hospital in London for nine months, suffering from depression. As she herself says: 'It was terrible because I'd had before this all that time when I was so, so close to the children and then I disappeared.'[41] To this day, just talking about those times brings tears to her eyes – particularly the thought of Boris and his siblings leaving her in hospital to return to Brussels after a brief visit. Friends say she used to worry terribly about her children's safety. 'I went to see her in hospital when she was painting these haunting pictures,' Howard recalled. 'She painted children climbing up trees – mad, very powerful pictures. In the background there was an idea of evil spirits.'

Until she and Stanley were divorced, Charlotte was often in and out of hospital. The depths of her depressions were undoubtedly frightening for everyone. Boris's life, which had revolved around the arty, sensitive, warm and cerebral mother known as 'Mama', would never be the same again. Her absence may account for much of the flamboyance, deliberate cheerfulness and resilience now associated with him and his siblings. 'If you're fearful when you're young, or you're growing up in a gloomy environment, you may well just decide to tap dance your way out of it,' says Sarah Sands, the journalist who knows both Rachel and Boris well. Maybe, as an adult, you try to overcompensate for the gaps in your childhood by almost obsessively seeking public acclaim in what Rachel's husband Ivo Dawnay only half-jokingly refers to as the Johnsons' 'severe case of Attention Deficit Disorder.' 'It was grim, there's no doubt about it,' confirms Rachel.

'We had a succession of deeply unpleasant Aunt Sponge and Aunt Spiker au pairs, who would gang up against us.'[42] Charlotte returned, but was not 'entirely well' for another two or three years.

Stanley, who had been absent during so much of their lives, was now sole parent in charge. However, this was not a role to which 'Dada' was accustomed and a solution was quickly found, at least for the eldest pair. 'My line on parenting has been very straightforward throughout,' he explains. 'It's too important to be left to parents.'[43] So in September 1975, when Boris was 11 (and Rachel merely 10), they were packed off to Ashdown House, a preparatory boarding school in Forest Row, East Sussex and known as a feeder for the great public schools. Charlotte hints it was Stanley's decision to send them away, rather than hers, largely absent as she was. 'It was kind of what my husband wanted and my grip on things was not great,' she says.[44] What's more, they were expected to make the cross-Channel journey to school by themselves, an experience that perhaps goes some way towards explaining their intolerance of weakness or hesitancy in others.

'My parents used to leave me and my 11-year-old brother at the Gare du Nord in Brussels with a packed lunch and a few francs to buy chips on the cross-Channel ferry,' chirps Rachel. 'We would take the train to Ostend, then the ferry to Dover and the train to Victoria; and after a brief pit stop at the paedophile-packed Cartoon Cinema, we would shovel ourselves and our trunks onto the train to East Grinstead. It took a whole day.'[45] Typically, the unusually resourceful pair made the trip without major incident but there was one hair-raising occasion when, returning at the end of a term, they managed to board the train to Moscow rather than Brussels. True to form, Rachel likes to recount the story with hoots of laughter, but she and Boris were certainly forced to face the misadventures of life from a very early age.

The family are all too aware of how difficult it must have been for Stanley to pick up the pieces after Charlotte's sudden departure. 'They're very loyal to their dad and protective of him. I suppose he had to do more than he expected because of Charlotte's illness,' says a close friend. Indeed, Rachel dedicated her novel *Shire Hell* to: 'My father, for everything'. But the same friend also believes the children inevitably suffered from the absence of their beloved Mama. What is certain is that Rachel took on an early cosseting role beyond her years, playing 'Wendy' to Boris's 'Peter Pan' and her younger brothers' 'Lost Boys'. 'There is something of the child-carer in both Boris and Rachel,' observes Sarah Sands. Another close friend adds, 'they all seem slightly in need of mothering, a bit vulnerable underneath the bluster. They became unusually close, all of them. Jo, for instance, became very attached to Rachel. When she had her first baby, he didn't seem to know how to react. He certainly behaved very oddly – I think he was jealous.'

Charlotte and Stanley separated just before the Christmas of 1978. On a grey December's afternoon, he drove her to Zaventem airport, on a desolate plain outside Brussels, returning alone to the former family home in Uccle. Afterwards, he wrote a poem about the split – it says much about the Johnsonian approach to life:

> So even though I smile and smile
> And pretend not to mind
> When I think of the good times
> I shall miss you.[46]

During reflective moments, Stanley has said he blames himself entirely for the breakdown of the marriage: 'I do not in any way wish to minimise the distress that can be caused to a family by separation and divorce. I felt desperately sorry for the children. Happily, Charlotte and I have tried to keep our relationship on the friendliest footing possible.'[47] It is to the credit of both that they are complimentary of each other as parents but friends of Charlotte, such as James Le Fanu, say she has never forgiven Stanley, rarely sees him by choice and was angry that she 'barely featured' in his autobiography. Boris has sought to avoid taking sides: it is instructive that he dedicates his novel, *Seventy-Two Virgins*, to both parents, with the Latin phrase 'optimus parentibus'.

At times, his father can sound astonishingly flippant about an event that ruptured Boris and his siblings' remaining childhood. 'I suppose

Charlotte and I grew apart – it is very hard to say, I never tried to analyse what happened in my first marriage. Look, I have no idea how much the children did or did not suffer, because I never asked them,' is vintage Stanley.[48] Four years later, when asked again why he separated from Charlotte, his stance was even more light-hearted: 'It seemed like a good idea at the time.'[49] And when pressed on whether he had strayed: 'These questions are not good – I was wholly faithful to Charlotte in all important respects.'[50]

Such quips could easily drop from Boris's own lips: seemingly, father and son share the same refusal to take conventional morals seriously or to abide by the same rules as anyone else. Both are fond of laddish banter and crude sexual references. At a book signing, Stanley once boasted to a woman about the frequency with which he had sex. His early novels offered numerous steamy encounters and a favourite game among the young Johnsons was to scour their father's books for the 'dirty bits.' But it wouldn't take long: 'You just open one of Stanley's novels at a random page, and there is inevitably something about sex. Good stuff!' chuckles Douglas Hurd. 'We needed only to snigger the words "rubbery nipples" to collapse in merriment,' recalls Rachel.[51]

Sex, sexual organs and sexual conquests are Johnsonian mainstays of conversation. Later, Boris infamously told a girlfriend that such was the number of his sexual partners that he hadn't had 'to have a wank for twenty years.'[52] Pretty much anything must be treated as a Johnson joke; once laughed about, however, it can be forgotten. The surprise must be that the son continues in the same vein after witnessing and being horrified by the intense suffering his father's philandering caused his mother.

Stanley's family certainly believe him to have been a serial adulterer. One of Rachel's close friends relates how she 'has moaned that Stanley was lecherous towards the au pairs, who were only a few years older than her.' Indeed, her father has expressed some disquieting enthusiasm for the constant supply of young girls in the house, particularly during the hot days of summer 1976. 'Our au pairs wore nothing – I do remember them certainly parading down by the river. Oliver Walston [a friend] says they wore nothing in the house, too –

he sent a card afterwards, saying, "'Thanks for the mammaries.'"[53] The Johnsons frequently took the precaution of hiring two au pairs in the hope both would not leave at once, although they sometimes did.

Even today, at parties Stanley's eyes constantly rove the room. Fellow guests often notice this unusual flirtatiousness in a man entering his eighth decade. Although there is no suggestion of infidelity to his second wife, Rachel's close friends – perhaps those with the greatest insight into this generally secretive family – have heard harrowing tales of the effect of his past affairs on Charlotte. Rachel herself has spoken a good deal about it over the years. 'She is very conscious of the damage Stanley had caused Charlotte through philandering,' says one of Rachel's former boyfriends. 'I don't think it made Rachel feel insecure, but it has made her feel more appreciative of her mother. She is also very fond of her father. I think he has indulged her and so she has come to terms with it. Maybe all the Johnson jesting is the way they all come to terms with it.'

Boris has told girlfriends that his way of coping was to make himself invulnerable so that he would never experience such pain again. True to form, however, he speaks less of it outside the family than Rachel. He once admitted to an interviewer that he had been 'upset' by the split, then immediately tried to close the open door by spluttering, 'No, it had some effect. They handled it brilliantly.'[54] Most acquaintances, even those who have known him for years, would have no inkling of the pain in his childhood: he has the hard outer shell of a child from a broken home, who has also had to deal with grave family illness.

Stanley told the children of the divorce when they were all at Nethercote for the holidays, prompting 14-year-old Boris to ask: 'Why did you have us?'[55] Charlotte, now 36, returned to London with her four children and moved into a top-floor maisonette on Elgin Crescent and Colville Terrace, Notting Hill paid for with the proceeds of the sale of the Regent's Park Road house. A bohemian home stuffed with oil paintings, exotic rugs, a doll's house and flowers, it was close to the fashionable markets and bars of Portobello Road and Westbourne Grove.

At last in her natural milieu, she found herself recovering mentally and able to live on the sales of her portraits of prominent characters such as Jilly Cooper and Joanna Lumley, worth thousands of pounds each. Compared to what she and the children were used to, however, money was tight as she refused to accept financial support from Stanley. Indeed, the roof leaked for a while and she also recalls, 'Once I sent the boys to the market to buy a turkey for Christmas and they came back with a capon because turkey was too expensive. So, Christmas dinner was rather small that year. It was like something out of Dickens. So, it's not true when people say Boris is cut off from reality.'[56]

Boris and his brothers were banned from playing ball games in the communal gardens but instead made do with cricket and darts in the hallways. They would also hide behind the roof parapet to drop water bombs onto unsuspecting passers-by on the pavement below. Such childish fun notwithstanding, Boris now assumed a key role in the family, acting as confidant and emotional support to his mother. His position as alpha male was thus unassailable, as was his growing aptitude as an emotionally literate companion to women, one who would listen and strike the right note, even if he could not be faithful.

Charlotte makes it clear the marriage had been doomed, whatever her efforts. 'I couldn't stay with [Stanley]. He was so inaccessible, not to say completely unfaithful. I couldn't live with him never allowing anything to be serious. That's the essential difference between Boris and his father. I can talk to Boris about anything.'[57]

When her children's friends meet Charlotte for the first time, usually they are surprised at how different she is from them – and also from Stanley. 'I thought if there is one woman in this room who is least likely to be Boris's mother, then it is her,' recalls one. She is calm, whereas Stanley is excitable; gentle where he is boisterous; quiet where he is noisy; retiring while he likes to be the centre of orbit. 'She takes the Ma Rothschild view of publicity – that your name should appear in the newspapers no more than three times,' remarks Le Fanu. And then of course she is genuinely upper class in contrast to Stanley's more rackety family history.

Charlotte eventually found happiness in 1988 when she married an American academic, Nicholas (Nick) Wahl, a man several years her senior but with whom she had so much more in common than Stanley. She left for New York again, this time to live with him in an apartment in Washington Square. He, meanwhile, worked as a professor at New York University and toiled away on what he hoped would be the definitive biography of Charles de Gaulle although sadly, this was never finished.

Nick had no children of his own but doted on hers and the affection was mutual. 'They were all very fond of their step-dad, Nick Wahl,' says a close observer. 'He was gentle, and nice – totally different from Stanley, who is a show-off.' 'Nick was good to Charlotte,' recalls Brian Johnson.

The couple spent eight happy years together in New York before Nick's death from cancer in 1996. Once again Charlotte returned to Notting Hill, alone. Although still painting whenever she can, she has had to contend with Parkinson's disease for nearly 30 years. When visiting his mother, Boris is a loving son and talks up her painting talents with commendable filial loyalty. However, Rachel's friends say as Charlotte's only daughter, the responsibility of caring for an ailing mother has fallen unevenly on her. She will – and does – drop everything whenever there is another medical crisis, although she never reveals the pain and anguish this sometimes causes. In addition, she has also had to deal with her husband's chronic health problems that necessitated a liver transplant. Illness has stalked her family, it seems. 'I have never seen Rachel break down,' reveals one of her closest friends, 'whatever life throws at her – it is not the Johnsonian way. She doesn't want sympathy, but she does crave recognition.'

While home life leading up to the split was painful for Boris, school was not that much better. All four siblings attended Ashdown House, which Stanley describes in the following way: '. . . as far as I could tell – a very happy ship.' Boris's own recollections of his time there seem rather different and are a subject on which he becomes unusually emotional. Now a happy, highly successful establishment, the school has indeed played a large part in creating the Boris we know today.

Rachel was the first girl boarder, but was later joined by another. However, used to mixing with boys – and sometimes even requesting to be called 'Richard' – she completely ignored the other girl. Perhaps she may have decided she was the 'wrong sort' after learning her father drove a Rolls and lived in a mock Tudor house in Surrey. Rachel also believes her presence there finally persuaded the headmaster to give up beating pupils. Stanley is insouciant – supportive even – of corporal punishment as a means to impart a valuable lesson in how not to 'blub', but it deeply troubled Boris. In fact, his contempt for the beatings and the masters who administered them is very revealing of the hidden, softer side of his personality frequently lost in the heat and noise of everyday existence.

This concern impressed his future proprietor Conrad Black, who noted that Boris's schooldays were one of the few subjects on which he became serious, and a believable and passionate opponent of corporal punishment. He also told Black how he would hear the younger boys crying, in terrible pain, and just how distressing it was. 'He was outraged at the physical cruelty inflicted by the faculty. He never gave me the impression that he had often been the victim of such treatment, but I would not doubt the depth of his revulsion at the thought of small boys being terrorised and battered.' Lord Black also observes Boris's haunted, angry tone on the school beatings in contrast to the typically joking one with which he is more associated.

Boris has also written of his experiences, using the word 'idyllic' below in his characteristically ironic manner. 'It seems amazing that in our lifetimes otherwise humane teachers would roll up their sleeves, flex the Malacca and – with or without a pervy Terry-Thomas glint in the eye – administer violent corporal punishment to the children they were supposed to be instructing. My memory of an otherwise idyllic 1970s English prep school is that masters used virtually any weapon of discipline they could lay their hands on.' He goes on to reveal an uncharacteristically heartfelt conviction: 'I remember being so enraged at being whacked for talking at the wrong moment that it has probably given me a lifelong distrust of authority.'[58]

Away from home, his mother ill, the family's future uncertain and now confronted with the misery of beatings (and possibly worse), it was at this point that Boris came up with a formidable method of self-protection. It may not be irrelevant that he – and his siblings – had already read a great deal of PG Wodehouse at home. In any case, family observers detected a startling change in him not long after he began attending Ashdown House. One noted: 'I heard he had hard times at school for his Turkish lineage, coming under fire for being a foreigner and coming over the Channel from Brussels. So he created a dishevelled look and persona, this 1930s-style English eccentric who appears to be bumbling, but is actually fantastically well read. It was a survival tactic and it worked brilliantly.' The experience also equipped him with another of his most endearing qualities: a genuine empathy for outsiders of whatever national or racial origin that he has demonstrated throughout his life. Indeed, it's an important element of his popular appeal.

Whatever antipathy he might still harbour against some of his former masters, it was at this 'idyllic' prep school that Boris won a King's Scholarship to Eton, reinforcing his position as Johnson top dog. Then headmaster Clive Williams rated all the Johnson children very highly, but added Rachel, 'was not as brilliant as Boris.' Leo later became head boy at Ashdown, but narrowly missed out on an Eton scholarship. For all his distractions, Boris excelled in Greek and Latin, quickly outclassing boys who had studied the subjects far longer. He was also an enthusiastic, if not brilliant rugby player. By now, he was physically, intellectually and emotionally tough – and an impressive figure of remarkable assurance.

There was, though, another challenge for the four children, who had already endured so much. A year after his divorce came through (and following his election in 1979 as Conservative MEP for Wight and Hampshire East), Stanley met his future wife, Jenny. He married her on 27 February 1981 when Boris was 16. Doubtless happy that their father had found new contentment so quickly, nonetheless it is never easy for the children of a first marriage to deal with subsequent nuptials, particularly when they lead to further siblings.

Jenny, nine years Stanley's junior and the widow of the theatre director Robert Kidd, is widely hailed as charming, poised and intelligent. Before meeting Stanley, she worked as an editor at publisher Weidenfeld & Nicholson and is considered a good hostess but is also known for being reserved, someone who 'doesn't give much away.' (She is also said to lean to the Left of Stanley, leading Rachel to observe: 'My father tends to marry socialists.') Inheriting a large, cohesive troupe of wilful children cannot have been smooth sailing for her either. A year later, she gave birth to her own daughter Julia, followed three years on by a son, Max. Both share the Johnson blond trademark, as well as drive and confidence but observers say there have been tensions. A friend of the older Johnson offspring remarks: 'It was very difficult for them when Stanley had more children – they felt Jenny didn't want anything to do with them. They felt she treated them like visitors to her house rather than making it another home for them.' Even today there is competition between the two sets. At one of Stanley's book-signings in 2010 – attended by both his daughters – friends of Rachel recall her distress that Julia had a more prominent seat. Later on, she was sitting in the chair closest to Stanley and defiantly placed at right angles to Julia and Jenny.

No wonder Boris has sought security, both financial and emotional, ever since. As someone who has known both him and Rachel for years says: 'I feel genuinely sorry for the Johnsons, whatever their successes in life.' But surely they rarely feel sorry for themselves? Indeed, they collectively feel almost a duty to be determinedly funny, brave and entertaining. Stanley and his first brood of children in particular benefit from each other's pre-eminence and talent for self-promotion. Their father never ceases to trumpet their achievements, even ostentatiously counting the number of times his family appears in one day's papers in the public arena of his local newsagent. He himself admits one of his greatest pleasures is that he managed to send all his offspring to top-ranking public schools. And for Boris that could not mean his own mid-table alma mater Sherborne, it had to be Eton.

Chapter Two

'Hey, Hey, ABJ'

Eton, 1977-1982

A well-worn gag about the great old schools of England goes:

> A lady enters the room where there are three public schoolboys.
> The Harrovian (motto: *Stet Fortuna Domus* / Let Fortune of the House Stand) orders someone to get her a chair.
> The Wykehamist (*Manners Makyth Man*) fetches it.
> The Etonian (*Floreat Etona* / Let Eton Flourish) sits in it!

'That's pure Boris!' cries a childhood acquaintance. 'I was brought up with generations of arrogant Etonian boys but Boris's arrogance transcends any I've ever met. He is the ultimate Etonian product, an opportunist to the core.'

In fact, dig deeper and the story is more complicated. Boris Johnson shares the overwhelming sense of entitlement of many Old Etonians, as his friend says, but there also remain traces of the insecurities of the outsider. Even an Etonian education did not completely dispel them and in some ways reinforced his empathy with other lone wolves.

In the autumn term of 1977, Boris entered Eton as a King's Scholar, one of a group of thirteen or fourteen boys a year who pass a gruelling entrance exam. He was by no means at the top of this list of dauntingly clever 13-year-olds, having scraped in at thirteenth, but it confirmed him as a member of the intellectual elite. In the 1970s, when Boris was at School (as every Etonian must call it), King's Scholars were excused all or most of their fees. This meant several of the Scholars were of relatively modest means compared to the scions of landed and commercial dynasties making up the ranks of the other boys, known as Oppidans. But Stanley gets quite snippy if anyone mistakes this for an attempt on his part to save money rather than a natural demonstration of his son's superiority. 'Winning a scholarship is a matter of honour,' he insists. 'It wasn't because we couldn't afford the fees.'[1]

'We were intellectually superior, the Oppidans socially superior,' explains a fellow Scholar, who knows Boris and his family well. 'Traditionally, scholars were seen as swotty and downmarket, but it didn't matter to us – we revelled in it. Actually, we felt protected. There was still fagging in the other houses, for instance, when we were there, but not in College [the name for the Scholars' House].'

College also had a more liberal bent than other houses in what was an overwhelmingly Conservative-supporting school. 'There were lots of rabid Tories amongst the Oppidans, who all read the *Daily Mail*. College was much more cultured and diverse and in our view at least quite left wing,' the Labour-voting Scholar recalls. Often reared on a diet of 'breezy anti-intellectualism,' the brasher Oppidans viewed Scholars as nerdy and even had a pejorative name for them: 'Tugs'. The name is derived from the gowns or togas worn by Scholars at all times, thus distinguishing them from the Oppidans. Surprising as it may seem to more meritocratic minds, it's not unknown for those who win Scholarships to turn them down in favour of a fee-paying place to avoid any hint of social stigma. Those who narrowly missed a Scholarship then, including the journalist Marcus Warren (Boris's junior by two years), talk of being 'spared.'

Such thoughts were no doubt far from Boris's mind on his first glorious day at Eton that Michaelmas Half (term), back in September 1977. Even if his apparent bumbling fooled his soon-to-be friend Viscount Althorp (later Earl Spencer) into believing at least there was 'one boy at school thicker than me,'[2] it was, of course, an act. Resplendent in gown, white tie and tails, he would have been fully aware of his status as a direct heir to King Henry VI's Foundation, which set up the school in 1440. Scholars go to get 'gowned' – a formal investiture exclusive to them in a ceremony dating back to the school's medieval origins. It's an inspiring occasion; participants recall tingling with a certain excitement and awe.

'The Provost presided over it all,' recalls a fellow Scholar from Boris's time. 'He told us we were the future leaders, that we had a responsibility and a destiny that was not to be taken lightly. We were privileged, but we were also duty-bound to give back to society and contribute to it. There was an expectation of us, and also a feeling that nothing was too big a stage. You found yourself thinking of someone like Pitt the Elder and asking yourself, am I really potentially that great?'

Over the years, Boris has observed to friends how such exhortations affected his outlook and that he believes those lucky enough to be educated at the great public schools are indeed being groomed to 'rule' over others. He was, in any case, accustomed to being around 'great' men – including Lord Charteris, a former private secretary to the Queen, who became Provost shortly after Boris started and whom he had known since a young boy as a friend of his mother's family.

The 70 Scholars are not only treated differently, and look different, they also have their own accommodation in the most historic buildings in the school. Lower School, dating from the Middle Ages and with desks eaten away by centuries-old boys' carvings, is exclusively for Scholars and used for prayers in Latin on Sundays. As one former Scholar puts it: 'You do feel you need to live up to these grand old buildings.' Until relatively modern times, Oppidans would reside with private landladies, whose lodgings evolved into the houses where the majority of Etonians now live. Even in Boris's day, while many College bedrooms would look out over the sweeping central courtyard in the heart of the school, the other 1,180 boys would have rooms in less-exalted buildings dotted further away all round Eton. The sleeping arrangements serve to this day to reinforce the College versus Oppidan distinction.

However, A.B. Johnson, KS, as he was formally known, was not immediately admitted to the hallowed College rooms and for the first term had to muck in with the Oppidans. His low ranking in the Scholar league meant that he had to wait until sixth formers staying on for their seventh term Oxbridge exams finally left and vacated their rooms in College.

David Guilford was Boris's housemaster for that first term and taught him Classics until O-Levels, as the first set of formal qualifications taken in English schools were called before they were replaced with GCSEs from the autumn of 1986. Now retired, he was a housemaster for 16 years and taught hundreds of clever Etonians, but Boris Johnson still sticks out in his memory. 'I had him in Private Business [an Etonian tradition similar to tutorial time when reports and extra-mural subjects of interest are discussed among a small group of boys with a master], and he always wanted to do something more advanced," he recalls. 'He was streets ahead of other boys who were not Scholars. He was certainly not at the top of the Scholarship list and not always in the highest divisions [subject sets] either, but he was a very fine chap, quite remarkable really and a much better scholar than he made out. But at school, he didn't come on top of the list or in the top 10: he was instead an all-rounder, very good at rugby and the Wall Game, but perhaps less at cricket. He was a School figure – unusual for a Scholar.'

This crystal-clear recollection more than three decades on is all the more striking considering some of the other students Guilford encountered in his time. 'I also taught David Cameron, but I don't remember him at all – he must just have done what he was told.' Another master – Tim Connor – actually denied having taught Cameron, having no recollection of him. Presented with concrete evidence that he had indeed taken the future Prime Minister in the Upper Sixth, a dumbfounded Connor admitted it was still a 'complete blank.' With generations of upper middle-class heritage and financial security, Cameron of course did not have so much to prove. 'Cameron was posh, even by the standards of Eton,' says Marcus Warren, an exact contemporary.

The fact that Boris, in contrast to most Scholars, became such a prominent School figure is instructive as Tugs traditionally found security in separation. Arriving as 'Al' or Alex Johnson, he gradually became known as Boris – chosen for its greater distinctiveness – and so did he incrementally perfect the eccentric English persona so popular today. In an establishment of real toffs, Boris's confected version outshone them all for humour and bravado: here was a Scholar who was certainly not nerdy or weird, whose intelligence and chutzpah marked him out over time as something special across School. He seems determined not to have played the role of the outsider (indeed, at Eton he abandoned his mother's Catholicism in favour of the Church of England). His success in blending in was a remarkable achievement, as Marcus Warren explains: 'College was more of a hothouse than other houses, with a reputation for eccentric and bookish boys in a school of 1,250 teenagers, where such attributes were out of the ordinary. So, Boris was unusual in that his strength of character allowed him to survive and thrive outside College's protective environment. Unlike most other Scholars, he appealed to the rest of the school. He was a figure of fun but we weren't laughing at him, but with him. He had this gruff delivery, but great comic timing. He was a star! He was a figure much like he is now – I really don't recognise any great change at all.'

Boris joined Eton at a time of considerable change under the headmastership of Michael McCrum, when brains began to matter more than mere privileged birth, or at least take equal billing. Fagging (the custom of using younger boys as personal servants) was on the wane and beatings administered by boys had finally been banned, while learning was on the up. 'McCrum was very austere, but in the bigger historical context was responsible for a big improvement in the academic success of the school,' explains Warren. 'He recognised that Eton could no longer rely on its social cachet, that it would need galvanising academically so from the 1970s onwards, it became this academic hothouse.'

Boris started off his Eton career modestly. His academic and humorous abilities were quickly evident and at 13, he was already a formidable debater. He was also adept at deflecting questions with the deftest of non-committal answers. 'He could block hostile or difficult questions from masters even then,' recalls one contemporary. 'Great training for dealing with the media later on.' But news of his parents' divorce temporarily dampened the flamboyance of the young

Boris. Although his flaxen hair and undoubted intelligence marked him out, his place in school mythology would not come for another couple of years. For now, traces of his old shyness still remained. 'As a kid I was extremely spotty, extremely nerdy and horribly swotty,' he admits. 'My idea of a really good time was to travel across London on the tube to visit the British Museum.'[3]

Although popular, initially he was not seen to be particularly close to anyone. And academically, he was not always in the top sets or divisions, which are typically dominated by Scholars. In his second year, known in baffling Eton parlance as 'E Block', he was in the second division for English when almost all other Scholars were in 'Div One'. In Science, he mustered a lowly Div Five and even Div Six in maths, neither subject ever being his forte (his fellow Collegers were mainly in the top group for virtually all subjects). He quickly shone at Classics, though – which stood him in good stead in a school where they were revered.

Only in his third year, or 'D-Block', in the 1979 Michaelmas term was he promoted to Div One for English. His genius for the verbal pirouettes that would later help make him famous was finally recognised in the Lower Sixth, when he won the English prize in the summer of 1981 at the age of 17. He was also writing for the school magazine, *The Chronicle*, in a style not dissimilar to the one his public knows today. On 10 October 1980, he produced a description of former prime minister Sir Edward Heath on a visit to the Political Society: 'Edward Heath was lit up from behind, his face in shade and a halo of silver light extending from his temples, like some prophet of old.'

By this time he had become a fully-fledged school celebrity, known to everyone simply as Boris for the first time in his life. Here was the near-perfect prototype of the seemingly bumbling, shambolic persona wrapped round the rapier intellect that we know today. Already he had learned to conceal his ambition with humour and self-deprecation, but it took time and effort to hone the act and this apparently could only be completed at the expense of his schoolwork. His innate brilliance could get him only so far, particularly in those subjects where he was less of a natural. The masters were fond of, and exasperated with Boris in virtually equal measure, but towards the end of his Etonian career there are signs that their patience was beginning to wear thin.

Martin Hammond, who became a popular Master in College in 1980, came to know Boris well. A richly cultured, but grounded man with liberal sympathies, he wrote to Stanley in December that year saying that his son was 'a delightful person, a real life-enhancer. I like his open friendliness of manner, and his ready wit.'[4]

But the next report, dated 3 April 1981, expressed concerns that Boris had 'a finger in a wide variety of pies.'[5] Soon there are grumbles about lateness, non-appearance of work and a lack of organisation, plus a doubtful 'commitment to the real business of scholarship'.[6] Nevertheless he managed to scoop up some considerable trophies, such as the Newcastle Classical Prize, albeit by a 'narrow' margin.

On 10 April 1982, just weeks before his A-Levels, there follows another letter from Hammond, which, while still containing words of affection and praise for Boris, also gives some really quite alarming observations. It's the sort of mixed assessment frequently delivered by his associates today: so many start off by saying how fond they are of Boris before embarking on lengthy descriptions of his failings and the letter from Hammond follows precisely the same pattern. After praising the fact that Boris had achieved 'some success' in a divinity scholarship, he goes on to describe the tone of an assessment from personal tutor Andrew Hobson (a mentor chosen by Boris himself) as 'pretty damning.' He then rails about his protégé's 'disgracefully cavalier attitude' which he believes is in danger of evolving into 'sheer fecklessness' and continues in similarly hostile vein: 'Boris seems affronted when criticised for what amounts to a gross failure of responsibility and surprised at the same time that he was not appointed Captain of School [Head Boy] for next half. I think he honestly believes that it is churlish of us not to regard him as an exception, one who should be free of the network of obligation which binds everyone else. I am enormously fond of Boris and saddened that he should have brought upon himself this sort of report.'[7]

And then in July 1982, Hammond writes again to Stanley: 'Boris is pretty impressive when success can be achieved by pure intelligence unaccompanied by hard work. He is, in fact, pretty idle about it all.

Boris has something of a tendency to assume that success and honours will drop into his lap: not so, he must work for them. Efficiency and organisation have been constant problems (there was trouble this half with his running of the Political Society, and an unprecedented rebuke from the Provost).'[8]

Boris himself recalls the rebuke was prompted by his arriving 45 minutes late for a meeting with Lord Charteris, in what must have been seen as a breathtaking display of rudeness. And yet, in what can only be an indication of the power of his charm, Hammond writes in the very next sentence: 'It was perhaps a bit of a risk to make Boris Captain of the School but he clearly has the personality and the respect necessary for the job, and it's my hope that the imposition of a public responsibility will energise all else. It's a particularly important job in the Michaelmas and involves a number of administrative tasks which simply must be done well.' Indeed, the key to his redemption in Hammond's eyes comes in the next line: 'Certainly I look forward to working with him – he's excellent company, and has a mature understanding of people and things.'[9]

Boris may have been infuriating, but he already recognised the power of charm and energy, as well as the futility of being a rebel when you want to get on. Enthusiastically and cheerfully, he embraced all the Etonian traditions – House, hymns, the Wall Game, Latin prayers, rugby and searing competitiveness. (Indeed, unlike his sister Rachel – who became a punk and acquired a Mohican-styled boyfriend partial to black nail varnish – he never underwent a teenage rebellion stage.) He also revealed none of the apathy or lack of ambition of which Etonians were widely accused in newspapers of the time, being intent, as he himself puts it, on 'greedily filling himself up to the gills with the finest education that England could offer'.

Other Old Etonians from those years remember a number of boys simply 'gave up and did nothing' when they could no longer cope with the merciless and relentless ranking of their academic position. (Each term, every boy would be given a rank between one and 250, according to his exam results. The Scholars would expect to dominate the top slots, and inevitably did, while everyone knew the names of those falling behind.) Following the refusal of some 'lazy' boys to go on a theatre trip, Boris's contemporary, the celebrity chef Hugh Fearnley-Whittingstall, even wrote a poem – Whither Apathy – about the extent of the 'Eton problem' and it is worth repeating here as an insight into the Eton of the early-1980s.

Eton's problem nowadays
Is no-one wants to go to plays
Those chaps we thought heraldic snobs
Are just a bunch of lazy slobs!
So speaks our friend, the national press
"It's APATHY, no more, no less!"
The word instills a sordid fear
What must I do with my career?[10]

This was also when the great public schools were often under attack for being unworthy bastions of an elitist class system. Boris's future rival for Mayor of London, Ken Livingstone, then leader of the soon-to-be abolished Greater London Council, summed up the view of many in an interview in the Etonian school magazine, the *Chronicle*, on 4 June 1983 – shortly after Boris left.

'I think your school should be integrated into the state system, because I don't think you should have the right [through] what your parents can buy [to] a privileged start over the rest of society. I look at the people who have emerged from Eton and Harrow, Oxford and Cambridge and I think you're a load of bloody wallies.'

Boris, who confesses to having become conscious of Tory 'feelings' at around this time, wrote a spirited, if pompous defence of Eton and its privileged pupils in the same journal. Whatever his populist appeal may be now, he is nothing if not an elitist. The confident tone – astonishingly similar to his adult writing style – belies his 16 years: 'I tell you this. The Civilised World can ignore, must ignore entirely these idiots who tell us that by their very existence the public schools demolish all hopes most cherished for the Comprehensive System. Clearly, this is twaddle, utter bunkum, balderdash, tommyrot, piffle and fiddlesticks of the most insidious kind. So strain every nerve, parents of Britain, to send your son to this educational establishment (forget this socialist gibberish about the destruction of the State System). Exercise your freedom of choice because in this way you will imbue your son with the most important thing, a sense of his own importance.'[11]

Boris was certainly imbued with a sense of his own importance – and a near divine, or rather Etonian, sense of a right to rule. Such a feeling of superiority was no doubt reinforced by his starring role in the Wall Game, a sport unique to Eton and one, masters claim, that brings out leadership qualities although another Old Etonian view is that it's just a 'mindless scrum, but fun because of its history and uniqueness.' The game, which sets Scholars against Oppidans in an opaque test of cunning and brute force, was the perfect exhibitionist sport for Boris and in time, he came to captain the College team. The object is to drive an under-size football over a line and then attempt to score. Winning not only requires serious muscle, but also stealth and an ability to inflict and endure pain. The *Chronicle* ran a spoof of the 1960s Vietnam peace chant (the original was written in protest at the escalation of the war by President Lyndon B. Johnson, known simply as 'LBJ') in celebration of the legendary aggression of A.B. Johnson when pitted against the Oppidans. They were in no doubt, it seems, when it came to his ruthless purpose on (and off) the field.

Hey, Hey, ABJ
How many Oppidans did you kill today?

The *Chronicle* exhorted boys to 'watch the Blond Behemoth crud relentlessly through the steaming pile of purple-and-orange [Oppidan] heavyweights, until he's knocking on the Lower Master's Door.'[12] Playing rugby, Boris took a similarly reckless approach to his own safety and that of others – it is remarkable that they all emerged intact, although his nose took a bit of a beating.

He also showed an early interest in journalism and the attention that went with it. Here, too, he sought – and duly won – the top job: the editor's chair. In his sixth-form years, he was determined to bag the most prestigious positions to bulk out an already impressive CV. By the summer term of 1981, he was one of two editors of the *Chronicle*, along with another boy – Roger Clarke. As he would later do at the *Spectator*, he brought in many of his illustrious friends to pen the journal, including Charlie Spencer (Viscount Althorp and brother of Diana, Princess of Wales) on the arts pages, with features by Andrew Gilmour (son of the Conservative minister, Sir Ian Gilmour). Darius Guppy, an exuberant half-Iranian boy whose ancestors on his father's side included the naturalist who gave his name to the fish and Sir Francis Dashwood, founder of the eighteenth-century 'Hellfire Club', notorious for its pagan orgies, was also involved. By now Boris's cleverness and above all, humour had catapulted him into a tight-knit trio with Spencer and Guppy, two of the best-connected boys in the school.

Although Boris was Charlie Spencer's editor, this was a reversal of the original hierarchy. A close friend of Spencer's in his youth recalls: 'Charles and Darius were the leaders of the pack and Boris was very low down in the pecking order in the early days. I used to go to parties at Althorp [the Spencer family seat] and Boris was relatively invisible. Charles was the richest, Darius the wildest – and Boris the cleverest. But they were all clever, and Charles and Darius were very handsome and Boris was thinner and better-looking then, too – he quickly rose up the ranks.'

As if to the manor born, Boris was by now mixing with the upper echelons of society. The Spencers ranked as one of the leading aristocratic families in Britain and of course married into royalty during Boris's schooldays. Spencer and Guppy were among Boris's first close male friends as opposed to the dozens of friendly acquaintances he had previously cultivated and their support and loyalty would no doubt have meant a great deal to him.

In the autumn term of 1981, Boris entered 'Pop', the self-perpetuating group of the grandest Etonians and the definition of social success at the school. 'Pop was a self-selecting society of popular boys, like a private club,' explains another Scholar, who did not share such ambitions to be tribal chief. 'Teachers are not supposed to have influence on its conduct or composition and generally it is the coolest boys, the best at sport, the richest and most talented that get in. They then mark themselves apart with different, checked trousers, lavish waistcoats and the Pop swagger. I suppose it is much like the Bullingdon Club at Oxford, but with official blessing. They are supposed to administer discipline in the school, but in practice they don't.'

Pop had a private room, where members could go to watch videos on a Saturday night – still a fashionable novelty in the 1980s; Pop could also stay at Tap, Eton's school bar, later than the other boys. Such privileges marked out the elite of the elite and so in turn, Boris's arrival as a considerable force. To assume he mixed solely with the possessors of stately homes and ancient lineage, however, would be wrong: one of his most admirable qualities also came to the fore at Eton, which had only a smattering of black pupils in the 1970s. It was not easy to be other than white in the world's most famous school at this time, but Boris did his best to be friendly to everyone. With that gift of including the outsider without being patronising, one black contemporary speaks of how Boris conversed with boys from ethnic minorities while many of his contemporaries ignored them.

He extended his popular appeal – and fame – by taking on the secretary's position at the Debating Society, which among its attractions had the prospect of trips to girls' public schools for competitions. The experience allowed him a wider stage and he never lost an opportunity to exploit it. Emma Jenks remembers vividly the time he first came to her school, Wycombe Abbey: 'We were very excited about debating with Eton and spent ages preparing our speeches. Boris was the head of the Eton debating society – although I am not sure why as he was absolutely useless at organising it. But he was a fabulous debater. We had done all this work beforehand, and he turned up and said: "Ah! Yes, a speech." He wrote it there and then, resting a piece of paper on the back of a tree. We couldn't believe it – and it was a fantastic speech. I couldn't work out whether this show of disorganisation was genuine or a veneer.' After a pause, she continues: 'I think probably a veneer as I later saw him running for President of the Union at Oxford and he was very organised then.'

Boris's observation that Wycombe Abbey resembled a gothic horror movie set on a golf course won him roars of laughter and a great many female fans, but not every girl was impressed. 'Boris really quite polarised people. Some of the girls found him very attractive – one girl talked about him for days,' remembers Jenks. Contemporaries recognise the tones of the Eton Debating Society in his writing and speech-making to this day. 'It was probably the most influential forum of his life,' says one, who knows the Johnson family well. 'It was a place where stars could really shine and have a whale of a time. The debates were lively and funny – it was all the perfect stage for Boris and he has never really escaped it.'

Jenks' brother attended Eton and she saw Boris again at the annual Fourth of June festivities (celebrating the birthday of Eton's greatest patron, George III), where his platinum hair made him stand out. He certainly made an impression on her father – the late Sir Brian Jenks, Bt. – despite numerous clever young men at Eton at the time. 'My father saw him at school from time to time, including once speaking in a debate and right back then, he said, "He'll be PM." He just had this charisma and style,' she recalls.

Those qualities helped to propel Boris and his friend Hugo Dixon, now a dotcom businessman, to 'steamroller' their way to the final of the 1981 House Debating Competition on 28 November that year. Against the background of a Thatcherite recession laying waste to much of Britain's industrial heartland and sparking riots in major cities, the motion was: 'This House would Emigrate'.

Boris spoke in favour of the motion that night, urging his audience to seek out a new life in space, away from what he chose to refer to as 'the ghastly dregs' living on Earth. His side lost the competition as the judges decided that they 'preferred to be cajoled rather than berated.' Boris's anger at this result is reputedly still keenly felt today but at least the audience of boys divided 26-21 in favour of his team, sealing his reputation as a formidable populist. Tim Connor, a highly regarded history master who was one of the two judges, remembers: 'Boris could always speak readily and wittily but we would judge on the actual quality of debate. Boris did berate people then and I can imagine he does now.'

Sir Eric Anderson, formerly Tony Blair's housemaster at Fettes in Scotland, became headmaster of Eton in 1980 and once a week taught Boris in Sixth Form Select – a handpicked group of the brightest boys.

A favourite memory of Boris's wit was when Anderson once wrote 'Business, Industry, Commerce' up on the board and gave his pupils ten minutes to write down what these words suggested to them. If you want to know how Boris 'gets away with it', look no further than his brilliant answer: 'These three words suggest to me that the headmaster dined in London last night.' Of course, he was right and Anderson – who thinks the story sums up his former pupil's special brand of wit – could give only an indulgent smile in response. But Boris had made his mark. Anthony Howard remembers going to speak at Eton after Boris had left and asking Anderson: 'Who is the most interesting – rather than the cleverest – pupil you've ever had?' He replied: 'Without a doubt, Boris Johnson.' And according to Anderson: 'He's a very memorable person. Anyone who's spent an hour with Boris never forgets it. All I have to say to you about him is all good.' Privately, a different message sometimes emerges from the Etonian ranks, with grumbles that despite his undoubted cleverness and panache, Boris was too much of a 'showman' to tackle anything really serious.

In common with Blair, being interesting at school often came at the price of a lack of attention to detail: Boris's dislike of preparation undoubtedly annoyed his headmaster. When playing the lead in *Richard III*, he omitted to learn the lines so he had them pasted behind various pillars. It was funny for boys in the audience, but somewhat annoying for those who had invested a good deal of time and energy in the production. Since then, Boris has confined his acting performances to occasions when he can deliver his own lines.

David Guilford remembers that Boris was invited to join the Essay Society, a select group of clever boys convened by the head. 'He delivered a paper once off-the-cuff – he was clever enough to half get away with it. The headmaster thought it was only half thought-out, but Boris was always so busy with so many things. He was popular, got on with people, so he got away with it.'

Despite his masters' misgivings, Boris won a scholarship to Balliol College, Oxford, to read Classics. Hammond's final report, written on 2 January 1983, predicted that he would be 'easier prey than some to the temptations of Oxford life.' Displaying a weakness for upmarket laddish banter, Boris wrote under a photograph of himself toting a machine gun in the College Leaving Book of his determination to achieve, 'more notches on my phallocratic phallus.' Having stayed on to take his Oxbridge exam the previous autumn, he now set off on a gap year abroad.

He spent the year teaching English and Latin at Geelong Grammar School, Australia's answer to Eton – and now with annual fees of A$27,700 (around £18,000), the country's most exclusive school. This choice was another demonstration of the Johnsonian fondness for the wealthiest and best (no sign of building latrines for starving Africans). All four Johnson sons attended Eton. Five out of six of Stanley's children were to go to Oxford – it is what he says makes him proudest of his offspring. Only Julia, the younger, more rebellious daughter, broke out and went to Cambridge before giving up after less than a month and fleeing to University College London. This cannot have been an easy move and it's rarely alluded to by the family. 'Oh, it's alright,' her mother Jenny reassured a close friend afterwards, 'Julia got her First.'

In Australia, Boris was set to work on Geelong's famous Timbertop campus – a year-long outward bound course for its Year Nine boys and girls, once attended by HRH Prince Charles and set in the wilderness of the foothills of the Great Dividing Range. Not only was he expected to teach the scions of Australia's and New Zealand's wealthiest and most eminent families, but also to help maintain its 325-hectare site of bush and farming land, 2km from the nearest road. In return, he received pocket money, plus board and lodging. Most of the 25 teachers and 40 assistants of various sorts lived on campus, where no television was allowed, access to phones limited and alcohol strictly forbidden. The teenage students in their care were expected to confront, 'the challenges of something like a man's life under conditions they have to conquer'.[13] Heating came from wood-burning boilers and if not enough wood was collected, the residents (including the students themselves) went cold. It was a fairly tough regime designed to put backbone into the Antipodean ruling classes.

As ever, Boris – who happened to be the only non-Aussie assistant in his time – made an impact. An extract from the *Corian,* the school magazine, calls him both Boris and Alexander, and notes, 'he will, in particular, be remembered for his inimitably stolid style of tractor-driving. How such a rustic character could also have such a ready wit and such facility with Latin always remained a mystery.'[14] Master and Chaplain of Treetops was the Australian Anglican priest, Peter Thomson – a powerful and charismatic preacher, whom Tony Blair had met at Oxford and found to be 'spellbinding' (it was under Thomson's influence that Blair developed his faith in Christianity). Back in Australia, he also impressed Boris with his Aussie directness and charm, although he in turn remembered the Etonian on his team as being a 'bit wild.'[15]

During his gap year – although presumably not at Timbertop – Boris claims to have dabbled with a few illegal substances, such as the odd joint. Throughout adult life, he has always treated the subject of his drug taking – like most other serious matters – as a bit of a joke, with variations depending on the audience. In an interview with a women's magazine he claimed that yes, he did try drugs, but no, not all seriously, and anyway the illegal substances around in his youth were 'not the same as what the kids are having now. My drug-taking past is pathetic.'[16] However, in a more laddish encounter with Piers Morgan in *GQ* in 2007, he was more boastful of taking cocaine at the age of 19 at Oxford: 'I remember it vividly. And it achieved no pharmacological, psychotropic or any other effect on me whatsoever.'[17] And for comic effect on the BBC quiz show, *Have I Got News for You* in 2005, the story was, 'I think I was once given cocaine, but I sneezed and so it did not go up my nose. In fact, I may have been doing icing sugar.'[18]

Is this Boris's way of quashing any suggestion that he has not experienced 'real life' while managing to dodge the outrage of Middle England? As with his rival OE David Cameron, contemporaries question whether Boris ever really indulged. Since President Clinton admitted that he had tried, but 'not inhaled' marijuana, a confession of a minor drugs 'experience' in youth has become almost de rigueur for any ambitious politician. Both Boris and Cameron are highly self-disciplined characters, who grew up at a time when it was considered dull or odd not to at least give drugs a try. Both desire the appearance of being normal, but being iron-disciplined and self-focused, neither was anything of the sort.

Boris is strangely reticent about his gap year but it gave him the time and the distance to practise and perfect the Boris persona – with the 'ready wit' and 'facility with Latin' that made such an impact at Geelong. At the end of it, 'Al' was left 10,000 miles away in the Australian Outback and 'Boris' was to come to the fore at Oxford and thereafter.

Chapter Three
Toffs, Tugs and Stains
Oxford, 1983–1987

Boris could not be going up to Oxford at a better time. For the previous two decades the ancient University had lost ground to its great rival Cambridge in terms of political importance. In the 1960s, the 'other place' had produced most of the then rising Tory political elite, such as Ken Clarke, Norman Lamont and Michael Howard. The so-called 'Cambridge Mafia' produced a clutch of Cabinet ministers and a party leader, though not a prime minister. But by 1983, the year Boris went up, the balance of Varsity power was shifting: Margaret Thatcher, then Prime Minister and at the height of her powers, was an Oxford graduate.

The political winds were also changing, with tradition back in the ascendant and the Michael Foot-led Left in chaos. Toffs were back in favour and Sloane Rangers and Young Fogeys were the rising social tribes. Since Granada Television's adaptation of Evelyn Waugh's *Brideshead Revisited* had transmitted a romanticised view of Oxford life into the nation's living rooms in 1981, the town had once again been attracting the nation's brightest 'young things'. Could any young public schoolboy resist emulating the languid undergraduate style and charm of a young Lord Sebastian Flyte? The charismatic, but ultimately doomed character – or rather Anthony Andrews' seductive TV portrayal – spawned a thousand tank tops, male blonds (bottle or *au naturel*) and cut-glass accents (real or affected) across Waugh's 'city of aquatint' and 'cloistral hush'.[1] There were even a few teddy bears, too.

Boris found himself at the forefront of a gilded generation of Oxford undergraduates, who went on to dominate politics and the media in the early twenty-first century. While much of Britain languished in post-recession gloom with three million people on the dole, at Oxford the air fizzed with future potential. 'There was an arrogance and an ambition,' says another alumnus James Delingpole, now a writer, journalist and broadcaster. 'We all thought that we would be part of the ruling class; that we should be rewarded for being bright and working hard.' One forward-thinking Balliol student spent three years having his photograph taken with as many Oxford contemporaries as possible on the (correct) assumption that a good number of them would become famous or powerful.

The roll call of Boris's contemporaries at Oxford includes British Prime Minister David Cameron, Foreign Secretary William Hague, Polish Foreign Minister Radek Sikorski, Education Secretary Michael Gove, Conservative fixer and thinker Nick Boles MP, Culture Secretary Jeremy Hunt, PR tycoon Roland Rudd, BBC political editor Nick Robinson, Channel 4 political editor Gary Gibbon, Clinton press secretary George Stephanopoulos and US pollster Frank Luntz. Labour's post-Blair/Brown elite was also well represented by David Miliband (followed a few years later by his brother Ed), Shadow Chancellor Ed Balls and his wife Yvette Cooper. Ian Katz, who was to become deputy editor of the *Guardian*, was also a contemporary and would later become a neighbour of Boris's in Islington.

Boris talks of this time with affection, pride and a little faux horror. 'What a sharp-elbowed, thrusting and basically repellent lot we were. We were always bragging or shafting each other, and in a way we still are, with our pompous memoirs and calculated indiscretions. When Toby Young began an article in [university newspaper] *Cherwell* with the words, "I work harder and achieve more than anyone else I know," we all chortled in approval of this ghastly ethic.'[2]

So, young Boris was not alone in holding high expectations – but he was unusual in how he went about achieving them. It undoubtedly helped that he already knew many of his contemporaries from school. Eton then, as now, sends dozens of boys each year to Oxford. In Boris's time – and he was no exception in this – Old Etonians would often socialise with each other to the exclusion of others, join the same invitation-only clubs and support each other in student elections. Throughout his years at Oxford they represented a formidable tribal group and have, as we have seen, gone on to maximise the benefit of their school and university connections to become Britain's new, or perhaps renewed, ruling elite.

To a foreign student, no matter how well connected or popular, they appeared an unassailable force. 'It became clear to me how powerful Eton is as a manufacturer of cultural capital. It's disproportionately powerful, devastatingly so,' remarks Mark Carnegie, a wealthy Australian rower. 'It's like the Goldman Sachs of England but instead of financial capture, it has national capture. It makes you ponder, "Is Eton for the nation's benefit, or is the nation for Eton's benefit?" I'm a big Anglophile and I don't understand the hold it has over this country.'

True to form, Boris joined the Bullingdon Club, an upper-class drinking society stuffed with Old Etonians on the make. The 1987 photograph of Boris and his fellow members – including David Cameron – striking arrogant poses in their Bullingdon livery is now so infamous that the photographers Gillman and Soame have withdrawn the copyright. At one time it was believed this was at the Conservative party's request, so concerned were its image-protectors about the potential fall-out from such an image of brazen elitism, but it has since been denied.

The Bullingdon is a one-time hunting and cricket society founded in 1780 that evolved into a rumbustious – some would say repellent – social club for well-connected toffs. A version of it also features in *Brideshead*, where Waugh pours scorn on the 'hearties' as he calls them, telling a story of how they bully the ostentatiously camp Anthony Blanche by dunking him in the Mercury pond at the centre of Christ Church's Tom Quad. In their absurd Bullingdon livery of blue tailcoats with mustard waistcoats – that even in the 1980s were £500 a pop[3] – Waugh describes its members as resembling a bunch of 'very disorderly footmen.'[4]

The club, whose members are bound by a vow of omerta, was also portrayed on stage at the Royal Court theatre in London in early 2010, albeit disguised as the Riot Club. *Posh*, a play by Laura Wade, exposed some of the Bullingdon's worst excesses and what one reviewer described as its 'casual hatred of the proles'.[5] As Boris's sister Rachel, who went to watch it (but left before the scene showing the ritual trashing of a private dining room at the end), said afterwards: 'I think if the entire country was forced to sit through it there would never be a Conservative government again, let alone a Bullingdonian Old Etonian Prime Minister.'[6] Or, she might have added, a Bullingdonian Old Etonian Mayor of London.

Boris was now ensconced in a closeted upper-class world of entitlement and wealth, socially a million miles away from his family's Exmoor hill farm. 'What fascinates me is the ease with which he took to the grand life,' noted Anthony Howard. 'Stanley went to Sherborne – quite a respectable public school – but Boris was a first-generation Etonian. The way he adapted to the ways of the rich and grand, including people like Charlie Spencer and Darius Guppy, and the members of the Bullingdon was astonishing. It was not in his background at all.'

Boris was present at the now-infamous Bullingdon evening in Oxford when a pot plant was thrown through a restaurant window and a couple of members ended up in police cells – dramatised on TV in 2009 in the docudrama, *When Boris Met Dave*. Boris claims he was one of those locked up overnight, before being released without charge. Others, who were incarcerated, insist he is merely trying to play up his prankster past and that he was never in fact held in custody. There are several other discrepancies between Boris's and other accounts of what he describes as that 'deeply pathetic' evening.[7]

An exact contemporary from Eton who also joined the Bullingdon, remembers that Boris did not attend frequently and held reservations about the wildest alcohol-fuelled antics. 'He did not like the lack of control shown by others by drinking so much, and did not want to do the same himself. That is not his scene.' Indeed, many friends and college neighbours of Boris's from that time report never having seen him the worse for drink. Even as a student, he did not like 'losing it.' One contemporary remembers sharing a joint with Boris at Oxford, but says: 'It was clear that he had hardly ever smoked and certainly never more than a drag or two. He would never want to get stoned or in fact let it affect him at all.'

It is perhaps surprising that Boris joined 'The Buller' when many more thoughtful Etonians avoided it. Even one of his few close friends – Charlie Spencer – steered well clear. A number of those who did join now bitterly regret it – but not, it would seem, Boris. The 'Buller' was notorious for its casual vandalism of other people's rooms, property and feelings. Trashing bedrooms was the standard method of initiation. In the middle of the night at Pembroke College, Boris led the destruction of his friend Radek Sikorski's room when a dozen tail-coated members smashed furniture, books and hi-fi. At the end of the proceedings, Boris is reputed to have shaken Sikorski's hand and said: 'Congratulations, you've been elected.'[8]

Not everyone enjoyed the pointless vandalism. One now highly successful businessman at Oxford at the time remembers: 'I really didn't like the Bullingdon. I had a few run-ins with people from the Bull and there was an occasion when they decided to come round to my house in Oxford to play one of their irritating pranks on me. Fortunately I wasn't there, but I complained to Boris and he feigned some mock outrage. He wasn't there that time, but why did he join at all?'

Most believe that Boris's membership was a question of tribalism, a need to reinforce his upper-class credentials perhaps with an eye to securing the Old Etonian vote when he stood for student office. He certainly appears to have been keener to advertise his membership than adhere to some of the club's rules and rituals. Anthony Frieze, another Oxford contemporary, remembers once looking out of his window to see an open-top bus pass by on Broad Street. 'There was Boris with the others on the top deck with a case of Bollinger champagne, chanting "Buller! Buller! Buller!" at the top of their voices to bemused bystanders.'

Public exuberance was one thing, the financial extravagance quite another; Boris seems to have been less enthusiastic when it came to settling the club's hefty bills for meals, drink and 'collateral damage' caused by the ensuing high jinks. Smashed windows and vomit – known as 'parking a tiger' – were the expected outcome of any decent evening's entertainment. One of his fellow members ruefully recalls that Boris never made his £125 contribution to the cost of one lavish evening, leaving him to pick up the extra tab. Nearly twenty years later, at a smart Christmas party in Notting Hill, he even confronted Boris about the unpaid debt – albeit in a teasing manner. The Bullingdon pays its way out of trouble, but the expense is considerable and Boris had something of a reputation for being difficult to part from his money.

In stark contrast to his hearty Bullingdon pursuits, Boris chose to study at Balliol College – traditionally, a haven for bright young Lefties rather than dim hoorays – presumably because of its glittering reputation for Classics. Founded in 1263, it had also produced three former prime ministers: Herbert Asquith, Harold Macmillan and Edward Heath, as well as literary giants such as Matthew Arnold, Graham Greene and Robert Browning. More recently, it had become known for its periodic fits of left-wing agitation in favour of miners or Irish republicans and other modish causes. The JCR – the Junior Common Room (a sort of Oxbridge student union) – was an orange-painted hotbed of middle-class student activism, plotting the downfall of the Conservative government and generally rebelling against their parents. Sited in the Olav Room, a prominent bust of Lenin had been removed shortly before Boris's time from what was considered a bleak, but busy student hangout; the sticky brown flooring and tired G-plan seating around the walls remained, however.

The basement bar, with two wooden picnic benches under sun umbrellas, drew a regular crowd, many of whom would come to watch Boris hold court. Most Old Etonians gravitated to the grander, High Tory colleges such as Christ Church, Magdalen or Trinity. Boris continued to mix with his old school chums – notably Spencer and Guppy, who were both in the more 'obvious' Old Etonian surroundings of Magdalen. Although he was friendly with many others – and liked by the Balliol radicals as a harmless clown – he made few other genuine friends at university, sticking clannishly with the close-knit duo from Eton; boys he had known for the past six years and who, with their wealth, breeding and looks were redolent of the Brideshead era.

Mark Carnegie, who later watched Boris closely as he prepared to stand against him for Oxford Union President, was struck by his opponent's insularity, whatever his public persona of bonhomie. 'There was never any real depth of conversation with Boris – he's an intensely private guy. Other than Charlie and Darrie, he didn't open up to anyone. They were all locked in with each other in a tight triumvirate. A few people like Radek Sikorski were on the outskirts, but that's it.'

While Boris did not form close bonds with outsiders at Oxford, he knew hundreds of other undergraduates and quickly became a university celebrity. His over-the-top plummy speech, stage eye-rolling and frequent 'aaaaghs', 'errrs' and 'grrsss' became widely imitated. His distinctive dress style – sagging cords, ragged tweeds and haystack coiffeur – contrasted beautifully with the spiky-haired, post-punk look of many state-school undergraduates and the faux-Brideshead polished Young Fogey confections of others. It was an era when the pared-down monochrome look of The Smiths – led by self-confessed 'misery' Morrissey – was the inspiration for many student wardrobes. Against this drab cultural backdrop of post-New Romantics, pre-City Big Bang, Boris stood out like an eccentric, shambling throwback. He was widely ridiculed, yet liked and seen as essentially harmless because he made people laugh. As so often in his career, this was a perilous underestimate: the ascent of Boris was about to get underway in earnest.

In the early days at Oxford he played along with the rigid social caste system. At the apex were the toffs or 'socialites', with genuine aristocrats like Spencer mixing with an assortment of other upper-class undergraduates. They would refer to those who had attended what they viewed as minor public schools – in other words, almost anyone outside the big three of Eton, Harrow and Winchester – as 'Tugs', the contemptuous Etonian term for non-fee paying King's Scholars. One contemporary, who attended a middle-ranking private school, remembers, 'a great banging at my door one day, it was virtually knocked off its hinges. Then Guppy stormed in and issued his command: "Sellotape, Tug!" No preamble or hellos, and addressing me as "Tug" – you were made to feel your rank. I got the Sellotape for him.'

Below Tugs – encompassing virtually anyone who was grammar or state-educated – came Oxford's version of India's untouchables, known as 'Stains'. Lloyd Evans, a classicist from a south London state school, who went on to write for Boris at the *Spectator*, was one such Stain. He too was casually dispatched on errands by Guppy: on one occasion, he was expected to wait in the street, as if a servant or public school fag, while Guppy wrote a lengthy message to Boris. He then had to deliver it to Boris's pigeonhole. Evans remembers how class defined almost everything at Oxford in the early 1980s: 'He just presumed I would wait. Class was an issue, you see. It was all a question of which school you'd been to. Had you been to one of the top ones or not? Boris hung out with those public-school types – his best mate was Guppy. But if you'd been to a comp like me, then forget it, you were beyond the pale.

'There was probably a 50/50 split on state and public-school entrants across Oxford as a whole but the place was very much geared to the public-school ethos. There was a whole network of secret symbolism that I transgressed such as asking whether so and so had been to Harrow – of course you should just know, but how could I? I had also never heard of the Bullingdon all the time I was there, as no one would have mentioned it to someone like me.'

According to a neighbour of Boris's on Staircase V at Balliol, he rarely invited others to his double-width set of rooms (with views over Broad Street on one side and the library quad on the other). Apart from the occasional woman friend, Guppy was the only frequent visitor. Boris co-edited the Oxford University satirical magazine *Tributary* with Guppy, a stint that was not universally applauded. 'I edited the magazine after them and like them, did the usual thing of touring round the shops in Oxford, persuading them to take advertising,' recalls Evans. 'Some of the reaction we got was incredibly hostile. Guys would come out from behind the counter and say, "Get out of here!" Eventually one woman explained that she had had some "terrible man" in there before, selling advertising for the mag. He said he was going to do "something terrible" unless they advertised, she said, and now no one would touch it – that was Darius. The tutors used to take bets on how soon after Oxford he would end up in prison. He did, of course. He talked bullshit the whole time, while posing and preening. I was always writing nasty things about him after that, calling him, "Zorba the Creep". Boris told me he thought that was very funny. That's when I first thought, he's not really that loyal to his friends, is he?'

Although extravagantly handsome, many women undergraduates felt intimidated by Guppy and disliked his attentions, which could become too persistent. 'I would sometimes be asked to interrupt or rescue women from conversations with Guppy,' recalls one undergraduate puzzled by Boris's close friendship with this 'strange, oily character.' 'He was not someone you'd want to hang out with. I was always fascinated by that relationship, it seemed strange for an aspiring politician: Guppy was the fly in the ointment.'

Evans was frequently derogatory about Boris in the magazine, calling him, variously, an 'exiled Armenian chicken farmer', product of 'a hideous Nazi war experiment' and 'Aryan bull pig.' All was tolerated until he made the mistake of describing Boris as 'incompetent.' Boris stormed round in the middle of the night to where Evans' co-editor, Aidan Hartley, lived and delivered a stream of abuse: 'He went incandescent, really mad, grabbing the typewriter and re-writing the piece. I was surprised at how angry he was – it was coming from a deep, dark place.'

Boris's association with Guppy would go on to cause him far more serious problems and they rarely see each other now – particularly as Guppy has moved to South Africa. Later, Boris was publicly dismissive of the man to whom he had been so close. When commenting on the disgraced Conservative politician Jonathan Aitken being sentenced for perjury, he added: 'There is a touch of the Darius Guppy about him, a Walter Mittyish refusal to face up to reality, and an inability to sort out right from wrong.'[9] As Paul Goodman, a former colleague of Boris's astutely observes: 'Churchill surrounded himself with a galaxy of oddballs. He and Boris are similar in being drawn to larger-than-life characters: Guppy is a key example.'

Fraternising with the controversial Guppy certainly marked Boris out but it was really by dint of his extraordinary appearance and cartoon personality that he became a well-known figure at Oxford, even in that first Michaelmas (autumn) term of 1983. Boris wasted no time in exploiting his notoriety to launch his political career. Within weeks, he had put himself forward in the election for a lowly position on the Treasurer's Committee of the Oxford Union, the world-famous student debating society and politico nursery slope. 'There was a 9.30 p.m. deadline on the Sunday evening for nominations and Boris sauntered into the Union at 10, expecting to put his name down,' recalls a now-influential Tory. 'Of course it was too late and he wasn't allowed to stand – much to the amusement of those who rather hoped he wouldn't run against them. You see, he was already seen as a strong candidate – provided he could get his name on the ballot paper, of course.'

Boris was supposed to be the obscure young thing at the bottom of the ticket – a purely supporting role designed to ensure Balliol turned out and voted for (future investment banker) Larry Grafstein as President. Was he embarrassed about the faux pas? It seems not, unlike those he was supposed to be helping and whom he had now let down.

Grafstein, a Canadian post-graduate student, won the Michaelmas 1983 presidential election despite Boris's oversight. His shortcomings as a team player did not deter Boris from seeking greater glory for himself and he next stood for Secretary for Trinity term 1984, one of the four top jobs in the Union. It was a prize normally granted only after distinguished service lower down the pecking order. Boris, however, never climbs any figurative mountain by the conventional path. At Oxford, the Union Secretary leads a stage life tailor-made for an exhibitionist. His duties would include reading the minutes at the beginning of a debate – a gift-wrapped opportunity for putting his personal mix of wit and charm on public display – and hosting social events, where he could also energetically peddle 'brand Boris' to as wide an audience as possible.

Leapfrogging the lower slopes of Union politics was seen as 'rather cheeky' by Union hacks but this time Boris lodged his nomination for Secretary – a far greater prize in self-advancement – well before the deadline. He was running against Claire Copperman, a clever woman from St Hugh's College with hair almost as blonde as his. She was not quite so funny and certainly not so well known as Boris. After some energetic deployment of the Old Etonian forces, Boris won comfortably.

His ascent to the ultimate goal of the Union Presidency – previous incumbents include William Ewart Gladstone, Tony Benn and Benazir Bhutto – now seemed assured. The post was widely seen – including by Boris's predecessor as MP for Henley, Michael Heseltine – as the 'first step to being Prime Minister.'[10] However, it is worth noting that although the last two elected Prime Ministers – Tony Blair and David Cameron – were Oxford-educated, both eschewed an Oxford Union career. Heseltine, who invested a lot of his time in the Union and eventually became President at his second attempt, never made it to Number Ten. Indeed, in his memoirs, Peter Mandelson, the architect of Blair's New Labour, specifically advises young undergraduates interested in a political career to avoid the Union and political activism during university to focus instead on the academic opportunities. Back then, though, Boris badly wanted the Presidency and all it represented. But a formidable 'Stain' stood in his way in the shape of the talented and ferociously organised grammar-school boy Neil Sherlock, then newly elected Union Treasurer and later a senior partner at a City accountancy firm and Liberal Democrat grandee.

The looming contest between these two starkly divergent men – the sparky redhead from Surrey versus the glamorous blond chancer from Eton – would lead to a titanic and ill-tempered contest that strayed dangerously into class warfare. Those who fought in this battle in the Michaelmas term of 1984 are still in part shaped by it today – perhaps most of all Boris. After an interlude of a quarter of a century, Sherlock likes to joke that he and Boris now finally find themselves on the same side, through the broad-church of the Conservative-Liberal Democrat coalition. Back in those days, though, they were bitter opponents.

'Boris seemed to take victory for granted,' recalls a Sherlock supporter, now an influential left-wing Tory thinker. 'He assumed he would be a cult choice for the freshers coming in, whereas in fact they were very, very polarised in their view of him. This was Boris Mark

One – a witty high Tory of conventional right-of-centre views, whose only real distinguishing features from all the other Old Etonians were his hair and personality. The fact that he was most comfortable with people like Charlie Spencer and Darius Guppy meant that if you were from a state school like me, you just didn't want to know – there was a large element of class war at that time.'

Boris recruited the usual suspects of well-born public school alumnae to rally the vote, including his aristocratic girlfriend, Allegra Mostyn-Owen. Said to be the most desired girl in Oxford of her time, she was frequently compared to Sir Max Beerbohm's fictional femme fatale Zuleika Dobson, who drove undergraduates to despair with her beauty. In July 1984, she even graced the front cover of a resurgent *Tatler* magazine as her elegance, startling blue eyes and obvious intelligence seemed to encapsulate the perfect mid-1980s amalgam of brains, looks and breeding.

The newsagents opposite the gate to Trinity College, where she was studying PPE [Politics, Philosophy and Economics], was covered with billboards of her face. Such fame merely served to make her appear even more elevated and untouchable – except to the super-confident or the terribly deluded. 'There were plenty of posh, ambitious boys around, who looked at her amazing cheekbones and saw high-class breeding material,' recalls one of Allegra's college friends. Bagging this most glorious prize against such intense competition – particularly when he was neither rich nor landed and still confined to the lower ranks of the Union – raised Boris's university status considerably.

At this stage she was a far bigger figure than he was but now she was determined to help her man succeed by issuing an invitation to Sherlock to visit her rooms on Trinity College's Garden Quad on Armistice Day, November 1984 for afternoon tea. She pleaded with Sherlock – who could not help but be moved by such a fabulous young Sloane alternately showering him with praise and admonitions – not to stand against 'my Boris.' Though he very much enjoyed his cup of tea in fine bone china, Sherlock did not lose his head sufficiently to agree to make way; he also became more than a little suspicious when Boris turned up just as he was leaving. He knew then that his adversary must be running scared to have drafted in a secret weapon.

Boris was unable – or perhaps unwilling – to reach outside his natural Conservative heartland to non-core voters. Instead he relied on the traditional public school networks – mainly the invitation-only Old Etonian-dominated Gridiron and Bullingdon clubs – rather than running a proper campaign. On one occasion he even handed out bottles of red wine to Gridiron members in a particularly brazen, even crass attempt to 'buy' their votes. 'Such displays of naked ambition were totally out of place,' recalls one undergraduate there that day. So, for all his charm and fame, he lost out to Sherlock's hard graft and broad-appeal competence. Boris scooped a creditable 558 votes – or 46 per cent of the turnout. Sherlock, however, triumphed with 661 votes: a majority of 103.

The shock was palpable – Boris supporters talk of this time as if almost a bereavement. How could such a talent, with his sense of epic entitlement, be deprived of his rightful prize – and by, gasp, a *Stain*, too? A good deal of snobbish and unpleasant personal abuse was heaped on Sherlock by Boris supporters – who pulled faces and called him a 'horrible, spermy little man', who spoke with a 'funny accent' and who was 'patently uncharismatic.'

Boris was undoubtedly shaken up by this rare setback. Here was a boy whose only real other 'failure' to date had been his inability to master the recorder at primary school but it was, quite likely, the making of him as a politician. It taught him the unassailable truth that no one can truly succeed in politics if he relies entirely on his own cadre. Just as President Bill Clinton (one of Boris's role models) would later reach way beyond the natural base of the Democratic Party in the US through his personal charm and charisma, so Boris appreciated the Old Etonian networks in themselves were not enough to realise his ambitions. Hitherto regarded as the Establishment candidate, Boris saw, just as David Cameron would later with the Conservative party, that he would have to decontaminate his personal brand.

Thanks to a recruitment drive by ex-President Larry Grafstein, who had worked hard to democratise the Union and move it away from a public school enclave, it now had some 5,000 members. No longer could a few dozen Old Etonians fix the result in favour of one of their number as in the past, simply by voting tribally. The new Union was more representative of the University as a whole: class still mattered, but it was something that could no longer be allowed to define you if you sought political office. The Union's finances – previously so precarious that closure seemed imminent – had also been put on a surer footing so the new President would have to be seen as a safe financial guardian to boot.

'The new Union intake of people from normal schools, whose fathers, sisters and brothers had not been to Oxford, meant that Sherlock was able to run a devastating Meritocrat versus Toff argument,' recalls one Sherlock supporter. 'Neil put out the word that, "This is your Union now, do you want to keep it? Or give it back to nobs like Boris?" We also homed in on whether Boris was competent enough to look after the money.' Sherlock himself says that, 'It was easy to paint Boris as a particular type of character. Tim Hames [who went on to become special adviser to the Speaker of the House of Commons] ran the campaign and as he has said, if we ever hit above the belt, it was entirely unintentional.'

For a brief interlude after his defeat, Boris focused his attention on another area of his life. He had first won Allegra's affections through a classic episode of Boris bumbling – calculated or otherwise, one can only guess. One evening he pitched up for one of Allegra's parties in her rooms at Trinity, clutching the customary bottle of wine – a night early. She did not know him – although he, like virtually every male student at Oxford at the time, knew of her – but she invited him in, anyway. They drank the wine and got chatting.

To a girl sometimes isolated by her own beauty and instincts, according to her friends, here was someone who seemed thoroughly at ease with her looks and was also surprisingly emotionally switched on for his age. Boris made her laugh; they dined out at Indian restaurants and gradually became friends. He seemed to be – and *was* – different from the over-forward, arrogant young pups who had been her past suitors. And, at least at first, he did not seem to be making a play for her and was not then widely known for chasing women.

Soon Boris's infamous charm melted the 'Ice Maiden' as, according to one of her friends, 'all the jealous blokes used to call her.' Others left in the cold began to dub her Ms Allergic Mostyn-Owen in the university magazine *Cherwell*. Just as Boris polarised female opinion, Allegra was either worshipped or dismissed by men, some branding her histrionic, distant or even 'a little crazy' and 'over the top.' She was also known for holding fixed left-of-centre views and could be rather chilly with those who did not share them, including her boyfriend. Boris is said to have once told her: 'What I like about you is that you've got principles.'[11]

Admiring young undergraduates, all too aware she was out of their league, noted that she did not often speak to people outside a very narrow social circle. 'She didn't have to,' observes one. 'Just her presence made a magnificent contribution to any event, just being there, saying nothing. We used to congratulate ourselves if she merely acknowledged our existence.' However, Lloyd Evans believes her extraordinary good looks did little to make Allegra happy: 'I always found her strangely closed – I thought that her staggering beauty meant that she didn't really have to develop her social skills. I always thought she was a bit cursed by that. Women like Allegra probably feel that whatever gifts are showered on them, it's never quite enough. And so she came over terribly grand, and she talked to me as if she were launching a ship.'

In the circumstances, the attentive Boris must have seemed even more of a support and champion, and after she appeared on the *Tatler* cover, something of a refuge from unwanted attention. He frequently sent her letters through the university's pigeon post system, telling her in one that she reminded him more and more of his mother. Others have also observed a similarity over the years – particularly both women's brand of rather ethereal intelligence. On other occasions, he warned against men whom he accused of being 'all the same.' He finally persuaded her to go out with him by telling her that otherwise he could not continue to devote so much time to being friends with her, but would focus on his Union ambitions instead. Now dependent on her ambitious young suitor, she agreed, allowing Boris to start calling the shots.

⋆

In the second long vacation of their degree courses during the summer of 1985, Boris and Allegra went on an extended tour of Spain and Portugal with his sister Rachel (who was a year below Boris at Oxford) and Rachel's then boyfriend, Sebastian Shakespeare. The trip became known to them all as the 'Animal Atrocidades' tour and was in part financed by Boris and Rachel working on a report on Animal Cruelty commissioned by contacts of Stanley's at the World Wildlife Fund.

'We were going round the Iberian peninsula in a car investigating what we called "atrocidades,"' recalls Shakespeare, who so closely resembles the blond Johnsons that he likes to joke that he is their long-lost cousin. 'We had to research beach photography of monkeys, bull-fighting and the treatment of donkeys, take pictures, interview people and put together a film. Boris and Rachel had been commissioned to do it and Allegra and I were there for the ride.' With their genius for publicity, the Johnsons were even interviewed by an ex-pat British radio station in Torremolinos.

The trip was not entirely relaxed, however. 'Allegra could be brittle,' Shakespeare remembers. 'She came across as quite cold, supercilious. She wasn't. It was just an unfortunate manner she had; she was very beautiful and that accentuated it. It wasn't a stormy relationship between Allegra and Boris, but she was obviously quite besotted with him, quite evidently more besotted with him than he with her.

'And she was fabulously well-connected all over the place so wherever we were on this jaunt, she would set up all these wonderful houses for Boris and her to stay at. Rachel and I would have to stay in grotty B&Bs down the road. Maybe there wasn't room for all of us in these luxurious boltholes, but I think she was probably showing off to Boris.'

After about ten days of travelling together, Allegra left the party. Thereafter, Boris seemed deeply troubled. 'He would ask us every night whether he should marry Allegra,' recalls Shakespeare. 'So it was obviously playing on his mind even at that stage as to whether it was a good idea. I expressed caution for all the traditional reasons such as that he and she were a bit young. What puzzled me was that

I think he had already got engaged to Allegra without saying anything. Yet even then he was not only having doubts, but actually voicing them.'

Indeed, unbeknownst to Shakespeare at the time, the 21-year-old Boris had already hatched plans and was as good as engaged. On paper, at least, it seemed as if he was the one pursuing the idea more than Allegra. It is possible that after a difficult childhood, he wanted the security and comfort only marriage could bring. On 8 August, Boris wrote to Allegra from the Pension Amazonas in Lisbon to ask whether she had yet broached the subject of marriage with her socialite mother Gaia and wealthy Old Etonian father William, known as Willie.

It would have been understandable for him to feel nervous about being accepted by such an exalted family. Willie, who was chairman of the art auctioneer Christie's, had two real ancestral seats rather than a dilapidated hillfarm on Exmoor. One was Woodhouse, a stately home in Shropshire, and, until it was sold, the seventeenth-century Aberuchill Castle in Perthshire (about which Gaia once admitted to having 'not the slightest idea' how many rooms there were). Through her father, Allegra was firmly rooted in generations of minor English nobility – not for her or Willie the Johnsonian insecurity of tenure or lack of roots. Indeed, the Mostyn-Owens can trace their ancestry back to Owen Glendower, the last native Welshman to claim the title Prince of Wales and a Welsh nationalist hero on a par with King Arthur in England. For Boris, Allegra was properly posh and the omens were not entirely favourable. Gaia Servadio, a formidable character, is said to have 'scared the life' out of him, while Willie Mostyn-Owen is quoted as having coldly described Allegra's suitor as 'rapacious' and 'willfully scruffy'.

The engagement also prompted a minor stir of astonishment on the couple's return to Oxford. 'Boris's relationship with Allegra was rather difficult to understand,' recalls Anne McElvoy, an Oxford contemporary. 'Well, it was, and it wasn't. Of course, she was a very glamorous girl but there was always a sort of distance between them. I remember going to his rooms once when I was editor of *Cherwell* and he said, "I can't believe it says in your paper that Allegra is having a very glamorous party." "Well she is," I replied. "But she hasn't invited me!" he cried.

'I think getting engaged at Oxford was all too soon. It was like they were rehearsing, playing at being grown ups. I think he was a boy who had always done everything precociously early – in the same way as he wanted to be President of the Union so that he could play at being prime minister.'

Furthermore, already there was a strong – even destructive – streak of rivalry between Boris and Allegra. 'They used to compete on everything, even down to who had the best orgasm,' remembers one contemporary. Perhaps that explains why Boris told Allegra's mother that he had never skied when he joined the family on the French Alps one winter. Allegra and her brothers are acknowledged as accomplished skiers, but Boris, too was no slouch on the slopes: as a child, he had also gone on family skiing holidays.

'All my children ski very well, as did I in those days,' recalls Gaia. 'I had rented a flat and he came to join us, but I was quite concerned because he said he hadn't skied before and the slopes were difficult. But he threw himself down, and I kept thinking he's not going to make it, he doesn't know how! But he always did, and so I thought that boy must have enormous courage and determination. He takes things on and he will go far.' Evidently, Boris's little ruse had worked.

Meanwhile, Sebastian Shakespeare was being put through his paces by Stanley, who has always doted on his daughter, with her libidinous laugh, toothy smile and helmet of blonde hair. Although Sebastian went out with Rachel for most of his three years at Oxford, he formed the distinct impression that Stanley wanted his eldest daughter to advance the Johnson project by 'marrying above her station.' Stanley, he recalls, 'had no compunction' in making it clear that he felt Shakespeare – though thoroughly well-born and successful by non-Johnsonian standards – was neither rich nor grand enough to fit the bill. 'Charlotte was very sweet towards me, whereas Stanley went out of his way to discombobulate me,' he reveals. 'I got the impression that I didn't cut the mustard for him.'

Stanley had his unique ways of testing Sebastian's mettle that made the keen young suitor feel distinctly unwanted. On his first visit to

Nethercote, Stanley gave Sebastian and Rachel a lift, 'and drove us like the clappers, 90mph down these country lanes. I was absolutely terrified, but he was testing me, literally trying to shake me out. I was probably meant to crack. He wanted to see what I was made of.'

Indeed, this odd behaviour was not untypical. 'There was also the memorable Wellington boot episode. We went out for a walk one very wet day in Nethercote and he insisted I wear his boots, even though I had my own. I thought it was curious, but it seemed rude to turn him down. Within a few minutes, I was awash with water as they had a bloody great hole in them. He cackled with laughter – and so did Rachel. It's a Johnson jape, isn't it? He'd got one over on me in front of Rachel because I was being polite. My ego didn't just wilt, it comprehensively drowned.' And as someone else, who has suffered at the hands of a Johnson jape, puts it: 'They are much better at charm than they are at manners.'

Stanley's antics worked, it seemed. After Oxford, Sebastian – later editor of the *Evening Standard*'s 'Londoner's Diary' – and Rachel drifted apart. In 1992, she went on to marry the blue-blooded Ivo Dawnay, an Old Etonian former journalist whose father was a private secretary to Queen Elizabeth the Queen Mother, one grandfather Lawrence of Arabia's commanding officer and the other Eighth Earl of Glasgow. Rachel occasionally holds grand gatherings at the home of the current Earl of Glasgow – the thirteenth-century Kelburn Castle, with heart-stopping views over the Firth of Clyde. (She would also insist they live in uber-modish Notting Hill, when Ivo, with less to prove socially, was rooting for a cheaper house in the less-fashionable west London surburb of Acton. 'That insistence on the best is very Johnsonian,' says one of Rachel's closest friends.)

On their return to Oxford for the new Michaelmas term of 1985, Allegra became joint editor of *Isis*. Guppy was poetry editor, while Rachel reviewed books. Allegra also ran an interview with Anthony Goodman, then President of the Union, relaying his advice to any would-be successors that, 'you do have to be able to play off one clique against another and still look as though you're doing no such thing.'[12]

Meanwhile, Boris rapidly set about planning his second assault on the presidency, no doubt bearing those words in mind. Boris Mark II was far more ambiguous politically, no longer the central casting Tory and standard Old Etonian candidate. He became deft at dodging questions about his political allegiances and made more use of his humour, personality, appearance and nice line in self-deprecation. In effect, he put himself through a hugely successful one-man rebrand much closer to the *Have I Got News For You* Boris that was to emerge nearly two decades later.

This personal remodelling was not so difficult as it sounds. Then as now, part of Boris liked being an establishment figure but there was also another side that revelled in his more esoteric background. Boris was now seen far less often with Guppy – at least in public. Allegra, although still with him, was also less visible and, according to contemporaries, 'kept to her very narrow social circle just as Boris was realising he had to, for political reasons, spread out from his OE core.'

'Allegra didn't particularly hang on Boris's arm at Union events,' confirms a fellow Union activist and now prominent Tory, 'but her relationship with him was something everyone was aware of – although that didn't stop him from having a reputation as someone whom the ladies quite liked. It was more moths to the flame than flame to moths. Boris was slimmer then and really quite physically striking. Allegra, though, became completely off-bounds for everyone.'

Boris II would now spend time with a more mixed Oxford crowd, without actually becoming close to them. He was a more egalitarian creature, or perhaps more calculating. Certainly, he now sought out talent irrespective of background to help him take another pop at the top job. Many of them – often a little over-awed – were only too happy to be enlisted by a figure so glamorous and notorious.

This 'disciplined and deluded collection of stooges'[13] – as Boris himself has referred to them – did all the hard graft for him through the autumn of 1985 in return for little more than the reflected glory of the candidate remembering their name and a vague promise (usually forgotten) of returned support in the future. As Boris himself explains: 'The terrible art of the candidate is to coddle the self-deception of the stooge.' Or, as Abraham Lincoln once put it: 'If you would win a man to your cause, first convince him you are his sincere friend.'

Boris's new acolytes drew lessons from the Sherlock victory and replicated much of his formidable electoral machine. Amateurism was out, replaced by a driven professionalism, albeit cunningly concealed by Boris's buffoonery. As he conceded shortly afterwards, it is essential for a candidate of his background not to 'appear too gritty or thrusting, or too party political.'[14]

'We managed to reach our tentacles into parts of the university community that others weren't reaching,' observes Anthony Frieze, one of Boris's stooges-in-chief. 'Although it was against the Union rules, which banned campaigning, it was total politics. Out of sight in private rooms, we had lists and lists of people to canvass, and who controlled which cell. It was all driven by a very strong sense of coalition with the SDP-supporting Limehouse Group – which helped with the grammar-school boys. We let them think that we were all for the realignment of politics, that Boris was "one of them" – the whole thing was a game of flexible geometry.'

So much for Boris's legendary disorganisation; he also went out of his way to befriend fellow student Frank Luntz, who has gone on to become a key backroom figure in American polling and politics. Through a highly sophisticated poll conducted by Luntz, Boris was able to analyse his target audience in detail. Luntz's forensic involvement, which predicted the result to within 1 per cent, raised Boris's game well beyond the usual realm of student politics to a semi-professional status. A self-professed 'Reagan-Thatcher Conservative', Luntz informed Boris that he had no need to change – or *appear* to change – his politics to win. 'I told him he was so popular that even in Oxford, where Conservatives were hated, he could have run and won as an outspoken Tory. He could have changed the whole image of Conservatism but he just didn't want to do that.'

Instead Boris chose to reflect mid-80s realities by becoming a politically androgynous personality, seemingly offering something for everyone. One contemporary recalls: 'You could read anything you liked into this new Boris. So, if you were from a northern comprehensive like me, you liked the "I'm funny and you like funny, so vote for me" pitch. He promised an entertaining Presidency for the summer term when people want laughs rather than worthy debates on care for the elderly.'

Boris II also instinctively believed that he needed to rinse out the shades of blue from his electoral persona – that any kind of Thatcherite pedigree would now be the kiss of death to a Union campaign. On 29 January 1986, Oxford dons voted crushingly to refuse to give the Iron Lady an honorary degree in protest for her government's cuts in education funding. This was the first time since the Second World War that an Oxford-educated Prime Minister had been denied the honour and illustrated the depth and breadth of anti-Conservative hostility. Boris studiously avoided the confrontation advocated by Luntz. 'He was in a curious way both apolitical and extra-political,' recalls one undergraduate from the time. 'He did not appear partisan at all, but rather happily mushy in the middle. If you were left-wing Tory – and most Oxford Tories *were*, rather than Thatcherite – then you could say he was probably "one of us." If you were part of the SDP [Social Democratic Party] ascendancy or a Liberal, then you thought, "Well, he's hanging out with our lot, so he must be one of ours."' Such an astute observer as Nick Robinson, now the BBC's political editor but then President of the Oxford University Conservative Association, had no idea of Boris's true political loyalties. 'I had not the faintest clue that Boris was a Conservative. Indeed, I would have told you, if you had asked me at the time, that he was a supporter of the SDP/Liberal Alliance. I think he must have taken the decision not to be seen as a Tory because he knew that to do so would be to lose.' It also meant that Boris was able to avoid the poisonous Conservative factionalism at Oxford at the time, which could have badly divided his vote: he is not one to join cabals.

There has long been controversy over whether Boris actually became an SDP member as part of these manoeuvres. Launched by disaffected Labour 'moderates' Roy Jenkins, Bill Rodgers, Shirley Williams and David Owen shortly after their 'Limehouse Declaration' in January 1981, the SDP was then the rising political force at Oxford. Most politically active undergraduates signed up as a way of keeping tabs on interesting political events, but Boris is unlikely to have joined the national party. That did not stop him from adopting their most eye-catching and totemic policies when it suited – as well as attacking Conservative policies, including their uncritical support of the then right-wing US Government led by President Ronald Reagan.

The most illuminating example of how Boris could trim with the wind came in what was for him the most important speech he made to the Union. The Presidential Debate on 28 November 1985 was his chance to set out his manifesto for a second attempt on the Presidency in the vote to take place the following day. He knew he needed to harness SDP votes to win and therefore spoke passionately in favour of the motion: 'This house has had enough of two party politics.'

That night, he told the assembled Union masses: 'There are two reasons why we should vote for a vote that counts. There is an overwhelming case for some type of electoral reform, some form of proportional representation. What sort of democracy is it where one party can get only two per cent less of the vote than another party and end up with a hundred fewer seats in the House of Commons? People will point to places like Italy. For them, a change of government is like a minor reshuffle and it works. They have a standard of living higher than ours.

'[First past the post] causes a crude polarity, a Manichean dichotomy and is dividing the nation. The two old big parties are retreating into their heartlands and currying favour by adopting rigid politics. The ruthlessness of the current electoral system is forcing out views and opinions, which we may not take seriously until it is too late. This motion is no more than a statement of fact – we have had enough of two party politics. The country has shown it in general elections, local elections and by-elections.'[15] His finale met rapturous applause. When Mark Carnegie, his rival for the presidency, responded, 'There isn't room for more than two partics in politics,' he was hissed.

Carnegie, though able to count on the support of the largish group of student 'colonials' at Oxford, was unable to land punches on Boris. He was ultimately defeated by an emphatic margin: 809 votes to 466, a majority (in a high-turnout election) of 343. Boris had got the voters out, and got them to vote for him. Riding high after such a glorious victory, he never went beyond the briefest of courtesies with his defeated rival. Carnegie recalls, 'We never once had a proper conversation. I never realised until then just how intensely focused and determined he was. Sure, he's engaging, but this guy is an absolute fucking killer.'

By now, even the national press were taking notice of Boris and Allegra, running diary stories on their domination of Oxford – he as President of the Union and she the former editor of *Isis*, with Boris's sister Rachel the current editor. Such early fame notwithstanding, Boris now faced the usual scramble to come up with interesting speakers who would actually turn up to debate crowd-pleasing motions. He was moderately successful but his was not to be one of the great Union presidencies. There is just a suggestion that for Boris the prize was in the winning, rather than the doing as President. 'I don't remember anything about his Presidency,' says Toby Young. 'I don't remember it being a disaster, I just don't remember anything – he's certainly always been accused of not working as hard as he might in office.'

A President's term card was then typically a modest folded and stapled booklet, listing upcoming Union events, debates and speakers. As so often with the Johnsons, Boris's was a dynastic enterprise, the front cover adorned with a violent black-and-white depiction of angry people shouting – presumably during a Union debate – by his mother Charlotte. Allegra's mother, Gaia, was listed for a 'compulsory' lunchtime talk on 7 May on 'The Mafia Today'. His father, Stanley, came in to speak in the Farewell Debate in late June on the motion that 'Nuclear Power will Cause a Catastrophe' (and was frequently seen with Boris in Oxford, even when not speaking).

Today's listeners of recordings of father and son debating at the Union would be hard-pushed to recognise Stanley's voice. There is none of the characteristic 'bumbling plum' of the senior Johnson, just an ordinary home counties' timbre. In contrast, there is little to distinguish the 21-year-old Boris's enunciation and his Wodehousian delivery so familiar now: he was already the Boris we know. It is almost as if father has followed son in oral idiosyncrasy. 'I wouldn't be surprised if Stanley hadn't taken elocution lessons,' remarks family friend James Le Fanu. 'It's the sort of thing he'd do.'

But otherwise the line-up of debates is unremarkable, touching on the familiar mid-Eighties themes of feminism, Chernobyl and the Greenham Common peace protestors. Boris does not come close to matching the coup of Jeya Wilson, his predecessor as President, who drew in Michael Heseltine to make one of his first public speeches since resigning from the Cabinet over Westland in January 1986.

He did, though, display a Europhile touch in organising a 'ground-breaking' joint debate with the Union of Utrecht on 'this House prefers Dutch Courage to Double Dutch'. With one eye on the future, he brought in some personally very useful contacts such as Max Hastings, editor of the *Daily Telegraph*, and family friend Anthony Howard, then deputy editor of the *Observer*, to speak on the future of Fleet Street.

Most people at Oxford at the time remember far more about Boris as a person than what he did as President. He left little mark, although his famed lack of attention to detail almost led to disaster on one dicey occasion when he failed to record a Union meeting. 'There was a panic that he would be branded an incompetent if it ever got out,' recalls one supporter. 'He was obsessed about that accusation about him, so we were very careful to hush it up.'

These debates were not universally well attended but listening to the tapes of them twenty or so years later, there is still a discernible crackle of excitement emanating from the best of them in the grand old Victorian debating chamber, with its smell of leather, wood-polish and earnest teenage sweat. Despite all the pomposity of students, many no older than nineteen or twenty, addressing each other as 'honourable members', something more adolescent also comes across.

As President, Boris sat in a throne-like armchair at the head of the chamber. Famous for his shambolic and soiled clothes, he and other debaters were nevertheless expected to dress formally. That requirement was one of the reasons Allegra was so keen for him to pursue a Union career as she considered him handsome in evening dress. Unfailingly elegantly presented herself, from the Fiorucci tights on her long legs to the artfully cut hair designed to set off the shape of her face, she despaired of his normal ragged attire. They cut an odd couple – soon becoming known, rather unkindly, as 'the Beauty and the Beast'.

'She gently chided Boris about his dress sense and messiness,' recalls Sebastian Shakespeare. 'But part of her quite liked it as well. Maybe, like the old cliché, she thought she could reform him.' Union staff obliged them both by keeping a bottle of Tipp-ex on hand to paint over stains on his white shirt; polish was also kept to restore his shoes to the appearance of cleanliness, at least from a distance in poor light. But these emergency measures were not really fooling anyone and Boris's apparent sartorial hopelessness – combined with the allure of the Presidential position – inspired a strong reaction from Union 'groupies': it was the first sighting of Boris as sex god.

As one (male) observer puts it: 'His unkempt, not obviously good-looking manner was very good at dispelling jealousy but was also a form of vanity. A vanity that said that "I have such extraordinary magnetism and appeal, it doesn't matter what I look like."'

During one debate, a seemingly serious female student suggestively offered to wash the honourable member's clothes for him, perhaps the equivalent of underwear throwing at a Tom Jones' concert. Indeed, sexual banter traded across the floor of the chamber – Boris was getting a taste of what favours come with power. 'Women threw themselves at Boris when he was President – it's one of the perks of the job,' says a former associate. 'He may well have been receptive. You do get things thrown your way as President, there's a definite interest. Girls seemed to like the fact that you can write to the President of the USA and he will reply.'

Another former President adds: 'It's true that women do offer themselves to you, but it's not something you tell too many people about.' Such wanton offers may have prompted Allegra – who had been raised in considerable grandeur – to take on the subservient role of buying Boris's shampoo at Oxford and doing his laundry. She may well have feared that if she didn't, he would soon find one of any number of females curiously willing to do so.

The President of the Union is granted a grand 30ft-long book-lined office, the envy of many a government minister – or city mayor. He can invite his friends to join him in the leather armchairs and hold forth around the vast mahogany table in a room once repainted over a weekend by Benazir Bhutto and Alan Duncan, both former presidents. He has a staff of 14 and even back in the mid-1980s, an annual turnover of £250,000.[16]

Such precocious experience of power and the powerful does not, however, grant automatic access to a high-flying political career. Many ex-Presidents satisfy themselves with quieter lives in accountancy or the law. Indeed, no president of the Union has become British prime minister since Sir Edward Heath, who held the position back in 1939. As the political commentator Dominic Lawson suggests, Boris's determination to bag the presidency was something of a 'throwback' and 'quite old-fashioned' by the mid-1980s.

And while Boris had his fans, he was by no means universally seen as a natural candidate for high office in the real world. There was always this question of competence and seriousness, one that was (and in some ways still is) a sore point. Defeated by Boris and a keen observer of his progress ever since, Mark Carnegie never entertained the idea of his old adversary pursuing a career in politics. He admits to being 'amazed at how successful Boris has been. He's kept his individuality but he has this measure of Teflon. I never thought at Oxford he was destined for great things – I just couldn't see how his act would translate to prime time outside Oxford. Of all the political figures at Oxford, I didn't think he would go this far. His personal political franchise is truly remarkable.'

Neil Sherlock is equally astonished that Boris, however great his showman talents, has gone into politics at all. Most wannabe politicians have a burning mission that drives them – whether it is to reform the NHS, take Britain out of the EU or renew a political party. Boris did not seem to have one then – when politics was considerably more ideological and cause-driven – and does not appear to have one now. As Sherlock observes, 'Without those passions, it's not obvious why he would pursue a political career.'

Boris's flexibility soon meant returning to his true political colours. 'By the time of the 1987 General Election, Boris was perfectly happy to be campaigning as a blue rosette-wearing Conservative again. After being President, he could safely start edging back to his party,' observes a fellow Tory. 'I guess he didn't want people to think of him as the SDP person for ever. He'd got what he wanted out of the SDP and its voters.' After all, Boris had never abandoned his inner Tory instincts – just disguised them.

'I can remember exactly where I was when I experienced my first spasm of savage Right-wing indignation,' Boris later wrote. 'It was 1984, at breakfast time – about 10.40 a.m. – and I had a spoonful of Harvest Crunch halfway to my lips. The place was the Junior Common Room of my college.'[17] So, what was the issue that stoked such outrage? Being asked to donate to the miners, who were then engaged in a doomed, but hard-fought and painful strike over pit closures.

'I won't give any dosh to these blasted strikers because as far as I can see, they are being execrably led, haven't had a proper ballot and are plainly trying to bring down the elected government of the country,' is how Boris described his feelings.[18]

A fellow journalist – and an admirer – who has known Boris since Oxford was angered by what he sees as his political cynicism: 'After his election as President, he became known as someone who will do what he needs to do, say what he needs to say. People came to know that they could like him, but not trust him.' Others, however, have been less forgiving of what they saw as calculation followed by betrayal. 'Boris showed then that he was not loyal, that he does not have many real friends, as it is all about him,' said one Oxford contemporary who now deals regularly – but uneasily – with Boris in her professional life. 'People were wary of him. He was always fudging *everything*. So I could see that Boris wouldn't really keep friends because he doesn't have principles. I knew that bumbling thing was an act – he has a real "economical with the actualité" persona.'

Indeed, some of his so-called stooges who had done so much to help him win the Presidency also felt abandoned now that they were no longer useful. 'I didn't recognise the ruthlessness then, although it was clear that Boris was the number one fan of B. Johnson. And it's true that unless you could do something for him, he wasn't that interested,' says Anthony Frieze. 'After he had finished being President, he just disappeared into the library and you didn't really see him after that.' In fact, a number of Boris's fellow students believe he did put in considerable academic effort in his final year and paid little attention to the Union after his presidency, whatever impression he might have given to his dons.

When Boris started at Balliol, like his father he had set himself three immediate goals. His were becoming President of the Union, finding a wife and to get a First. He had achieved one and was well on his way to the second with Allegra. A top degree, though, was out of his reach. His dons, though recognising him as clever and amusing and capable of a First, despaired of what they perceived as his work rate. Boris specialised in Ancient Literature and Philosophy, rather than History, as most people believe. Jasper Griffin, then professor of Classical Literature at Balliol, was nevertheless an inspiration to him. A genial fellow, he was tolerant of Boris's absences and late or non-existent work, but his patience was not universally shared. 'There was a dividing line between tutors who liked Boris the Great and those who disliked him,' he recalls.

Jonathan Barnes – brother of the novelist Julian and a don known for not tolerating playboys, however brainy – taught Boris Ancient Philosophy at Oxford: 'He was clever, enthusiastic, he had excellent Greek and Latin. He was what I probably called in my outdated fashion, a first-class man.' So why did he not get a First? 'You don't get a First on intelligence alone – you also need to work like stink; he miscalculated slightly and left things too late. I guess that had he started burning the midnight oil in March rather than in May (in his final year), he would have made it. He sometimes annoyed the dons – as he sometimes annoyed me – but he was so evidently a good egg that it was hard not to get on with him. He might have written his essay between getting up and his 10 o'clock tutorial, but at least it was stylishly done and usually had some good jokes in it.'

As Oxford undergraduates are expected to read out their essays in tutorial, it gave Boris the opportunity to enhance his work and ad-lib as he went along. Few of his peers would have been so daring but when there was nothing at all to read out, he would simply admit: 'I haven't done it.' 'His disarming frankness was his ultimate weapon,' adds Griffin.

Oswyn Murray, who also taught Classics at Balliol and was at Oxford as a student with Stanley, remembers Boris attending one of his classes on the subject of Thucydides, shortly before his finals. 'He promptly fell asleep – presumably because of a heavy night at the Union. It was this that caused the event that both he and I remember so vividly, at his last end-of-term report before the Master of Balliol. I said: "Well, Master, if Mr Johnson works very hard between now and finals, he might just manage a third." He was not, I think, a serious scholar in the academic sense.'

Actually, for all his 'fooling around in the Union,' as Griffin and others assumed, Boris only narrowly missed the top mark. 'He was viva-ed for a First, as his marks were on the cusp, but he didn't have quite enough alphas. It was quite a long viva, and you might have expected him to get through with his charm and dazzle, but it didn't work that time: vivas are very intimidating, with eight members of staff all in white tie and gowns interviewing you. A lot of tutors saw him as irritating, as they felt he didn't take their subject seriously. When he didn't scrape through, the Professor of Latin kept saying, "He was so close," with a certain gusto.'

Griffin doted on Boris. Even if his former student did not come away with the top-drawer degree he hoped for, Boris's inspiring education and his passion for Classics have stood him in good stead: for years, his classical allusions were a key element of Brand Boris. He would, for example, draw parallels between the modern and ancient worlds. Casting America as enlightened Athens to the Soviet Union's harsh and militaristic Sparta was one; talking about how the transformation from idealistic Republic to brutal Empire in the *Star Wars'* movie series mirrored similar changes in ancient Rome, is another.

Like his mentor Griffin, Boris has that rare talent for making an esoteric subject fun. In an age of relentless dumbing down, Boris can be credited with making learning if not exactly 'cool with the kids' then not a deal-breaker either. No doubt Griffin winced, though, when during a 2008 mayoral hustling on the Vanessa Feltz BBC

London Radio Show, Boris appeared to confuse Shakespeare's Pericles with the Classical Pericles, who rejuvenated Athens.[19]

Ken Livingstone, who had taken it on himself to study the classics in order to understand his opponent better, wrong-footed Boris by picking him up on his error. 'I think Boris knew exactly what he was doing, but didn't think anyone else would know and was shocked when I caught him out,' says Livingstone. In any case, it certainly raised the debate from the usual infantile level of British political discourse.

Boris is well known for inserting classical tags into his newspaper columns and even his speech – since university this has become his trademark, a quick way of distinguishing himself from more mundane politicians (and making himself money, too). The schtick may now have worn thin: Pericles and co. are quoted less often than they were. But for most of his career since Oxford, he has ostentatiously worn his classical learning on his sleeve. Peter Guilford, who knew Boris well after university, once went on a skiing trip and (perfectly innocently) shared a hotel bed with him to save money. 'He kept me awake all night reading Homer,' Guilford recalls. 'Are the Classics some sort of affectation for him, some way of turning up the toff?'

Any pretensions aside, the use that Boris has made of his education has set him apart. It is hard to see him making the same crashing mistake as David Cameron who, just after being elected Prime Minister in May 2010, described Britain as America's junior partner in the war against Germany in 1940. Or, indeed, needing to ask the same question as Tony Blair when confronted with news of atrocities in Kosovo: 'Where is it?'

If Eton had seen 'new Boris' emerge from his inner 'Al', a near-finished version of 'brand Boris' was perfected at Oxford. Most importantly of all, his brush with democracy in the Oxford Union had demonstrated the need for the brand to extend its appeal beyond traditional Tory heartlands. Boris had to be much more than a public-school stereotype; he must be a man for all people, as well as all seasons. Now he was to enter the world of work, it was time to put this ever-evolving brand to the test.

Chapter Four
World on Speed Dial
Starting Work, 1987–1989

When they took their vows on 5 September 1987, Boris and Allegra (both just 23) were the youngest of their Oxford set to marry. The relationship had survived a year of being conducted from either end of the M40: Allegra had finished her three-year PPE degree in 1986 with a 2:2 and returned to London, while Boris stayed on for the fourth and final year of his Classics course in Oxford. It had also lasted through Boris's undoubtedly bitter disappointment at missing out on a First, which lost him sleep then and still rankles to this day. Now finally, the golden pair were reunited with much to celebrate.

'They made a very charismatic couple, and it seemed that everything would happen for them,' recalls Sarah Sands, a friend and former colleague of Allegra's. On the big day, the smiling bride dazzled in her white veil and flower-strewn hair. But Boris failed to turn up with anything suitable to wear and had to be lent trousers, even cufflinks, by an astonished guest: John Biffen, the kindly and humorous Tory MP. The only reason why Boris wore his own, worn-out shoes was that Biffen's were too small for him. To add insult to sartorial injury, he lost his wedding ring within an hour of the ceremony.

'I was standing there when Boris said he had lost the ring,' recalls Emma Jenks, a tutorial partner of Allegra's at Trinity. 'I laughed, but Allegra thought he had done it on purpose. And I can well imagine Boris thinking that he didn't want to wear it.' His nonchalance was noted, not least by his bride and her parents. It struck a slight jarring note on what was a grand occasion, with guests from London, Oxford and Italy all flocking in to a reception at Woodhouse, the Mostyn-Owen country seat. One stylish cosmopolitan note was that the confetti was made of sugared almonds. Another that Anna Steiger, daughter of Rod Steiger and Claire Bloom, sang from the *Marriage of Figaro*.

A piece for violin was commissioned from a highly regarded living composer, Hans Werner Henze, entitled *Allegra e Boris – Duetto Concertante per Violino e Viola all'Occasione delle loro Faustissime Nozze il 5 Settembre, 1987*. Henze was an interesting choice, being a gay German composer, avowed Marxist and member of the Communist Party of Italy. He had produced compositions honouring Ho Chi Minh and Che Guevara but was now marking the nuptials of a rising English Tory and alumnus of the Bullingdon Club and his wealthy heiress fiancée.

During the ceremony itself, the vicar at St Michael's and All Angels counselled the congregation at length on the sanctity of marriage and the evils of divorce. Several guests could not help but notice how many broken families were present as the cleric warmed to his theme. Boris's parents had split, Allegra's parents' marriage was also disintegrating and there they were, all sitting in church. 'I remember a distinct feeling of discomfort,' says one guest. Not that Charlotte and Stanley would have found it easy to counsel Boris against marrying so young: after all, they themselves had ignored Stanley's father's mumbled concern about 'lambs to the slaughter' and married straight after university. However, friends of Stanley's have made it clear that he was privately worried that Allegra was not right for Boris. She was widely considered both beautiful and clever, but some quickly tired of her undoubted sensitivity. 'I always took Stanley's side on that,' said Anthony Howard, a long-standing friend of the family. 'I think she was a very tricky customer, that girl.' Another close friend of Stanley's, the unrelated Brian Johnson, said that Boris's father simply thought Allegra was 'nuts.'

In another strange footnote to the day, the guests were presented with a mug decorated with a picture of Woodhouse, but inscribed with the names of Allegra and her brother Owen rather than Allegra and Boris. On the Johnson side, it was also kept in the family: rather than a friend, Boris's brother Leo had been chosen to act as best man.

After a honeymoon in Egypt (reputedly paid for by Allegra), the newlyweds bought a flat in Sinclair Road, in Olympia, west London. A scruffy road of large Victorian terraces crudely divided into starter-home flats and bedsits, it was not what either of them was accustomed to, but it was the golden boy's first home of his own and marked his entry into the real adult world. The direction of travel was not, however, in the slightest bit clear: how could he match, let alone improve on, the glories of his formative years?

A decade earlier, he just might have set his sights – as Classics graduates had done for a century before him – on serving his country as a Sir Humphrey-style mandarin, with a respectable salary, index-linked pension and eventual knighthood. Sir Boris Johnson of the Foreign Office, our man in Caracas, has a certain ring to it. In the end, he chose to follow the lucre, a path trodden by many 1980s Oxbridge products. At the high-tide mark of the 'Loadsamoney' 1980s, City banks and management consultants were a more appealing prospect than decades composing memoranda in a Whitehall department: they promised prospects and riches unimaginable in the Civil Service with starting salaries of up to £20,000 compared to the graduate average of around £8,000 at the time. As a result, they sucked in the best brains from the top universities. In any case, public service was out of fashion – it was the age of red braces, sharp suits and Porsches. From his plate-glass palace *Wall Street*'s Gordon Gekko preached 'greed is good' while stock markets were soaring.

Boris went for a number of interviews with blue chip companies but he started his working life at one of the smartest management consultancies, LEK (Lawrence, Evans, Koch) Consulting. It is said that he looked the part, even turning up in a smart new pair of red braces on his first day in the autumn of 1987. No doubt the LEK recruitment chiefs realised that they had hired an exceptional young man on what was then a considerable starting salary of £18,000, but it would appear that Boris was not quite so well informed about what his new life offered.

An Oxford contemporary, who managed to stay the course, reveals the lot of the management consultant as 'grinding numbers, detailed analysis, and working and socialising for long hours with your team.' It is difficult to imagine a job description less suited to a free spirit with a dislike of detail and team playing. Whatever the financial rewards, LEK life was a nasty shock and as Boris famously later recalled, 'Try as I might, I could not look at an overhead projection of a growth profit matrix and stay conscious.'

Boris bolted after only a week – staying just long enough to collect the joining fee. It was a good time to head for the exit: the twin storms of the great hurricane and the stock market crash were about to hit the Square Mile, sending stocks and shares into a spectacular nosedive and quickly snuffing out the nascent careers of many of the red-braces brigade. Suddenly the City did not look such a great bet after all. Instead Boris's connections to the world of journalism – through family and his time in the Oxford Union – allowed him to pull off an early and fortuitous career change.

Even at such a young age there were few, if any high-flying circles that Boris did not have on the equivalent of speed dial. Through his mother, for instance, his godmother was Rachel Billington, daughter of Lord Longford, and cousin of the writer Ferdinand Mount, former head of Margaret Thatcher's policy unit at Number Ten. Ferdy's cousin is Mary, David Cameron's mother. Billington's sister is Lady Antonia Fraser, whose husband was the socialist playwright Harold Pinter – who had played tennis with Boris. Colin Lucas, one of Stanley's friends from Oxford and a distinguished academic, was his godfather, while another of his father's friends was Sir Crispin Tickell, former chef de cabinet for (Lord) Roy Jenkins when he was president of the European Commission. His stepmother Jenny is the independently wealthy stepdaughter of Edward Sieff, a scion of the founding family and former chairman of Marks & Spencer. From school and university, he knew many other blue-blooded types likely to be of interest to newspaper editors such as Viscount Althorp, plus a raft of senior politicians, campaigners, lobbyists and assorted other famous people from his time as President of the Union. In short, he had astonishing access to the drawing rooms of power and his dynastic tentacles went further than almost any young graduate of his age. Armed with these connections and many more, plus recommendations from established journalistic hands such as the *Daily Telegraph*'s columnist T.E. Utley and its arts editor Miriam Gross, he was swiftly taken on by *The Times* towards the end of 1987 as a graduate trainee.

Although undoubtedly a prestigious title for his first job in journalism, this was not quite the unqualified blessing it might sound. *The Times* was still recovering from the trauma of its bitter battles with the print unions, which had previously enjoyed a destructive stranglehold over the newspaper. The angry and sometimes violent clashes outside its new home in Wapping, east London, had only come to an end in February 1987. Proprietor Rupert Murdoch had secretly hired more compliant print-workers from a different union at Wapping and then sacked the old Gray's Inn Road printers en masse. There was also bad blood between those journalists who refused to move with the paper in support of the old printers and those who defied their union to do so. Memories of these divisions were painful and still raw. Nor was the work environment inside the new office much better: housed in a windowless former wine warehouse on the News International site known as 'the Fortress', it was protected by barbed wire and sat cheerlessly on a traffic-infested four-lane urban highway with few shops or other signs of life.

Overseeing the regime change was Charlie Wilson, a no-nonsense Glaswegian former Royal Marines boxing champion, who became editor in 1985. He had replaced the aristocratic Charles Douglas-Home, who was remembered as a charming boss in the old establishment traditions of what was once dubbed *The Thunderer*. Wilson was considerably less charming and like Murdoch, certainly no respecter of 'the old ways.' He was feared and respected by his staff in equal measure. 'Charlie Wilson replaced the old effete atmosphere of languor and privilege with more than a trace of Glaswegian menace,' recalls Mark Law, who served under both regimes.

The Times initially sent Boris to work on the *Express & Star* in Wolverhampton for a three-month baptism of fire in reporting. It was not Boris's happiest time: already his marriage was coming under strain and the separation prompted by his new career was only making it worse. Allegra, meanwhile, was struggling to find a life purpose: by the time of their wedding, she had already abandoned journalism and was in search of something to which she was more temperamentally suited. Her experiences of the hard grind of Fleet Street – mostly spent on the *Evening Standard*'s 'Londoner's Diary' – had not suited her. She had in any case suffered capricious treatment by some of her superiors, who had resented the presence of someone they unfairly dismissed as a mere well-connected Sloane. Perhaps too it was difficult to follow in the footsteps of her larger-than-life mother Gaia, who at one time wrote so frequently about food for the *Standard* that the satirical magazine *Private Eye* began referring to the editor Charles Wintour as Sir Charles Mostyn-Wintour.

'Allegra seemed rather brittle psychologically, somewhat earnest, probably insecure and rather unhappy,' recalls one of her then colleagues Nigel Reynolds, who says she rarely socialised with colleagues. 'Here was this rather beautiful girl, who on initial meeting maybe seemed a little bit spoiled and stuck up, but I don't think that was the case at all. Her diffidence was, I think, some sort of private anguish. She didn't fit in with Fleet Street's rather bullish ways and perhaps felt herself to be an outsider. She tried to please and engage people round her in the way that a puppy does, but somehow she always seemed to come unstuck.'

Allegra's confidence was not boosted when a *Sunday Telegraph* piece on which she collaborated with Boris in the summer of 1986 caused her profound embarrassment. In the article under her name she had made out that she had been present at an event that she had, in fact, not attended, although Boris had. The article accused Tina Brown, former editor of *Tatler*, of devoting a lunch to the pursuit of 'tasteless details'[1] about the notorious death of Olivia Channon, daughter of the then Cabinet minister Paul Channon, who had choked on her own vomit at a smart Oxford party. As Allegra had not been present at the occasion, Brown was able to dismiss the entire article as fiction. The row must have been wounding for Allegra and is also revealing about Boris's occasionally cavalier take on journalism. And yet she still garnered praise from high quarters. Sarah Sands, another colleague, remembers that the then Diary editor Geoffrey Wheatcroft thought

Allegra so glorious, he used to say: 'There goes the future editor of *The Times*.' 'But in fact,' says Sands, 'Allegra was not really a born journalist – she didn't have the scrappiness, the competitiveness, cunning or low-mindedness. Boris did. He was a force of nature; she was shy, cooler.'

Despite her success on the cover of *Tatler* – and on another occasion, a Terence Donovan shoot for *Vogue* – Allegra had also given up on modelling. Incidents such as the time she had been told to hide her copy of *War and Peace* because a fashion editor would think it indicative of a lack of commitment had convinced her that it was all 'superficial, personally unfulfilling, and even pernicious.'[2] The opinionated Allegra, who was on the books of the renowned Models One agency, also railed against being repeatedly told of the need to be efficient, punctilious, polite and cheerful, regarding it as 'personality prostitution.'[3]

Attracted by the orderliness of the law after the unpredictability of journalism and modelling, Allegra decided to train as a solicitor. But while embarking on this hopefully more promising new career coincided with a new life married to Boris, there were already cracks in the edifice. Boris had won his marital prize; now he was in an excellent position to begin the pursuit of his next one: a brilliant career. It turned out that the two were incompatible. 'When we got married, that was the end of the relationship, instead of the beginning,' is how Allegra puts it. Friends agree it was less a question of violent arguments between them, more a mis-matching of ambitions: Allegra wanted a marriage; Boris wanted glory. 'I never saw them row,' says Noonie Minogue, one of Allegra's closest friends for nearly 25 years. 'They didn't.' And nor did Boris see any major trouble brewing. On a skiing trip in the French Alps with eight other friends, including Minogue, at that time, he told the rest of the group how 'ridiculous' divorce was and how he didn't 'believe in it.'

In Wolverhampton the local newspaper repertoire of non-stories about stranded pets, dreary council meetings and petty crime was sapping Boris's habitual cheerfulness. He lived in digs with two other lodgers and a landlady called Brenda, who wore a wig and mules. In his misery, he wrote to Allegra, saying that life without her was a 'cold cup of urine.'[4] Brenda, meanwhile, told Boris that he needed to treat his beautiful young wife 'like porcelain' but he was in too much of a hurry to take her advice.

Derek Turner, then news editor, remembers Boris as 'the most disorganised person I've ever encountered; he was clearly not cut out for life in the Black Country.' Many of the trainees sent up from *The Times* – Boris among them – were not exactly given 'rapturous welcomes' as 'they seemed selected for their connections rather than their suitability for [journalism.]' But typically, Boris won them over with his 'easy manner' and 'likeability.' Even so, after the three months were up, Turner recalls writing a report in which he concluded that Boris would 'never make it as a reporter and any future he had in journalism would be as a specialist writer.' It was hardly a glowing endorsement.

At last, the call came to return to London and the glamour of reporting for the world's most famous paper of record. The red braces reappeared from the wardrobe and an exciting future seemed assured, but his shambolic manner did not impress the hard-faced *Times'* news editors. Boris continued to be deployed in the backwaters of journalism and given low-grade jobs, such as rewriting copy from wire news agencies for the inside news pages. One can only imagine how desperate the star of Eton and Oxford must have been for an opportunity to shine.

As one of two graduate trainees that year, he was assigned to shadow a senior reporter to observe how the professionals did it and he was lucky enough to be teamed up with seasoned Fleet Street legend and future *Telegraph* news editor David Sapsted. Unlike some of his less-indulgent colleagues, he warmed to the young Boris. 'We were chalk and cheese – he, breathlessly posh and educated in the classics, me a hardened hack who had left school at 16 to become a trainee reporter on my local paper in Romford,' says Sapsted. 'But I took to the guy. For anyone with a penchant for dishevelled English eccentrics, it was hard not to.' Sapsted took Boris on his first outside reporting job, an interview with the traumatised daughter of an African dictator, who had escaped death threats in her home country. A natural bantering joker, Sapsted found a way to encourage his interviewee to relax and got the story in the bag. Boris was clearly uncomfortable with the whole process, however, sitting on a sofa in virtual silence throughout.

As Turner had warned, it quickly became clear that he was not cut out for the role of news reporter, with its requirements of physical stamina, easy familiarity with people from all backgrounds and foot-in-the-door bravado. He would rather other people did the 'dirty work.' 'I got a call from John Jinks, the *Times* news editor, at home one evening,' recalls Sapsted. '"Sappers," he said, "Charlie [Wilson – the editor] wants you in Dover first thing in the morning to cover the National Union of Seamen's strike. We sent Boris, but it's kicking off down there and he can't cope, so we want you to take over. Tell Boris to get his arse back to Wapping but do it nicely, will you – don't make him feel bad."' In fact, he seemed only too pleased to be recalled. 'When I broke the news to Boris outside the ferry port entrance the following morning, he was more than happy to return to London,' Sapsted recalls. "I got the feeling – and not for the first time – that Boris preferred sitting, thinking and writing, rather than being on the front line.'

By spring 1988 and coming up to the age of 24, Boris could not have been feeling entirely comfortable about his second career choice. Not least because his younger sister Rachel, although still a student, was now outshining him by editing the *Oxford Myth*, a collection of deliberately provocative and pretentious essays about life at the university – probably the best of which was written by Boris. The tome garnered 45 reviews in the national press – not all of them bad – and provided Rachel rather than her brother with some useful notoriety. Meanwhile, there was Boris on a paper whose editor was rooted in the values of hard news and prized most the reporters who delivered it, but according to Sapsted, 'could never quite get his head round Boris. The two were simply from different planets.' Indeed, perhaps it was the pressure to make some sort of impact on *The Times* that led Boris to make the first public howler of his career.

The story was a harmless tale involving the discovery of the long-lost palace of Edward II by archaeologists digging on a building site on the south bank of the Thames. Boris had been assigned because he seemed to know his history. So far so good, but he could not resist inserting a titillating paragraph about how the King would use the palace to cavort with his catamite, Piers Gaveston. The quote he used was sourced to a certain Dr Colin Lucas of Balliol College, Oxford. Suddenly the story became far more exciting than mere archaeology and was promoted to the front page.

Lucas had been a friend and housemate of Stanley's at Oxford and was Boris's godfather. Over breakfast on 20 May 1988, he came in for a bit of a shock. Not only had Boris not checked the quotation with him, it was, simply put, pure historical tosh. Piers Gaveston was beheaded in 1312, making it hard for him to cavort round a palace not constructed until 1325. Lucas, an ambitious fast-track academic on his way to a professorship at Chicago University and eventually the vice-chancellorship of Oxford, did not see the funny side. In any case, an expert on the French Revolution rather than medieval English kings, he risked becoming the laughing stock of history departments around the world. He complained to Charlie Wilson, the editor, who in turn replied: 'Our reporter stands by his story.' Lucas wrote back, saying there was no way that Boris could have obtained this quote from him because it was not right. His letter began: 'Much as I would hate to damage the career prospects of a young journalist (particularly when he is one's godson), but . . .'

Four days later, Boris penned another story, which aimed to defuse the row by backtracking on the original. It's not clear whether this second quote from the historian is any more accurate a reflection of anything he actually said than the first: 'Edward II is reputed to have led a life of wine and song with his catamite Piers Gaveston. But if 1325 (the date of the palace) is correct, that could hardly have taken place in this building since Gaveston was executed in 1312.' In any case, it sealed Boris's fate. He was summoned to appear before the editor, who told him that it was a 'heinous crime' to make up quotes on *The Times*. According to one account, rather than being contrite Boris pointed out that 'most' of the quotes on the paper were made up. Following this heroic but futile Last Stand, he was sacked. Wilson was one of very few bosses throughout Boris's professional life not to indulge him: from the school of hard knocks rather than Eton, he seemed immune to his protégé's charms.

As Boris himself admits: 'I left *The Times* in inglorious circumstances.'[5] But he has never truly repented, instead seeking to blame 'whingeing historians' and Lucas's 'ruthlessness'. Eight years after the event, he said: 'I was asked to provide detail about Edward II. In desperation, I rang up Colin. He brilliantly extemporised some stuff about silken-haired youths and Piers Gaveston, which I put in. The problem was that the castle had not been constructed while Gaveston was still alive. A lot of whingeing, snivelling, fact-grubbing historians wrote asking sarcastically was this the same Colin Lucas who was an expert on the French Revolution. I had applied Colin's description of life in Edward II's court to the palace, which he did not intend. Colin showed his ruthlessness in vindicating the accuracy of his remarks.'[6]

Boris also got his own back on his first editor. Later he was to describe Wilson as 'a man straight from a Britflick gangster movie'[7] but long before that, he was to triumph over his nemesis by walking virtually straight from Wapping into a job on *The Times*' arch rival, the *Daily Telegraph*. Boris knew the editor Max Hastings because as President of the Oxford Union, he had invited the distinguished former war correspondent to speak at a debate on 21 May 1986. He must have known he had made an impression that night and ever the consummate networker, he immediately contacted Hastings after being ejected from *The Times* and asked for a job (around this time, he was also offered a role by the Conservative Research Department but still fancying his chances in journalism, turned it down).[8] Hastings decided to take a gamble on this unknown quantity: after all, seeing him in action at the Oxford Union had persuaded him of Boris's potential. It was not necessarily his glittering academic prizes that made Boris an appealing catch – as Hastings has noted, 'a brilliant career at Eton and Oxford [is] so often the precursor of a lifetime of obscurity.'[9] It was more a question of standing out from the crowd, as he recollected from that Union debate: 'I remember feeling cross that the evening seemed a benefit match for the presidential ego. No, let us be frank: I realised that this callow white lump in formal evening dress was a lot better at playing an audience than I was.' And he went on: 'Over the next few years, he developed the persona which has become famous today, a façade resembling that of PG Wodehouse's Gussie Fink-Nottle, allied to wit, charm, brilliance and startling flashes of instability.'[10]

It was Boris's great good fortune that Hastings hired *The Times'* reject. No longer the star graduate with an unblemished record, without Hastings' patronage, it is quite possible that Boris would have been lost forever to journalism at this point. Don Berry – Hastings' right-hand man, known as 'Uncle Don' for his friendly unflappability – remembers his editor's interest in 'bright young Oxbridge types.' 'Why did Max take him on? He said he would take any of them and give them a chance – he would be approached by lots of well-connected people. But if their kids didn't have talent, they would soon be out.'

The status-conscious Hastings' regime on the *Telegraph* was far more suited to Boris's editorial strengths than the Wilson administration in Wapping. He was moved straight onto the leader-writing desk, staffed almost entirely by public schoolboys similar to himself and collectively known to colleagues as 'Club Class'. Here, he was spared the rough and tumble of the newsroom – where state-school products then predominated – and was able to spread his wings in civilised calm next to the font of power, the editor's office. At long last, Boris seemed to have found his niche. Finally, he had been identified as a 'brilliant mind' and began to be treated with the indulgence he sought.

'Boris suited the *Telegraph* and the *Telegraph* – full of eccentrics, sub-edited by Marxists, read by Middle England – suited him,' says the distinguished journalist Mark Law, who by now had also made the switch to comment editor after a stint on *The Times*. Individuality, even eccentricity was positively encouraged, or at the very least easily tolerated. 'Middle England might have been surprised at what went on in its favourite paper,' adds Law. 'I know that I was. At the end of my first day at the *Telegraph*, the chief sub-editor of my section put away his papers and lit a joint.'

At first, Boris was seen as yet another clever eccentric who could be left alone to get on with the job of crafting leaders. But with time to make up, he set out with single-minded determination to reboot his faltering career; there was little time for office socialising or collaboration. Quentin Letts, then editor of the *Peterborough* diary column and another rising star, recalls the arrival of Boris – whom he described as 'quite good-looking then, with a certain Nordic ruthlessness about him' – after *The Times*' débâcle. 'Boris turned up at the *Telegraph* offices, then in South Quay. He sat in the leader writers' bit on the other side of the pot plants from *Peterborough*, but he never used to come round and give us stories. He was not a natural newspaperman, actually. He would never come to the pub – even though we were all the same age as him, for God's sake. He's not clubbable. You would think given he was in disgrace, he might come and wag his tail at us, but he didn't. I don't think it was a question of scorning the diary for being a downmarket, sleazy news-getting operation although there was an element of that.'

Rather, Letts thought Boris might be shy – he certainly did not appear to be chatting up any of the several attractive young women around the place. 'He's not a leaning-against-the-lamp-post type,' he observes. But Boris was evidently ferociously driven and Letts noticed that he viewed the world from the other end of the telescope to the typical journalist. 'He was already part of the establishment, friends with Lord Spencer and so on and consequently he saw journalists as birds of carrion rather than fine upstanding, investigative types. He never did the investigative thing or proper news. And he was always alive to money – money was very important to him. He was mixing with bankers, who saw the world as a business opportunity. So it was clear that he was never going to be just a passive observer, which is what the rest of us are. I think there was always in his mind the idea of going and doing something, to try to be part of public life. He was therefore very careful not to upset important people in the land.'

Colleagues were given the clear impression that Boris was very keen not to get on the wrong side of the wealthy and powerful friends he had collected since his time at Eton. On Saturday, 16 September 1989, his friend Charles Spencer married his first wife Victoria Lockwood in a grand ceremony at which Prince Harry served as a page and his parents, the Prince and Princess of Wales, were also guests. The next day, the *Peterborough* column got wind of a story bound to be of interest to *Telegraph* readers: the word was that disaster had only been narrowly averted when the best man – the other of Boris's two closest chums from Eton, Darius Guppy – failed to deliver his speech. Another guest had had to stand in at the very last moment with a few off-the-cuff words.

Boris was in the office that Sunday writing leaders and knowing he must have been at the wedding, the *Peterborough* staff approached him for confirmation of the story. It was totally normal newspaper procedure but it seemed to put Boris in a difficult spot. 'He just blustered, did the wobbly blancmange act,' recalls one of the diarists present. 'So we went with the story without his help and Darius phoned us a few days later and told us very charmingly that we had got the facts right.'

Boris soon made a good impression, however, on the important people on the paper – either by making them laugh (such as one humorous piece he wrote about skiing etiquette) or his increasingly sophisticated political leaders. His desk was appallingly untidy, sprawled with piles of papers, letters, empty sandwich boxes and old coffee cups but he would simply sweep them all to one side when he needed to write and after some heavy pacing up and down the corridor, he would produce a beautiful piece of writing, virtually without hesitation.

Bernice Davison, a senior colleague who sat on the features desk nearby, was taken aback. 'I've seen only a few other people – Max Hastings, A.N. Wilson and Robert Fox – write like that under pressure. It's an amazing feat of concentration, being able to produce 1,200 or 1,500 flowing words without a trace of the angst it would cause most of us.' But while Boris's star was finally in the ascendant, his ruthless focus earned him something of a reputation among the junior staff. 'I do remember people saying that Boris Johnson was very demanding of the editorial assistants or young undergraduates on work experience, or even colleagues, in fact anyone who was around,' adds Davison. 'He somehow expected them to fall into a "servant" kind of role, producing drinks, food, research, whatever.' He would then win some of them round again, of course, with carefully timed dollops of charm. One remembers feeling very grateful when on one occasion Boris offered to "do the tea round."'

He also had a reputation for displaying an extraordinary self-confidence – some would say arrogance – in senior editorial meetings, given he was still only in his mid-twenties. 'He was well known for "talking over" people. Boris was so sure about his own point of view that he'd often not let other people have a say, or would cleverly, possibly even cruelly, insinuate, or just state that their viewpoint was either wrong or idiotic,' recalls Davison. But self-belief is a highly prized asset in a leader writer and did Boris's reputation no harm at all among those who counted. He was competing for his 'place in the sun' against other 'brilliant minds,' such as his great rival Simon Heffer. One former colleague recalls: 'I suspect that many of the "Oh God, Boris is so full of himself!" comments current at the *Telegraph* at that time probably came from older staff members schooled in years of stiff-upper-lipness, who did not appreciate Boris's ability to be very demanding one minute, then very charming the next.'

Boris began to hone his individual writing style, using gloriously old-fashioned phrases, words and humour that set him apart from the other, more earnest young men on the leader writers' desk. His copy was fun to read; it literally sounded good. One of his favourite words was 'glutinous', an adjective he has summoned time and again over the years, variously to describe James Blunt's singing ('glutinous aspartame-flavoured schmaltz'[11]); traditional parents (swimming against the 'glutinous tide of political correctness'[12]) and Tony Blair's poll ratings ('glutinous and extravagant approval'[13]). On his appointment to the editorship of the *Spectator* in July 1999, he vowed to challenge the 'glutinous consensus' in British politics;[14] a decade later he used the same phrase to describe David Cameron's control over the Tory party.[15] 'Boris always managed to come up with wonderful fantastically obscure words – I often wondered how he got hold of them, but he knows how to craft them into the text,' notes Mark Law.

Another Boris trademark was dusting down long out-of-favour vocabulary such as 'goof' or phrases such as 'big girl's blouse'. He plays with words, selecting them as much for their pleasing sounds as their meaning. Sometimes he would simply invent a word to fill a gap in the dictionary: the evocative 'scabophobic' said everything necessary about the health and safety industry.[16]

He also developed the habit of saying the opposite to what he meant, but somehow letting the reader in on the secret. It's a clever device that takes the confrontational sting out of controversial opinions while at the same time appearing amusingly self-mocking. For example, when he wrote that he was 'speaking as an ardent feminist,' before sternly warning high-flying graduate women that they risked ending up childless and alone, it was pretty clear where his real sympathies lay.[17] Another effective tool was describing as 'my friend' someone who was nothing of the sort. Sparring partners such as the Labour MP Keith Vaz (who has crossed swords with Boris on more than one occasion) and the *Guardian* commentator Polly Toynbee (whose politics he ridicules) have both been subtly addressed in this way. It is an adept technique that unleashes the attack dogs while disguising them as Andrex puppies. However, when he addresses readers as 'my friends', another frequent mannerism, it is used as an ingenious device to appear conspiratorially on the side of his audience, almost as if addressing them personally.

In the space of just a few years, he addressed readers as 'my friends' more than 70 times in the *Telegraph* alone, and on many other occasions rang the changes with 'amigos' or 'mes amis'. It is a marvellous way of establishing a rapport, giving readers (and now voters) a sense of Boris-ownership that persists to this day. He would go on to adapt this device in his speeches as a politician, particularly to his devoted followers at party conference. The obvious point of comparison is John McCain, who was widely mocked for overuse of the 'my friends' schtick in his 2008 US presidential campaign. He failed to pull it off because he lacked a genuine sense of warmth and rapport with his audience, something that has always come naturally to Boris but was honed during these years in his writing.

Another Boris trademark was seasoning his copy with the odd Wodehousian 'crumbs' or 'cripes' tailored nicely to go with the bumbling persona he was busy perfecting for public consumption.

Double negatives – 'not unreasonable' became a favourite – somehow making the point without sounding didactic. 'Dog-in-the-mangerish', a classic Boris-ism, has also made an appearance several times – a phrase said to hail from an Ancient Greek fable meaning someone who spitefully prevents others from having something they have no use for, and applied by Boris to, among others, Britain's perceived attitude to Europe, Scottish MPs and former French President Jacques Chirac.

In full-scale attack mode his language can be both amusing and crushing in a way that few writers of his generation can match (although many may try). He dismissed Michael Portillo as 'the pompadoured whippersnapper of the right'[18] and Tony Blair as having a constantly lurking smile in which 'his lips twitch upwards, waiting to burst open in a glistening crescent of confidence.'[19] The trademark Latin tags soon began to appear – a Treasury official in Brussels was 'the locus classicus of British limpwristedness'[20], while the Christian Lacroix-wearing President of the European Commission, Jacques Delors is described as 'homo foederalis.'[21]

Boris appealed brilliantly to the 'country's going to the dogs' traditionalist instincts of the middle-class, middle-aged, middle-England readership of the *Telegraph*, with observations such as, 'No French politician would dream of succumbing to the mushy-minded inversion that has beset the British establishment since Gladstone, that in any dispute their country is more likely to be in the wrong.'[22] He was finding a voice, and one that his audience very much wanted to hear.

Between banging out leaders, he would sometimes find time to wind up his colleagues. A favourite target was the ever-affable Mark Law, a dedicated judo practitioner. Although Law omits to mention his name in his book, *The Pyjama Game*, Boris was one of the leader writers mentioned below. 'I have had to put up with a lot of that narrowing of the eyes and expulsion of the breath from the back of the throat which passes for oriental impersonation. Two *Telegraph* leader writers would sometimes circle around me, singing in its entirety, complete with gong sounds, the title song of *Hong Kong Phooey* in flat, nasal we-are-Siamee-eese voices. 'Hong Kong Phooey, faster than the human eye; Hong Kong Phooey, number one super guy.' I tried to feign laughter, but I was amused to note the point at which my sense of humour failed.'[23]

The amusement stopped entirely, though, when the boot was on the other foot and Law spiked Boris's work. 'Getting the copy from Boris was like blood out of a stone,' he recalls. 'His pieces were very good, but they were usually very late. We would be screaming at him to file but then eventually when he did, there were times when I wasn't able to use it. Something big might have happened and we would have to use a piece about that instead. At first he would be very angry but then he'd brush it off with a big jokey number about me taking revenge for him filing late.'

Finally, Boris was making his way in the newspaper business and when a vacancy came up in the *Telegraph*'s Brussels bureau in the spring of 1989, he was the obvious choice. He knew the city and its European institutions extremely well, having been familiar with them since childhood; he also spoke good French and Italian and passed muster in Spanish and German. But before he left for Belgium, he astonished his superiors by asking for more money. 'I well remember ushering the young Boris in to talk terms with Jeremy Deedes, our managing editor,' recalls the then foreign editor Nigel Wade, who was to be Boris's immediate boss. 'We fixed his salary and allowances, and I thought the meeting was over when Boris asked, "What about my wife and family?" Neither Jeremy nor I had the slightest idea that the young brainbox sent to us from on high was anything but a recent, unmarried graduate.'

In fact, Boris did not as yet have a family. He did, however, have a wife and consequentially, his accommodation and other allowances were substantially increased. From then on, he had a reputation within the *Telegraph* for being a hard negotiator on pay. After finishing off her law exams, Allegra followed him over the Channel in the summer. It was a difficult time to be moving abroad as her family back home was breaking up. After 28 years and three children together, Willie and Gaia were going their separate ways. Boris, now sensing that his career was finally motoring, seemed incapable of providing the emotional support she needed. He seldom, if ever, did household chores such as shopping or washing up, and according to her friends paid scant attention to his beautiful wife. After a while, he was rarely at home at all.

Boris had entered into a transformative new phase of his rise to fame. For some time, Brussels had not been viewed as a particularly interesting posting on the paper – news from the bureaucratic Belgian capital tended to be lacking in drama. But Johnson serendipity struck again. Six months before his departure, Margaret Thatcher had drawn the battle-lines with Europe in her notorious speech in the Belgian city of Bruges, in which she declared: 'We have not successfully rolled back the frontiers of the state in Britain, only to see them reimposed at a European level, with a European super state exercising a new dominance from Brussels.' Then, just six months after Boris arrived in Brussels in March 1989, the Berlin Wall fell – and communism swiftly with it.

Thatcher summoned an emergency summit at Chequers, the country residence of the British Prime Minister, to try and halt what seemed to be inevitable German reunification. As the geopolitical map was radically redrawn, with Britain's role on the continent also in flux, Europe and European politics took centre stage. Meanwhile, at home hostility to a newly invigorated Germany began to harden into full-blown Euroscepticism, widening the rifts in an increasingly divided government. Boris – after just 18 roller-coaster months in journalism – had landed in the midst of a perfect storm.

Chapter Five
I Fought Delors . . . and I Won

Brussels, 1989–1994

Boris likes to make a dramatic entrance and as the *Daily Telegraph*'s new man in Brussels, his arrival was no exception.

Geoff Meade, the experienced reporter from the *Press Association* wire service, and his first wife Sandra had been invited to Sunday lunch one warm April day in 1989 by Boris's father Stanley and stepmother Jenny. The two couples were chatting over aperitifs at the Johnsons' grand house with tennis court in the wealthy Brussels enclave near Waterloo when there was the crunching sound of a taxi pulling up sharply on the gravel driveway outside.

'We hadn't been led to expect anyone else so it was a surprise to see this outstandingly blond chap jump out in the loudest pair of Bermuda shorts possible. I'll never forget it,' recalls Meade. The scene was made even more memorable when a striking young woman followed him out of the cab – they made an attention-grabbing pair. 'It turned out to be Boris and Allegra, of course but it was Johnsonian cliché not to mention that they were coming,' continues Meade. After all, it added to the theatrical effect. 'But it became clear over lunch that I had been invited there as the established hand to meet and help Boris – and I duly did drive him round for the first few weeks, as was expected of me.'

In the early days, Boris certainly seemed to need the help that his father so deftly arranged and with characteristic selflessness, Meade provided for his new rival. As a family, the Johnsons have developed a useful knack of enlisting loyal helpers, whenever needed.

At the age of 24, Boris had been – through his father – steeped in the ways of the EU since childhood and knew many of the key characters personally, having holidayed with some of them. But while he did not let on about his 'insider' knowledge, it was clear after working on the *Telegraph* for barely a year, he still knew very little about news reporting. He was now confronted with a fast-moving, wide-ranging and fiendishly complex story without the journalistic tool-kit to deal with it, although it was quickly apparent that the newcomer was quite different from the established ranks of Brussels' reporters. 'Boris didn't immediately shine,' is how Meade gently puts it. In fact, his arrival in Brussels coincided with the first major cracks in the Thatcher government over Britain's role in Europe back in London, leading to Nigel Lawson's dramatic resignation as Chancellor of the Exchequer just six months later, on 26 October 1989. So, it was undoubtedly a leap of faith to send over someone so green to cover events now driving the domestic political agenda – a gamble that very nearly failed to pay off.

As a fellow reporter and rival who also lent him a hand explains: 'Boris said that Max [Hastings, the editor] had told him to come over to Brussels to see what was going on. As a reporter, he was shite. As a writer of intellectual ability, of course, he became something else.' Apart from goings on at the EU, Boris was also expected to cover general news stories, in and around Belgium, but his lack of experience in straight news reporting left him vulnerable. 'I remember the story in 1990 when some Australian tourists were mistaken for British soldiers by the IRA in Roermond, in Holland,' says one broadcast reporter. 'We all had to scramble from Brussels to do that story as the Dutch police chased the IRA. Boris was out of his depth and survived only by relying on the others.'

Boris's charm, unruly custard coiffure and apparent bumbling meant that his erstwhile rivals were happy to lend a hand, however, and in those early days, he greatly furthered his cause by cultivating this image of intelligent helplessness. Even his Brussels home suggested a modest, slightly impoverished man who cared little for the material life. Unlike his father's resplendent residence, Boris and (reluctantly) Allegra made do with a flat above a dentist's practice in

Woluwe-St-Pierre, an unfashionable district known for its petit bourgeois distrust of outsiders. More accustomed to the grandeur of the family seat in Shropshire and a gilded life in Oxford, Allegra disliked the place but it suited her husband's purpose well.

'Boris was very clever at creating an image and downplaying expectations so that colleagues thought he was way off-beam, and didn't know what he was doing,' recalls Michael Binyon, then working for *The Times* in Brussels. 'He put rivals off the scent and then would come up with a cracker of a story; the others then wondered where that had come from. He seemed like a bumbler to us to begin with, but his news desk back in London always knew what he really was. He used to infuriate colleagues in Brussels by persuading them to take pity on him, help him and then find themselves completely outsmarted.'

Another former rival notes how Boris was fond of combining artful bumbling with a craving for an audience. 'He exploited everything to get noticed. He would ask questions in comically bad French [the language in which EU business was then conducted]. Yet I discovered by chance that he could actually speak it very well, with a very good accent – it was part of the act.'

Even his driving proved ostentatiously eye-catching: Boris became legendary for Mr Toad-like frantic darting through the congested Brussels highways in his beloved flame-red Alfa Romeo, heavy metal band AC-DC blaring out unsociably through the wound-down windows. As well as a certain flamboyance his cars usually showed signs of strain – doors were tied on with string, wing mirrors had long since been lost. But they complemented his equally ragged wardrobe well.

His unusual appearance caused a particular stir at the European Commission's daily press briefings, attended by the media from all member states. He would wait for the other journalists to take their seats at midday precisely – with the Brits traditionally occupying the centre front rows – before making his own belated, but scene-stealing entrance. When not dressed for a Malibu beach party, he favoured soiled and frequently whiffy jackets with ripped pockets and trousers with fraying seams – this in a city where the work uniform was one of sober European elegance and polish. An impeccably attired *grande dame* of the French press corps once famously leant over to the comfortingly urbane Michael Binyon to enquire, '*Qui est ce monstre*?' Soon, he cut such an infamous figure of intelligent hopelessness that no one, not even from other EU countries, needed to ask. Boris was notorious across the different national press packs: from the Italians to the Danes, they recognised a star when they saw one. He was known to all and sundry as just Boris, his writings as the 'English position' and he lapped up the attention.

David Usborne of the *Independent*, another knowledgeable old hand, gives further insight into the Johnsonian 'winning friends' and 'getting noticed' technique: 'He was very young and in a slightly deranged way, he looked up to me.' However, with hindsight, Usborne recognises he was being worked. 'At least,' he says, 'he was very good at *flattering* me.' Flattery is another cunning family tactic – making others feel good while simultaneously making use of them and what they know, at least until they tire of the game. Like many of his ruses, Boris honed the art to perfection in Brussels. As soon as he had recruited an army of sympathetic helpers – or as his critics, remembering his Oxford antics, would put it, 'stooges' – he began to focus on a strategy that would pluck him out of obscurity, seize the glory from his generous cohorts and in turn elevate him to become both Margaret Thatcher's and the nation's favourite journalist. In taking a different stance from his peers, he would eventually, at least in his own estimation, alter the course of history and earn himself fame and fortune in the process.

Boris's genius lay in recognising that Brussels reporting had become a cosy cartel, in which the various correspondents produced broadly sympathetic accounts of the EU's activities. He spotted a commercial opportunity – the chance to make his name by doing what he does best: being different. He has subsequently obliquely confirmed that this was his Brussels game plan in the afterword of a collection of his journalism, *Lend Me Your Ears* (2004). Indeed, it's a telling insight into how strategically Boris thinks: 'Because it is a free market, there will always be someone to buck the conventional opinion, ready to buy when the market is low. If someone spots that gap and starts to offer another stock, there will be one of those tipping points. Suddenly, everyone will stop selling and start buying.'

At first, his was a relatively lonely Eurosceptic voice in Brussels, but by the time he left after five years there were only a few brave souls left who still felt it safe to present themselves as unquestioning pro-Europeans, at least in public. The 'tipping point' had emphatically been passed and that was in part down to Boris's early and consistent investment in sceptic stock. Of course, Boris did not invent Euroscepticism – there were others who had long been hostile to the Euro-project – but he helped to take it out of the hands of its traditional proponents from the Left, such as veteran Labour MPs Tony Benn and Peter Shore, and make it an attractive and emotionally resonant cause for the Right.

A spokesman from UKIP (United Kingdom Independence Party), which campaigns for Britain's withdrawal from the EU, says that Boris's writings 'helped to pave' the way for the rise of his party. Its leader Nigel Farage goes further by saying that before Boris made them a fashionable cause, Eurosceptic leanings were 'something that would only be shared amongst close personal friends. They were a minority pursuit.' After Boris, there were few on the Right who did not join the Eurosceptic bandwagon. Of course there were other writers, mainly based in London, also starting to peddle the anti-European cause but Boris whipped up Eurosceptic fervour in the most devilishly clever way, using a potent cocktail of humour and gross exaggeration. Quickly realising it was imperative to become an amusing, as well as hostile writer, to stand out, he could already see that humour was perhaps his most devastating weapon.

'EC CHEESE ROW TAKES THE BISCUIT,' was the headline on one of his *Telegraph* stories. Another noted, 'the Italian rubber industry has fallen foul of EC rules by making undersized condoms.'[1] His copy was full of 'plots' and 'traps' laid by the dastardly French against the 'limp-wristed' English with their 'shy grins' and 'corrugated soled shoes.' Within a couple of years of his arrival, Boris had developed a whole new mode of journalism, one that the rest of the media were swiftly compelled to adopt. The 'straight banana' school of Eurosceptic reporting saw fishermen made to wear hairnets, prawn cocktail crisps banned and a two-mile high Eurocrat folly built at taxpayers' expense, all under the auspices of an insanely grandiose and imperialist European Commission.

'He was very inventive and creative. What he would say would never be simply untrue, but would be on the edge of what might happen,' says Michael Binyon. 'The skyscraper story, for instance, was based on just a hint that such a building would be nice. It was hard to deny these stories outright so we were all forced to follow them up. It was good to be a leading Eurosceptic in a consensus of Europhile correspondents. Everyone was then mocking Maggie and cheering [Jacques] Delors [president of the Commission]. Boris played a brilliant spoiler card by following the reverse stance.'

Journalists chasing the same story frequently resort to hunting in packs but Boris, despite his convivial air, was still a loner at heart. 'He wasn't the best of the bunch, but one of the most likely to cause a stir, to get a good story,' recalls a distinguished rival. 'He always had a different line, angle, or piece of information. But was that because he had better stories or was he just better at showcasing them? Or perhaps it was that he was simply better at making them up?' Boris's energy, his inventiveness, opportunism and dogged self-belief combined to make him an unstoppable force. As a close friend of the Johnson family recalls: 'Everyone in the Brussels press bought into it, this Euro-loony thing; there came about a basic assumption that if it came from the EU, it must be loony. Even the BBC were doing it, and that was down to Boris.'

Most of Boris's stories speculated on the latest schemes of Jacques Delors, President of the European Commission, who was then determinedly driving forward the process of European integration. During his extensive term of office, from 1985–1994, his career outlived that of his arch enemy Margaret Thatcher, British Prime Minister. He also pulled off some historic achievements. These included the Single European Market in 1986 (making the entire EU an open area for the free movement of goods and services), the Schengen Agreement of 1990 (under which most EU nations, but not Britain, removed systematic border controls between participating countries) and above all, the Maastricht Treaty – which, when finally ratified in 1993, set in train greater political integration and the process towards the introduction of the Euro in 1999.

In 1989, Delors had set the agenda for reaching economic and monetary union in what was known as the Delors Report (with political union added to the mix as a result of a bargain between German Chancellor Helmut Kohl and the French President, François Mitterrand). 'The single European market needs a single European currency was their cry. We should not have been surprised. It had been their ambition for a long time,' wrote John Major, after leaving office following the General Election of 1997.[2] With his sights set so high, Delors' highly tuned political manoeuvring skills came into play. The diminutive, yet formidable Frenchman frequently triumphed over the entire British government and diplomatic service, leaving them looking flat-footed and foolish. In hostile British tabloid land, however, he was regarded as dastardly, with the *Sun* resorting to the infamous splash headline of 'UP YOURS DELORS!'

Even this semi-mythical Frenchman was eventually outsmarted by Boris, who won his battles where HM Government had failed, through speed, wit and his own brand of brilliant invective. Delors and his team of otherwise gifted advisers, though trained in the schemer's academy of Parisian politics, seemed bereft of weapons with which to fight back. Both men shared the ability to charm, to flatter and to plan strategically – plus a feel for the ways and means of the EU derived from years of association therewith. But Delors specifically lacked Boris's winning sense of fun, colour and the absurd, making this ultimately an uneven contest. 'We answer his attacks,' fretted one EU official, 'but the problem is that our answers are not funny.'

Indeed, so powerful did Boris become while still in his twenties that some visiting Ministers of the Crown would delay press conferences until he deigned to turn up (while others fearing his difficult questioning would secretly pray he would not show at all). Virtually all would spend hours deliberating on how to 'Boris-proof' their policies or announcements. He was by no means universally popular within government circles, despite his self-appointed championing of the British cause, because his natural wit, mischief and ambition made him impossible to control. There were rumours at the time that, at least on one occasion, the then Foreign Secretary Douglas Hurd tried to get his friend Max Hastings to sack Boris. Hurd himself dismisses this as 'rubbish' and 'not my style' – and Hastings also says that he 'never complained.'

Indeed, Hurd recalls that they had a relatively 'joshy' relationship, finding that joking with his fellow Old Etonian King's Scholar, 'helped to keep him off my back. Max and I had lunch at Wiltons once with Boris, and he went through his paces. But that was perfectly friendly.'

Hurd's characteristic laid-back and generous approach was hardly met with reciprocal loyalty, however. Boris in turn accused him of 'capitulating' in key negotiations with the Europeans over a range of subjects, from lifting the export ban on British post-BSE beef, the talks on Maastricht and even the failure to send the troops into the former Yugoslavia early enough to avert catastrophe.[3] And yet Hurd says Boris's attacks were 'within reasonable bounds.' It is as if the former foreign secretary, who describes himself as neither 'original' nor 'brilliant',[4] decided to indulge Boris because he saw in him the sort of sparkling young man he himself might have wished to be. Boris seems to have sensed – correctly – that Hurd was one important person he could attack with impunity.

But Boris was becoming 'an issue' for the British Government as a whole and undermining its negotiating position. Officials from that time talk of the 'constant headaches' he caused them, and there are elements of distrust that remain to this day. 'The Foreign Office even set up a Boris unit, a team of people tasked with rebutting negative Boris stories or trying to stop them appearing in the first place,' claims one well-informed Brussels source from the time. 'They were utterly obsessed with him,' confirms another. 'Sir John Kerr [then Britain's Ambassador to the EU] told guests at a private lunch that "we're working on Boris."'

A key Government source confirms Boris was a source of constant concern not only within the Foreign Office but right across the Major administration. 'We were struggling to maintain our position in Europe,' recalls one high-flying official on the Boris brief. Boris and the

Telegraph newspapers were 'key factors' in the 'presentation of policy,' he confirms, but whatever the Government's efforts to advance its arguments, 'he still managed to put us on the back foot.' Another Government source recalls: 'He has a brilliant talent with words – and a great imagination [and] he wasn't deterred if the facts didn't quite sustain his line of argument. I would sometimes phone him up, astonished, and ask, "What was all that about?" He would just waffle [with vague excuses such as] "that's the way I saw it"'.

Sir Richard Stagg, who went on to become High Commissioner in Delhi, but was then the British government's press secretary in Brussels, remembers how Boris stood out from the rest of the British press corps – even those who quickly followed his anti-Delorian stance – by straddling the dividing line between reporter and politician. 'He used these dull technical EU matters to sustain his thesis that a Delorian super-state was being created, but in a very entertaining way,' explains Sir Richard. 'The difference between Boris and most of the rest of the press corps was perhaps that he had a clearer intellectual idea of what he thought was right or wrong. Others wanted to lead the agenda journalistically. They just wanted a hell of a story, he had more of a political purpose.'

Hurd has vivid memories from the receiving end of what became known in Government circles as Boris's 'grenades': 'The image that stays in my mind is the end of a bloody day in the Council of Ministers [the meeting of EU foreign ministers]. It has been rough-going and you're tired. Your private secretary says to you, "Now it's the press, Secretary of State." I heave a sigh. I go into the room and there is Boris, with his shaggy locks, in the front row. He is the best informed of the press corps; he grew up with the whole EU/EC thing. He usually puts his question late, well after my platitudinous opening remarks – I wait for it, I know it will come. The word "dread" is a bit high – it is more like a sparring match. The question is always critical, from some extra piece of knowledge that he has. I can still see him waiting to throw his grenade, and he does.' Boris, he says warmly, was one of a group of people who saw it as their duty to make life 'more difficult for me.'

*

Of course Boris was lucky to enough to find himself at the centre of such a big story. Margaret Thatcher, who cherished Boris's reports from the Euro-front line, fell from power 17 months after he arrived in town as a direct result of the EU summit in October 1990, in Rome. She had been the victim of an ambush by the Italians, who sprang on her the date of 1999 for the launch of the euro. Returning to the House of Commons on 30 October 1990, Thatcher famously declared: 'No, no, no' in response to what she saw as many and various European integrationist plots.

Two days later, Sir Geoffrey Howe resigned as Deputy Prime Minister in protest at her intransigent European policy – and within a month, she too had gone after failing to garner sufficient support in the inevitable leadership contest. The putsch was of seismic political significance and the end of an era. Boris greatly benefited from it. (He famously wrote that, while he disputed the account, his 'wife Marina' claimed to have found him sobbing in the street over Thatcher's downfall, claiming it was if 'someone had shot Nanny.'[5] It is intriguing to note that in 1990, he was still married to Allegra.)

After Thatcher's demise, the battle lines were drawn deeper between Britain's ever-hardening Euro-reluctance and the enthusiastic Euro empire-builders on the continent. Europe dominated the agenda and Boris found himself on the front line. All the British newspapers staffed full-time offices in the city and there was a buzz to the place that suited him well. Many journalists sent to Brussels in the late 1980s and early 90s were, like Boris, rising stars. Some have indeed gone on to great things – Lionel Barber was to edit the *Financial Times* (he was then its Brussels bureau chief), Sarah Lambert (formerly of the *Independent*) later headed the European Commission mission in London and David Gardner of the *FT* became an internationally renowned authority on the Middle East. Yet his status as maverick-in-chief ensured only Boris emerged as a true household name and national figure. Under the Canadian-born tycoon Lord (Conrad) Black, who had been ennobled by Thatcher and mourned her loss, the *Daily Telegraph* and *Sunday Telegraph* newspapers became increasingly virulently anti-Europe. Boris, as ever, seized his chance to up the ante. 'He was feeding the appetite to make Delors and Brussels look stupid,' recalls David Usborne.

While Boris's stories were becoming apparently more heavyweight and certainly more influential on the affairs of the entire EU, his fellow journalists and former helpers were now seeing through the bumbling façade and becoming increasingly uneasy. Usborne continues: 'He wasn't making things up necessarily, just over-egging to a degree that was dishonest. I always assumed he didn't believe that stuff. He couldn't do! But he played the *Telegraph* game brilliantly. It was always clear he was going for the main prize but he compromised his intellectual integrity to get on. And I assume he has done that in the rest of his career since. I was irritated by it – not least because his father was an EU bureaucrat. I told Boris in a jokey way – you're writing out of your ass.'

Boris's opportunistic – some might say, pragmatic – approach to politics came to the fore in Brussels. Despite his supposed tears after the shooting of 'Nanny', it's fair to say that he did not share her sense of ideological conviction. Indeed, it is very telling that few of his close associates believe that his Euroscepticism is anything like as rabid as it seems. Some don't hold with the idea that Boris is actually Eurosceptic at all – but that he, in fact, felt much sympathy for the ambitions of Brussels, not least because of his father's Euro-career and his own childhood and schooling in the city. David Gardner of the *Financial Times* recalls, 'whenever Boris got on my nerves, I would threaten to out him as a federast. Under that confected exterior lurks a committed Europhile!' Even Douglas Hurd, so often the brunt of his anti-European crusades, observes that although Boris 'wasn't one for wearing his opinions on his sleeve,' he did not believe that he held 'entirely negative' views on the EU.

On one occasion, when an EU directive was criticised as invasive by Gardner in the normally pro-European *Financial Times*, its Brussels office was besieged by complaints from Boris. 'Britain had just signed off what we thought was arguably the single most intrusive bit of legislation ever devised in Brussels – the Habitats Directive, which took central control over the status and future of whole swathes of the European landmass, particularly in countries like Spain,' says

Gardner, occupying for once what might have been expected to be Boris-friendly territory. But Boris himself was incensed. 'He jammed the *FT*'s fax machine with reams and reams of pages complaining about this "outrageous slur". It got to the point where the fax actually ran out of paper and we decided not to replace it.' So here was Boris in manic defence of the same interventionist EU he had created a top-flight career from attacking. Interestingly, in clannish Johnsonian style, he was also defending the directive's author: his father Stanley.

Charles Grant, then the *Economist*'s correspondent in Brussels – and now director of the pro-Europe Centre for European Reform – started in town at the same time as Boris: 1989. He recalls how Boris's stance changed. 'He was not writing very Eurosceptic stuff for the first year or two. I always felt that even later, he just wrote that way to make a name for himself. He didn't like that point of view when I put it to him.' 'Far from being a hardline Eurosceptic, I actually had the impression that he was really a federalist,' agrees Peter Guilford, who used to play ferociously competitive squash with Boris when working as spokesman for Sir Leon Brittan, EU Commissioner from 1989 to 1999. Guilford was one of the few who Boris occasionally confided in, not viewing him as a potential rival. 'But Boris also saw his job as to entertain, to please his editors' prejudices and thereby advance his career. He put that before accurate news judgement and he was clever enough to get away with it. Boris brought the entertainment factor of Brussels coverage up, but the quality and accuracy down,' he adds.

Indeed, many of those accompanying him during those heady years in Brussels could not fail to note that his published words were in stark contrast to the way in which Boris spoke privately about the EU and its dramatis personae. He was far more sympathetic, even affectionate in person than the anti-Brussels rants under his name in print. In truth, he can be said to be neither truly anti-European nor a little Englander. As Guilford puts it: 'He was never quintessentially English, not in Brussels nor afterwards.' In Brussels some began to feel annoyed about this apparent contradiction. It is telling that he rarely worked alongside other journalists but typically sought a quiet corner out of sight to write, or when he could, would absent himself from the pack entirely to seek refuge in the *Telegraph* office. Like Superman, he would then undergo a startling and virtually instantaneous transformation from Bumbling Boris to Bilious Boris before penning yet another explosive tract.

Most days, just before copy deadline, he would do this by a tried-and-tested method known as the 'four o'clock rant'. Cannily, he would first wait for Thérèse, the motherly Flemish secretary who spoilt her youthful charge with Lion d'Or chocolates, to go home. After locking his door, he would then work himself up into a frenzy by hurling repeated four-letter abuse at a ragged yucca plant near his desk. Indeed, he still bears a scar on his hand where the force of his emotions snapped a biro he was holding at the time. Formerly the drawing room of a grand parquet-floored apartment, his office overlooked a normally peaceful scene of fountain and lake ringed by weeping willows and presided over by a statue of Artemis, the Greek goddess of hunting, in the centre of the belle époque Square Marie Louise. Yet anyone passing by around teatime could not help but be alarmed at the torrent of guttural roars and full-volume expletives from the bay window above. His outburst spent, he would settle down to his keyboard to dash off at hurtling speed – and with a violent fist-handed typing style – another brilliantly damaging and inventive thousand words. This bizarre ritual, to those who witnessed it, was an insight into the torrent of focus and drive that lies beneath Boris's affable exterior. When relaxed, he would gossip with colleagues and counterparts on other papers and would be amusing and stimulating company. (Although strangely, more than once, a jokey comment from these sessions would later appear in a story, immediately after the words: 'One Brussels source said . . .') At his keyboard, however, his mood would alter. He would brook distraction from no one. 'If you ever interrupted him when writing on his grubby Tandy 300 [the antiquated brick-like laptop he favoured], he got incredibly angry,' reports a senior European Parliament source. 'He would literally yell at you to leave him alone – he never lost focus on what he was trying to do.'

These frenzied stories on the threat the EU apparently posed to the British way of life began to dominate the domestic news agenda. As

Boris later recalled on BBC Radio's *Desert Island Discs* (in October 2005), he was 'sort of chucking these rocks over the garden wall and I listened to this amazing crash from the greenhouse next door over in England as everything I wrote from Brussels was having this amazing, explosive effect on the Tory party. And it really gave me this, I suppose, rather weird sense of power.'[6] Indeed, Boris's Brussels' despatches were widening existing splits in the Tory party over Europe into great yawning chasms – rendering the frenetic attempts of Thatcher's successor, John Major, to create unity futile and his government ultimately unelectable. It took Major what he described as a 'year of gruesome trench warfare'[7] to win the narrowest of votes in the House of Commons for the bill that finally ratified the Maastricht Treaty in July 1993 – and Boris's antics had undoubtedly played a part in the pain the Prime Minister experienced. His Government was repeatedly taken to the point of collapse by Eurosceptic rebels and at one point he did not sleep for more than 60 hours as he tried to restore order.

Major was frequently infuriated by Boris and had 'cross words'[8] about the political fallout from Boris' writings with an unreceptive Max Hastings. The Prime Minister also liked to make his point – perhaps rather more successfully – by publicly teasing Boris at press conferences about becoming EU obsessive. In contrast, Major's many critics among the Eurosceptics adored and applauded the havoc Boris was wreaking on their behalf. As Major knew only too well, however, it all came at a price – rendering the very party that Boris professed to support political pariahs for over a decade. Major would never square the circle with the anti-Europeans in his party; their divisions would see the Conservatives dumped by the electorate at the 1997 general election, ironically paving the way for a more Euro-friendly Labour administration under Tony Blair. For fuelling the rift Boris continues to be regarded as 'suspect' by many pro-European, moderate or loyalist Tories to this very day.

Until the end of his five-year stay in Brussels, Boris continued to satisfy the British appetite for stories of sinister continental plots. Just as his marriage to Allegra began to fray under the pressure of his obsession with his career – which made him both distant and intolerably selfish at times – so did his professional fortunes take off and his influence grow. His reporting gradually progressed from the dangers of EU interference with Britain's favourite crisp flavours to what he portrayed as a direct and broad-based attack on the very essence of the nation's sovereignty and soul.

The ferocious fighting over the closer European integration introduced by the Maastricht Treaty, constant rows over Britain's half-hearted involvement and its ignominious exit from the Exchange Rate Mechanism (a precursor to the single currency) on 16 September 1992 (known as 'Black Wednesday') gave him plenty of material to cast Delors in the role of über-villain. And the plaudits poured in – not least in the form of 'herograms' – notes of congratulation – from Hastings. Most journalists quietly place such professional *billets-doux* in a drawer, but Boris pasted his large collection up on the wall as a triumphal arch over the office doorway for all to see.

Guilford recalls once reading the 'herograms' at a drinks party at the *Telegraph* offices. 'There was one from Max, saying, "we all think you're doing a wonderful job if only you'd learn to be a little more pompous." I think he was pompous enough already.'

Boris's writing was becoming so prolific and so eye-catching – both in the *Daily* and *Sunday Telegraph* plus their stable-mate, the *Spectator* – that by 1991 he had truly become a star. Meanwhile, other journalists on rival newspapers were instructed to follow up his stories, even when there seemed to have little basis in fact.

'When they discovered asbestos in the Berlaymont [the Commission HQ], Boris wrote a colourful story that teams of sappers were going to mine the building and blow it up,' recalls one long-suffering EU official. 'The story really took off. Another paper made their poor correspondent ring up to see whether they could press the trigger for the dynamite but it just wasn't true. There was asbestos and there were various options to deal with it, including removing the asbestos or destroying the building, but there was never any suggestion of sappers – it would have been done by specialist demolition men, piece by piece.' For the record, the star-shaped Berlaymont is still there, asbestos-free and now coated in a smart new glass-and-steel façade. Boris's thrilling image of soldiers and explosions never made it into reality.

'He consequently set the pace, even if the stories weren't exactly right,' says a well-known broadcaster also in Brussels at the time. 'The others had to play catch-up – it made them very cross.' Another highly diligent journalist remembers a comment from Boris around this time that speaks volumes about his cavalier approach. 'Some of his stories were simply not true,' he says. 'When I mentioned this to him, Boris just wagged his finger and said, "There'll come a day when you'll write a story without picking up the phone – we all do." What he was doing, he was doing by reflex. It was a clear insight into how he was thinking towards the end of his time in Brussels. Early Boris was far better than later Boris.'

It is not clear whether he picked up the phone for his most explosive story, which he wrote in May 1992 at a meeting of European foreign ministers at Guimarães in Portugal. The Maastricht Treaty had been signed but not ratified by the individual member states. Some countries were holding referenda first. A 'yes' vote from one of those countries – Denmark – was crucial to the treaty, but although closely fought, was widely thought to be in the bag.

Boris himself likes to revel in the havoc following the Guimarães story. A decade later, he crowed in his *Telegraph* column: 'All journalists probably delude themselves that they may have influenced the history they are paid to observe. My boast is that I probably did contribute to the Danish rejection of Maastricht. I thought it was quite good stuff.'[9]

The *Sunday Telegraph* thought it good stuff indeed and ran it as the front-page splash under a banner headline, 'DELORS' PLANS TO RULE EUROPE'. Boris reported that Delors wanted to scrap rotation of the EU presidency and to centralise power in Brussels. The Danish 'Nej' campaign held up Boris's story as proof of their long-running claims that the new treaty would deprive small countries such as Denmark of their rights. Boris recalls: 'With less than a month until [the Danish] referendum, and with mounting paranoia about the erosion of Danish independence, the story was seized on by the No campaign. They photocopied it a thousandfold. They marched the streets of Copenhagen with my story fixed to their banners. And on

June 2nd, a spectacularly sunny day, they joyously rejected the Treaty and derailed the project. Jacques Delors was not the only victim of the disaster; the aftershocks were felt across Europe, and above all in Britain.'[10]

Two decades on, controversy still rages. Arguably, without Boris, the Danes would have voted 'yes' to Maastricht (polls before his article pointed to a narrow vote in favour of the Treaty) and the EU would have cantered rather than crawled closer to becoming a superstate. After the piece appeared, the polls dramatically switched to a narrow vote against Maastricht. Charles Grant, author of an authoritative tome on Delors and a man not given to hyperbole, agrees with Boris that his article did indeed change the course of history, derailing the march towards ever-greater integration and stronger EU institutions. The Danish Government even threatened to block Delors' reappointment to the commission presidency unless he disowned the ideas quoted in Boris's piece. Delors was seen looking distraught afterwards, 'the pallor of his skin suggested he had received an electric shock.'[11] Others, including Douglas Hurd and Geoff Meade, believe that Boris likes to overplay his role in the events of Denmark.

The incident certainly raised Boris's fame to new heights, however, both back in Britain and now across Europe. A despairing John Major observed, 'not since the heyday of the Vikings had the Danes precipitated such disruption'[12] – stirring up Eurosceptics back home and increasing the pressure on a struggling pound being just two unwelcome consequences.

John Palmer, then the *Guardian*'s Brussels bureau chief and loyal Europhile, is incensed to this day. He claims Boris's story was an inflated and distorted version of his own sober and accurate account, published just a few days earlier. In contrast, Boris had told his bosses on the *Sunday Telegraph* foreign desk that he received the story from EU sources. 'I have no personal animus against him whatsoever – I'm friendly with his family – but as a journalist he is thoroughly irresponsible, inventing stories. Just before the Danish referendum, I wrote a story about Delors' thinking on the next stages of political integration in the *Guardian*,' Palmer says. 'Boris came up to me when it appeared and asked whether I'd seen the relevant document. He then rewrote my story and completely distorted it to say "Delors' Plans to Rule Europe."

'In fact, it was all about mere *ideas* on more majority voting, more powers for the European Parliament and that sort of thing. Then what happened was that the extreme Europhobes in Denmark took Boris's inaccurate version and produced it as a leaflet. Whenever he was challenged about his rubbish, he would never actually defend his corner – he just blamed London, he was quite shameless. But what Boris wrote was taken as gospel by the zealots. It fuelled the whole UKIP phenomenon.'

More extraordinary is the fact that even one of Boris's own supporters confirms the tale's shaky foundations: 'These were not plans, as he said, but merely thoughts and ideas. [But the story] caused the government enormous grief. And he could see what it was doing to the Conservative party, which arguably took a decade to recover. The irony is that Boris is a pro-European at heart. So why did he do it? Just pure opportunism – it made him feel powerful.'

It is essential to note that while these ideas were merely subjects for discussion at the time – rather than plans, as claimed by Boris – many of them, such as more powers for the European Parliament and a permanent rather than rotating Presidency, have now come to fruition through the Lisbon Treaty of 2007. Boris's instincts – if not his attention to hard facts – were spot-on.

The fall-out at the time, however, was disturbing not only for the London government, but Boris too. Adulation from the European Far Right in countries like Denmark and Holland did concern him, as did the feeling that he was becoming too closely identified with one tribe back in Britain. Boris is the ultimate individualist – he is not a clubbable man, but a secretive one. On his well-trodden route up to the Commission from the *Telegraph* office in Square Marie Louise, he would occasionally point to a street sign. 'Ah, rue du Taciturne,' he would smile, tapping his nose. 'The road of the silent one, quite right.'

Although now a legendary figure, few people in Brussels knew Boris well. He was obsessively silent about himself, or at least the real Boris, rather than the act. Even Allegra was unable to keep tabs on him and more than once discovered his whereabouts only by reading his articles in the paper from Baghdad, say, or Zagreb. It was doubtless humiliating when she had to phone the *Telegraph*'s London office to ask where her husband was. His career was all consuming, leaving little space for his marriage. 'You get past caring and you start drinking malt whisky,' she says of that time.[13] In her solitude, she began to fear that, like Boris's mother Charlotte, she too was heading for a breakdown.

'There was a feeling that Allegra was a troubled person,' recalls Peter Guilford. Boris seems to have been insensitive at best, incapable or unwilling to do anything about her increasing unhappiness. Tony Robinson, spokesman for the Socialist Group in the European Parliament, recalls having a drink with him one evening to discuss a potential story. 'It was the 22nd of March, and after a while I said I had to go as it was my wife's birthday. Boris said, "Oh no! It's my wife's birthday too!" He'd totally forgotten.' Not long after, Boris told a colleague that he realised he had blown it with Allegra when he asked her what she thought of 'subsidiarity' – a piece of esoteric Euro-babble referring to devolving decisions to national or regional governments. It excited Eurobores but no one with anything resembling a normal life. 'Boris would tell me that that had been the trigger for the whole breakdown in the marriage,' the colleague says. While this seems unlikely, another obfuscatory joke, it is clear that Boris's ruthless focus on his war with Delors came first.

Allegra packed her bags and fled back to London in February 1990. Charles Grant says: 'Boris was distraught – he desperately wanted Allegra; that was probably the only time the comic mask dropped. He was very, very unhappy.'[14] It was also one of the few occasions when he relaxed his self-control and drank more than a glass or two of wine. Charles Grant remembers inviting Boris to a party at his apartment in the rue de Calle just after Allegra had left. 'That was the last time I vomited from drinking too much – and it was because of Boris. He didn't want to go home when everyone else did because he was on his own. He said, "Let's open another bottle." I was persuaded to drink it with him – and then I was ill.'

'Very unusually, we had one or two heart to hearts when he was disentangling himself from Allegra,' recalls David Usborne. 'We got very drunk on Duvel (a strong Belgian beer) when we went away for a weekend and stayed in a log cabin in the Ardennes.'

Other guests were surprised when Boris also got 'very distressed' in public over dinner with his uncle Edmund Fawcett – his mother's brother – in late June 1990, while he was covering an EU summit in Dublin for the *Telegraph*.

The period of the break-up, which stretched over two years, is a rare example of Boris reaching out to other men in what has otherwise been a remarkably self-sufficient life. On occasion, he would also be uncharacteristically open with professional rivals. He once asked one: 'Do you think I'm a difficult person?' It was not 'a Boris sort of question.' Divorce proceedings had begun and even reached the decree nisi or provisional stage, but in September 1990 there was something of a reconciliation. At weekends, Allegra began flying to Brussels (before the days of the Channel Tunnel) to be with Boris while taking her Law Society finals in London during the week. A full year later, she enrolled at the Université Libre in Brussels for a Masters in EU law, in one last attempt to repair their ailing marriage.

For Boris, never a man to be alone for long, it was already too late. Although in some ways a loner, he has never enjoyed bachelorhood. While Allegra had been slogging over her law books in London, he had already begun a dedicated pursuit of his childhood friend Marina Wheeler, whom he had known since they were both in nappies in Washington. He had first fallen for her a few years later at the age of nine – when she had turned up from America sporting an 'Impeach Nixon' badge and been able to teach an impressionable young 'Al' what it meant. As we have seen, she was less enamoured back then.

Their halting relationship suffered another false start when the pair were both 16 and Boris discovered how he could take Marina out in London without having to pay for it. 'I found out that Hare Krishna devotees would give you a free lunch if you attended a session at the centre near Shaftesbury Avenue. I thought the food was delicious but she didn't think much of it and has never forgiven me.'[15] As if trust is a constant issue for him, Boris gravitates towards people he has known a long time. Marina came back to Brussels in 1990, just as Allegra was leaving, and was working only a short walk away as a lawyer for the EU practice of Stanbrook & Hooper. The ex-pat community in Brussels is close-knit but she found Boris at his most lonesome. Even when he reunited with Allegra in the autumn of that year, his wife's studies in London meant he was by himself most of the time.

Where Allegra had become more emotionally needy, Marina with her steady career, sense of purpose and quiet steeliness was a reassuring presence. Here at last was a woman who was a model of stability and independence. He was attracted to her unusual self-sufficiency and calm, inherited from her unflappable Indian mother, Dip. 'Marina was always so grounded, such a balanced person,' remembers a close female colleague. 'She was a star on the fast track. She was very interested in people in a genuine way but she's also someone who doesn't need attention.' Certainly, Rachel's friends have said how Marina has been accepted into the family in a way that Allegra, thought to be neurotic, never was.

Despairing of his marriage, Boris pursued Marina devotedly, bombarding her with phone calls and flattery. 'Boris was obviously smitten and she fell madly in love with him,' recalls the colleague. 'When he was pursuing her, he didn't play it cool at all. It was full out, lots of phone calls all the time. Boris would be very open about his feelings, he wasn't coy once he decided that Marina was the one.' Fatefully, when she was in town, Allegra frequently invited Marina round to dinner at the flat she shared with Boris because Marina lived in 'crappy digs.'

This time Marina responded in the way that he had hoped. Although she and her family – particularly her ever-loyal mother – insist she did not become romantically involved with Boris until it was all over with Allegra, observers are equally sure that the line between Allegra finishing and Marina beginning is fuzzy at best. 'It was a sort of natural progression,' says one. 'Or rather there was no real line at all.' 'I often went to Allegra and Boris's house for lunch or drinks and Marina would be there too,' recalls another ex-pat. 'There was clearly something between Boris and Marina in terms of attachment and affinity. It was like visiting a ménage à trois – I wondered how Allegra dealt with that.'

Another frequent visitor puts it: 'It was clear Marina was obsessed by Boris. When I went round to Allegra and Boris's house, Marina would often be there. She was clearly in love with him. Her familiarity with him, the way she treated him, it was hard to see where the friendship stopped and the love began. One week I was going round to Boris and Allegra's house with Marina there. The next week, I was going round to Boris and Marina's house with Allegra nowhere to be seen. It was if nothing had happened. I don't think Boris would have let Allegra go if he hadn't had someone else lined up, but Allegra's growing disenchantment had made it uncomfortable for Boris.'

Really there is little justice in blaming Marina for the breakdown of Boris's first marriage – and it is clear that Allegra does not hold a grudge. According to one Brussels friend who had also known them in Oxford, relations with Allegra had by then become 'acrimonious.' She was telling friends that Boris was behaving 'shockingly.' 'It upset both of them a lot, and there were unpleasant accusations. It was really very bad.' Allegra left Brussels for the last time in early 1992, taking the furniture with her – down to, and including the egg spoons. Marina helped Boris refurnish his home – and rebuild his life. And then she moved in.

'She dropped everything for him,' remembers one of Marina's friends. 'Then the pregnancy happened very quickly and she was absolutely delighted.' By October 1992, Marina was engaged to Boris as well as expecting his child. His charm, wit, intelligence, charisma and growing fame were undoubtedly a potent mix. Life with Boris promised glamour, excitement, lots of laughs and a whiff of danger. No doubt he was a refreshing antidote to the stuffiness and tedium of EU directives, conventions and articles that filled her working life. She in turn was more indulgent of him. Visitors to the flat now inhabited by Boris with Marina observed theirs was a very different liaison: 'The relationship must have been founded on much greater tolerance than with Allegra from the start,' one frequent visitor noted. 'She seems to see amusing foibles in Boris, whereas Allegra wanted to change him. Boris was never going to change. Maybe Marina knew what she was getting into with Boris, because of how she had come to be with him in the first place.'

Allegra had long attempted to smarten Boris up with an expensive wardrobe in which he took no interest whatsoever. 'She wanted a stylish Boris,' explains an old friend. 'She wanted everything ordered and organised. She wanted to remould him, but that wasn't possible.' In contrast, Marina would merely laugh indulgently at Boris's ragged attire and leave it to him to decide on his own style. Under her influence their home was designed for practicality and cheerfulness rather than elegance. This laissez-faire approach was immensely helpful to Boris's freewheeling style and in part explains the longevity of this much-tested and unconventional partnership. 'When I was round at their house, Marina was always calm and calming, while he was volatile,' recalls a one-time regular visitor. 'It was a good match. He also provided her with something. He is witty, clever with words, recites poetry brilliantly and has a high level of emotional intelligence. He's quite empathetic when he wants to be, clever at judging other people's moods. His roguish thing also works – she actually enjoys it. Marina is also bright, although outwardly less assertive, confident and outgoing than he. So overall, I get the impression it is a marriage of equal parts.'

Nonetheless there were also indications that Marina, the liberal Lefty lawyer, had serious doubts, not only about the divergence between her own and Boris's political views – but also the extent of his overweening ambition. Indeed, she once pumped me as a colleague and someone who had observed her husband at the closest quarters for information on him and was keen to know what I *really* thought of him. Some observers believe she was also wary of Stanley's extra-marital past and the circumstances of the breakdown of his marriage with Charlotte – plus, of course, Boris's own failed relationship with Allegra.

There was, however, an immediate practical problem. Boris was still married. Once Allegra learned about the baby, she agreed to an accelerated divorce but Boris was also required to produce various crucial items of paperwork speedily – a challenge that has frequently defeated him. One EU official recalls finding him head in hands on the steps of the European Parliament building in Strasbourg, groaning loudly at his own ineptitude. 'He said he had great problems because he was getting divorced,' the official recalls. '"Allegra is very angry because I forgot to send in the papers," he said. I asked him why he had married her. He said she had pushed him into it.'

The divorce finally came through on 26 April 1993. There was no time to lose, as Belgian doctors were beginning to question whether the now heavily pregnant Marina would be able to cross the Channel for her wedding on 8 May. She just about managed it, following a party in Brussels where, resplendent in a smart fuchsia and black maternity dress and a beatific smile, she lugged a magnum of champagne around for her guests. Boris performed his usual bumbling glad-handing routine in a smelly brown jacket with shredded pockets. Sunlight filtered down through the glass kitchen ceiling and Boris's paintings lined the shelves down one whole wall. It was a happy scene in their new home together – unlike Allegra, Marina had been successful in winkling Boris out of the old flat to a house that was capacious and homely. They were now living at 76 rue van Campenhout in a fashionable central area just a few minutes' walk from the *Telegraph* offices and the European Commission.

The wedding, a few days later at Horsham town hall in Sussex, was low-key compared to Boris's first with a small reception in the Wheelers' nearby garden. 'It was a very simple affair, without any big names there,' says one of a handful of close friends invited. 'It was just a lovely, sunny day in the garden without ceremony or fuss and not at all an English society wedding with top hats and tails. Marina, although heavily pregnant, took everything in her stride and both Boris's mum and dad turned up.' True to Johnsonian form, the honeymoon was modest – consisting of one night in a hotel in unromantic East Grinstead.

Back in Brussels a month later, on 12 June Marina went into labour. But Boris was nowhere to be found and not answering his pager. In desperation, she repeatedly phoned the *Telegraph* office in Brussels to try and track him down. As usual, he had left no indication as to his whereabouts, so London was called in. This caused further consternation, as Boris, in typically secretive mode, had omitted to tell his bosses that he was an expectant father, let alone that his wife was on the verge of giving birth. Eventually he was located on a remote North Sea beach on the 'Belgian Riviera' covering a far from thrilling tale about a ship that looked as if it might go down in high seas – but didn't. He still insisted on filing before hurtling back to Brussels. Soon afterwards a baby girl was born – followed by a fierce battle of wills between the couple over her name. 'I've got to win this one,' Marina told friends and, significantly, she did. Boris had been set on calling her 'Lettice' while Marina preferred the less outlandish Lara. The compromise was that she was to be known as Lara Lettice but for many years now she has been known, to her mother's pleasure, as simply Lara.

Lara's birth was before the days of automatic paternity leave. Even so, as a brand new first-time father, Boris was unusual in barely skipping a beat in his gruelling near seven-day-a-week work schedule. It was a portent of how life was to be for Marina, where despite working full-time as a lawyer and becoming an eminent name in many legal fields including privacy, the EU, divorce and mental health, she has been the key family ball juggler. Home has never been a refuge from work – and certainly wasn't after Lara's arrival. 'Boris is extremely clever, but he's also a workaholic. He's done it by sheer hard work at the exclusion of everything, including other people,' recalls Peter Guilford. 'I remember a dinner party when he spent the whole time writing an article. At a requiem concert in the cathedral, he spent his whole time writing notes. At a wedding disco, Boris was going round interviewing people for his column while Marina was breast-feeding. He is completely driven. He has an ability to focus on one thing, no matter what human beings may be in the way.'

Boris had genuinely been upset at the failure of his marriage – but with a new wife, a new baby and soaring career he moved on quickly. Allegra's wounds took longer to heal, however. Many of her old friends from college who knew her before she married Boris claim she has been 'destroyed' by what happened. Several were 'shocked' when they met her at a college reunion, not least because of how beautiful and full of promise she had been as a student. 'She has changed inside and outside,' said one. She withdrew from society circles and took up first drink and then art.

'When she was younger, people would say that with her beauty and wealth, she would have the world at her feet,' her mother reflects. 'And after she married Boris, it seemed they would, indeed, have it all. But they were not compatible. Boris is a man who needed someone very obedient and silent, who would be willing to stay in the background and create a soothing home life, while giving him space to build a glittering career. My daughter wasn't that kind of person. She's not always been the most self-confident person, but she's very strong-minded. Boris was very ambitious and Allegra is very sensitive.'[16]

For some time, Allegra was very angry about the split. Two sources at *Private Eye* claim she tried to sell stories on her former husband, insisting the satirical magazine, 'expose Boris before it is too late.' Whether this is true remains unclear, but unflattering articles did indeed appear at this time, including a little-noticed one in August 1995 under the headline: 'THE CROOK, THE *SPECTATOR*, THE HITMAN & HIS EX-WIFE (PART 94)'. First it noted that in the previous week's *Spectator* Boris had written that the problem with the modern Briton was, 'his reluctance or inability to take control of his woman and be head of a household.' Considering its alleged source, the piece is worth quoting at length. It continues: 'These moral lectures sound a little odd when one learns that Johnson had to arrange a quickie divorce from his first wife, Allegra Mostyn-Owen, after discovering that he had impregnated his lover, Marina Wheeler. Johnson's belief that a man should take charge in the household scarcely tallies with his own domestic habits. He is notoriously reluctant to pay for anything (he wasn't even prepared to foot the bill for his first honeymoon) and is almost incapable of dealing with income tax, insurance policies and other such duties that often fall to a head of the household. "The modern British male," Johnson concluded in the *Spectator* last week, "is useless." Speak for yourself, matey.'

Meanwhile, Allegra took to drink to fight her demons. She went through a tempestuous time, with some of her less-constant friends dropping her, claiming she had 'changed.' The ever-loyal Noonie

Minogue observed Allegra's troubles were 'very complex' and that, 'things were going to be hard anyway, not just because of what happened with Boris.' But Allegra's plight and condition was doubtless in stark contrast to Boris's own marital bliss.

If anything, Boris became more self-sufficient and private once he recovered from the breakdown of his first marriage. It is as if the hurt he experienced made him determined to be ever more invulnerable. 'Boris never once let his hair down,' recalls Chris McLaughlin, who worked out in Brussels for the *Scotsman*. 'He was never that matey with anyone; he never stayed long when we all got together. He liked to go off and have posh dinners but I don't know who with. We used to wonder whether he might be shy, but surely he can't have been given everything that he's done? He was certainly a character and we would all talk about him a lot. We were trying to work out where he was coming from and never really found out.'

Many other journalists formed close friendships, living as they did far from home in a foreign city. But while Boris would sometimes be present at a gathering, say, in the Irish pub near the Berlaymont called Kitty O'Shea's or the press bar at the European Parliament, he would never quite join in. Some took exception to his aloofness, interpreting it as arrogance. One senior rival, quoted elsewhere in these pages but who declined to be named here, decries what he sees as Boris's 'contempt of people he considers inferior in any way. He has a profound sense of class and hierarchy. He always went to receptions far less well-dressed than the rest of us because he believed he didn't have to make an effort.'

Chris McLaughlin takes a more benign view despite Boris's reputation for never standing a round: 'He never bought drinks at the bar. I don't think it was meanness, but perhaps he didn't know the rules.' Lunch was rarely, if ever, on Boris either. 'He was amusing in his cups, but you were always wary,' adds a senior EU official, who had observed Boris since his early days in Brussels. 'I was told never to lend him money as he never paid it back – so when he asked for the equivalent of £50, I refused.'

He played the buffoon with new arrivals right up to the end of his time in Brussels, even when he was already a star. 'I arrived in 1993 as the foolish new boy,' recalls James Landale, then the bureau junior for *The Times*. 'Boris had been there four years by then, but came into press conferences very late, dishevelled, bumbling and groaning to me, "Oh, god, have I missed anything?" Not knowing better, I would fill him in on a story that got four paragraphs on page 27 in my paper, but with Boris's spin made the splash and a page two lead in the *Telegraph*. I soon discovered that Boris's ability to do this to people was going to be a real pain but that these stories were, shall we say, more speculative than full of actual content.' There was another incident with David Gardner, who protested to Boris over his direct lifting of six paragraphs from his story in the *Financial Times*, commas and all. Boris cheekily replied that such slavish copying was surely permissible, 'because we consider the *FT* to be a primary source.' Of course, through flattery and fun, he got away with it.

Peter Guilford explains how Boris worked: 'The key was, he did use people, he used everybody. It was in a charming, buffoonish way. But he used them. The reason people put up with it, by and large, is that at a certain time, when he sensed he had to, he would make time for everybody. It would be at some unorthodox time, like during a squash match or skiing down a mountain. And now that he's famous, everyone remembers it.' (Or at a funeral – Boris is also remembered for being kind to his original mentor Geoff Meade at the funeral of his first wife Sandra, giving a fine eulogy in her memory.)

Even when Boris embarrassed Guilford by badly misquoting him, he was forgiven. 'I rang Boris and gave him a bollocking. He didn't fight, never does – he rolls over and asks for his tummy to be tickled. I went along with it because I didn't want to spoil my friendship. It's the same for everyone.' A well-known broadcaster based in Brussels at the time summarises Boris well: 'He gets away with murder because he is very charming.' Despite the charm, Boris's rivals eventually became more circumspect in his company. Even Geoff Meade, who had done so much to launch him in Brussels, became wary and combines talk of his affection for Boris with disdain for his 'lying, conniving' side. 'I'm always very careful what I say to Boris as I know he'll always try to benefit from it,' he says.

Certainly, the information exchange tended to be one-way: he was not a sharer. He disliked colleagues entering his office when he was working and even avoided cooperating on stories, as is the norm in journalism. Sometimes he could be outright obstructive with those instructed to assist him.

However, charm, manipulation and sheer individualism had served Boris well. When he finally packed his bags for London in 1994, he was leaving as a star. But in truth, his departure also saved him from embarrassment among his peers in Brussels, who by now were openly laughing at the latest 'Borisism'. James Landale witnessed his declining powers: 'There was a sense by the time I got out there that it was the end of an era – that Boris had become such a pariah amongst the EU officials that no one would talk to him any more. He was by then a caricature figure, and he had to go.'

Tony Robinson remembers Boris as unfailingly courteous (and, unlike many of his peers, polite to Mrs Robinson) but also the author of 'complete inventions' that undermined him as a serious player. 'The stories generated a simmering annoyance amongst his peers, but that never spilled over into real anger. What did happen though was perhaps worse, as his conduct invited them not to take him seriously as a journalist capable of producing actual facts.'

To mark his departure in 1994, his fellow journalists performed a revue, for which Landale penned a poem mocking Boris's flexible relationship with the *actualité*. Based on another infamous Boris non-story that proclaimed Britain was about to quit the EU in favour of EFTA – the Swiss-dominated, loosely-knit European Free Trade Association – it was closely modelled on *Matilda* by Hilaire Belloc. The *Telegraph*'s foreign desk takes the place of Matilda's aunt. It began:

Boris told such dreadful lies
It made one gasp and stretch one's eyes.
His desk, which from its earliest youth
Had kept a strict regard for truth,
Attempted to believe each scoop
Until they landed in the soup.

Landale then writes about one of Boris's stories having been found to be false and concludes:

> The moral is, it is indeed,
> It might be wrong but it's a damn fine read.

Afterwards, Boris sent Landale a note: 'Dear James, Thank you very much for your poem – I think. Yours, Boris.' 'Well,' says Landale. 'We'd all suffered from Boris's antics, so there was an element of payback in it – I guess he knew that.'

His credibility shot, Boris started his search for an escape route from Brussels. Back in London, there was also the feeling that it was time for fresh blood. In any case, the spotlight was moving a thousand kilometres to the southeast and the bloody events in the Balkans. Sensing the winds of change Boris had been lobbying bosses in London to allow him to reinvent himself as a war reporter – considered the most macho assignment in journalism. He managed to talk himself, along with one other journalist, onto a high-powered last-minute delegation to Belgrade and Croatia during an EU summit in Luxembourg. His sense of nervous excitement was palpable. 'We were only gone for about 15 hours, but we met Milosevic and were in the room when a lot of the talks were going on,' another journalist recalls. The trip clearly inspired Boris, but the *Telegraph* newspapers never agreed to his requests. They knew that he was far more valuable in the political – where interpretation was allowed, even encouraged – than military arena, where such creativity with the facts might actually prove dangerous.

Boris surmises that his lack of success in becoming a war reporter may have been linked to his notoriety as a prodigious spender of the *Telegraph*'s money. Long before he sought to portray himself as a paragon of thrift during his mayoral campaign, he described the newspaper's reaction and his own wry interpretation of its response: '"Nay Boris,"' the Foreign Editor Frank Taylor eventually returned, "if you go to Yugoslavia, you'll just take them all out to lunch." This seems to be some sort of reference to my expenses claims,'[17] he wrote sheepishly but with an element of journalistic pride; his expertise in this area was legendary. 'Boris was indeed a major claimer of expenses,' Taylor confirms. 'It may have been a bit extravagant, but that was Boris. The bean-counters would go on about it, but I took a pretty liberal view.'

For the next few years, he would regularly travel back to Brussels but it was clear that he was ready for new challenges. His departure in 1994, although not mourned by all, certainly left the Belgian capital a duller place. Many, especially those not subscribing to the view that all Eurocrats were power-crazed empire-builders, had been outraged at his creative licence. And yet, his personal charm prevented them from becoming enemies. One rival, who grew exasperated with Boris's antics, nevertheless remembers: 'The French press railed against Boris, but they also loved him. He had a real panache and made the press room a more interesting place to be. When he came back to Brussels a few years after leaving and made an appearance at the Commission, the atmosphere was electric. Everyone was pleased to see him, even Bruno de Thomas [the rabidly French spokesman for Jacques Delors], despite the run-ins they had.'

'Oh yes,' agrees Geoff Meade. 'When Boris was here, it was a golden era. We will never see his like again.'

But times had changed, and now Boris would have to change, too.

Chapter Six
M'learned Wife
Islington Life, 1994–2008

Boris and Marina make a couple of extraordinary contrasts. He is ursine, blond, exuberant and tweedily scruffy. She is tiny, bird-like, with a curtain of jet-black hair and a neat wardrobe of colourful designer clothes. But although he may be twice as big and twice as loud as Marina, in some ways she is arguably the steelier of the two. She can certainly thrash him on the tennis court with some dastardly shots and whatever the outward appearances, she has scored many notable victories against him since the start of their marriage.

When they arrived back in London in 1994, many expected the pair to settle in the fashionable west London district of Notting Hill. Boris's sister Rachel lived there and it would soon lend its name to the new generation of rising Tories, notably David Cameron. But Marina favoured the New Labour heartland of Islington in north London and that is where they quickly headed. The choice turned out to be far more influential in Boris's life and political outlook than just any ordinary and random house move. And, together with Marina's growing influence, it is part of what has made him over the past few years such a curious and interesting political mix – and arguably electable as mayor.

They settled in busy, redbrick Calabria Road in Islington N5, near the grassy play spaces and tennis courts of Highbury Fields. Although a socially mixed street, where yuppy homes jostle with run-down flats, the houses are quite substantial. Boris settled on one after annoying the vendor of a smarter, but smaller house nearby, who had once been a colleague of Stanley's. 'Boris came in, looked round, told me it wasn't good enough for him and left,' says the vendor. 'He was the rudest viewer I've ever known.'

Visitors remarked on the warm, liberal and loving atmosphere that Marina soon created in Calabria Road. Her homes have a welcoming, lived-in appearance with no off-bounds areas for children and an appealing assortment of the detritus of family life. Children's paintings were exhibited proudly alongside Boris's impressive efforts; colours and fabrics chosen with child-friendliness and a cheerful practicality in mind. Guests inevitably described Calabria Road as a 'happy' rather than a smart or ostentatious home. It was noticeable, however, for its lack of pets. Boris believes that cats, in particular, are a 'sure index of unsatisfied human cravings.'

While he embarked on his new career back in London, Marina rejoined the English bar, but was soon pregnant again. Their first son, Milo Arthur, was born the following year in 1995, Cassia Peaches arrived a couple of years later and Theodore Apollo, known as Theo, in 1999. The youngest narrowly escaped also being called Washington, which had seemed a good idea for a while following a glass of bedside celebratory champagne. One or two of the middle names reflected Boris's exotic tastes, but the first names were perfectly serviceable for most school playgrounds, as Marina had intended. Although routinely known as Johnson, Marina ensured that her children, at least on formal occasions such as her father's memorial service in Westminster Abbey, are known as Johnson-Wheeler; she also kept her maiden name for herself.

Of course, she has been able to do nothing about the fact that her offspring resemble their father far more than they do her. Cassia and Theo have the trademark white-blond Johnson hair, with Cassia taking so much after her father that she is frequently recognised as his daughter in a crowd. 'She showed me round her school on an open day,' said one parent, who had not previously met the Johnsons. 'I had no idea Boris sent his kids to that school, but I knew immediately she must be related to him – the similarity was uncanny.' Lara and Milo are a little darker, with honey-coloured hair, but also share their face-shape and stature with Boris. The similarities are so intense that the half-Indian Marina is fond of protesting: 'I've been genetically removed from my children's life!' Boris's mother Charlotte also agrees that the blond hair gene is so strong in the Johnson family, 'it defies attack from anyone else.'

Largely through their tribe of children, the couple put down extensive roots in an area dominated by scions of the liberal intelligentsia – people who mostly shared Marina's political views on education, in particular, but racial and sexual discrimination, too. She had been brought up in an intellectual family with a long track record of Labour voting and support for liberal causes. Her father, Charles Wheeler, was an avid campaigner against capital punishment in America right up to his death from lung cancer at the age of 85 in 2008. Her mother, Dip, worked for Amnesty International and comes from a top-drawer Sikh family of highbrow liberals and knights of the British Empire from the Punjab, who were accustomed to a grand life with servants.

While her parents lived in Brussels, Marina was sent over the Channel to board at a public school in England with the motto of 'Work of Each for the Wealth of all'. Bedales, now charging similar fees to Eton of up to £30,000 a year, has been renowned over the years for turning out upper-class bohemians. Hollywood actor Daniel Day-Lewis, model Sophie Dahl and singer Lily Allen are all alumnae. Co-educational and laid-back, it's about as far removed from Eton in terms of public schools as it is possible to be. The informal ethos is one of collaboration over competition and a determination to be 'different'. Marina earned a reputation for being a slightly intense, cerebral girl, who won a place to read Law at Fitzwilliam, one of the more modern, low-key colleges at Cambridge and some distance from the main university quarter.

At 'Fitz' she was awarded a lowly third in her first year of studies, but raised her game to 2:1 level in her second year and graduated in 1986 with an overall upper second degree. Another Cambridge law contemporary observes Marina was already accustomed to being linked with a famous alpha male through her father Charles, but that seemed to make her only the more formidable. 'A lot of people at Cambridge knew who her father was,' he says. 'She already seemed so determined, someone who would surely not take any shit.'

In those early days, Boris had little time for Marina's very different political heritage. When asked by the journalist Adam Raphael – an old Wheeler friend – how he had formulated his right-wing views, Boris replied, only half-jokingly, that he studied what Marina's family thought on any particular subject and took a position exactly 180 degrees opposite. 'I can't go wrong,' he exclaimed.

Their next move – to a cream-stucco mid-Victorian semi-detached villa in Furlong Road – was even further into what Boris calls the great north London 'media gulch' inhabited by newspaper editors and TV producers. But the house, which they bought in March 1999 for £470,000, was still not the grandiose residence inhabited by many of his far wealthier Old Etonian friends. Beyond the jungle of a front garden and crimson-painted front door was an obstacle course of ageing bicycles, musical instruments and piles of books, newspapers and coats. To the left, on the raised ground floor, was the sitting room, with its collection of 'unplotted' furniture and stripped pine floors. Downstairs was a fairly cluttered, well-used kitchen playroom. Upstairs, five bedrooms arranged over two floors. 'The whole place was a domestic version of Boris's desk at work,' recalls Mark Law fondly.

A leading American journalist from *Vanity Fair* was sent over to interview Boris as a rising social and political British phenomenon. He arrived at Furlong Road at the appointed hour of 8 a.m. to find the house in disarray and Boris apparently still in bed. Michael Wolff saw through what he considered to be an 'artful presentation' that included Boris ostentatiously looking for yesterday's discarded trousers on the sitting-room floor while dressed in not much more than a pair of boxers. In what was mainly a panegyric introduction to the American public, Wolff judged that 'he quite clearly invites underestimation.'[1]

Indeed, Boris habitually rises early, often at 5 a.m., pacing his kitchen with a newspaper in one hand while munching a slice of toast in the other, or sometimes last night's leftover chops. As with the early bird and the worm, this way Boris has read the papers and plotted the day before most people are even awake. Like Margaret Thatcher, he needs less sleep than most of us.

Although Furlong Road is one of the prettiest in the area, it also suffered from its proximity to what one local described as the 'Holloway badlands.' Crime – and fear of crime – was an ever-present issue, with one close neighbour coming home to find a burglar still at work in her kitchen. This again would shape his political views. But Boris also now found himself physically at the centre of a group of cerebral liberal thinkers who would dominate the couple's social lives. Ian Katz, for one, a senior editor at the *Guardian*, occupied the other half of their Victorian villa. There were moments of tension when the paper ran critical pieces on Boris, who would register a protest by leaving his copy on Katz's doorstep. But Katz has also been a loyal friend on the paper. Opposite lived Marina's close friend Lucy Kellaway, author and columnist on the *Financial Times*, and married with four children to the liberal commentator David Goodhart.

(Lord) Andrew Adonis, who was later to become a highly influential Labour schools minister and driving force behind its academy programme, lived just around the corner with his wife Kathryn. (The Adonis link came in very useful – Boris was able to seek advice from him on specialist education for the disabled son of a former Brussels colleague, who was returning to Britain. This gesture earned Boris credit among the now-dissipated Brussels press corps.) Tim Allan, one of Tony Blair's spin doctors for most of the 1990s, also lived close by and was another member of what evolved into a high-powered, Left-leaning dinner party set.

Marina became a prominent 'Islington mum' through the state-run Canonbury Primary, where the local media and political types sent their children. This was no typical inner-city primary, however. In 2006, Boris acted as the celebrity auctioneer at a school fundraising evening. Coldplay's business manager Paul Makin was a fellow parent and had offered the star lot: a promise that Chris Martin would play in the living room of the highest bidder. One parent put up £5,000 to secure the prize, while Boris is said to have offered another £5,000 to be shown around the House of Lords by Adonis. The evening raised tens of thousands.

Yet despite the glitz, the truth was that the school was struggling. It could not have been much more removed from the style of education that Boris – and Marina – had enjoyed. Pupils called staff by their first names and Boris himself remarked in 2002 on how 'teachers have no power whatsoever to discipline [the children].' [2] Although it had enjoyed a reputation for friendliness, extra-curricular clubs and good Year Six results, within a few years Canonbury was in crisis, with a headteacher of four years, Jay Henderson, suspended from the school in October 2008 while investigations into his conduct were carried out. He had been praised by Ofsted for 'providing clear direction' but was later sacked in May 2009 for gross misconduct after allegations that he had been accessing pornography on school premises.

The whole tawdry experience no doubt confirmed Boris in his desire to move his own children into the private sector. He is unrepentent in his choice of independent secondaries, stating in an interview that, 'because we live in Islington, I extracted them. I have no embarrassment about it whatever.' But at the same time he has talked increasingly passionately about the problems caused by middle-class flight from state education. 'It becomes a self-fulfilling problem, self-generating, because the middle classes not having confidence in the schools perpetuates the trouble they experience.'[3]

Indeed, many evenings with the Islington set were spent discussing education – specifically state schools – with Marina railing about the poor provision locally at secondary level, in particular. At first, Boris wanted to part-solve the problem by sending his sons to Eton. 'Marina put her foot down,' says one local friend. 'She did not want another Old Etonian in the house. And of course, like so many other battles, she won that one, too.' Indeed, although the Johnson children are now all privately educated, Marina's choice of schools are popular with the higher-earning, London-based liberal professional and media classes rather than Eton's international plutocrats or landed gentry.

But the whole, if relatively brief experience of state education – and the problems it faces – was undoubtedly a sobering one for Boris and one that certainly, under Marina's influence, shaped his views. For him too now, improving state provision became a political priority that he reflected in his writing. He called for more male teachers in the primary sector, synthetic phonics to teach reading, learning multiplication tables by heart, academic competition including grammar schools, a 'grand smashing of PlayStations' and making all children learn two poems a term.

Marina – and her local set – also influenced his thinking on other issues such as race, homosexuality and, to some extent, global warming during those Islington years. 'Like the other Left-wing women who have married Johnson men, Marina provides humanity,' notes journalist Sarah Sands. But she does far more than that: Marina Claire Wheeler, with her Indian mother and different outlook, is a large part of what makes Boris such a fascinating figure. A Boris married to a 'central casting' Tory wife plying the boutiques of Notting Hill would still be a formidable politician, but it is Marina who provided him with the alternative Islington world-view without which he might just have been too strong meat for a mainstream electorate. So, when in 1999, Lord Macpherson of Cluny's inquiry into the murder of black teenager Stephen Lawrence uncovered 'institutional racism' at the heart of the Metropolitan Police, Boris's reaction had been predictable in its contempt, dismissing the findings as 'Orwellian,' 'weird' and 'crazy.' But, by January 2001 he revealed: 'I have had savage arguments with my nearest and dearest, and, slowly, I have begun to see things (Macpherson's) way. The Laird of Cluny is no loony.'[4] He also softened his views on homosexuality and climate change during these years, gradually moving away from his Tory shire-ish traditions to a far more metropolitan outlook. It is as if Marina, whom Boris used to refer to as 'M'learned wife', took on 'educating' Boris in liberal thinking where his mother had once laid off.

Robert Seabrook QC, her head of chambers, notes that Marina has a 'steely core' in her beliefs on issues such as justice and race. 'It's not a protective steeliness, but a principled one,' he says. 'She will stick up for her core values and stand up for those who deserve to be stood up for.' Indeed, she has travelled to China with Seabrook to deliver lectures on administrative law there – 'in the hope that we might in some way advance benign reform.' She was paid expenses but donated the lectures as part of an 'outreach' project.

But while she was not only challenging Boris intellectually, Marina impressed friends and neighbours with her devotion to her children. 'Marina is the sort of mother who will paint with them, swim with them, read, build things, just generally get down on the floor and get stuck in,' says one admirer. She has also over the years manned the odd stall at a school fête. But giving so much of herself – while holding down a full-time job in the law and coping with Boris's frenetic work rate – resulted in a certain degree of chaos when the kids were still little and over the years, a great deal of strain.

'We were all going out to Chequers for lunch with Tony Blair,' recalls George Jones, a former colleague at the *Telegraph*. 'So we were going round to Boris's house to pick him up on the way. It was absolutely full of young children, they were all over the place. Boris was late, his life is chaotic. There were books and toys everywhere and Marina was trying to keep order. One toddler was crying, but Boris didn't seem to be doing anything to help.'

Dominic Lawson, the former editor of the *Sunday Telegraph*, once invited Boris and his family to stay at his house in Sussex for the weekend but says he barely remembers Marina. She was clearly kept busy parenting and consequently had virtually no time to socialise with the other adults. 'I didn't have great conversations with her, there were several children flying all over the place and I think she was trying to keep them under control,' he says. Chris McLaughlin, now editor of *Tribune*, recalls bumping into Boris and Marina in a newsagent's one Sunday morning when Lara was very small. 'He had a baby under one arm and a stack of papers under another, and was busy handing over the baby as quickly as possible.'

A friend of Marina's elder sister Shirin, who has two children, said that Marina's frantic life during these years when they were young was a matter of concern for her family. 'She has brought up the children singlehandedly, according to Shirin. In fact, Shirin once told me that she didn't want more children precisely because she had seen Marina run ragged with hers.'

It seems universally acknowledged that while Boris is inordinately fond of his children – and they of him – most of the burden of childcare or domestic duties has fallen to Marina, whatever his professions to be a multi-tasking 'careerist, nappy-changing MP-cum-journalist-cum-house-husband,' father.[5] She has made sacrifices to leave him free to pursue his career – or rather, careers. Boris is not one to discuss domestic matters and Marina is the one to cook. 'I've only ever seen him fry an onion,' says one dinner party guest, 'and I don't think he enjoyed that much.' Boris was also spotted at least once happily reading the magazines on sale at the local Waitrose branch in Holloway Road while Marina single-handedly pushed the trolley round the aisles.

Marina's keypin role at home may well explain the fact that she has not taken silk despite her obvious talents and intelligence. She had still not put her name forward for consideration by the time she reached her mid-forties whereas real frontrunners are typically elevated at, or even before the age of 40. Her head of chambers, Robert Seabrook, says it has been entirely her decision: 'She would get it, if she applied. I am a great fan of Marina's – she must just be biding her time.'

Boris may also be in no rush for Marina to be elevated. While he has changed dramatically on other issues such as race, he continues to hold jurassic views on the higher education of women, blaming the prevalence of hoodies and NEETS ready to 'mug you on the street corner' on 'the colossal expansion in the numbers of female graduates.' The fact that they marry other graduates, his argument runs, means the wealth gap forces women from lower-income families to work 'often with adverse consequences for family life and society as a whole' as their 'unloved and undisciplined children' go on to terrorise everyone else.[6] It is certainly fair to say that Boris is really quite a traditionalist on gender and he confesses that 'a Neanderthal corner of my heart worries about some aspects of the coming feminisation. Will we all become even more namby-pamby, elf-n-safety-conscious regulation-prone and generally incapable of beating the Australians at anything than we already are?'[7] He has also raged about 'that ridiculous, compulsorily paid paternity leave' [8] and been overheard complaining that the fact Marina was working was to blame for his shortage of matching socks.

Marina's ability to cope is nevertheless much admired. She deals virtually solely with the challenges of domestic life, such as paying bills, dealing with the taxman or negotiating with estate agents. Her joint income with Boris – which during the Islington years rose rapidly to around £600,000 or £700,000 – soon provided the wherewithal. 'I do remember thinking how does Marina do it,' says a friend of Rachel's. 'She had four kids and worked full-time as a lawyer, with Boris never there. But the answer is staff. Over the years, they had a housekeeper, someone to help with cleaning, maybe even a weekend housekeeper plus a nanny or au pair.'

Bar the odd blip, the Johnson children seem to have inherited the resilient gene from both parents and have coped well. They are confident but not overly so. 'All the children are physically and emotionally stocky and robust,' says a close friend of Marina's. 'They are very grounded, very well balanced, despite everything. That's down to Marina and I feel quite jealous of it.' Another Islingtonian accused Boris of 'only turning up for the jolly bits of parenting.' But she also concedes that when he is around, his children adore being with him and largely enjoy a good life. 'The children may not see Boris very much, but I got the impression they really enjoy his company when they do,' says an old friend of Marina's.

As they have grown older, he appears to love the fun as much as they do – which sometimes gets him into trouble, such as in August 2006 when he squeezed both Milo and Theo onto the front seat of a two-seater Lamborghini Gallardo Spyder that he was test-driving in the fast lane of the M6. They were photographed by another motorist and the safety lobby condemned his actions as 'stupid'. But Boris insisted they were in no danger as they were wearing a seatbelt – the same one, as it happens – and the boys looked as if they were having the time of their lives. There is no doubt they enjoy quite a few of Boris's professional perks – he had a motoring column at the time, which gave him access to some of the world's fastest and most glamorous cars – and he has taken rugby-mad Milo on corporate jollies to Twickenham. He is also prepared to shell out, where his children are concerned. A family trip to Athens in June 2007 was nearly ruined when it turned out once they arrived at Luton airport that there was not enough room on the plane for all of his children.

He stood on a chair and theatrically offered fellow passengers £2,000 in return for two low-cost tickets – and crisis was averted when a couple took up his offer.

But one significant (male) political figure, whose approval Boris would be keen to court, notes that it's not all about 'flash and cash'. 'I see Boris playing tennis with his son sometimes on Sunday mornings – in very odd shorts. I'm always struck that he seems to pass the good dad test, as his son seems to be having a good time. And although he says "hi" to me, there are some politicians who would forget their children entirely to have a half-hour gossip. He says hello, has a quick exchange, then gets back to the tennis.'

When the children were smaller, Boris had that gift of seemingly being able to forget the rest of the world for the short spaces of time he could devote to them. At a wedding in Ireland, Peter Guilford – who did not have children at the time – was struck by Boris's behaviour. He remembers: 'Boris turned up for a walk with his kids. As he walked along the pebbles on the beach with them, he was a different guy. He was holding one by the hand and had the other on his shoulders. He looked like a hands-on parent, but was he play-acting or simply throwing himself in for the moment? He was very convincing when he told me that this was what it was all about, but then immediately after that he spent the whole evening interviewing people at the wedding and writing his column.'

For all his ambition and his absences, Boris is a devoted and emotional father and family man. Like almost every parent, he suffers the odd twinge of doubt about his relationship with his children. 'A propos of nothing, he once just started talking about his relationship with his children,' recalls Lloyd Evans, who remembers him sounding anxious. 'Boris said he didn't feel that his kids respected him.' And later, on another occasion, when asked by a journalist whether he had always possessed natural authority, he replied: 'The sad truth is that my children would find that question satirical.'[9]

While Boris's childhood was sometimes lonely, and certainly hard-working, his own children have a sociable existence. Parents of Lara's friends say she is very talkative and 'really is the life and soul of any party.' And of course, like any parent Boris has been greatly influenced by having children and listening to what they have to say. He is not by nature a strict disciplinarian and far from being kept away during adult gatherings, his children are encouraged to join in. Anthony Howard recalled driving Boris's mother Charlotte over to a dinner party at Furlong Road, to be joined by Marina's parents and her friends and neighbours, Goodhart and Kellaway. 'Marina had cooked and there were a good deal of interruptions, with children coming down and this kind of thing. It was all very amiable, very nice,' he said. Boris is undoubtedly proud of his children – and indeed the fact he has so many seems in his eyes to be a badge of pride, even political virility. He has often made it clear that he would like even more.

Yet Boris has on occasion been attacked by fellow parents – often Islingtonians – who have accused him of being 'eccentrically liberal', particularly in regard to what he has allowed them to view on television. He sees nothing wrong in 11-year olds watching Roger Moore in old James Bond movies. Indeed their tame sex scenes, usually involving Moore's wrinkly knees, parodic violence and complete lack of swearing, made them in his view 'wholesome family viewing.' The fairly violent cult films, *Hot Fuzz* and *Shaun of the Dead*, were similarly suitably entertaining for all the family despite their 15 certificates, because, 'like families across Britain, our family has been richly entertained by the bit where they bludgeon the zombies with cricket bats, and the bit in *Hot Fuzz* where the spire falls from the church and skewers someone.'

Perhaps realising that his views – particularly on the latter two films – were a little controversial, he drew on his own childhood in support: 'I have been racking my brains for a defence, and the first point to make is that we are always slightly stunned to discover what the younger generation is reading or watching. I remember my grandmother being amazed that I was reading David Niven's risqué memoir, *The Moon's a Balloon*; and no one stopped me picking up *Flashman*, at the age of eleven, and discovering that the hero gets off to a cracking start in life by being expelled from school and raping his father's mistress.'

He then concludes: 'Sometimes I think our censoriousness is not so much about protecting children as it is about preventing them from seeing the embarrassing silliness of adult behaviour.'[10]

But there is one embarrassing aspect of adult – or semi-adult – behaviour that Boris seems particularly eager for his children to avoid. It's an area in which he himself exercises an iron self-discipline: he has frequently lambasted the binge-drinking culture, its protagonists of bladdered lads and ladettes and the accompanying trophy of an ill-won hangover. Neither Boris nor Marina is a big drinker – although both enjoy the odd glass of champagne or decent red wine: he abhors the loss of control – and dignity – inherent in drunkenness and the British tolerance, even admiration, of inebriation. He takes a more Continental view of savouring a drink rather than downing it. In quieter moments he admits to being able to handle only a couple of glasses at a time – and in the course of hundreds of interviews for this book relating to all stages of his life, only one person claimed to recall Boris being 'hammered.' Stanley's father drank, as we saw in an earlier chapter, and that may well have had its effect on the habits of future Johnson generations, making them far more careful.

What is curious is that during the Islington years, Boris developed a habit of attributing his lateness, inability to answer awkward questions, ill-temper or apparent lack of preparedness in interviews to a debiliating hangover. Yet a real hangover seems unlikely in the extreme, as those who know him best will testify. Perhaps it's just a convenient ruse – giving an impression of conviviality and 'normalness' to put interviewers off their guard while Boris's razor mind is, in fact, as sharp as ever. If so, it is certainly an effective act and many have been taken in by it. Whether his children, with all the pressures they endure, can be equally controlled remains to be seen; they also have to contend with being in his shadow.

Despite their own achievements through hard graft and talent, Marina and Boris are not seen as obsessively pushy parents, although inevitably they must be ambitious for their children. In print, Boris has frequently referred to his distaste for parents who fight their own battles or inadequacies through the auspices of their offspring. One couple they are close to are habitually called the 'pushiest parents in North London.' In what is perhaps also a token rebellion against the ultra-competitiveness of his own upbringing, when TV was largely banned and coming second not acceptable, he wrote and illustrated a little-noticed book of verse entitled *Perils of the Pushy Parents – A Cautionary Tale*. It contains the following revealing passages:

> Even if your life's a bitch
> Watching all your friends get rich,
> Isn't it a kind of cheat
> Using children to compete?

And then on the folly of preventing your offspring from watching television, he writes:

> Every child's a human being,
> not a piece of Plasticine.
> Loving parents, learn from me.
> If your children crave TV
> Tell them, OK, what the hell
> You can watch it for a spell . . .
> IF YOU READ A BOOK AS WELL.
> (A proper book, you'll understand
> Like the volume in your hand.)

Rather unkindly, the *Guardian* reviewed it as 'the most cringe-making book ever published'[11]. No doubt Boris deposited his copy of that morning's edition on Ian Katz's doorstep. Fortunately, early evidence suggests his children are bright and energetic enough themselves to succeed without the need for too much sharp-elbowed parenting.

Boris is pushy in one way, however, in expecting his offspring to show independence and initiative from an early age. He allowed them to travel unaccompanied by an adult on public transport from the age of eight (to the horror of some of Marina's friends); he has instructed them 'to look after themselves' and walk away from any trouble rather than attempt to get involved.[12] But there are limits to his laissez-faire regime, and in one area he is far stricter than most parents: he is fanatically against games consoles, whose addictive powers he compares to the highest grade of narcotics. There are few subjects on which he writes in such vehement and emotional language and on which the outrage seems entirely real rather than column- or headline-driven. It's not a stance likely to curry the youth vote (and has not recently been re-aired).

'Millions of seven- to 15-year-olds are hooked, especially boys, and it is time someone had the guts to stand up, cross the room and just say no to Nintendo. It is time to garrotte the Game Boy and paralyse the PlayStation, and it is about time, as a society, that we admitted the catastrophic effect these blasted gizmos are having on the literacy and the prospects of young males,' he opined in one column.[13]

Boris issued a call to action to other parents to deal with what he calls this 'electronic opiate' and 'cause of ignorance and under-achievement and poverty.' 'Summon up all your strength, all your courage. Steel yourself for the screams and yank out that plug. And if they still kick up a fuss, then get out the sledgehammer and strike a blow for literacy.'

It gave all the impression of a compelling *cri de coeur* – and demonstrates only too well how brilliant Boris can be when he has real conviction. Readers could not help feeling that they were hearing from the real man. But the intimacy that Boris sometimes offers in print he often appears to be incapable of in the flesh. Indeed, while Marina arranged an active social life in Islington – with all the access it gave Boris to an alternative way of thinking – he retained a certain distance even while he was busy observing. Many people from Islington – and other spheres of his life – might describe themselves as Boris's friends but while he is friendly to them, they are almost all mistaken about the friendship. As one of his fiercest critics acidly observes: 'Like Lord Palmerston, Boris does not have friends, merely interests.' One of his closest former aides puts it another way: 'He is a detached person. A lot of people think that he's their friend, but it's funny because I've noticed that he never mentions them.' It is as if he fears intimacy with people in case they find out what he really thinks, or perhaps that they might discover that he is not sure what he really thinks at all. Boris is unusually, almost uniquely, determined to keep people at arm's length, it seems.

The few exceptions tend to be women, such as Nell Butler, wife of his Oxford friend Justin Rushbrooke (who has been unfailingly supportive of him and has grown in importance since university). With almost all other men, Boris rarely if ever relaxes. His former neighbour David Goodhart, whose wife Lucy Kellaway is very close to Marina, found the difficulty of getting behind the Boris public persona frustrating. The two couples spent many Islington evenings together and their respective children are also friendly, particularly the eldest daughters. However, Goodhart believes that genuine two-way conversations with Boris where there is a real mutual confidence are near impossible.

'You never really get to know him,' she says. 'He never lets his hair down, even in these circumstances. We had very drunken evenings round at their house in Furlong Road but not one was memorable. They, and he, were always the same. He always speaks at the same pitch. He mocks everything, particularly ideas and thoughts that he calls –isms. He is fanatically anti-intellectual. I would never go for a pint to the pub with him, as you might expect with a neighbour or the husband of one of your wife's greatest friends – there is no point unless there is likely to be some level of intimacy with someone. That is never the case with Boris.'

Lloyd Evans, who has known him since Oxford, makes the point that Boris rarely stops moving long enough for a proper chat. 'People grumble that he won't have a conversation with anyone – he's always thinking about the next thing. At a party he's always introducing you to someone else.' Evans does not presume to call Boris a friend but as he is not seen as a potential rival, he has perhaps got a little closer then most. 'What I've found when you do occasionally have conversations with him is that you get this sense that you are in his confidence. That is a particularly warm or pleasing place to be. Are the conversations two-way, is he interested in you and your relationships? No, no, I don't think he is. Maybe it is a bit of a monologue. You can list his vices endlessly – the egomania, the vanity, the ruthless ambition, and probably, you don't detect that there would be any great loyalty coming from him. But all those failings make him seem all the more lovable. It's just the way he is, some sort of exotic species.' 'It's partly a competitive thing, alpha-man stuff but he's not into other men at all,' confirms Michael Binyon, who has known him for more than twenty years.

Boris's wariness has another bizarre manifestation. For all his quick-fire wit, he does not really laugh. He looks amused – particularly at the reaction to his own jokes – and occasionally his shoulders move a little and his eyes crease. But few can recall a full-throttle Boris chuckle, let alone an abandoned guffaw. Attempts at laughter can sound a little forced. To laugh – as to cry – involves a loss of control, almost an admission of vulnerability and that is something he is unwilling to allow. 'Who really knows Boris as a person?' says a friend of Marina's. 'You never get to see his vulnerabilities. Perhaps Marina is the only one who does.'

What is certain is that the Islington years with Marina and the children have given Boris a sense of secure and consistent home life that he has probably never experienced before. They gave him an insight into another, more liberal world-view and an experience of the lives led by people outside the charmed circles of Eton and Oxford. What's more, they underlined the great value to his life of his second wife, who not only indulged but also 'educated' him and who over those years, would on occasion refer to Boris as her 'fifth child'. It was this tried-and-tested bedrock that allowed him to launch the next phase of his claim, if not to be 'world king' then surely the next best thing.

Chapter Seven
Untouchable
Boris the Celebrity, 1994–1999

On his return to London in early 1994, Boris was recognised as having fought a good war in Brussels. For the Eurosceptic forces in the Tory party he had proved a valiant Fleet Street ally in the face of a bitter and interminable battle over national sovereignty. The pro-European Conservatives were left a reduced and ragged group who did not enjoy the benefit of a charismatic journalistic champion. Boris revelled in the glory. In what he himself conceded was a 'babyish way,' he appeared to be proud that his dispatches from Brussels might be at 'the root' of the Conservative Government's misfortunes. He liked to recite the verdicts of others who thought they were, before trailing off with an unconvincing, 'It's all nonsense, of course.'[1]

But not everyone enjoyed the chaos. The bitterness of the Conservative civil war between pro- and anti-Europeans bewildered and bored the voters: the Prime Minister John Major annoyed or alienated both camps in turn by not conclusively aligning himself with either stance. He had famously called the awkward squad on the Right of the party the 'Bastards' – a label they appeared to relish but which betrayed the extent of his frustration. Meanwhile, the Cabinet pro-Europeans led by Kenneth Clarke and Douglas Hurd bridled at Major's anti-Brussels rhetoric – which would raise exultant cheers in the House of Commons before the inevitable retreat once his isolated ministers entered *mano à mano* combat with their EU counterparts.

Major had never really recovered from the trauma of Black Wednesday, when the pound crashed out of the Exchange Rate

Mechanism (which tied European currencies to an agreed exchange rate band as a precursor to the single currency). Interest rates flickered briefly at 15 per cent, and the Treasury had thrown away £27 billion in trying to prop up sterling against the deutschmark; both were devastating failures. Major could not beat the markets, the pound was devalued anyway, while the American speculator George Soros walked away with a $1 billion profit at the taxpayers' expense.

Major had eventually sacked his Chancellor, Norman Lamont, in a desperate bid for self-preservation and then in late 1993 launched a new political campaign that would ultimately render his government a laughing stock. The 'Back to Basics' theme was a well-meaning attempt to shift the emphasis away from the toxic subject of Europe to the more certain ground of law and order, education and public probity. But as Lamont, who went on to become one of Major's fiercest critics, pointed out, it was: 'extremely ill thought-out, and an example of [Major's] tendency to think he had found a policy when he had merely found a phrase.'[2] It also gave the press the green light to highlight Tory sleaze – of which there was plenty.

By the time Boris was settling into domestic life in Islington, his party was well on the road to electoral self-immolation. In February that year, the Tory MP Stephen Milligan had been found dead with an orange in his mouth as an apparent victim of erotic asphyxiation. The cash-for-questions scandal followed a few months later, in which Tory MPs were accused of accepting money in brown paper envelopes from Mohammed Fayed to table helpful Parliamentary questions. Cabinet minister Jonathan Aitken was later immersed in a complex scandal involving free stays at the Paris Ritz, Arab businessmen and arms dealers – which ended in his imprisonment for perjury. (Lord) Jeffrey Archer, a one-time deputy party chairman, who would also later go to jail for perjury, was being investigated by the Government for alleged insider dealing. It seemed that every other week another middle-aged Tory MP would be exposed as having an affair or fathering love children – to the point where political commentators observed Conservative sleaze had become Britain's most productive industry.

Appalled by this display of ineptitude and then moral decay, voters took any opportunity to punish John Major's government – first, in the local elections of May 1994, when the Conservatives lost 429 seats and 18 councils. Then the following month, the party suffered its worst results of the twentieth century, winning only 18 out of 87 seats in the European Parliament compared to Labour's 62. To cap it all, the young and presentable Tony Blair was elected Labour leader in July and after months of revelations of Tory sleaze, by December his party was 39 points ahead in the polls.

It was not a pretty picture for a young man no longer just 'conscious of Tory feelings,' but who had firmly, if secretly, decided to become an active Conservative politician. Perhaps for the first – but certainly not the last – time, the conflicting interests of the journalist and politician came into play. No longer could he just enjoy the sensation of throwing the rocks over the wall and hearing the greenhouse glass shatter; he himself was in danger of being cut by a flying shard.

However bad the political timing, it suited Boris to return to London to pursue his dream of a political career but he was actually given no choice by the *Telegraph*. Max Hastings wanted a different approach to the Brussels story, one less frightening to the horses. It was suggested that Boris's editor, a moderate Euro-realist by instinct, was tired of the explosive line on Europe that his young correspondent had adopted. As Hastings himself puts it: 'I fear it was the Brussels posting [that made] Boris the rabid Eurosceptic he later became.'[3]

'The decision was taken to move Boris on,' confirms Frank Taylor, foreign editor of the *Sunday Telegraph*, who had been one of Boris's greatest supporters. 'There was nothing wrong in terms of the coverage. I wouldn't have been instrumental in the move but they did like to make changes. I don't think any fault lay with him.' Indeed his star was still in the ascendant and Hastings took another gamble on his celebrated young protégé. At the age of just 30, Boris was crowned assistant editor and chief political columnist. They were grand titles, and challenging ones: he had never managed a staff or worked with a team, and he had been out of the country for the previous five years. In the meantime, much had changed socially – the brash, flash Eighties had given way to the arguably Nicer Nineties, but the City boom had also withered into recession and record numbers of repossessions. Domestic politics moved on accordingly.

Having been subsumed in the relatively one-track world of European affairs, Boris told an astonished colleague that he was a 'bit worried [as] I haven't got any political opinions.'[4] When pushed, all he could come up with was that he was anti-Europe and anti-capital punishment. Boris – and his editor – must have sensed he was in danger of becoming branded a one-trick pony, confined to the EU corral; he continued to return frequently to Brussels to write sketches or commentaries on summits. Certainly, his knowledge of the people and processes of Europe made him a formidable opponent for Labour when it came into power in 1997, including Tony Blair and his pugilistic spin doctor Alastair Campbell .

'Campbell had run-ins with Boris, and so did Blair over Brussels,' recalls Toby Helm, who was the next-but-one EU correspondent for the *Telegraph* after Boris. 'They had been warned about Boris because he knew his stuff so well but they fell into the usual trap and came out unprepared. Boris asked detailed questions, which Campbell just couldn't handle so they realised they had to sharpen up – and they did. Six months later at the next summit, Campbell came back very knowledgeable and sharp. He must have learned practically every treaty by heart – that was partly down to Boris.'

Unbeknown to his colleagues, though, Boris had been busy working on his next move for some time. Most people assume that his political career began comparatively late in life when, as he turned 33, he fought a no-hope Parliamentary seat in the 1997 general election. In fact, he had been applying to become a candidate since 1993, when he was still in Brussels. It just took him a long and frustrating seven years to land a winnable one, and so he kept his efforts under wraps for as long as he could.

Although he did not act immediately, Boris likes to date the birth of his Parliamentary ambitions at least as far back as 1990. The then Foreign Secretary Douglas Hurd gave a speech in which, says Boris, he drew a 'cunning distinction between achievers and commentators.' Hurd argued that journalists should be seen, in Boris's words, as 'people living like parasites in Grub Street' as distinct from those 'clean-limbed, honourable fellows trying to improve the world' and known as politicians.[5] But Boris's political dreams were not universally shared: the creatively polemical style of his Brussels' reporting meant that not everyone in the Conservative party saw him as either honourable or trying to improve the world, or even possibly clean-limbed. And, crucially, that included the then Prime Minister John Major.

Bloodied by those relentless internecine battles over Europe, he blamed Boris for recklessly fanning the Eurosceptic insurgency in the *Telegraph*. A then senior Whitehall official describes the Major government's private view of Boris as an electoral assassin: 'He caused a great deal of teeth-grinding amongst Major and his ministers and created enemies in the Tory party. He was both denouncing government policy in a persuasive way and also indirectly picking holes in its majority, making it more difficult to govern. Boris gave evident support, succour and ammunition to the anti-European [anti-Major] tendency of the Tory party. And reflective ministers thought that his line of attack was making them ultimately unelectable. It is *certain* that Boris had a long-term strategic effect on Tory fortunes – even if no one can exactly quantify the damage he caused.'

Douglas Hurd, who still harbours some affection for his fellow Eton Scholar, argues that Boris was simply the most *effective* of the many Eurosceptic journalists of the time whose EU output damaged the government. 'The *Mail, Express, Telegraph*, the *Sun* were all part of one's daily penance. They were all anti-British membership of the EU and they all employed people who overflowed on this subject, of whom Boris was the best informed. Boris was handed out with the rations; he was part of the problem.'

But Major shared little of Hurd's fellow Old Etonian indulgence and saw Boris as a uniquely damaging figure for the Tories. Downing Street was aghast at the thought that Boris would continue his campaign as a Conservative MP. Although the ex-Prime Minister says he has no recollection of the incident, others recall him actually prepared to take the extraordinary step of banning Boris from the candidates' list. 'John Major complained about Boris and he could be outspoken about him,' recalls (Lord) Norman Fowler, then chairman of the party. '[The Prime Minister] didn't much care for Boris or his views on Europe. Major thought the best way to explain his views on this was head-on. He was not, shall we say, over the moon about Boris standing.'

Major was not alone in his distaste for Boris's ambitions. The Boris backlash began at a Parliamentary selection board held over one weekend in 1993 at an unremarkable hotel near Heathrow airport attended by some sixty people. Andrew Mitchell, then vice-chairman of the party in charge of candidates and also a government whip, was in the chair. Likened by many to an Army's officers' recruitment board – but without the assault course – the occasion cannot have been a comfortable experience for Boris. A number of MEPs who violently disagreed with his approach on Europe were there as assessors and officials. The thought of Boris, the notorious scourge of federalists and Europhiles everywhere, staking rightful claim to the Parliamentary palaces of Brussels, Strasbourg and Luxembourg was, for some, too much to bear.

Although he was not one of the protestors, James Elles, a Conservative MEP, viewed Boris as an '*enfant terrible* always looking for the headline.' Like many of his colleagues, he had known Stanley Johnson when he was an official at the European Commission and an MEP, which intensified the feelings of betrayal. It is clear that Mitchell came under great pressure to refuse Boris a place on the candidates' list but he stood his ground, insisting the professional assessors should be allowed to get on with their job of selecting good-quality candidates from across the whole spectrum of Conservative political views. And so Boris's name went through but his troubles were far from over.

After the meeting, Mitchell recalls a group of MEPs led by their chief whip in Europe, Richard Simmonds, raised the temperature by protesting about Boris in writing, both to Fowler and even the man credited with inspiring Boris to become an MEP: Douglas Hurd. The next night, Fowler took Mitchell aside in the Lobby of the House of Commons to warn that the Prime Minister was also seething at any suggestion Boris should become a candidate and that he was to see Major in person immediately.

Mitchell duly made his way to Major's Commons office behind the Speaker's Chair. The Prime Minister was indeed very angry but Mitchell warned that if he excluded Boris from the list, there was a danger the whole selection process would be brought into disrepute. He argued the list had to be seen to be a 'broad church of Conservatism' from which local associations could then choose. Mitchell's arguments won the day: undesirous of yet another row over Europe, Major eventually agreed to back down. 'It is to his credit that he did not exercise a Prime Ministerial veto,' says Mitchell. 'After all, Boris had been persistently beastly to him and repeatedly taken the mickey out of his European policy in the *Telegraph*.'

Fowler agrees that Major was never a vengeful man and in that, Boris was indeed lucky to escape the consequences of his wrath. Those 'big beast' politicians, such as Major, Hurd or Michael Heseltine, worst affected by his antics, have all now departed the stage. Pragmatism has replaced attrition in the Conservative party and Boris, whatever his past, has earned his electoral spurs. 'I don't think Boris made the rifts over Europe worse – if he hadn't written this stuff from Brussels, someone else would have done but he wrote it rather more elegantly,' Mitchell concludes before acknowledging, 'The whole era was a dark night of the soul for the Tory party. We paid a terrible electoral price for what happened.'

The MEPs thought differently at the time, however, and continued their fight against Boris right up to the final decision-making stage, which was then presided over by the candidates' advisory committee, chaired by Lord [Basil] Feldman. But Feldman backed Mitchell's view and Boris finally officially joined the candidates' list that summer. Even at that late stage his success was far from a foregone conclusion – it was widely understood that Mitchell would have resigned as Conservative vice-chairman, had the selection board's decision been overturned.

What the episode does make clear is how sharply Boris divided the Tory party. Some, such as Mitchell, were prepared to take extraordinary steps to back someone they saw as uniquely gifted. Others sought to take similarly vigorous action to prevent his advance. Boris recalls one 'normally genial minister' going red with anger upon seeing him and shrieking profanities at him over his writings that turned heads twenty yards away. His supporters, though, are not always rewarded with equal loyalty on Boris's part.

Mindful of the row, Mitchell – ever the government whip – had extracted a promise from Boris that he would not seek a safe seat in the forthcoming Euro-elections of 1994. Boris duly agreed to put his name down for a 'hopeless' constituency, that time round. Naturally Mitchell was surprised to spot Boris's name on a list of names applying for a plum Conservative seat and rang to suggest there must have been some sort of 'mistake.' Boris's response consisted of a volley of exclamations and splutters then finally an agreement of withdrawal. In the event, he never did stand as an MEP and after returning to London from Brussels in 1994, quickly translated his name to the Westminster candidates' list. Years later, he did take the time to send an effusive letter of thanks to Mitchell when he won the selection for the safe Westminster seat of Henley in 2000. It was a well-judged gesture that has stood him in good stead with a man who has since entered the Cabinet.

While Boris was battling against Europhiles for a seat in the Conservative party, he was also determined to find a new niche in journalism but one – or more than one – that suited him more than his employers. His intransigence angered the man who had done so much for him and would continue to be his editor until autumn 1995. 'Max Hastings thought there was a very good journalist inside Boris that was trying to get out,' recalls George Jones, one of Hastings' trusted lieutenants and the *Telegraph*'s then political editor. 'Max used to row with Boris because he was trying to turn him from a wild Brussels correspondent into a serious political commentator. But Boris wasn't – and isn't – the sort of person to take instruction or guidance. And Max has a very short attention span. If you don't answer his question immediately, he loses interest. He couldn't take Boris's shambolic and rambling delivery, and his unwillingness to conform; he couldn't wait. And Boris wouldn't listen. There was simply no meeting of minds.'

Boris was notorious for letting his mind wander in what were typically rather earnest gatherings of the 'thinkers' on the paper. He would make little pen-sketches of the people in the room rather than listen to what they were saying. There was one odd occasion when he seemed unfamiliar with the existence of President Clinton. Asked what he thought of Clinton's latest escapade, 'Boris just looked up and replied: "Who? Aaaarrrgh, who? Who?" remembers ex-*Telegraph* man and former MP Paul Goodman, 'He seemed to be somewhere else entirely, a place a long way away.'

Goodman, comment editor on the paper at the time, remembers another illustrative conversation: 'What are you going to write about today, Boris?'

'Aaaarrrrggghhh! Cripes! Erm. . . .'

'Well?'

'I thought . . . sort of . . . eeerrrhhhmmm.'

'Sorry?'

'I mean . . . um . . . Blair.'

'What about him?'

'Sort of . . . gosh! . . . Europe . . . and . . .'

'And?'

'Hague . . . I mean, Hague! . . . er . . . sort of . . .'

'So, I'm to tell the Editor that you're writing about sort of Blair, Europe and Hague, sort of?'

'No . . . well . . . um . . . Yah! . . . er . . . That's it!'

And seven hours or so later, an immaculately composed and piratically arresting essay would appear.'[6]

But it was not just Hastings who Johnson annoyed with his bumbling buffoon routine. At one point Boris – now a senior *Telegraph* executive – was sent over to Belfast to cover a landmark in the Northern Irish peace process. David Trimble, the Unionist leader, emerged from the talks to give waiting journalists a briefing on progress. 'Boris goes, "Er, David, you want to stay, you know, in the United Kingdom, and er, that other chappie over there wants to go with Ireland," recalls Nick Robinson, one of the other journalists present. 'And David Trimble just says: "Fuck off Boris."'

'That was Boris's old trick, you see but one at which women are much better than men. Men generally want to show off how clever they are; clever women are rather good in my experience at fluttering their eyelashes a bit and going, "Oh well, I don't really understand this" and then getting amazing stories. I think Boris was playing the dumb blond trick in the hope of getting something but Trimble spotted it and refused to play along.'

In the circumstances, Boris was once again lucky to be offered a column on the *Telegraph*'s sister publication, the *Spectator*. 'Max brought Boris back from Brussels, but had not yet really reassigned him,' Dominic Lawson, the *Spectator*'s then editor, recalls. 'There was a strange hiatus and I was looking for someone to write a political column. Of course Boris seemed ideal – he was a fantastic writer. So I gave him his first column, under a formal weekly arrangement. He got paid extra for it, and Max was fine with that.'

The column drew mixed reviews, with some claiming it read as if it had been rushed. Loyally, Lawson thought Boris's work was 'absolutely fantastic' and Boris made sure he was equally flattering in return. 'He said in some piece that "Dominic was the best copy-editor I've ever had to work with,"' Lawson recalls. 'But I don't remember ever having to do much copy-editing because it always worked, it hung together perfectly.'

Soon Boris was also building up his profile in the *Telegraph* itself. He set to work on developing a persona as a political columnist – although as yet without the worldview ideology or convictions on a whole range of subjects that informed many of his rivals. In some ways this was his greatest asset: his pieces were eclectic, often humorous and with a conversational style all of his own. Within three years, he had been named Commentator of the Year at the What the Papers Say awards. But it was also during these years that Boris wrote many of the pieces that have since come back to haunt him – and which provided his metropolitan critics with the brush to paint him as an extreme right-winger and closet racist.

He had not yet developed the political antennae to detect words or phrases that were mad, bad or just plain dangerous to use outside 'Tory boy' circles. It is worth looking at what he wrote then – to marvel at the success of the personal rebranding since. Had he continued to expound these views in the way that he did, it is hard to imagine him clasped to London's bosom as Mayor (or indeed, being received into the Islington dinner party circuit). So, on the Scott report on British arms sales to Iraq, he wrote in 1996 that MPs in the Chamber were 'toting Sir Richard's oeuvre like puffing coolies,' an offensive term from the vocabulary of Britain's imperialist past used to describe Chinese workers.[7] Worse still was his repeated use of the word 'piccaninny' – a racist term for black children previously most famous for being used by Enoch Powell in his Rivers of Blood speech against immigration.

On the fall of Jonathan Aitken, he wrote in the *Telegraph* on 25 June 1997, 'news reaches us, perhaps brought into a cleft stick by some piccaninny from the steaming Mato Grosso' that the disgraced MP had resigned from the Privy Council. Some time later, he compounded the offence by supposing 'that the Queen has come to love the Commonwealth, partly because it supplies her with regular cheering crowds of flag-waving piccaninnies.' The piece continued: 'One can imagine that Blair, twice victor abroad but enmired at home, is similarly seduced by foreign politeness. They say he is shortly off to the Congo. No doubt the AK47s will fall silent, and the pangas will stop their hacking of human flesh, and the tribal warriors will all break out in watermelon smiles to see the big white chief touch down in his big white British taxpayer-funded bird.'[8]

No one can doubt the sheer chutzpah of his writing – or the probability that he was using such language in irony – but the judgment is still open to question. In another article entitled 'Cancel the guilt trip. Africa is a mess, but it is simply not credible to blame colonialism,' Boris appeared to be advocating a new imperialism – 'The Continent may be a blot but it is not a blot on our conscience. The problem is not that we were once in charge, but that we are not in charge any more.'[9]

He also defended 'sickeningly rich people' on the grounds that 'if British history had not allowed outrageous financial rewards for a few top people, there would be no Chatsworth, no Longleat.' (This may be one view Boris has not fundamentally changed – he has been one of the staunchest defenders of the bonus-earning bankers in the City – but he now cites the more democratic benefits, notably jobs and tax revenues.)[10] In another claim of questionable wisdom he once wrote that Silvio Berlusconi towered above the ranks of 'bossy, high-taxing European politicians.' Echoing the narrator's verdict on Gatsby and the complacently rich in F. Scott Fitzgerald's novel, Boris decreed that Berlusconi, who was later charged with, among other misdemeanours, sex with a minor (which the Italian president denies), was 'better than the whole damn lot of them.'[11]

Looking back, even Boris occasionally winces. He has admitted to embarrassment about a particularly tasteless piece in May 1999 on the Serbian warlord Arkan, in which he treats the 'famous thug and mass killer' as 'if he were some buffoonish backbench rebel.' However, he was also capable of executing sharp handbrake turns once he realised he had called it wrong. On George W. Bush for example, in 2001 Boris wrote that he found 'a cheer rising inexorably in my throat' whenever he saw the President's 'buzzard squint and his Ronald Reagan side-nod.'[12] Three years later, he started to waver: 'It's just maddening that when asked to form a simple declarative sentence on child literacy the leader of the free world is less articulate than my seven-year-old.'[13] When Bush was re-elected shortly afterwards, the U-turn was complete and Boris was happy to admit it in typically amusing style: 'Not four more years of a man so serially incompetent that he only narrowly escaped self-assassination by pretzel, and also managed to introduce American torturers to Iraqi jails. Who on earth, I moaned, can conceivably have supported this maniac? And then I remembered. I backed him, come to think of it. In fact, not only did I want Bush to win, but we threw the entire weight of the *Spectator* behind him.'[14]

Boris's references to women suggest he thinks of them as either wet or power-crazed. He once tacked a Pirelli calendar above his desk at the *Telegraph* in a gesture of defiance against the '*Daily Mail* women' he said were running the paper but when mentioned at all in his writing, women were portrayed as rather feeble 'blubbing blondes'[15] or 'collapsing with emotion, disappearing from the ranks like a soldier shot in a Napoleonic battle.'[16] Even the 'generally tough-minded American,' Kimberly Fortier, publisher of the *Spectator* (somewhat implausibly) appeared to be brushing away a tear when the 'suave' and 'sorrowful' Stephen Byers was dispatched from the Cabinet by Tony Blair[17] and Bianca Jagger, 'the hot-lipped disco queen from Managua' weeps on a sofa about Bosnian atrocities – 'and I don't think she's faking.' [18]

'We live in an age where feminism is a fact, where giving vent to emotion in public wins votes,'[19] he writes, appalled at the grief fest after Princess Diana's death. It is clear whom he blames: 'The Princess is a symbol for every woman who has ever felt wronged by a man.' Women who held opposing views or did not sufficiently appreciate Boris were in contrast inevitably written up as bossy or harridans, or both, such as the commentator Polly Toynbee and a high-flying Swedish Social Democrat and pro-Euro minister Anna Lindh, a rare female figure on the international stage, who was later assassinated.

Meanwhile, other 'blubbers' included the 'tank-topped bumboys' distressed by Peter Mandelson's first departure from government. [20] (In the same vein, Boris referred to the new Labour government's attempts to repeal the notorious Section 28, as 'Labour's appalling agenda, encouraging the teaching of homosexuality in schools, and all the rest of it.'[21])

This period of his life also saw Boris's fixation with sexually charged language revealed in his motoring column for the men's magazine *GQ*, which he added to his growing portfolio in 1999. It provided him with a list of 'babe magnet' motors, from the Bentley Arnage Red Label to the Lotus Exige S2, to test drive at his leisure. The reviews relied on words such as 'filly', 'chicks' and 'flapping kimonos' and were garnished with plenty of 'gearstick' gags. Read now, the *GQ* output comes across as the outpourings of a sex-obsessed cross between Jeremy Clarkson and Toad of Toad Hall. There is talk of blonde drivers 'waggling their rumps,' his own superior horsepower 'taking them from behind,' aided by tantalising thoughts of the imaginary 'ample bosoms' of the female Sat Nav voice.

On driving a Ferrari F430, he wrote: 'it was as though the whole county of Hampshire was lying back and opening her well-bred legs to be ravished by the Italian stallion.'[22] Overtaken while driving an Alfa Romeo 156 Selespeed by a beautiful blonde in a 'poxy little Citroen or Peugeot thing,' Boris described how his 'whole endocrine orchestra said: "Go. Take." You can't be dissed by some blonde in a 305.'[23] He also enjoyed the virile superiority of driving the Nissan Murano, a sort of fat-lipped SUV on steroids. 'Tee-hee! What was it saying, with the plutocratic sneer of that gleaming grille? It was saying "out of my way, small car driven by ordinary person on modest income. Make way for Murano!"'[24] Later, even Boris was to admit these pieces suffered from a 'sprinkling of desperate sexual metaphors.'

His then editor at *GQ*, Dylan Jones, believes the column to be probably the most expensive in magazine history. Boris was certainly paid handsomely for his work but he would hugely increase the cost through majestic indifference to the normal rules of car use. He collected dozens of parking tickets and fines by casually double parking the cars outside the likes of New Scotland Yard or the Royal Festival Hall. Penalty notices were, in Boris's own words, 'building up like drifting snow on the windshield' and more than once an underling had to be dispatched to rescue the car from the pound. Boris would never dream of paying these fines himself, of course. *GQ* paid up, one of the reasons why Jones recalls that Boris managed to reduce three managing editors to tears during his association with the magazine. He would revel in what he describes as 'my crass sexism,' exchanging smutty jokes with the handful of men he had known for a long time. Before his political ambitions taught him otherwise, he was often shamelessly chauvinist in public and no doubt this was at times embarrassing for Marina. He wrote in the *Spectator* about developing his own Tottometer, 'the Geiger-counter that detects good-looking women'[25] and the wife of the editor of the *Economist*, Boris proudly announced, had cancelled her subscription in protest. He also devoted almost an entire leaving speech for a departing female colleague to the proportions of her embonpoint.

But at a time when it was fashionable to rail against political correctness what was certainly crude sexism to some was seen as mere jolly banter by many others in his readership, not to mention the wider Conservative Party. He was courting fans beyond, in his words, the 'foam-flecked' ranks of Eurosceptics, reaching out to more mainstream right-of-centre opinion. Boris was on the verge of something big. Then, on 16 July 1995, an article appeared in the *Mail on Sunday* that would have finished off the careers of most aspiring politicians.

It involved his Eton and Oxford chum Darius Guppy, who had got himself into deep trouble following a brief stint as a bond dealer after university. In March 1990, he arranged to have himself and his business partner tied up in a New York hotel room to make it look as if they had been robbed of jewels worth £1.8 million. They then claimed the money under an insurance policy from Lloyd's of London. Later that year, Stuart Collier, a reporter at the *News of the World*, began to annoy Guppy by making inquiries into the affair. Guppy decided to frighten him off by having him beaten him up and phoned Boris in Brussels for Collier's home address and phone number. The 21-minute conversation was taped by an accomplice, Peter Risdon, who had been paid £10,000 to tie up Guppy in the hotel room, but had then turned against him. Risdon co-operated with the police and became chief prosecution witness when Guppy was tried for the fraud in 1993. The hugely incriminating tape, however, was kept secret from the public for five years.

The conversation begins with friendly greetings, in which Boris makes it clear that he is expecting Guppy's call and tells him that he has been going 'through his files.' He also leads Guppy to believe that he has arranged for a number of contacts to try and get Collier's details. Boris, by now a married man of 26 with a promising career, seems most concerned at the possibility of being found out. He also talks as if he is fully aware of Guppy's plans, asking for assurances that the 'beating up' would not be too severe. In return, Guppy explains why he wants violent revenge on Collier and how important Boris's help is to his plan. Guppy's tone ranges from exclamatory to cajoling, explaining all the while that he cannot afford to 'look stupid' by delaying the attack. He gives Boris 'his word of honour' that his role in the assault will remain undetected. Boris repeatedly asks how severely Collier is to be injured. Guppy tells him 'not badly at all.'

Boris: 'I really, I want to know.'

Guppy: 'I guarantee you he will not be seriously hurt.'

Boris: 'How badly will he . . .'

Guppy, interrupting: 'He will not have a broken limb or broken arm, he will not be put into intensive care or anything like that. He will probably get a couple of black eyes and a . . . a cracked rib or something.'

Boris: 'Cracked rib?'

Guppy: 'Nothing which you didn't suffer at rugby, OK? But he'll get scared and that's what I want . . . I want him to get scared, I want him to have no idea who's behind it, OK? And I want him to realise that he's fucked someone off and that whoever he's fucked off is not the sort of person he wants to mess around with.'

Boris's greatest fear appears to be detection: 'If you fuck up, in any way,' he tells Guppy, 'if he suspects I'm involved . . .'

Guppy: 'No, no, he won't.'

Boris frets about the fact that he has used four contacts to track down information about Collier and is worried one of them 'might put two and two together, if he heard that this guy [Collier] had been beaten up.' Guppy reassures him that he will have an alibi as he will be in Brussels on the day of the attack. Guppy insists: 'As far as I'm concerned, I have never told you what I require this number for. You do not know at all so you are totally off the hook.' By the end of the conversation, Boris is volunteering to do what he can to help.

Guppy: 'Well, do it discreetly. That's all I require – just the address: the address and the phone number . . . all right?'

Boris replies: 'OK, Darry, I said I'll do it and I'll do it. Don't worry.'

When Guppy was convicted of the insurance scam and jailed for five years in 1993, the pair remained firm friends. Back then, Boris described Guppy in the *Telegraph* as living, 'by his own Homeric code of honour, loyalty and revenge' and praising his 'ascetic, contemplative intelligence.' Shortly afterwards Boris's editor Max Hastings, considered by reporters a harsh disciplinarian, received a copy of the tape through the post. Hastings' response was to fly Boris back to London from Brussels 'for a serious discussion.' Anyone might have expected a dramatic showdown – and even a resignation or a sacking at the end of it. But it appears from Hastings' account that the 'interrogation' brought out 'all [Boris's] self-parodying skills as a waffler. Words stumbled forth: loyalty . . . never intended . . . old friend . . . took no action . . . misunderstanding. None of us seriously supposed that Boris was a prospective assassin's fingerman. We dispatched him back to Brussels with a rebuke.'[26]

And so Bumbling Boris won the day. That was the end of the matter as far as his employers were concerned, the affair was kept under wraps and Boris appeared to have got away, Scot-free. But someone was determined to get the story out. Two years later, in the spring of 1995, an unnamed police officer handed a transcript of the tape to a *Daily Telegraph* reporter. It was passed on up the line to Hastings, who had already heard of it, of course. No further action was taken. 'I stood back for the fireworks,' says David Sapsted, Boris's former mentor at *The Times* and now the *Telegraph*'s news editor, who had sent the papers to the editor. 'But none came.' Parts of the transcript were finally published in the *Mail on Sunday* in July 1995, however, prompting a furore – not least because Boris was beginning to position himself as a prominent voice on law and order. He had just written a *Spectator* piece attacking the legal system titled 'Law unto Themselves'. And in that month's edition of *Vogue* magazine he was championed as one of the new leading commentators, popular for his 'geniality, humour and lack of pomposity'. The geniality was now in question. One apt description at the time of the overall tone of the tape is 'ludicrous, but chilling.'

Boris's defence was that he had never supplied Collier's details to his friend. 'I certainly did not attempt to find the address,' he told the *Mail on Sunday*. 'He's obviously in cloud cuckoo land. It was all a bit of a joke. It was all rather harmless. It was – just Darry.' Indeed, he dealt with the whole affair as 'a bit of a joke.' Max Hastings' right-hand man at the *Telegraph* (and subsequently at the *Standard*) Don Berry ('Uncle Don') remembers teasing him the day the story was published and 'he just made a rueful face, as if the beaks at Eton had just caught him raiding the tuck-box.'

It is true that Collier, who has since left journalism, was never attacked. But was Boris right to dismiss 'Guppygate' as merely 'a tale told by an idiot, signifying nothing'? [27] He must also have told Marina that it was inconsequential and like an indulgent parent confronted by an adored child, she clearly wanted to believe him. Marcus Scriven, author of the *Mail on Sunday* piece, recalls meeting her – and reencountering Boris, whom he had met when working at the *Daily Telegraph* – two years later. All three were among the guests invited to a corporate hospitality box at a Newbury race meeting; their host was Max Hastings, by then editor of the *Evening Standard*. During the course of the afternoon, Boris approached Scriven. 'I'd been tipped off that he was going to be there,' recalls Scriven, 'so I'd taken the tape just in case he chose to mention it or Guppy. He came up and said, "Why do you keep writing about me?" I said that anyone who wrote apologia for Guppy, as he had, was fair game and that if he really wanted to be a good friend to Guppy, he wouldn't indulge him by having conversations in which he asked how badly people were going to be beaten up. He said, "I'm sure I didn't say that," then Marina said that, yes, she was sure Boris would never say anything like that. So I got the tape out and said, "Let's listen, shall we?" She and Boris took off.' Later in the afternoon, Boris quietly suggested: 'Let's call it pax, shall we?' 'It was all very Johnsonian,' Scriven recalls.

For years, Boris was nicknamed the 'Jackal' by Matthew Norman on the *Guardian*, but it seemed the Guppygate file had otherwise been closed. Hastings moved on and Boris moved up the ladder at the *Telegraph*, where he became comment editor under new editor Charles Moore, who remembers him performing the role with 'maximum idleness.' Three years on, Guppygate must have been far from Boris's mind when he was invited in April 1998 to appear on *Have I Got News For You*, the BBC programme that was to bring him to the attention of vast new audiences beyond 'Planet Telegraph.' The ensuing celebrity could only help his ever more glorious journalistic career – and surely his chances of landing a safe Parliamentary seat.

Ian Hislop, editor of *Private Eye*, who captains one of the teams on the quiz, decided to spring a nasty surprise on Boris, however, by digging up the by-now largely forgotten Guppy tape. Boris responded with: 'Ha ha ha, richly comic' but his facial expression, despite the fixed smiles, suggested he thought it anything but. He was forced into admitting that the plan to beat up a journalist 'did come up' but to raucous laughter insisted, 'I am not ashamed of it.' Hislop has since described just how angry Boris was at the show's 'elephant trap.' He even took his revenge with an article in the *Spectator* under the headline 'I WAS STITCHED UP', in which he claimed the show constituted a 'fraud' on the watching public because all the apparent ad-libbing of amusing lines was in fact meticulously prepared.

The affair might have ended up with Boris in deep trouble. He risked looking a bad loser – and making enemies of both *Private Eye* and the *HIGNFY* teams. But he is far too canny to enter into feuds with people with such influence over popular opinion. Hislop recalls how Boris's apology, which came soon afterwards, was so charming it was irresistible. Together with his fellow regular panelist Paul Merton, he realised Boris's value as a ratings draw and forgave him. Hislop suggested Boris must have been drunk when he wrote the *Spectator* piece and as ever with the subject of drink, Boris allowed him to think so. The spat became a national talking point and if anything, it was Boris who benefited most. He had escaped the confines of the *Telegraph* and *Spectator* to reach millions of viewers with no Tory instincts at all. Some were even too young to vote but they would now remember him as a full-throttle celebrity. And if they lived in London, based almost entirely on Boris's total of seven *HIGNFY* appearances, not a few would later support him as mayor.

Whenever Boris was invited back, he disarmed Hislop and Merton by his cheerful willingness to play the hapless fall guy, mercilessly lampooned but always coming back for more. On his third appearance, when he introduced himself with the words 'My name is Boris Johnson,' the host Angus Deayton corrected him by reeling off his full moniker 'Alexander Boris de Pfeffel Johnson'. But Boris took all the relentless teasing in good humour, giving the impression of being an easy target while actually handling it all with aplomb. It was a compelling masterclass in how to win over your audience while making it all look effortless. 'It's like watching someone about to fall off the high wire but somehow they always stay on. He's very, very good at that,' says one admirer. Audiences thought him unusually game and somehow authentic; and that his monumental ineptitude when he became guest presenter – fluffing his lines on the autocue and awarding points to the wrong team – was endearing. His phone went off on air and he answered it with the words: 'I can't talk now,

I'm on the television.' Just a handful of cynics questioned whether the timing was purely coincidental.

Hislop and Merton deliberately upped the mayhem factor with their usual quips, while Boris shamelessly plugged his books. It was win, win all round. Boris ceased being Boris Johnson: from here on in, it was Just Boris. No one could believe this jolly fellow could have been caught up in anything sinister involving professional beatings and cracked ribs. He may have come over as a 1930s upper-class twit, but he was box office. He lapped it up – and the TV bosses did, too. Soon he was on *Top Gear, Parkinson, Breakfast with Frost* and *Question Time*. There was no one else quite like him. In an age of airbrushed, politically correct, classless sound-bite merchants, he was literally a class act. Tony Blair may have beaten him to become arguably Britain's first celebrity politician (the early Blair was certainly influential on Boris), but Boris was the first one to make people laugh – and they loved him for it.

It was an act, but a brilliant one. The haystack hair would be artfully arranged in a mess just before the cameras started to roll. He would turn up outrageously late. But *HIGNFY* rendered the Etonian Bullingdon Club product a man of the people, someone who appeared to belong to the masses. He was high-fived in the street by students, hailed by white van man and let off failing to buy a ticket by the train inspector because 'You're that Bozza off the telly.' Failing to take life seriously was no longer a flaw – it was his most valuable asset.

He continued these appearances after he eventually became an MP, although he drew criticism from some quarters who believed such antics to compromise the dignity of his position. Charles Kennedy, the former leader of the Liberal Democrat party, had endured the unflattering tag 'Chatshow Charlie' after putting in a good *HIGNFY* performance but Boris just retorted that the £1,000 fee came in handy for paying for 'approximately' two of his children to go skiing and suggested it would be cowardly not to use the opportunity to reach a wider public. Realising the importance of popularity if you want to govern, he was unapologetic. As so often, his stance on going on a TV quiz show was the Borissian 'Why Shouldn't I?'

Max Hastings was one who counselled caution, suggesting in a letter published in the *Telegraph* that Boris's 'mania for publicity threatened to turn him into a latterday Rector of Stiffkey, who earned undying fame for his sexual dalliances in the 1930s, but was eventually eaten by a lion.' In classic style, Boris rounded on his old boss. He first lauded his target – whom in this case he described as 'one of my journalistic heroes' – before twisting the knife. Hastings, he said, was guilty of 'rank cowardice' for not going on *HIGNFY*. In hardly the most generous display of loyalty to the man who had rescued his career at least twice, he mocked him in the *Telegraph* of all places (after Hastings had left): 'I do not know whether the Liberator of Port Stanley went all yellow-bellied as he contemplated an hour of tart rejoinders from Ian Hislop. I do not know whether his knees knock. Only the great war reporter can tell us if he secretly trembles at the idea of coming off second best to Paul Merton.'[28]

Boris now had an adoring public, but there was not quite such universal veneration among colleagues back at the *Telegraph* and *Spectator*. While basking in the lights of the TV cameras, he was spreading himself thinly to the point of invisibility in his day jobs. He left his commitments to write major sections of the newspaper and magazine, for which he was being paid handsomely, to the last minute. 'He was a complete nightmare on timing,' recalls Dominic Lawson. 'He took things right to the wire, and beyond, and beyond and beyond. He was always absolutely the last to file. He always had this rather disarming thing of saying when I berated him, "Oh, Dommers, come on!" But I used to get incredibly cross with him. With him, it was a pathological problem. There was that sense of entitlement, he'd been President of the Union and won the glittering prizes at Eton. That's bound to give you a deep sense of self-belief.'

But again, Boris was forgiven, as one would a wayward child. 'I've always felt that Boris was like a hyper-intelligent two-year old,' observes Lawson. 'You know that thing about very young boys, it's immensely charming and lovable, they do genuinely believe they are the centre of the universe. As you grow up, you realise that the world does not centre on you. Boris, I think, has not escaped that two-year-old mentality but there is a strange charm to it.'

Indeed, Boris became notorious for filing late – keeping section heads, sub-editors and even editors themselves tapping their fingers and counting the seconds before the presses had to start rolling. Charles Moore recounts how he would phone his star at 5.30 p.m., half an hour before the deadline, to find out how he was getting on. Quite often, Boris would not have even started writing then. Or even know what he was going to write about. Each week Boris would apologise with humour and bravado, and so it would go on. 'I can't believe I've been so disgraceful again,' was a favourite apology. 'He would say sorry, admit he was wrong and make a self-deprecating joke. You felt unable to say any more because you didn't want to lose what you thought was his friendship,' recalls one of his 'handlers'.

His charm and fame were bewitching – he had a curious hold over people. There were clearly plenty of other public schoolboys who secretly wished they possessed the same freewheeling, serendipitous, unbelievably charmed and charming life as him. Some tried to copy Boris and his style but of course they could not pull it off; one or two even blushed when he talked to them. A couple of senior editors thought that Boris's behaviour was simply unacceptable and believed it was time to get really tough, but this was not the predominant view. 'I was one of the few journalists – male or female – not in love with Boris,' says one. 'I saw too much and I knew how much he was being paid and was in awe of it.' Another recalled: 'I told Boris we couldn't run his column because it was simply too late, but he got straight on the phone to Charles Moore, who came round to my desk to instruct me to put it in. I felt powerless to do anything about it – he always got special treatment.'

Week after week, people were staying late just waiting for Boris, asking him politely to file on time and being ignored. If they ever threatened not to use his copy, he would 'get very nasty.' So sometimes they lied and told him the deadline was an hour earlier than it really was but he would still be late for the real deadline. Such was his fame, Boris was by now virtually untouchable. 'I didn't want him flouncing off on my watch and me getting the blame,' explains one executive of the paper, who did not wish to be named. 'Boris knew he had us where he wanted us so regretfully we put up with it.'

And publicly, Boris liked to make a joke of it. 'Dark Forces dragged me away from the keyboard, swirling forces of irresistible intensity and power,' he quipped to a newspaper in July 2000.[29]

On only one occasion did an editor actually dare confront the superstar and carry through his threats. Boris's sub-editor Mark Stanway had complained bitterly about the delay yet again. Others had young children waiting at home; the entire newspaper was in danger of missing its slot on the presses. Charles Moore, one of his greatest fans, realising that Boris had exhausted his handlers' patience, decided he would spike (or discard) his column unless it arrived on time. The copy was even later than usual, so Moore took the decision that if it hadn't arrived by 8.30, it would not be used. At the allotted time, there was no sign of it and the section editors ran another piece instead.

'Boris went completely ape,' recalls the long-suffering Stanway, who was kept late into the evening by Boris for years. 'He phoned me, f-ing and c-ing. I said it wasn't my decision. He came back ten minutes later full of apologies. But Boris has a ferocious temper – he is not a cuddly teddy bear all the time.'

Boris started to file on time for a couple of months but soon afterwards, slipped back into his old way. He was angry, however, about what he saw as an outrageous slight. 'Boris would have been unhappy about Charles spiking his column,' remembers Paul Goodman. 'His way of getting his own back was to refer to Charles in print as the Greatest Living Englishman. Charles will have seen the flash of the stiletto at once, but many readers would have missed it – an example of Boris's capacity to exact revenge without anyone much noticing other than the victim.'

Yet Moore is forgiving of his fellow Etonian and he explains why: '[Boris] is an original. And he is exceptionally bright and exceptionally gifted and exceptionally imaginative. And so that does make you forgive a lot and that's just as well because there often is a lot to forgive. But, of course, he knew that he could more or less get away with it because, again, it's the genius – it's different, it's unique. He has a way of turning a thought upside down in an illuminating manner. In a funny way he does have the interests of, if you like, ordinary people at heart – by which I mean he has a completely non-bureaucratic, non-party way of looking at things. He gets a sort of intuition about what it is like to be someone on a bicycle in the streets, what it is like to have a problem about getting your child into a school. He's actually remarkably good at that for someone who you might think of in some ways as an elitist. It's very funny, of course, but the funny-ness is to do with the fact that in some weird way he's on your side.'[30]

Stanway was also an admirer, for all his irritation. 'Boris is a superlative writer. It's seamless – if you take just one word out, it all falls apart.' In fact, Boris would typically write 50 words under the required length so that no one would actually be able to cut his prose. But Stanway also observed that far from finding it easy, in the early days he 'had to work very hard at it. It's wrong to think that he just messes about. There was quite a lot of pacing and shouting too.' Stanway was grateful for a number of well-timed gestures from Boris that prevented him ever feeling quite so cross again. Not only was he invited to a convivial lunch at the *Spectator* – a popular date in anyone's diary – but Stanway's 'kindness' was also acknowledged by Boris in one of his books. Boris even let him smoke in his office when he was not there. 'If he kept me fairly sweet, I probably wouldn't complain about him quite as much than if he treated me as dirt under his feet,' Stanway suggests. He was snubbed, however, as soon as he was made redundant in 2010. After 13 years of subbing his copy and enduring his foibles, he never heard from Boris again.

While his copy was late, Boris himself was frequently not there at all. In the autumn of 1995, he was responsible for commissioning copy for the comment pages on the *Telegraph* if Simon Heffer took a day off. On more than one occasion he failed to do so, and a panic-stricken office would have to track down Heffer to ask what to do. One notorious occasion during the Conservative party conference that year, Boris disappeared for longer than usual. He could not be found anywhere, but was needed to write an emergency leader on the death of a prominent politician. He did not answer his mobile phone – a capital offence for most journalists – and had not booked into his hotel. In the end, he was found at the eleventh hour, but again it went right up to the wire. It transpired that he had spent the weekend staying with the Eurosceptic politician Bill Cash at his house in Shropshire. His lack of team spirit was more than some of his colleagues could endure; he could not claim to be close to any of them. His political sights were perhaps now being put first – and some felt very angry about having to cover for him while he was busy building a Conservative power base.

'People could never find him and he was always perennially late, even for things he had arranged,' George Jones remembers. And once again he developed a reputation for forming an army of stooges, people with useful knowledge, contacts, influence or just patience. 'Boris is friendly with people who are useful to him,' says Jones, whose familiarity with the ways of the Conservative party was then second to none. 'I no longer am. But when I was political editor of the *Daily Telegraph*, he used to phone me every Wednesday at four when he was writing his column for the next day. He would expect a total rundown on what was happening. And then I would read his interpretation of exactly what I'd said the next day. He was shameless the way he used people.'

Another colleague, Quentin Letts, who was 'pummelled' for information and analysis by Boris, described his antics as 'grand larceny.' Yet another former colleague, a very senior man who perhaps understandably wishes to remain anonymous, sums it up: 'There is an inverse relationship: the greater the proximity to Boris, the less you like him. If you just see him cracking jokes on *Have I Got News For You*, you think he's a great bloke. If you've worked with him or relied on him, it's a different matter.'

Paul Goodman, his comment editor from late 1995, agrees: 'Boris has a selfish streak – he's like the kid in the playground who always goes for the ice cream no matter who else wants it, owns it, or gets hurt in the process.' But Goodman also noticed that he was far from a gung-ho politician with no consideration of human cost or pain. 'For instance, he didn't like the line that Charles Moore, Dean Godson and I took on Northern Ireland. He thought we were glorifying in conflict, whereas he just wanted everyone to sit down and sort it out peaceably.' That said, Boris wasn't always easy to work with. 'He was capable of switching on great charm, but the off-switch got a certain amount of use too,' Goodman adds.

Publicly adored, privately indulged, and earning good money, Boris might have been content with his lot but the political bug refused to go away – even during these years of Tory rout. In an ill-fated election for the Conservatives, now was the time for Boris to pay his dues in a hopeless seat before he could lay claim to a winnable one when the political pendulum swung the other way. But when Boris's plans for a political life finally became public ahead of the 1997 election, there was widespread astonishment. Nick Robinson privately asked Boris why he was intent on entering Parliament – the graveyard of so many hopes and ambitions – when he was making such a splash as a journalist. Boris's answer was unexpectedly serious and revealing – 'Look, you don't change anything as a journalist. The guys in [Parliament] actually change things.' Robinson came away, thinking: 'So there is probably a genuine sense of duty and public service there. And there is also an arrogance and ambition that he is capable of these things – and I could see that he's also easily bored.'

An impressive raft of journalists tried to dissuade him. One concern was Boris's evident lack of self-discipline but there was also the great, still unanswered question: Could Boris ever be *un homme sérieux*? 'Not only would [a Parliamentary career] be a waste of his journalistic talents, I have always thought that a penchant for comedy is an almost insuperable obstacle to achieving political office, which seems the only point of becoming a member of the House of Commons,' Max Hastings wrote in his memoir.[31] Douglas Hurd agreed Boris's clowning tendencies could come in the way of political advance: 'The problem has always been keeping his sense of humour under control. He wrestles with that day by day.'

Clearly frustrated with the limits of journalism – and perhaps sensing the waning powers of newspapers in the Internet age – Boris's serious side had made up his mind. Later he explained that while he 'loves journalism,' it is not 'taking responsibility. It's an extended mid-life crisis really.'[32] On another occasion, he attributed his ambitions to the fact that no one erects statues to journalists. Indeed, it's clear that from quite early on he had been thinking like a politician – by adopting that almost universal political obsession with 'legacy.' Only politics would give him the opportunity to create one.

The entreaties were to no avail. Against the backdrop of New Labour's political tsunami – which many claim he helped to create – Boris was selected to fight the Labour fortress of Clwyd South. Although a largely rural constituency in north Wales, it is also home to communities of redundant miners and steelworkers hostile to Tories in general (and toffs, in particular). This was a classic piece of political mis-casting – an urbane public-school polymath fighting a largely Welsh-speaking Labour stronghold. It is astonishing that he won the selection, not least because his hand-written application letter arrived late, was barely legible and did not even include a CV. Indeed, such a mark of disrespect and disorganisation would have ruled him out had it not been for another stroke of Johnsonian good fortune – an intervention from Conservative Central Office apparently keen to promote (or perhaps more accurately, test) a would-be star. Boris had already been rejected by the London seat of Holborn and St Pancras because of a 'badly typed' CV; someone obviously felt the rules would have to be bent, if he was to have his chance.

'I was absolutely staggered. Boris appeared to take absolutely no real interest in the detail and his letter was a shocker,' recalled Ian Reynolds, then chairman of Clwyd South Conservative Association. 'However, I was primed by Central Office that he had applied and that although we'd drawn up our shortlist, if I would consider him they'd be grateful so he was put in to be seen with the other candidates.

'But the initial impression was rather like Boris is now: everything is haphazard. It isn't just his hair that's blowing around in the wind, it's also that his thoughts don't seem to be concentrated on the things that count. And so it wasn't a good first impression. He always looked like a tramp – he was expected as a Conservative candidate to go around in a suit and a tie, and actually he went around in a pair of – well, anything really. For someone who'd been at Oxford and a member of the Bullingdon Club, he wasn't what people expected.'

What won the day, said Reynolds, was Boris's undoubted

intelligence, which eventually shone through and secured him the candidacy. 'He fought a very good election, although some people saw him as being aloof; they didn't seem to think he was an appropriate person for a North Wales constituency. But I personally was very much in favour of him. I accompanied him on a lot of the meetings he attended and he performed extremely well.'

After his selection, Boris finally began to do his homework. 'Where I think he excelled here was his mastery of the detail. He knew nothing about farming when he came up here and obviously, a large section of the vote were people who run sheep and cattle farms. But he really read the red book [the Conservative party handbook] on farming and the C.A.P., which was critical. He hadn't looked at it before but read it when he stayed with us, which he did for quite a lot of his six weeks of campaigning. At home, we've got plenty of accommodation as it's an estate.'

And so Boris was spared the expense or bother of renting a property in the constituency, unlike many of the other candidates. His willingness to learn and his ability to get on with people from all walks of life won him many admirers locally, even among non-Tories. Even so, this was clearly a battle he could not win. 'It was not easy for him [but] he endeared himself very much to the people up here. But in my mind I felt that he didn't fit the token image of what a Conservative MP in a country seat should be like,' added Reynolds.

Boris nevertheless conducted his campaign with some energy and humour. In fact, too much humour on occasion – including the time he addressed a group of farmers about the BSE crisis at the Hanmer Arms in Wrexham Maelor. He allowed his love of *double entendres* – not so much mad cows as bum steers was his line on the media handling of the crisis – to get the better of him. They made clear their displeasure at his treating their pain as a 'laughing matter.' It was a lesson in the difference between punditry – the same jokes had gone down a storm in the *Telegraph* – and politics. And it is a distinction he has struggled with ever since.

But Boris was sufficiently astute both to learn enough Welsh to sing the national anthem and order fish and chips; also to visit plenty of other farms and pubs without offending the locals. But even though this was a newly created constituency, as with Canute and the tide, Boris's efforts against the political odds were doomed. Despite its sprawling size and rural appearance, many of the constituency's 70,000 population actually live in urban Wrexham. One in five speaks Welsh; many are tribally Labour. Boris cut an incongruous Conservative figure, a throwback cast into contrast by the fresh-faced, clean-cut, sharp-suited Blair proclaiming the dawning of a 'new day.'

He drew a mere 9,091 or 23 per cent of the votes (down seven points on the previous election) against Labour's 22,901 or 58 per cent. Still, it must have been some comfort in the small hours of 2 May at the Plas Madoc sports centre in Acrefair, where the count took place, to compare his performance with that of Michael Portillo, who managed to lose a 15,545 majority in Enfield Southgate. As Boris himself says, it was the worst Tory defeat for 160 years – the party's version of Cannae. So he took up the returning officer's invitation to say a few words after the result and proceeded to make what Marina later dubbed 'the most graceless speech she had ever heard from a defeated candidate.' Once back in London, though, he allowed himself to jest again, cracking the well-worn politico joke: 'I fought Clwyd South . . . and Clwyd South fought back.'

It must have been a relief when it was all over. Shortly afterwards, Boris held a 'Come What May' party at home in Furlong Road, Islington. Those who attended the jolly occasion – where Marina's father Charles Wheeler cooked an enormous lasagne – noted some of the guests crammed into the drawing room and basement kitchen had clearly been invited as a 'thank you' gesture for their part in the campaign. 'But there also seemed to be a celebratory element that it was all over and now he could look forward to something better,' one guest observed. There was also a recognition that he would have to evolve the Boris brand in line with the change of political landscape.

For someone who branded himself as a 'Young Man in a Hurry', the going was proving painfully slow. At Oxford, he had said it was his ambition to be in the Cabinet by the age of 35. Just short of his 33rd birthday, Boris had lost his first stab at a Parliamentary seat. For now, he would have to content himself with journalism until the political weather changed. Fortunately, his career was looking good. On occasion, he was put in charge of the paper on days when Charles Moore was not around.

'One week Boris was given the chance to edit the *Telegraph* on a Sunday,' Don Berry recalls. 'But he wandered in looking completely baffled. He seemed to have no idea what his role would be – he hadn't bothered to find out. So everyone helped him. Perhaps he just had enough confidence to take it on without finding out what it entailed. Perhaps he just knew that like the Berlin Philharmonic, the amount of conducting needed was pretty minimal. But anyone else would have boned up. Not Boris. He relied on others.'

And it is his good fortune that throughout his life people have flocked to help. Stephen Robinson, formerly *Telegraph* foreign editor, recalls Boris going off to Kosovo to write a piece. 'I got an email from a name I'd never heard of saying, "I've just been given a memory stick by someone called Boris Johnson and he gave me your email address."' It transpired Boris was too busy doing something else to file so he had approached a complete stranger in the airport and said, "Would you mind awfully emailing it to London." Most people just wouldn't get away with it. I suppose you just look like someone who good things happen to, and good things do happen to you.'

Another good thing was to happen to Boris. In July 1999, just after his 35th birthday, he was appointed editor of the weekly political magazine, the *Spectator*. The proprietor Conrad Black, who also owned the *Telegraph*, gave him the much-prized job on the explicit understanding that he had given up on chasing a Parliamentary seat. One of the most desirable jobs in journalism had at last cured him of a passion for political office – or had it?

Chapter Eight
'Sack me!'
The *Spectator*, 1999–2005

In a pub car park in Henley-on-Thames, the cloud of 40 blue 'Vote Conservative' balloons had become hopelessly entangled. A hapless but devoted party worker was valiantly trying to separate the strings with the only method available to him – his cigarette lighter – leading to a round of mini explosions reminiscent of the 'gunfight at the OK Corral.' Sparks then set off a small fire in a pile of Tory leaflets and several onlookers turned purple with laughter. It was a suitably comic opening, recorded in his political memoirs, *Friends, Voters, Countrymen*,[1] to Boris's successful bid in the May 2001 general election to become a Conservative MP.

Yes, less than two years after he had promised Conrad Black that he would drop his political ambitions if he became editor of the *Spectator*, Boris had been elected to Parliament. It was the most spectacular deception from the start. 'We found out within a couple of months [of appointing him in July 1999] that he had sought selection as a Conservative MP in two different constituencies,' sighs Black. 'We thought that it was Boris being Boris – doing whatever he wanted and assuming that his disarming personality would carry him through any consequences.'

And it was. No doubt Boris had calculated that the likelihood of being allowed to keep his cake while eating it was very high. And he was right. A furious Black branded him 'ineffably duplicitous.' Yet he still indulged his young editor and so Boris got away with it with his well-rehearsed routine of grovelling apology, super-abundant charm and humour. He introduced a new, but soon well-used, element of inviting his boss to dismiss him – on the basis that this would massively reduce the chances of him doing so. It did, and he didn't. But to any outsider, it looked increasingly as if Boris was pursuing a career by death wish.

'We had him in and invited him to explain what he had done,' recalls Black. 'He said that it was outrageous and that we would be quite within our rights to sack him, that the opportunities had arisen after his promise had been given, that he really wanted to be an MP more than anything else and that he was going to tell us when he was more confident of being chosen as a candidate. His plan was to argue that he could do both. He cited Iain Macleod as his evidence of this, as he had been an MP while editor of the *Spectator*. He explained how he would make a success of both jobs and we said we would give him a try.'

In the end, Black thought it worth taking a gamble: 'Boris was, and is a talent, as well as a likeable man and the last thing we wanted to do was to get rid of him. He was a capable editor, kept morale up, raised back the quality of the magazine, recruited good writers for imaginative stories and helped promote the magazine and raise its circulation.'

Dan Colson, Black's chief executive, eventually came to the same conclusion but could not disguise his anger at this personal betrayal. Boris had continued to deny the rumours about his seeking another seat, even when Colson interrogated him about them over a good lunch – and paid for it. Finally, when it officially came out that he was seeking selection in Henley, Colson was furious and left a series of messages for the ever-absent Boris about his displeasure. He raged at his editor, reminding him that the *Spectator* was 'not some magazine on pig-farming in Wales' but a highly influential political journal that required his full attention. 'You gave us your assurance,' he roared. But then Colson too recalibrated his opinion and decided that Boris's *Spectator* role could indeed be carried out on a part-time basis. In fact, this was already the case.

'Boris wasn't exactly working 18-hour days but he was on radio, on TV, in the papers talking about the magazine,' he says, shrugging his shoulders. 'We recognised that Boris's rise in the Tory party would give us even more exposure.' It is testament to Boris's extraordinary sense of self-worth that he stood up to Black and Colson – two formidable characters who would have been within their rights to cast him adrift. He almost seemed to enjoy the danger. But by now, thanks to his fame and popularity, Boris was such a figure in his own right he no doubt deduced that the normal rules no longer applied to him: he was a brand that sold the magazine.

He had been summoned by the Prime Minister Tony Blair to the famous Downing Street sofa room to be congratulated on his appointment in person. By the time he could no longer deny the rumours that he was seeking a Parliamentary seat, he had raised circulation by 10 per cent to around 62,000 (and later it reached nearly 70,000.)[2] He had achieved the Holy Grail for any editor – a profit – and taking the magazine into the black allowed him to take liberties. But Black and Colson also seemed powerless to stop him, as if in awe of their young editor and his growing fame and popularity. Once again Boris had survived through the extraordinary indulgence of others.

In any case, Black and Colson had long since brought in a formidable duo to 'mind' Boris. 'Stuart Reid made sure the magazine came out on time and Kimberly Fortier sold advertising,' says Colson. With Boris not so much at the helm as a pennant from the mast, the magazine was making waves. It was witty, often surprising, eclectic, capricious and occasionally scored a dramatic hit. Reid, a languid, considered figure, with a couple of decades on Boris and a distinguished career at the *Sunday Telegraph*, was an inspired choice. 'They said they needed a mature, responsible chap to keep an eye on Boris,' he recalls. 'So it seemed an ideal job for me, really. We ended up egging each other on – but Boris is braver than me.'

One of Boris's first acts as editor was to go on two weeks' leave (his fourth child, Theodore Apollo had just been born), leaving Reid to edit from the Monday he started. For the next six years, the pair worked together and Boris's regime continued to be unorthodox. There were few conventional editorial meetings. 'Boris was his own man and didn't operate as a conscientious, form-filling, tradition-observing editor with lots of conferences, notes and brainstorming,' recalls Reid, 'And thank God for that!'

Only once a week on Thursdays, the beginning of the *Spectator* editorial week, would there be a meeting of all the key characters – Boris and Reid, of course, but at various times the cast also included associate editor Rod Liddle, the political editor Peter Oborne and columnist Petronella Wyatt. Sometimes visitors would drop in, too. 'It was always a lot of laughs, but we didn't very often settle on anything and then we'd go to lunch,' recalls Reid. 'In an ideal world, we would have known what was going in the magazine by Friday night but often, it wasn't until Sunday evening that Boris would call me and say, "What can we cook up, Stuart? What's going on?" We didn't allow ourselves to get too alarmed until Tuesday afternoon. The ultimate deadline was, of course, Wednesday morning.'

Leaving everything to the last minute was no way to run a magazine and there were plenty who tutted over Boris's management style – or 'no-management style,' as his critics put it. But the talented and tolerant Reid appears to have enjoyed the challenge, and certainly rose to it. Behind the heavy black door and brass plaque at 56 Doughty Street, Holborn, the *Spectator* was a fun, even thrilling, place to work. 'Boris was great company and a popular editor,' says Reid. 'He was sweet to the staff – but that was because he couldn't really be a bastard if he wasn't around the office. He was an absentee editor because he had other interests; he certainly wasn't nine to five. I used to get frustrated from time to time. Sometimes when I wanted to talk to Boris, I wasn't able to. He just wouldn't answer his phone.'

In fact, many contributors – even the stars such as Matthew Parris – dealt almost exclusively with Reid. 'There were long stretches of time when Stuart was the editor,' recalls Parris. 'If Stuart was the workhorse, then Boris was the plumed horse: the dressage. Boris usually has a team of intensely loyal people around him who are carrying the can for him, whose importance is only half-recognised and who appear to be content that Boris continues to get the credit for things. The general public just don't know about them. He must inspire in people this strange loyalty.'

To this day Reid insists, 'It was absolutely Boris's magazine. Boris has helped create the myth that I did all the work at the *Spectator* and he had all the fun. But the myth has no basis in fact: Boris did a lot of the work and I had a lot of fun.' However, the consensus is that Reid curbed some of Boris's wilder excesses, just as Conrad Black had hoped, and doggedly kept the show on the road. Certainly, Colson is in no doubt where credit is due, knowing Boris was not up to it on his own. 'Stuart Reid has consistently undersold himself. I don't believe the success of the *Spectator* was all down to Boris for one minute. Stuart made the train run on time, a job Boris couldn't have done in a hundred years. Stuart had no desire for the limelight, but was methodical, reliable and tolerant. We always had grave reservations on Boris's ability to see things through but he was clever enough to realise his strong and not so strong points. So he enthusiastically welcomed Stuart Reid and they made a brilliant team.'

Boris's persistent absences meant that mistakes were made that a more meticulous editor might have avoided. It was Reid rather than Boris who removed offensive references by the notorious *High Life* columnist Taki to the skin colour of the 'stink pot crowd' who moored their 'gin palace' next to his boat. On another occasion in 2003 Taki's comments on 'black hoodlums' as the root of Britain's social ills[3] were not excised. Still Boris would not shoulder the blame.

'He has form on blaming others,' says one otherwise admiring former colleague. 'Very embarrassing,' Boris said at the time. 'I was on holiday, of course. It should never have gone in. It was a terrible thing. But what can you do?'[4] Well, Boris could have taken responsibility. He could have dispensed with Taki – who frequently courted controversy on race and religion – but consistently chose not to, despite entreaties from many critics, including his own father-in-law Charles Wheeler. It is down to Boris that Taki was able to run columns on 'bongo-bongo land,'[5] West Indians 'multiplying like flies,'[6] and one on the world Jewish conspiracy, in which he described himself as a 'soi-disant anti-semite,'[7] that prompted even Taki's friend, proprietor Conrad Black, to protest.

It was Boris who chose to celebrate Taki's '25 glorious years' as a *Spectator* columnist in October 2000. (Boris got into even more trouble on race when his columnist Rod Liddle recalled a tour of Unicef work in Uganda, where Boris boomed to the Swedish workers and their black driver: 'Right, let's go and look at some more piccaninnies!'[8])

Boris also had a habit of making promises to contributors that he could not keep. It is more than likely that Reid would then have to deal with a disappointed writer when the story did not merit the prominence promised. On one occasion, Boris commissioned 2,000 words from a journalist on an aspect of the murder of eight-year-old Victoria Climbié and insisted it would be trailed on the front cover. He was overheard saying to another guest at the party where the commitment was made: 'It's quite easy, this magazine editing lark!' Only the story never made the front, nor did it run to anything like 2,000 words.

Reid, although obsessively modest about his own role, remembers another occasion when Boris disappeared during the biggest news story in living memory. 'He didn't turn up till pretty late on 9/11. We'd all been sitting there in his office watching television and he came in and said, "Crikey, why's everyone sitting in my bloody office?" We said, "Don't you know?" and he said, "Crikey, I think we've got a cover here. Spike that piece on school vouchers!"' His absences were thus regularly nail-biting and infuriating for the magazine's staff. He would habitually not answer his phone, commission articles, turn up to lunches, or meet dignitaries, important advertisers or even his own deadlines. 'Any *Spectator* columnist will tell you about the difficulties of being Boris's accident and emergency service,' says Parris. 'You'd receive the sudden phone call with Boris saying, "Oh my God, we've got a page to fill and I promised to ask someone to do it. I can't find anybody, could you do it?" There were dozens of stories like that of Boris presuming on other people's goodwill.'

On two occasions, Parris was a last-minute stand in for Boris at major *Spectator* dinners but disliked seeing the disappointment of guests when the editor failed to show. Andy McSmith, another contributor, remembers rescuing Boris when he failed to arrange a promised interview with the TUC general secretary John Monks. 'Boris had phoned Monks and left a message on the answerphone, which he had played to everyone at the TUC because he thought Boris came over as this blithering idiot. Then I got a message on my mobile, which made me fall about laughing. Boris was saying, "Oh my God, I've messed up. Go down and sort it out. You know how to talk to these people!" What he wanted was for me to cover for the fact that he had failed to nail down an appointment, do a Monks' interview myself and then smooth over relations between the *Spectator* and the TUC. He appeared to have completely lost control of events, and so of course you end up doing it. Monks was amused by it all but scathing. His view was: "These people with their expensive education who can't hold it together!" Boris was playing up to what they wanted to hear and it made them feel better about him.' Indeed, far from resenting Boris's apparent bumbling, it rendered him more likeable to McSmith and somehow less of an unwavering enemy to the TUC.

When there was no escape from writing a piece he would typically leave it to the eleventh hour and then dash it off. 'Because I have no time to do it, I do it in no time – you just whack it out,' he told the *New York Times*. Or occasionally he would offer to pay someone else to do it for him. It just added to the sense of barely controlled chaos. On one occasion, Boris had interviewed someone in Somerset and had then gone on to Sussex to stay the weekend with Dominic Lawson, a previous *Spectator* editor. Only he had left his notebook in Somerset, so the office had to dispatch a taxi at great expense first to his interviewee and then across half of southern England to Sussex. 'It was all very Boris-ish,' recalls Lawson.

Boris's secretary – the redoubtable, crop-haired Ann Sindall from Batley, West Yorkshire – was another long-serving member of his accident and emergency team. She was accustomed to many a crisis such as this. He had plucked her out of the *Telegraph*, where she was unhappy – although with her crisp Northern humour and 'socialist' tendencies she may not be what most would expect of Boris's secretary. But then Boris likes to avoid the predictable. 'Ann Sindall is almost a pantomime Northerner,' observes a former colleague, 'like Boris is a pantomime toff.' She is said to have presided over the *Spectator* office, 'with the implacable demeanour of a headmistress trained by the SAS.'[9]

Boris remained loyal to her, affectionately nicknaming her 'be-all and Sindall' and giving her a special mention in his Christmas address to the staff. She was also permitted to bring her beloved Jack Russell, Harry, into the office, whom Boris liked to refer to as 'certainly no smellier than anyone else in the building.'[10]

Sindall has more than repaid his constancy by putting up with Boris's demands (although not one request to sew up a rip in his trousers) and enduring his absences. 'Ann's tolerance of Boris's misbehaviour does surprise me,' notes Parris. 'I adore Ann, she's been terrifically helpful to me over the years. But I would have thought she could be rather severe with people – even Boris. But she has never dropped him. You'd have to have a huge sense of humour to work with Boris. But if you appreciate intelligence in a human being, it's hard not to admire him.'

For over a decade Sindall has been his gatekeeper – fall foul of her and reaching Boris himself becomes impossible – and his organiser-in-chief. Parking tickets, unpaid tax demands, bills, threats from bailiffs, requests for interviews, publishers, irate proprietors, irate colleagues, pleading contributors, members of his family, high society and low society – she has dealt with them all. During the *Spectator* years, Boris was a journalist (he also wrote regular columns for the *Telegraph* and *GQ*), novelist (*Seventy Two Virgins*), media personality (*Have I Got News For You* plus an assortment of other chat shows and TV and radio outings) and, of course, politician (applying for at least two seats and succeeding in one).

Sindall's job was to help keep all these balls in the air. No one believes it was easy, not least because Boris has a habit of saying 'yes' to people without any intention of doing what they ask. With customary skill, Sindall then had to extricate him. She has admitted to, on occasion, wanting to 'kill Boris' or 'hating his guts' after he had gone AWOL once too often. And she would scream at callers who phoned looking for him: 'If you want Boris, why the hell are you wasting your time ringing the *Spectator*? You won't find him here.' But like many others in his life, she has been won back so often by the fact that he makes her laugh.

Reid, too, jokes that it is the fun of being with Boris that has ensured his survival. The frustration of his casual attitude to deadlines, promises, decisions, his sheer and persistent unreliability, he says, would otherwise mean 'that he would be dead by now.' He also believes that Boris 'does feel guilty about things, about letting people down. But Charles Moore once said there's one thing you can rely on Boris for and that's to let you down – and it's true. Boris does not like to take things seriously. It's part of his brand although he does take his own career seriously, of course. But at the same time it's genuine, too. He sees the absurdity in just about everything, even himself.'

There were also occasional flashes of kindness. Reid remembers Boris taking the time to write a handwritten and sweetly personal letter to the mother of a boy with whom he had been to prep school who had died. The mother was very touched.

With Stuart Reid and Ann Sindall shouldering much of the load, overall Boris admits to having had 'more fun than is strictly proper'[11] (although not all of it within the confines of the *Spectator*'s offices). He would pop into the magazine's ramshackle Georgian townhouse with holes in the wall and push past the dog leads, champagne bottles, umbrellas and bicycles parked under a 'No Bicycles' sign in the hall to join in the gaiety. But rarely before lunch – which, at least for his guests, was often long and liquid. There always seemed to be a bevy of attractive young women hanging around and games of ping pong in the garden. The door to his spacious, but chaotic first-floor office – presided over by a Pericles bust and a crystal chandelier – would be left open and, recalls Reid, 'people would wander in and read the papers. If you were having an attack of the vapours, you could lie on his sofa.'

Some of the furniture was quite distinguished, including the striped Chesterfield settee of a perfect length to lie on and a valuable Persian rug, but the rest was 'distressed'. The editor's desk was suitably dark and colossal with two phones, one white and one black, and was warmed by a cosy gas fire. The place reeked of prep-school pencil shavings and decaying orange peel – with overtones of comfortable elitism. (Indeed, for all his latterly acquired 'man of the people' credentials, Boris unashamedly used the *Spectator* to peddle his Darwinian creed. In 2000, for instance, he ran a leader under the headline 'LONG LIVE ELITISM' saying, 'without elites and elitism, man would still be in his caves.'[12])

But for all that, Boris also allowed a culture to develop of inspiring creative libertarianism. He prevented the *Spectator* from simply acting as some sort of predictably constipated Tory salon by bringing in a range of ideas and opinions. For his columnists, at least, he was more mascot than master. 'It was total anarchy, just a feeling of letting a thousand flowers bloom,' says Parris. 'I was never steered by Boris in any way; he never asked me to change a word I had written. My line was often different from the others, but there was no censorship. I don't think that was inattention on Boris's part. I believe he believes in free speech in a rather intense and profound way.'

There were few pre-conceptions, Reid explains, but rather a healthy general scepticism that few, if any other politically aligned journals achieve. 'Boris is very attached to a certain journalistic principle. This is that you go along with something until everyone else does, and then you distance yourself.'

The *Spectator* was, for instance, perhaps the sole Conservative outlet regularly to give a platform to those who had doubts about sending the troops into Iraq. Its editorial position was broadly in favour of the war and as an MP, Boris voted for it – although he has since said he regrets doing so. But he hired Andrew Gilligan, the former BBC correspondent at the centre of the 'September dossier' row (involving the government's exaggerated claims over weapons of mass destruction in Iraq) and, according to Reid, 'the man probably most hated by the general hawkish establishment – Tory and Labour. Boris hired him because he liked him and because he could see what Gilligan had said was true. The dossier *had* been sexed up.' Indeed, in December 2003 the *Spectator* even hosted a 'Save Andrew Gilligan' dinner at Luigi's restaurant in Covent Garden.

Perhaps in part reflecting his Islington home life, Boris liked to take the counter-intuitive position whenever possible. For instance, in September 2001 he commissioned a piece arguing Britons should be grateful and proud that protectionism on the continent made asylum-seekers choose Britain for a fresh start. It was the very antithesis of the abrasive nationalism of the *Daily Mail*, which was commonplace among right-wingers at the time. And Boris would commission work from talented people, no matter what their political persuasions, such as the *Guardian* cartoonist Steve Bell. 'Boris was a great admirer of Steve Bell and they don't come more left wing than he is,' says Reid. 'He did some good covers for us.' Bell was given virtually free rein to poke fun on a total of 17 front covers – including two on Michael Howard, once portrayed as a vampire and the other time as a bat, and William Hague, drawn as Napoleon.

But there was one institution that could not be mocked. In July 2005, Bell was commissioned to illustrate a piece about Etonians being an abused minority. He drew a pig in Eton collar behind barbed wire with the school gateway in the background. Boris took one look and said: 'No, no, no, I can take a lot but not that!' He paid Bell, but spiked the drawing, although no lasting resentment rankles between the pair. 'I do like Boris – even though politically he's as far from me as I can conceive,' admits Bell. 'He's genuinely enthusiastic for my work.'

Since Boris left, the *Spectator* has become more unilateral in its tastes and Bell has not been asked to work for it again. Nor has Andy McSmith, a writer from the left, who joined the roster because Boris wanted someone who knew the Labour party to write about it. 'Boris is very intellectually confident so he doesn't worry about people writing from different viewpoints,' says McSmith. 'He's intellectually curious, so he wants to know what other people are thinking. I find him a very friendly character even now.'

Boris also delighted in pursuing some pretty whacky ideas – which he liked to describe as 'wheezes.' Many of the whackiest wheezes he directed at Lloyd Evans, the 'Stain' he had known since Oxford. 'He was always asking me to leave the country on idiotic missions such as an inquiry into Swedish lavatorial habits,' sighs Evans. 'He had a strange obsession lasting nearly ten years that men in Sweden weren't allowed to pee standing up. I refused to do it – and it turned out it was Switzerland anyway, but only in flats, because of the noise for the downstairs neighbours.'

Boris also wanted to take revenge on the tabloids (in what was perhaps the opening salvo of his war with our more salacious newspapers) for 'ruining' the Earl of Hardwicke by ensnaring him with the offer of some Class A drugs. So he also instructed Evans to mount an absurd counter-sting on a *News of the World* reporter. In an exercise doomed to failure, Evans demanded £5,000 for evidence that Boris was not only dealing in cocaine but heavily using it in what had become a hotbed of illicit drug-taking at the *Spectator*. Not surprisingly, Evans was rumbled by the *News of the World* and the wheeze was dropped. But Boris soon came up with more mad schemes for him, from deliberately trying to get himself thrown out of a top-notch restaurant to infiltrating gangs of animal rights terrorists. Few were successful. Evans went to two restaurants – Gary Rhodes in the City and 'some place full of prostitutes in Shepherd Market' – 'but didn't have the guts to cause a scene' and so failed to get ejected from either. But Boris's enthusiasm for such 'investigations' suggests that in another life he might have made a fine tabloid editor himself – he was very serious about frivolity.

Evans was also given the job of poetry editor – involving in his own words 'sifting through a mountain of tosh' – for which the fee was a twice-yearly crate of cheap plonk. Despite negotiating a good salary for himself, Boris was not known for paying his contributors well. In fact, most were paid no more than £500 for a piece and some, like Evans, considerably less.

Boris once sacked Evans as poetry editor for writing a scathing piece in the *Mail on Sunday* about a private *Spectator* lunch attended by a 'group of save-the-planet freaks', whom he described as 'a threat to civilised conversation.' The 'Chatham House rule' was that guests at these lunches would not be identified afterwards to encourage the free flow of conversation. Keen to 'out' these bores, Evans ignored the stricture and wrote a lengthy article naming them. One of the guests, Zac Goldsmith, complained to Boris, who published his letter in the next issue. Soon afterwards, Boris put in a call to Evans, who knew what was coming. 'Here's the bad news,' said Boris. 'You're fired as poetry editor.' And then seconds later: 'Now the good news – you're reinstated!'

Evans deduced that Boris would not be able to find another poetry editor quite so cheaply and in any case was an energetic rule-breaker himself and could hardly punish others for playing the same game. And it *was* a game: Boris despised tedium and those who talked it. Evans was indeed actually promoted and Boris continued to urge his contributors to excite and even incite. 'He harassed me to write about India,' recalls David Gardner of the *Financial Times*, whom Boris knew from Brussels. 'I did a few pieces for him, one of which was on Hindu fundamentalism. "Give us a bit more oomph," he said, "I want to see newsagents go up in flames!"'

As lord of his manor Boris drew in a whole crowd of people he knew from Brussels, Oxford, Eton, the *Telegraph* and of course, his extended family. In a provocative move, he gave Toby Young from his Oxford days the magazine's theatre column when Young himself admitted he knew 'nothing' about theatre. No doubt Boris enjoyed the furore this prompted in theatre critic circles when he removed the veteran Sheridan Morley, blaming orders from Conrad Black. Young certainly enjoyed his new berth, describing it in the *Evening Standard* as 'one of the last bastions of cavalier individualism, a chaotic haven of bohemian self-indulgence and aristocratic broad-mindedness.'[13]

Earl Spencer was invited to pen a diary (and hosted *Spectator* cricket matches at Althorp), Boris's brother Leo wrote a few times, Rachel a great deal, and on occasion her husband, Ivo Dawnay; Stanley wrote about the environment and brother Jo contributed on a variety of subjects. His father-in-law Charles Wheeler was also a contributor. Paul and Frank Johnson (neither related to each other, nor Boris and his clan) were also frequent contributors, adding to the general Johnsonian confusion but Boris was shrewd enough to leaven this abundance of Johnsons with an unlikely but winning combination of younger lad-mag journalists, the angry Leftie Rod Liddle, Joan Collins, Anna Ford and Nicky Haslam.

He avoided long, worthy or turgid pieces by instructing at least one contributor that no *Spectator* piece should take more than three calls and a total of 45 minutes. The result was a wisecracking, pistol-paced magazine that was provocative and funny though perhaps not terribly serious – or in the purest meaning of the term, 'political'. Pompous discussions of –isms did not interest him. In February 2001, Matthew Parris wrote a piece that might have been Boris's personal manifesto when he declared 'the correct approach for a sound fellow is a faintly amused disinterestedness. [The] importance of not being earnest is, among the Right, hard to overstate. [And] we [should] never be personally rude to one whose persuasions we described in print as poisonous.'

Boris took great care about whom he 'described in print as poisonous.' His targets were those in no position either to champion or to block his ambitions. One such was the former prime minister and arch Europhile, Sir Edward Heath – a figure of scorn for Eurosceptics and a spent force politically. Just before the 2001 General Election Boris let rip, referring to how Heath's 'belly [was] cantilevered between us like some decked whale.' 'It would be utterly magnificent,' he went on, 'if I could tell you, my friends, that Sir Edward, at 84, has got over his Incredible Sulk and become a piping geyser of optimism about the party under whose banner I am about to fight. Alas, amigos, it is not to be, he wants to gloom me out. Here we are, two fat Balliol Blonds, and the older one wants to rock the confidence of the younger. Well, I won't let him.'[14]

But sometimes his laid-back approach meant that his writers got him into trouble anyway. One such occasion was when Petronella Wyatt described Fawley Court, a Polish religious order on the borders of the Henley constituency, as resembling 'an inverted bus shelter', where the resident monks dressed like 'narcotics abusers.' Worse still was her declaration that a list of Polish achievements would 'not cover a cheeseboard.' The ensuing deluge of complaints from Poles and Catholics included a particularly angry missive from the Duke of Norfolk. Realising the gravity of the offence and the appalling timing (it was September 2000, a few months after his selection in the run-up to the 2001 election) Boris went to apologise in person and sent dozens of grovelling letters.

Sometimes the darts were carefully targeted, however. In November 2002 he ran a piece by Mary Kenny that gave an insight into his thoughts on so-called self-appointed moral arbiters to the nation. Dubbed the Mothers of Morality, the piece named a group of fierce and forthright journalists such as Melanie Phillips and Janet Daley who it said saw themselves as embattled voices against a loose-living liberal establishment.[15] Although as an anti-abortion pro-marriage Catholic, Kenny was naturally one of the group, it was pretty clear that Boris did not share (or care for) their moralising.

Sarah Sands, a journalist and friend of Marina's whom the article claimed was 'showing promising signs' of Moral Motherhood, was horrified to be included. 'For Boris, it was the rudest thing he could say about anyone,' she says. Perhaps this was merely a warning shot across her bows that he would not take kindly to any 'moralising' about his own life.

Boris also liked to joke that 'scoops are us' but in fact the *Spectator* did not break many stories, with two honourable exceptions. The first was Peter Oborne's revelation in April 2002 that Tony Blair had tried to 'muscle in on the mourning' for Queen Elizabeth The Queen Mother[16] which although strenuously denied was widely believed. Its gist was later confirmed by evidence from Black Rod but before then Boris was treated to the full fury of Downing Street, which brought in the Press Complaints Commission. Then director Guy Black first tried to make an informal resolution by going to see Boris at the *Spectator*.

'I think it was Boris's first difficult PCC complaint. He was in a bit of a panic about it, asking me, "What should I do?"' recalls Black. Never having met Boris before, he felt obliged to take the apparently struggling young editor through the routine process of establishing with the writer the strength of his material and sources. 'My impression was that he was slightly scatty and in need of help and advice to get through it but now I don't believe that to be the real Boris at all. In essence, it's all done to get you onside. His behaviour didn't affect the outcome of the complaint or the dispute, but it is true that I came away with a sympathetic feeling for him. The act is very effective. And that was the first time I'd seen it in action.'

The second scoop came from Boris's sister Rachel, who in July that year, revealed that the Blairs were hiring private tutors, teachers from the local top public school, Westminster, to help their children through A-Levels. It was a good story. Both revelations took their toll on Labour's body politic but did they make the *Spectator* a true power in the land? Did they establish Boris as a political sage or thinker? They undoubtedly showed up the failings of the Conservative leadership of the time, which was struggling to land any punches on the government; they also attracted oodles of publicity for Boris and his writers but they were accompanied by a series of unfortunately inaccurate predictions that undermined both his and the magazine's status as consistently reliable political pundits.

Boris predicted, for instance, that Peter Mandelson would survive his first political saga in 1998 over a mortgage (which he didn't) and that there was no way back in 2001 from his second, Hindujagate (which there was, in 2008). He forecast a swift Tory revival after 1997 (which there wasn't) and then in 2001 promised to eat his hat if Tony Blair did not go to the country during the foot-and-mouth crisis. Well he didn't (the election was delayed, for the first time since the Second World War, until the disease was on the retreat). Four years before Gordon Brown became Prime Minister in 2007, he also predicted there would never be another Scot in Number 10. Fortunately, no one much noticed because of the ever-present lashings of humour – and according to his critics, no one took Boris seriously anyway. One said he had created an 'ideological vacuum' on the magazine, another claimed *Spectator* leaders were regarded as so insubstantial that even leader-writers on the sister *Telegraph* newspaper did not bother to read them.

A *Telegraph* writer herself, Cristina Odone wrote when Boris left the *Spectator* in December 2005, shortly after David Cameron became Leader: 'A weekly political magazine ought to have more than circulation in its sights: it should have an impact on the life of the nation. The *Spectator*, hijacked for nearly six years by an editor who saw life as a big joke, instead sidestepped the serious issues of the day and missed out on shaping the most important transformation of the Tory party since Margaret Thatcher.'[17]

Long after leaving the *Spectator*, Boris continued his record of poor punditry when he predicted the Conservatives would win outright in 2010, and of course they didn't.

Odone's judgment may have been harsh but it is fair to say she was not the only one to consider Boris short on gravity. One of his many sidelines was presenting BBC Radio 4's *The Week in Westminster*, which was meant to be a fairly weighty analysis of political events. In October 1999, a few months after he took over at *the Spectator*, he was sacked from the job. Such a dismissal might have tarnished the golden boy's reputation, but Boris deployed his formidable public relations skills to turn an evident negative into a glowing endorsement. Oh, and at least one column. If ever there was proof all publicity is good publicity, this must be it.

The 'brutal sacking' had, he told his readers, been due to his irredeemably posh accent, which had offended the egalitarian ears of the BBC and Radio 4's boss James Boyle. He had thus, Boris argued in the *Spectator*, been fashionably elevated to become a victim of discrimination 'just because I lacked the chameleon skills of Tony Blair, who knows just how to perform a perfect glottal stop and drop an aitch on *Richard and Judy*.' Knowing his audience to a tee, he went on: 'Of course he is right to sack me. What is this voice but the inherited result of aspiration and education, acquired in the belief that it would invariably speed the advancement of its user? [But] if any of us are so lazy and complacent as to refuse to accept the tyrannical voice correctness of our new masters, then we only have ourselves to blame.'[18]

This was splendid stuff – irony, wit and doubled-edged mockery pouring out from the page. Once again, Boris did not mean what he said, certainly not blaming himself. But now readers could be in no doubt but that his dismissal was unjustified on the grounds of talent or commitment but rather the outrageous result of a virulent outbreak of vocal tyranny. There is only one problem: it may not have been true. Boyle actually rather liked his voice, but wanted to make changes for reasons of 'tone and adaptability.' 'I'm afraid Boris just made that up,' says Boyle, who has now left the BBC. 'The only correspondence as I recall (on the matter) was a subsequent letter of apology from him to me. It's all part of the game.'

And Boris loved the game even when it involved turning on those who had helped him most. That included Dominic Lawson, who had given him his first political column and tolerated his foibles. Based on the testimony of a renegade spy called Richard Tomlinson, in January 2001 Boris outed him on the front page of the *Spectator* as Agent Smallbrow of MI6. Lawson, who was by then editor of the sister title, the *Sunday Telegraph*, was not impressed at this gross disloyalty, not least the fact that Boris failed to warn him.

'He knew me, we were friendly – it was intensely annoying. And apart from anything else, if you're running a newspaper with foreign correspondents in strange parts of the world, as I was then, it's potentially a physical threat to them if it's believed that they're working for British intelligence. You can imagine how angry I was. I rang him up, but there was just this sense of "Never mind, Dommers, I just did it for a laugh." And the thing about Boris is that because in some strange way he is adorable, one forgives him. It's not just women; men too fall for that charm. He is not at all a malicious person, and he was on the make as editors are, and he wanted to sell his magazine. He exudes a general bonhomie and it's contagious. After a week of being furious, I didn't give it another moment's thought.'

Boris also repeatedly upset Charles Moore, then editor of the *Daily Telegraph* and arguably his most ardent long-term supporter. The well-known rule within the *Telegraph* group was that any article published in the magazine would also be offered to its sister newspapers without charge, before being made available to other publications for money. 'The *Spectator* was a huge beneficiary of the *Telegraph*'s generosity,' explains Dan Colson. 'But one day I got an hysterical call from Charles Moore. He was incandescent with rage. "That's it, he's done it again! He's sold a piece to the *Daily Mail* for £1,000! We wanted it for the *Telegraph*!" I phoned Boris, who was perfectly aware of the arrangement [on making articles available]. Of course he wasn't there, so I left a message. Half an hour later, Boris rings and starts straight off, "I cannot believe I've been so monumentally stupid. I should be immediately sacked, my pay confiscated retrospectively, marched out to the square outside Canary Wharf, hung, drawn and quartered on the flagstaff." I hadn't had the opportunity to say a word. Well, what could I say after that? I just said, "Let's see if we can retrieve the situation but don't plan any major expenditure in the next 48 hours."'

Again, the 'sack me!' defence worked. It was, rather charitably, decided that Boris had simply 'not been thinking.' The *Mail* was duly warned off and did not run the piece. Boris lived for another day, and the storm, as always, passed. But how did he get away with it that time and so many others? 'I did threaten to sack him at least a couple of times,' admits Colson, 'but he's like a mischievous child. You want to wring his neck but somehow you never do. You still love him. It's like dealing with one of my own kids. His buffoonery is an act, but it works for him. He puts you on the defensive. He's brilliant at it, and he knows he is.'

It was not the only time Moore was driven mad with fury by Boris's pursuit of cash. Although he paid Boris well for his column on the *Telegraph*, which was also the paper that had rescued and promoted his career, in September 2001 Boris sold the serialisation of his political memoirs *Friends, Voters, Countrymen* to the paper's deadly rivals at *The Times*. Sarah Sands, then Charles Moore's deputy, remembers, 'Charles being furious that Boris had done that. I saw Boris with his head in his hands, saying that the *Telegraph* had simply not made a good enough offer. But I thought he'd behaved disgracefully. Yet Marina was very robust in his defence. I've no idea what her argument for doing so was. Perhaps it was just the fact that she loves him, or perhaps pride, or perhaps just the idea that it was nobody else's business.'

Boris also used the 'sack me!' ploy with Conrad Black, who called him one Saturday evening to complain about 'an outrageous' piece in the *Spectator.* 'I asked if he were out for dinner. Boris replied, "No, I am at the top of the most dangerous piste in Gstaad staring into the face of death, about to decide, depending on why you are calling me, if my intention is to survive my next run or not."' Black laughed and forgot his anger. As Boris himself puts it, he has survived more than once thanks to 'the blessed sponge of amnesia' wiping 'the chalkboard of history.'

Indeed, a few months after Boris was elected in Henley, Black and his wife Barbara Amiel hosted a party in honour of the 'Boris Phenomenon' at their 11-bedroom double-fronted mansion in Cottesmore Gardens. Guests included the French ambassador, who compared the whole event to the cult of Pol Pot. There were cardboard cutouts and pictures of Boris everywhere. His treachery in seeking a Parliamentary seat after promising not to was celebrated at considerable expense by the very people he had betrayed; his unreliability was even the subject of a jolly and specially commissioned song performed at the occasion. Boris took the score without asking, annoying its composer. But in Black's eyes, Boris seemed to do no wrong: he had his proprietor dangling off his fingertips and Black looked to be enjoying the ride. Sometimes Boris's thoughtlessness was breathtaking, though.

'It was the *Spectator*'s 175th birthday and there was a grand dinner to celebrate,' recalls one female guest. 'There were drinks first at the *Spectator* offices and the Tory leader Iain Duncan Smith was there, as were all the *Telegraph* grandees such as Algy Cluff and Dan Colson. Conrad Black, this great bear of a man who was Boris's proprietor arrived, and nobody, including Boris who was busy holding court, took any notice. Conrad looked bewildered and so *I* went over, welcomed him and led him in. No one else was going to.

'That same year I also went to the *Spectator* summer party and bumped into Conrad on the pavement outside. He had been there for ten minutes as it was so full inside with all Boris's cronies that he literally couldn't get in. I felt that Boris didn't give a damn about the man who had so indulged him. He never for a moment thought, "The most important person here is the owner, not me."'

Some of the credit for the *Spectator*'s success (without which such lassitude towards Boris would not have been possible) must go to the other key figure in Doughty Street. Los Angeles-born Kimberly Fortier, three years Boris's senior, was an A-list schmoozer and raven-haired force of nature, as well as the magazine's publisher. Dan Colson hired her because 'I figured no one could resist Kimberly Fortier's efforts to sell an ad. Once she was in someone's office, there would be no escape. Unquestionably she was one of the most charming and relentless crusaders I have ever met.' Indeed, she was sexy, flirtatious and did something to middle-aged men. Editor and publisher made a formidable pair.

There are suggestions, though, that Boris was not quite so enamoured. Fortier's job was to make money for the magazine, so she did not take kindly to having to chase its executives to come into work; she also wanted Boris to attend promotional dinners with advertisers or even people prepared to pay for the privilege. Boris hated what he considered to be 'meat-trading.' There were tensions and he would take pleasure in mocking her high falsetto American voice behind her back.

'Boris's relationship with Kimberly was fraught,' confirms Colson. 'She found him very difficult, but loved the guy at the same time.' Boris never takes kindly to being bossed about by women and Kimberly could be rather imperial, barking orders such as 'Boris! Lunch!' pointing to someone she wanted invited to one of the magazine's infamous gatherings. He liked to refer to her disparagingly as 'Little Bo Peep' because she had small fluffy white dogs and would wear outlandish designer costumes. She, in turn, wished he would focus on his job full-time.

It was a forlorn hope: an even bigger prize was now occupying his thoughts. It was no longer the prospect of one day editing a national newspaper – a job for which the *Spectator* was traditionally seen as the natural training ground. No, he was a Young Man in a Hurry for *political* office – having decided at Oxford that it was his ambition to be in the Cabinet by the age of 35. Boris had clearly overshot yet another deadline, but catching up consumed far more of his time than he let on. No doubt he knew he now had much to offer the Conservative party in its hour of electoral need. No longer a callow youth, he was by 2000 a popular national figure, he had already paid his dues in a hopeless constituency and he was married with four kids. But perhaps most helpfully of all, he was the favoured son of the now-dominant Tory tribe: the Eurosceptics.

Once again, though, other people rather than his own hard graft sealed his fate and landed him a safe seat. And what a seat it was. Centred on a prosperous riverside town, Henley-on-Thames has been held by the Conservatives since 1910. Only 37 miles from Westminster, it can be reached in a speed-limit breaking 60 minutes, yet its ambiance is decidedly unmetropolitan. Henley folk rightly view their town as a particularly blessed corner of England and they are determined to keep it that way. The outside world can only envy their good fortune each year at the end of June, when crowds descend on the riverbanks to watch the Royal Regatta; the mansions, with lawns rolling down to the water, command some of the highest property prices in the land.

The lordly Michael Heseltine had served as Henley's distinguished MP for the past 27 years. Clever, glamorous and ambitious, he had risen to the rank of Deputy Prime Minister – and might have become Conservative leader without an ill-timed heart scare in 1997. His political glory reflected on the good burghers of Henley but now he was retiring and the local Conservatives were determined to attract someone of similar calibre to represent them. It was their double good fortune that the replacement was also known for his crop of luxuriant blond hair – even if it did not possess the tamed, swept-back elegance of Heseltine's. (There were other similarities – both had been President of the Oxford Union; both had worked in magazine publishing; both were intensely ambitious and popular with the party grass roots yet somehow detached from them. Both natural showmen, they were also keen to make serious money. And where Boris had been deaf in childhood, Heseltine had struggled with dyslexia.)

As ever with Boris, although he won through in the end his candidacy was not universally welcomed. His selection prompted more than one party resignation and several allegations of dirty tricks. In fact, the rules were again deliberately broken on his behalf to allow him to stand at all.

It started off well. Boris, famous from *Have I Got News For You* and his *Telegraph* column, was actually invited to put his name forward. 'My wife said, "Why don't we invite Boris in as a candidate?"' recalls Peter Sutherland, president of the Henley branch of the Conservatives. 'There was the usual thing of a lot of people thinking he was just a buffoon and had no depth but it proved to be entirely wrong.'

A number of Tories were not convinced. Boris failed to show the constituency elders the respect that some of them felt that they and Henley deserved. Maggie Pullen, then president of the South

Oxfordshire Tories (the party's umbrella organisation in the constituency) was one. 'We were used to Michael Heseltine, a very serious and visionary politician with a high profile. To find a serious politician to follow him, who would climb to the highest levels, but also with experience outside politics, was obviously going to be a challenge.'

By the time of the deadline, there were over 200 applications for the seat and this was quickly whittled down to around 20. 'Then Boris's application came in a week late. It was outrageous,' says Pullen, 'but the committee decided to allow it because he had broad appeal with the members.' Granted such leniency (again), Boris must have quickly realised that he had a captive audience in Henley – a group of largely middle-aged, affluent activists, most of whom were particularly susceptible to his brand of charm. 'Boris was incredibly funny. He came with no preparation at all and with a torn pocket and grubby shoes,' Pullen remembers. 'Everybody thought it was very amusing. We had very good, well-prepared, serious contenders plus a number of local candidates, but of course Boris still got through. But if he hadn't been Boris, he wouldn't have stood a chance considering the lack of effort he put in. He was a star and many Conservatives in Henley follow the *Telegraph*, so he had his fans before he even started. And the fact that he was so anti-European helped – or he allowed people to think he was.'

The clear front-runner had been a clever and ambitious lawyer, David Platt, who assiduously researched and cultivated the constituency. Moderate on Europe and agnostic on the Euro, he was seen by many as an asset to a party still reeling from the 1997 election disaster and needing to reach out beyond its narrow core. He was known for being a witty speaker but one also able to argue his case authoritatively. His many admirers considered him certain to join the political fast track as soon as he entered Parliament. Platt was a formidable opponent for Boris and, as he garnered more votes than him until the final stages, the main obstacle to his success. The other notable candidate was the leading woman contender: another resourceful lawyer, Jill Andrew. Boris was up against stiff competition.

Consequently, his success in reaching the final selection committee shocked some Henley members. 'His grasp of policies, his grasp of Henley was completely non-existent,' said one. 'He hadn't done any research at all. The others had been down, knew where all the villages were, talked to people – not Boris.' But others were seduced by his humour. 'This process is normally so boring it was good to have something that was fun and light,' said a fan. 'He made it fun, and that's why I voted for him.' In any case, in Henley such an omission – usually fatal to an aspiring MP – proved of little consequence. Not least because of the devoted support of such eminent Conservatives as Baroness Buscombe (who was the following year commissioned by Boris to write in the *Spectator*).

The hot and sticky night of the final selection – Thursday, 13 July 2000 – saw an estimated 200 members piling into a smart new hall in the village of Benson to cast their votes. Even here Boris was hard to pin down. At least once, Buscombe was frantically looking for him among the ranks of Jaguars and Mercedes parked outside. There was a palpable sense of excitement and tension. Conservatives who had never previously attended meetings now turned up in force to see Boris the celebrity in close-up. They outnumbered the regular activists, many of whom were evidently not so star-struck.

Jill Andrew remembers turning up that evening in the anteroom made available for candidates and their partners. 'Boris had this huge pile of papers on his desk, which he was furiously thumbing through. And he called out, "Jill, what do you think about waste targets?" He was deliberately trying to unnerve me. I think he wanted me to believe that he knew all about waste and that I would be shown up.' Marina, who knew Platt from her days at Cambridge University, was there too but furiously preparing for a legal case the next day. Only later did she take her place in the front row of the main hall.

'I was at the door that night,' recalls Pullen. 'People were streaming in and saying, "Hello Maggie, we've come to vote for Boris." But I replied: "You haven't even heard him speak yet." Their minds were made up.' Whatever his talents, Boris did not shine as a serious politician that evening; he did excel as a comic act, though. Many laughed uproariously at his bumbling and amusing personal anecdotes while ignoring the lack of political content. Because he was of a certain class, they looked indulgently on his loose tie and untidily rolled-up shirtsleeves.

'Boris looked scruffy, his hair needed a cut but it didn't put people off,' recalls Lorraine Hillier, then vice-chairman of the Henley branch. 'Because of his breeding and his Eton background, it was acceptable. If you saw frayed shirts on anyone else, you'd think they're not very smart but if you're upper class like Boris, you can get away with it.' But there were others present who felt alarmed at the prospect of an MP with what they felt was a thoroughly flippant attitude to serious issues, not to mention the state of his dress. In the general mayhem, it is unlikely that Boris noticed, but a handful of Tory members even walked out in disgust.

'When he was asked a serious question that night about what reforms he would make to the NHS, he told his now-notorious toast story,' recalls Pullen. 'It was about how he had eaten his wife's toast when she was sleeping in hospital after just giving birth, and how disgusted he was that the NHS was unable to provide her with replacement toast when she woke up. He used this as the chief – if not only – reason as to why he wanted to change the health service. Some members found this amusing.' And it did, as he has admitted himself, achieve 'one sneaky psychological trick [of] putting the selectors in mind of Marina.'[19]

'But you can only compare it with the thoughtful, considered answer given by David Platt, who, of course, wasn't married at the time,' continues Pullen. 'But I know people who wouldn't vote for Boris again because of that toast story. It became a cause célèbre locally – three Conservatives in my village alone were furious. Several others have told me that in the general election the following year, they spoilt their ballot paper. They couldn't vote for Boris after that.'

The toast tale was not the only divisive moment that night: another member brought up Guppygate. Astonishingly, this was the only time the issue was raised throughout the selection process. Boris's defiant response actually drew more sympathy than opprobrium. 'As it happens I really, honestly, truly don't think I have any skeletons to speak of in the cupboard,' he recalls saying that night.[20]

Later, Boris related that he had dismissed Guppygate as 'a tale told by an idiot, signifying nothing. But the point was that this chap felt he had me skewered, and for one terrible millisecond it seemed he might be right. [But] his question was so long, so venomous, and so full of recondite detail about a decade-old non-scandal, that by the end of it I guess some people were rather hoping I'd be able to bat the ball back.'[21] And this is what Boris did, with a successful retort along the lines of: 'In so far as you accuse me of keeping this Guppy business a secret, well, that seems a bit thin, since I have actually been questioned about it on a TV game show watched by I don't know how many millions. I don't think you could get much more public than that.'[22]

It was Borissian magic: deflect a serious question, with potentially serious consequences, with a little humour and a good deal of bravado. The questioner was subsequently booed and afterwards became the target of abusive letters and comments for daring to bring up the subject. Most constituents had no idea what he was referring to, seeing his intervention merely as negative and unhelpful. 'It was very difficult for him after that,' recalls Pullen. 'He was almost fussed out of the association. In the end, he gave up his membership. The atmosphere was not very pleasant that night.'

While the supportive Hillier thought Boris had performed impressively, not everyone agreed. The mood became even more febrile when Platt's then girlfriend, Sarah Morris, an interior designer, became distressed at some loudly disparaging remarks about his appearance from a group of rowdy Boris supporters at the front of the hall. But what happened that evening was merely the culmination of a long and troubling story that has never fully come out.

Of course there is no suggestion that Boris knew, let alone approved of the actions of some of his supporters in the preceding weeks. What is clear is that a handful, viewing Platt as a serious threat, had decided to 'go all out for him.' Boris undoubtedly benefited from the false rumours circulating about his chief opponents and the related view – which he allowed to go unchallenged – that he was the only 'sound' contender on Europe.

Like so many that year, the Henley selection took place against the almost-McCarthyite national campaign by supporters of Michael

Portillo to drive out anyone from the party who showed even the slightest Europhile tendencies. Boris's staunch Eurosceptic reputation from his Brussels days as a reporter made him a standard bearer among the Portillistas. Conversely, Platt's pragmatic 'One Nation' style of mild Europhilia undoubtedly made him 'suspect' and a target. He has since told friends how, despite failing to win other safe seats such as Major's former constituency Huntingdon, for similar reasons, 'Henley was undoubtedly the most extraordinary selection process of all.'

'There was great in-fighting between the [Eurosceptic] Conservative Way Forward and the [broadly Europhile] Tory Reform Group at the time,' recalls James Landale, who reported Boris's selection in Henley for *The Times*. 'You would see little old ladies in selection meetings quizzing David Platt, someone who should so evidently have been an MP, with hostile questions supplied by the Eurosceptics. The sort of loaded thing they asked was, "Explain what you once said at a meeting in 1985, as it sounds pro-European to me."'

In a town like Henley, there was another issue. MPs are traditionally required to possess both devoted wives and a brood of appealing children to prove their suitability for politics. With Marina and a four-strong tribe of flaxen-haired offspring in tow, Boris fitted the bill perfectly. Photographs of him triumphantly holding up yet another offspring beside a hospital maternity bed were soon circulating among local Tories, who clucked in approval at this proof of Conservative fecundity. Meanwhile, completely unfounded rumours that Platt was homosexual were also doing the rounds. His girlfriend, Morris, was wrongly said to be mere 'window dressing' – a friend who turned up to give him much-needed heterosexual credentials. In the Eurosceptic press he was referred to as the 'bachelor barrister' who 'supported the Euro' – and consequently became a natural hate figure for one whole wing of the party, including many in Henley. Indeed, so persistent were the reports on his sexuality, that many senior Henley Tories still casually describe Platt – now happily married to Jess Perks, a successful singer – as 'that gay man' to this day. And one gay newspaper reporter sent to Henley to cover the story was reliably said to have actually made a pass at him.

Hillier's memories of the other contenders are typical. 'The favourite was this young man, [Platt], who was very good. They were a bit concerned [at the beginning] that Boris might be a loose cannon. But the other chap – I think he was gay actually. They were concerned about that; they wanted a family person. Somebody did mention it, that that was the trouble. When [Platt] had his final interview there was a young woman who turned up with him, but I think that that was just a friend he'd brought along to make it look like something. That did go against him.'

Peter Sutherland also appears to have been in receipt of false information. 'I don't remember who the other [candidates] were but one of the men was rather inclined to prefer men to women,' he recalls. 'If I tell you I went through the whole of school, university and army without being aware of anyone being homosexual, perhaps I'm rather impervious to things that other people see. Some people are far more observant.' (Ironically, within a few years homosexuality would no longer be seen as politically disadvantageous in the Tory party.)

Of course, no one owns up to spreading these false reports – and there is no suggestion either Hillier or Sutherland was the author of any of them. Or those about Jill Andrew: she was wrongly branded a heavy drinker, who had been wildly promiscuous at university (two mortal allegations for any woman candidate). An anonymous letter was even sent to the local paper, the *Henley Standard*, accusing her of being a friend of Cherie Blair and 'being so indiscreet the party could never feel that its secrets would be safe again.' It went on to allege an even greater crime, that 'on Europe she says different things to different people,' taking money from the Eurosceptics while branding herself, 'a Major loyalist in the Heseltine tradition.' Even her commitment to the party was questioned, with the suggestion she might be concealing her real past from the selectors; suggested questions about her record as a Conservative councillor in Bromley were also circulated anonymously to those in the constituency as well as the other candidates by 'a friend'.

Without a shred of evidence, Boris's opponents found their names smeared in innuendo and suggestion in stark contrast to the growing adulation of the evidently heterosexual and legendarily Eurosceptic Balliol Blond.

It is clear that Boris understood the importance of playing up his marital status. 'My single greatest advantage over David Platt was that I had a wife beaming up at me from the front row, with every appearance of interest, and wearing a suitably colourful flowery coat,' he admitted shortly afterwards.[23] And he must surely have been only too aware of the allegations of dirty tricks during the selection process. He has even dropped a hint that he too might have been the victim of smears from the Europhile camp, although there is little evidence that that was so. 'Well, I don't know if there was any serious effort by allies of Michael Heseltine to interfere with the selection, but I doubt it. As for Hezza, he was far too dignified – and too fly – to get involved.'[24]

Despite the rumour mill, the result was still not a foregone conclusion. It went to a second vote, with Andrew in third place being eliminated and the drawn-out proceedings soon saw a gradual exodus from the increasingly over-heated hall. 'But the ladies from Henley didn't leave,' recalls Pullen. 'They waited until the bitter end to make sure they got their man.' Boris won – apparently to his surprise – by just a handful of votes. It was an emotional moment and not just for team Boris: tears were shed.

'But for Boris, David would have won. He would have been fantastic,' says Pullen. 'I was absolutely devastated for him.' But Hillier explains Boris's appeal on the night: 'The others gave nice presentations and Boris clearly worried some people. When I looked round, I could see that not all the faces were happy when he won, but Boris made you laugh and that's what a lot of people wanted. Many of us realised then he was destined for great things, that he was going to be bigger than Henley, that nothing would hold him back.'

So began Boris's ascent as politico-comedian. It was perhaps the first time that laughter won someone a safe seat, but not the first time that he had profited from humour. Of course, in reality there was far less to divide Boris and David Platt in their views on Europe than might have been apparent but Brussels was still the ultra-toxic and divisive issue in Conservative politics and Boris rather than Platt benefited from the fall-out. It was another stunning display of breathtaking Johnsonian good fortune largely designed by others.

Pullen's husband Richard, another senior local Tory, sums up a common view: 'He didn't deserve it. A good 50 per cent of the activists in the constituency would probably have wanted someone else.' One can only speculate how much effect the rumours had in drumming up support for Boris. There is no doubt they were helpful in getting him selected – and that they also left a bitter taste.

Anthony Howard, a great friend of the Europhile Heseltine who helped him write his memoirs, was clear that 'Boris was jolly lucky to win that seat as it was very much against the will of Heseltine. He had a pro-European candidate lined up, David Platt. Heseltine went through the courtesies and asked Boris to lunch, and they got on alright but it wasn't what he wanted, having a Eurosceptic installed in his own old seat.'

Despite the euphoria, there was one final bizarre twist in what had been a turbulent evening. Feeling sympathy for Andrew, and even more for the golden boy Platt, the Pullens invited the pair back to their home, where they had put champagne on ice to celebrate the expected Platt victory. They presumed that Boris would have been swept off to a victory party by his army of supporters and so did not invite him. But oddly, with the cheers to his triumph still ringing in his ears, Boris did not embark on raucous celebration. They later found out that he had been left largely alone, with just Marina for company. It was already clear that he had not won all the hearts and minds of Henley.

The Pullens were fully supportive of Boris as their MP although there were a number of detractors who continued to feel let down. Once again, he would attract a hoard of devoted supporters for whom he could do no wrong. He was charming, funny, energetic and complimentary – but in truth, no unifying force. Importantly, the critics included those outside the constituency who had once been his most ardent fans. Max Hastings, now editor of the *Evening Standard*, had tried to dissuade Boris from going for a seat. Now he had landed a safe one, Hastings ran a leader that displayed a dramatic shift in his view of his one-time protégé. Hastings had been researching into

Boris's character with some of his former teachers. Tucked away at the bottom of the page, few may have noticed the Hastings' verdict. In any case, it's likely that Hastings only had one reader in mind when he placed it in the paper:

> Boris Wooster
>
> The selection of Boris Johnson, the *Spectator* editor, as the Tory candidate for Michael Heseltine's Henley constituency, confirms the Tory Party's increasing weakness for celebrity personalities over the dreary exigencies of politics. Johnson, for all his gifts, is unlikely to grace any future Tory cabinet. Indeed, he is not known for his excessive interest in serious policy matters, and it is hard to see him grubbing away at administrative detail as an obscure, hardworking junior minister for social security. To maintain his funny man reputation he will no doubt find himself refining his Bertie Wooster interpretation to the point where the impersonation becomes the man.[25]

Boris was straight on the phone to the *Standard*, and in Hastings' absence vented his fury on a shocked 'uncle' Don Berry. 'Boris had always been the lovable buffoon – that was how he had always got out of a whole lot of trouble; that was his public image,' recalls Berry. 'But now I was seeing the steely side of Boris. He was extremely serious and extremely angry. He kept demanding to know who had written it. I wouldn't tell him. It was in any case a direct reflection of Max's views that Boris couldn't help playing to the crowd. I tried to calm him down by saying it was meant as a bit of fun. He obviously felt it was going to harm his political rise; someone was out to get him. Afterwards, I asked myself, is this really the same lovable Boris?'

In a far more placatory mood, Boris also rang up Pullen to say he knew she was not 'happy' at the outcome. Shortly afterwards, the pair met in London, where they agreed to work together. 'Boris made his peace with me, and I did everything I could to make it work from then on,' she explains. 'As the constituency got used to him, things settled down. You had some people who just loved Boris and we probably made more money at dinners and other events because of him. When he gave up, there were a lot of people who were genuinely sad but you still had Tories in the constituency who wouldn't ever vote for him.'

At the same time, Boris set about soothing ruffled feathers, pouring praise on Jill Andrew. 'To his credit, Boris wrote in his book that I was far better than him, but that I was a chick and Tory associations don't "groove to chicks,"' she says, although the compliment was marred by the fact he got her name wrong. What is disturbing, though, is that in large part because of the dirty tricks in Henley, both Andrew and Platt subsequently gave up their quest for seats, depriving the Parliamentary party of two considerable talents.

Somewhat ostentatiously, Boris also paid homage to Michael Heseltine and the most colourful moment in his political career when he brandished the Parliamentary mace at Labour left-wingers. In March 2001, he seized the less-impressive Henley Town Council's version at the Mayor's Annual Dinner, providing an arresting photograph for the front page of the *Henley Standard*. Not for the last time would Boris court and play the local press with all the skills and insider understanding of a consummate journalist.

When the general election was called in mid-May, Boris handed over the reins of the *Spectator* to his deputy, suspended his *Telegraph* column and began his campaign in Henley in earnest. Many in the constituency were allowed to believe that when he became MP – as seemed certain – he would permanently resign from both posts to focus on his political life. Boris went down well on the streets of Henley, providing plenty of laughter. When one woman offered him her vote, he enchanted her with the reply: 'But madam, why?' Life with Boris certainly seemed to be more fun – he was the light relief in a tale of almost unremitting Tory gloom. On occasion, it was only Heseltine who would sit through Boris's joke-fests straight-faced, valiantly trying (and failing) to introduce a serious discussion of policy.

Boris endured the candidate's usual lot of door-slamming and ferocious dogs, but his fame and bonhomie mostly drew handshakes, back slapping and outbreaks of general geniality. He discovered that appearances on a programme such as *Have I Got News For You* genuinely made people feel that they knew him; that he was one of them. In the end his TV career may have proved his greatest electoral asset, even trumping Marina and the children in boosting his popularity.

AA Gill was dispatched by the *Sunday Times* to cover the fun. First, he insulted Henley as a 'faux rural' area, where the main industry was 'cutting barrels in half and stuffing them with pansies' and then he started on Boris, or 'Quisling Boris,' as he called him for crossing the border from journalism into politics. There followed an amusing series of canvassing mishaps and the soon-to-be notorious conclusion: 'Boris Johnson is without doubt the very worst putative politician I've ever seen in action. He is utterly, chronically useless – and I can't think of a higher compliment.'[26]

At last it came to election day itself: Thursday, 7 June, and a final tour of the constituency after a breakfast of decaying Asda cheese – the only edible item left in the fridge of his rented cottage in Swyncombe. Later, following a nap and supper at the Shepherd's Hut in Ewelme, Marina and Boris made their way to Icknield Community College in Watlington for the count. It was a gruelling night for the Conservatives generally, unexpectedly losing affluent southeast England seats such as Guildford to the Liberal Democrats while failing to make inroads into Blair's 1997 majority.

The count dragged on and on, past two, three then four in the morning towards the sort of territory normally occupied by hard-to-call marginal seats rather than the foregone conclusions of a constituency like Henley. The Liberal Democrats allowed themselves a little cheer by noticing a rise in support in some areas, but there was never any real doubt. Watching the piles of Boris votes grow ever-bigger, he allowed himself to let rip with an enormous yawn, unveiling his epiglottis to a Press Association photographer.

As dawn broke outside, Boris was confirmed as Henley's new MP – albeit with a majority down to just under 8,500 compared to Heseltine's 11,167 of 1997. But it was more than enough. Boris advised the poor souls still in the hall with him to 'go back home and prepare for breakfast.'[27] In a rare quote, Marina said she and the rest of the family were 'very proud. I am so pleased for him. I think he will be a brilliant MP and I am looking forward to being an MP's wife.'[28] But Anna Ford from the BBC – whom Boris had been ogling all evening – was not so sold on the idea. 'How can you expect to look after this constituency,' she asked him in all seriousness, 'when you can't even look after yourself?'[29] The bookies took a different view of his prospects, though, immediately setting the odds on his becoming Conservative Party Leader at 50:1.

Chapter Nine
On Yer Bike!
MP, 2001–2004

Boris found his first day in Parliament on the Tuesday after the June 2001 election like starting at a new school. He was by far the most famous among the batch of Tory newcomers but in turn he also knew a few of his fellow novices. David Cameron was a familiar face from Eton and Oxford, Mark Field had been active in the Oxford Union and Hugo Swire, although older than the others, was also an Old Etonian. When they met over coffee and biscuits following an induction meeting in one of the Commons committee rooms with the Chief Whip James Arbuthnot, many greeted him like old friends.

It was not only his fame that set him apart from the other new Conservative MPs that day, however: he was about to take yet another 'death wish' decision that could derail his fledgling political career. William Hague had already resigned as Conservative Leader after his party's drubbing at the polls, sparking a five-way race to succeed him. Iain Duncan Smith was a leading candidate and standard-bearer for the Thatcherite legacy (and had previously been praised by Boris as the 'future of Conservatism.') Boris was expected to back him or Michael Portillo, although the latter was now losing some of his lustre through an ill-judged campaign. Portillo was accused by some party supporters of 'treachery and trickery' and specifically of having undermined William Hague while he was Leader. Margaret Thatcher was also angered at what she thought were Portillo's attempts to use her in his campaign, when in fact she did not support him.

Boris had conversely praised father-of-four IDS for being young, affable and able – and having 'oodles' of children (always a virility badge worthy of praise in his book). But unaccountably for many, Boris immediately threw his weight – and that of the *Spectator* – not behind IDS, but behind the only pro-European in the pack, Ken Clarke. He was the only new entrant to do so. A week after he was elected to Henley on a Eurosceptic tide of support, Boris plastered the front cover of his magazine with: 'The Case for Ken. Peter Oborne says Clarke is a winner'. As the contest drew to the final vote in September that year, Boris's consistent support culminated in a rallying leader entitled 'THE APPEAL OF CLARKE'. 'By choosing Ken Clarke,' it read, 'Tories would be addressing their most serious defects in the eyes of the electorate: that they are only really interested in their own problems, and in themselves.' Clarke, who never had any real chance with the party at large, lost the final ballot to IDS (60 to 40 per cent in the popular vote).

On more than one level, it was a strange and even provocative decision to back him. Boris and Clarke were seen to be poles apart on Europe and Clarke's views on the subject were always going to count against him in the Conservative party of that time, whatever his obvious talents. Politically, IDS or Portillo seemed far more at one with Boris. So why did he opt for Clarke? Was it a case of the journalist in Boris trumping the politician? Certainly it made a better story to back the 'Big Beast' although a lot of other journalists attributed his choice to a 'streak of contrariness'. Others believed that Boris identified a kindred spirit in Clarke and genuinely liked and hoped to influence him. 'There's that issue of discipline, they both shoot from the hip,' says one senior commentator. 'They both like being contrary, they both have affectations. If Ken had been leader, he would, like Boris, have struggled with the discipline.' But what would this do to Boris's reputation in the Commons as a serious and consistent Eurosceptic? Indeed, was it the beginning of a realisation that he needed to move on from self-destructive European sectarianism and align with a more liberal, (Islington-friendly) broad-brush political creed? What seems most likely was that this *was* the start of another reinvention of the Boris brand, risky though it was.

After the event, Boris was worried that his vote for Clarke had damaged his career and repeatedly asked others whether they thought it had. Several Eurosceptic MPs who had previously considered Boris 'sound' now saw him as suspect and 'unserious'. There were questions of consistency and loyalty. Did Boris believe in anything? However entertaining, his own rendition of his particular Conservative credo failed to answer all the questions. His beliefs were, he said, 'free-market, tolerant, broadly libertarian (though perhaps not ultra-libertarian), inclined to see the merit of traditions, anti-regulation, pro-immigrant, pro-standing on your own two feet, pro-alcohol, pro-hunting, pro-motorist and ready to defend to the death the right of [football manager] Glenn Hoddle to believe in reincarnation.'[1]

In the meantime, he was struggling with the drudgery of back-bench life. With so few new MPs to choose from – the Tories had added only a single net seat to their Parliamentary tally – the new intake had been swiftly put to work. The whips ensured that Boris would be broken into Parliamentary ways by being treated the same as the other new boys and girls. He was assigned to a standing committee on the Proceeds of Crime Bill, a giant 462-clause piece of legislation that set up the Assets Recovery Agency and was packed with complex new provisions on money laundering. The committee's job was to grind through every letter of the bill, line by line, two-and-a-half hours a day every Tuesday and Thursday over two whole months. It was an important task, but not a glamorous one and a rather dreary comedown compared to Boris's celebrity outside life.

As Mark Field, who sat on the same committee and is still an MP, recalls: 'It wasn't very Boris. He was so thinly spread with all his other commitments, too. I remember thinking back then that he wouldn't last more than two terms here.' Boris was also unused to the committee's early starts (nine sharp!) and did not always make them, or indeed all of the sessions. It seems the experience confirmed him in his dislike of detail, even when it comes to policy, and by association, his antipathy to a backbench existence. Boris did not pop up on one of the prestigious select committees, such as Home Affairs (which Cameron joined almost straightaway), which are often seen as useful showcases for rising young talent. Gradually the feeling began within Westminster that Boris, like his hero Disraeli, was similarly a 'loose cannon on the backbenches, whose devotion to self was greater than that to his party or his leader.'[2]

Field had not been a particular friend of Boris's at university, but he felt sympathy for him now. 'For the first two or three years here, he was like a fish out of water,' he recalls. 'Boris was a big personality as editor of the *Spectator*, writing a *Telegraph* column and appearing a lot on TV. He was put in a similar category to [businessman] Archie Norman and [Olympian] Sebastian Coe, well-known outside and subject to an institutional put down inside from older Parliamentarians, people from the other side of the House, even from the Whips Office. It's one of the worst elements of this place, and Boris fell victim to it.'

His cause was not helped when he allowed his mobile phone to ring in the chamber during a debate on the Bristol heart babies' scandal, earning him a rebuke from the Deputy Speaker. But perhaps what really counted against Boris was the fact that – against all expectations – he did not give up the *Spectator*, the *Telegraph* column, his TV appearances or his motoring column on *GQ*. It is also fair to say that he would on occasion rile his colleagues by flaunting whatever Maserati, Ferrari or Bentley he was test-driving that month. His multi-tasking did not go down well in his constituency either. 'There were people who were angry that he had short-changed Henley,' recalls Richard Pullen. 'He never gave up the *Telegraph* or *Spectator* and he did say he would.'

To try and placate his critics, and illustrate his commitment to politics over journalism, Boris told the *Henley Standard* in October 2001 that he had given up part of his salary at the *Spectator* to reflect his reduced role there. But that is not Dan Colson's recollection. 'I don't recall any discussion about a pay cut after he was elected,' says Colson, who settled his salary. 'Boris always came in and said he was impecunious [and] he always did very well in negotiations – don't worry about him. My assistant at the *Telegraph* had a picture of Boris behind her desk; I asked her to take it down – it wasn't helpful when I was renegotiating his pay.' Even Stuart Reid, ever the loyal deputy, is critical of Boris for not stepping down from the magazine. 'Boris promised Conrad that he wouldn't run for Parliament, and Henley that he would give up the *Spectator*,' he says. 'He betrayed them both.'

There were also mutterings of *folie de grandeur* when he publicly invoked the names of two of Britain's most admired prime ministers in his defence. Their illustrious careers were proof, he argued, that there was no 'conflict of interest' in him continuing to serve as editor of the *Spectator* while being an MP. 'It is not an unprecedented career path – I could mention Winston Churchill and Disraeli,' Boris declared. 'My plan is not to leave my job, not least because I would be broke.' (That last comment might surprise Boris's many other employers as well as Marina's clients as a barrister. By now the couple must have together been pulling in several hundred thousand pounds a year.)

Both Churchill and Disraeli had indeed been writers in flurries of activity throughout their lives, although neither had edited a weekly magazine. But these exalted comparisons would not have surprised those who had worked closely with Boris, as he was known to be a devoted student of both. And indeed, Boris also drew on Churchill's example privately in other ways, telling the influential wife of a senior Tory politician that he held a similar feeling of destiny to be leader of his country. Far from laughing at this presumptuousness, she recognised his leadership qualities and encouraged him to pursue his dream.

Meanwhile, political commentators and politicians alike saw it differently and shook their heads. Practically to a man they predicted that Boris would either be forced out of the *Spectator* or fail to build a career in the Commons – or possibly both. But Boris continued to keep all his plates spinning. Just. His life at this point was full to overflowing; few could have stood the pace. One associate remarked that even thinking about Boris's huge range of commitments at this time made him feel 'physically sick.' Boris himself would admit sometimes to being down and overwhelmed. Occasionally, he would be found asleep on the sofa in his Commons office. With four children, the youngest only two years old, he got very, very tired indeed. He is rarely ill – and does not tolerate illness in others – but he does enjoy his food and now in his late thirties was finding it harder to avoid the consequences. Boris's weight is linked to his state of mind and the stresses were beginning to tell. 'There is absolutely no one, apart from yourself, who can prevent you, in the middle of the night, from sneaking down to tidy up the edges of that hunk of cheese at the back of the fridge,' he wrote.[3]

This was when he discovered the benefits of a half-hour jog. He has been a devoted runner ever since, often making it a theatrical event with an array of colourful surfer shorts. He also began to cycle around London to save time in the congestion, making phone calls with one hand while steering with the other. No moment went unused. His mobile 'office' occasionally gave rise to rows with pedestrians who thought it was dangerous but he knew all too well the public relations dividend of being photographed regularly on two wheels. It re-aligned him with liberal, good, caring, free-spirited people with a life rather than boss-eyed right-wingers obsessed with fighting EU sub-clauses, who needed to get one. (Boris, with neat hair in his own Jaguar, for instance, conjures up a very different image.) It was another, but important stage in the gradual Islingtonian rebranding but amid all this activity, it is hard to imagine how he ever made time for the everyday needs of a young family. 'The fatal thing is boredom,' he explained, 'so I try to have as much on my plate as possible.'[4]

It is therefore not surprising that he did not work the tearooms and bars of Westminster – a convention observed by most ambitious MPs intent on building up support. In any case, Boris finds making genuine conversation with people – and particularly women on an equal professional footing – difficult. Indeed, one female assistant talks of how she dreaded car journeys with him because of the long, awkward silences. He is better talking *at* people in performance-mode than talking *to* them over a coffee table. To this day, he struggles with private dinner parties, for instance, often offering to make a speech rather than be cornered in the agony of a personal 'cosy' chat. Clubbing up with possible future 'Johnsonites' was therefore never going to be his forte. Nor did Boris, like many of his contemporaries, 'keep in touch' through email – 'I don't believe in it,' he said. Meanwhile, Cameron, having been a special adviser, already knew the place 'to his fingertips' and was busy establishing his credentials in the tearooms and elsewhere as a very modern, professional, 'in-touch' politician and the emerging leader of a like-minded group.

When in Parliament – as opposed to the *Spectator* – Boris was frequently to be found in his office, alone. It was not a room where other members felt welcome if they dropped in –with the occasional exception of fellow Tory MP Andrew Tyrie – despite the fact that there was plenty of room. A former aide explains: 'I think Boris would have gone completely mad if he'd had to share his office. He liked being on his own for significant periods of time.'

The then accommodation whip (responsible for doling out desk space to new and existing MPs according to rank) insists Boris was granted no special favours. And yet, for a brand new member he was allocated a particularly generous office with a fireplace, green sofa and yet another capacious desk. Even more unusually, he bagged a smaller, but separate annexe room for his staff on the floor below in the Norman Shaw North office building and so was left in sole occupancy upstairs. In contrast, despite all the important jobs Peter Mandelson had already done for the Labour party when elected in 1992, he was allocated a 'narrow and rather dark room' in an adjacent block and had to share with another MP.

Boris appointed Melissa Crawshay-Williams as his secretary after meeting her at a Conservative dinner. From the off, she had to cope with the enormous workload such a well-known and multi-tasking MP generated. 'I worked very long hours for Boris,' she recalls. 'There was a minimum of 200 emails a day, plus quite often 200 letters. His mailbag was twice the size of a normal MP's. Sometimes I'd be up to four in the morning dealing with it all; sometimes other secretaries would have to help me. Eighty per cent of the time, working with him was wonderful.' But in common with other former colleagues, she also remembers his temper. 'The other 20 per cent was terrible – Boris would swear a lot when he was frustrated, but it was quite contained and then he'd move on.' She remains loyal to her boss but his temper is still an issue with many he has worked with: he frequently bangs the table in anger, on at least one occasion so hard that he nearly broke a bone.

Despite this frantic activity, Boris was making little impact in the Commons. With his bonhomie, charm and quick wit, he was widely expected to become an instant star yet he gave only two speeches in his first five months. By convention, new MPs heap praise on their predecessors in their maiden speech but in his, on 12 July, Boris chose an oddly comic – and perhaps disrespectful – way of 'honouring' Michael Heseltine. He compared himself to Simba (the cub in the Disney cartoon, *Lion King*) to Heseltine's regal Mufasa. It was a puzzling comparison, despite the obvious reference to the former deputy prime minister's celebrated locks. The movie sees Mufasa killed and Simba forced into exile after a coup involving his treacherous uncle and a pack of hyenas. Unlike Cameron in his maiden address a fortnight earlier, Boris was not able to draw on any deeper political experience – or observe some of the finer Parliamentary niceties.

In his first four years as an MP, Boris managed to attend only slightly over half of the votes and he was ranked 525th out of 659 MPs on attendance. By his second Parliament, from 2005 to 2008, this had slipped further still to just 45 per cent, a cause of resentment among his colleagues and party whips. It perhaps did not help that within four months of being elected to Westminster he had followed the first Johnsonian rule that all life's events must be exploited for financial gain in publishing the first of his political memoirs. *Friends, Voters, Countrymen* was a slight volume, covering merely his selection and election as there was nothing else to say, but it was fun and pacy. At the launch party in Politicos, the Westminster political bookshop, Boris secretly teased his publishers and mocked his own insubstantial volume in ancient Greek – repeatedly saying '*mega biblion, mega kakon*' or 'a great book is a great evil.' No one could imagine, even so, how he had found the time to write it. No doubt it helped that he was given more 'slack' by the whips than other, less glittering MPs. 'We didn't see that much of him,' confirms the former MP and whip Andrew Mackay. 'He had a pretty full-time second job. But because he looked so different from everyone else, when he was here everybody noticed it. A drabber backbencher might have to be here full-time to be noticed as much as Boris half-time.'

For a maverick, he rebelled against his party a puny five times in his seven years as an MP. When he did so, it was usually taking a more liberal line than the leadership (and, indeed, his own previous positions), such as backing the repeal of the infamous Section 28 ban on the promotion of homosexuality and voting in favour of giving legal status to change of gender for transsexuals.

When he did appear in the chamber, Boris's style seemed particularly unfit for purpose and he came over as awkward and exposed. He would annoy rather than amuse by addressing other members as 'old boy' rather than the 'honourable gentleman' that etiquette required. What's more, he looked fidgety sitting on the Commons' green benches for more than a few minutes, once acidly noting, 'It is a great pleasure to follow Dr Palmer. I congratulate him on speaking for more than half an hour.' Labour MPs took delight in taking shot at his divided loyalties and the rumours soon circulating about Boris's 'other' interests: 'I am happy to follow Mr Johnson, who is glancing at his watch. Clearly, he wants to go and put the *Spectator* to bed and I am sure that he will do it very well,' said one, back in February 2002.

Unwisely, Boris once peppered a long speech about holiday entitlement in 2003 with classical references to Hammurabi, Moses, Plato and Cicero. 'He's definitely a credit to Eton education,' said the Labour MP Anne McGuire in a tone that suggested this was not necessarily a good thing. Indeed, in the days before Old Etonians came to dominate the Tory front bench, Boris's schooling was frequently commented on by the other side and used regularly to taunt him. The old Labour Parliamentary warhorse Dennis Skinner passed comment on Etonians being 'educated beyond their intelligence.' Eye-rolling and bumbling routines did not pass muster in this environment; on the Commons floor, there was no indulgence of the golden boy.

Still he persisted with his buffoonish bag of tricks, including the hair mussing. 'It's the Hair behind the Chair again,' chortles Mackay. 'When a young David Owen was about to come into the chamber as foreign secretary in the [1970s] Callaghan government, he was seen combing his hair behind the Speaker's chair. It showed a vanity, just like with Boris. The only difference was that he was seen *ruffling* his hair. It's designer scruff!' But the barnet routine did not allay the nerves, and after 18 months Boris conceded that he was still to 'land any blows' on Blair – in Parliament, at least. 'The Speaker won't call you unless you stand up every time. Your heart is thudding and you try to remember your question. I asked Patricia Hewitt a question on nuclear energy, but I wrapped it in so many subordinate clauses that she was able to knock it straight back,' he told an interviewer in 2002.[5] No wonder he found it easier to score political points in the familiar territory of the pages of the *Spectator*.

Sensing something not quite right, the newspaper sketch-writers, who can define MPs' careers with putdowns or praise, began to watch him with care. The cult of Boris had built him up as a showman par excellence, but somehow one audience that perhaps really mattered to him was left cold. Quentin Letts, sketch-writing doyen and a former colleague of Boris's, explains why he failed to shine.

'He was terrible in the chamber, an echoing parody of himself. The Commons sees through you in a way that other institutions don't. So they could see through the accent, and the fact that he was trying to ventilate false anxieties about matters in which he wasn't really very interested. The reaction was quite often silence. You see, Boris isn't angry. You've got to be angry: you've got to feel things as an MP, but there's no soul, no church in him. No belief. Most people don't just go into politics out of vanity, but maybe he has. The only good speech I ever heard him give in Parliament was not even in the chamber but in a minor debate in Westminster Hall that nobody attended. It was on pig slaughter and – because he has a slight resentment against the big state – he was outraged on behalf of his constituents about the regulatory burden and so had actually done the research.

'It's not a class thing. [The new MP] Jacob Rees-Mogg, who's similar in some ways, holds the Commons. He's very clever, he's done his homework, and he *feels* it. Labour MPs stand up and ask for more. Boris can make very good party conference speeches but the Commons is a different arena. You're being challenged. You're quite often playing to an empty house, which is difficult, or you're looking straight at your opponents. Boris was obviously good on *HIGNFY* but then that was as a show-business character. He's not very good when he's up against an audience of real people, looking at Labour MPs from places like Mansfield and Nottingham with whom he has no affinity at all. You can't suddenly start making wisecracks in a Bertie Woosterish manner – it doesn't work. Gravity is unavoidable in the House of Commons and he didn't have it.'

Boris's difficulties in adapting were all the more marked because of the contrast with his predecessor, Michael Heseltine. The fact was that Boris's style – so brilliant on TV – lent itself, when it came to the Commons, to local or esoteric detail better than to national-stage policy. He was becoming stuck in a side role. James Landale of the BBC observes: 'MPs like the crisp, efficient wit of William Hague, not the bumbling of Boris interspersed with the occasional one-liner. He is a much better writer on paper than in person. He can be too slow and elaborate in speech.' Even Andrew Mitchell, who had done much to propel Boris into politics, is guarded about his ability as a Parliamentary performer. 'The House of Commons is a tremendous leveller. Boris was best either when he was being incredibly funny or when he was standing up for his constituents,' he says. After he had resigned his seat in 2008, even Boris described his own performances as 'crap.'

Eager to win more favourable reviews, he would on occasion offer some of the more critical journalists such as AA Gill the chance to write on the *Spectator*. He won over Matthew Parris – who already wrote for the magazine and whose good opinion was particularly invaluable – by accident or design another way. 'There is a side of him which is possibly calculating or just humanly generous or a complicated alloy of both, but is capable of doing very big favours for people in circumstances where it is not immediately obvious that there is a return for him,' says Parris. 'I once made a Boris-style cock-up of forgetting that I was speaking at a book launch. I realised only 25 minutes before it started and I simply couldn't go. In despair, I rang Boris, who happened to be in the area and he dropped everything and did it for me. True, I was a *Spectator* columnist but I had never done him any particular favour. True, it was no skin off his nose. But because of that one incident, I've always stayed my hand when I've been contemplating attacking him in anything other than a routine sort of way. This is the corruption of journalism – he purchased my goodwill.'

It was nevertheless a disappointing start. Boris had vowed in *Spectator* promotional literature to 'stir the blood and stiffen the sinews' of the Tory faithful, but his relationship with IDS was visibly strained. It was not helped by the fact that he barely bothered to disguise his lack of support or respect. Within a year, in September 2002, the *Spectator* was running the line that the Conservative party was in chaos under IDS's leadership and predicting he could soon be replaced by the sacked party chairman, David Davis. He even commissioned a front cover from Steve Bell depicting Michael Portillo peeing on IDS's head. Stuart Reid was surprised at how far Boris would push it. 'I thoroughly approved but I wouldn't have dared do it myself,' he admits.

Naturally this was seen as mutiny by IDS's people, who were quoted anonymously in the press threatening to 'deal with' Boris although the chief anti-IDS piece again carried Peter Oborne's by-line rather than Boris's – conveniently allowing him to distance himself, if necessary. There was now, however, a real danger of a formal challenge to the leader, who had disastrously dubbed himself the 'quiet man.' Yet with bitter irony, the more IDS sunk into the mire, the more he *needed* Boris because he recognised that his tormentor was one of the few stars his party could muster. The *HIGNFY* headliner – who had broken down the barriers of party, class, age and apathy through TV performances now considered popular culture classics – was of far more use onside than cast into the wilderness. Such was his popularity that he could command £25,000 per appearance.

Fan clubs and websites in praise of Boris were springing up all over the place – run by both Home Counties mothers and northern university students. (The Durham University Fan Club was just one that had as its mission 'the admiration, promotion and discussion of Boris Johnson.') Plus which other MP, let alone Tory MP, would merit an indulgent interview in *GQ*? It was an opportunity seized by Boris to peddle his ever-clever concoction of jollity and laddishness. 'I try to cheer people up. Life isn't all that bad,' he had said, in a sideswipe at what he considered a particularly joyless Labour regime before promising a no doubt receptive audience that voting Tory would mean 'your car will go faster, and your girlfriend will have a bigger bra size.' The joke went down so well it endured several more outings. Here was a Conservative who actually appeared to be fun. Only later in the interview does he let slip a far more revealing remark: 'I make what I think is a very cunning calculation. If you clown around, you may be able to creep up on people with your ideas, and spring them on them unexpectedly.'[6]

It was this lightness of touch, this ability to reach the politics-averse – so rare in politicians – that made him such a valuable commodity. Michael Portillo, the defeated leadership contender, advised Boris to choose between 'politics and comedy.' But Boris could not see why. And while Portillo's career was fading fast, Boris's star seemed to shine ever more brightly – at least with the public at large. There was even the first mention in print that he might be destined one day to become Prime Minister, as Tories despaired of IDS ever wounding Blair any more than his predecessor, William Hague.[7]

So Boris's 'punishment' for his disloyalty was nugatory – a summons for a 'conversation' about the *Spectator*'s 'unhelpful' take. The more significant outcome was that he was to attend IDS every Wednesday morning, ostensibly to work on preparing him for Prime Minister's Questions but in reality for a much broader purpose. With Boris came the tantalising prospect of some of his stardust rubbing off on his lacklustre leader and he continued to be brought in even when he committed another act of gross party disloyalty in the *Spectator* only a couple of months later.

Boris had gathered eminent political journalists into the magazine's tiny third-floor dining room, as he did every autumn, to discuss the *Spectator* Parliamentarian of the Year awards. As editor, one of his most important jobs was to conjure up an appropriate list of recipients. In 2002, he arrived characteristically late but fatally without his own favoured options. This may well be why over a raucous lunch he agreed to back Tony Blair as *Spectator* Parliamentarian of the Year – an astonishing decision, not only because he was a *Labour* Prime Minister who had inflicted two catastrophic defeats on Boris's party but also because he was widely seen to hold Parliament in contempt.

'By the time Boris got there, Blair's name had already come up,' recalls George Jones, one of those present. 'He didn't like it but he didn't have any ideas of his own. It was certainly something he came to regret.' At the awards ceremony – which fortunately Blair was unable to attend – Boris went on to heap praise on the man he dubbed 'the coolest cat in town': 'Time after time, the Labour benches threaten to rebel, and he quells them as Zeus quells sea nymphs.'

It was all too much for the Conservative grandees. 'The Blair award directly clashed with his political career,' says Jones. 'It dramatically highlighted once again the problem of having an active politician editing a magazine like the *Spectator*. When he got the raspberry from senior Tories he then tried to offload the blame.' Indeed, Frank Johnson, the son of an East End pastry cook who was Boris's predecessor as *Spectator* editor, and who had relentlessly teased Boris in his Parliamentary sketch and elsewhere, was the chosen target. Boris wrote in the *Telegraph* on 12 December: 'In a fit of madness, a group error for which I principally blame Frank Johnson, the jurors of the *Spectator* parliamentarian awards gave [Blair] not the wooden spoon, not the booby prize, but the Top Gong.'

Such was the desperation of the IDS team, even this latest outrage was overlooked, however. For the next year, until the Leader's defenestration in autumn 2003, Boris continued to be asked to advise IDS alongside the other two leading young Turks, David Cameron and George Osborne. It confirmed his importance within the party and was in fact a great compliment. But as ever Boris was unable – or unwilling – to work as part of a team and many opportunities were lost. Blair was soon on the retreat over a botched reshuffle, the Hutton inquiry into David Kelly's death, a row over taxes and another over the Euro – but it was largely the Liberal Democrats who were taking advantage of his woes. Meanwhile, IDS needed all the help he could find but it did not come from Boris.

'Osborne and Cameron worked hard on finding subjects on which to press Blair and scripting the questions and turned up on time,' recalls a source close to Duncan Smith. 'But Wednesday was press day at the *Spectator* so Boris would turn up for five minutes, read the newspaper, do a routine on the lines of "marvellous! This will really slay Blair" before disappearing. The rest of the team worked for another three or four hours. His contribution was, frankly, negligible.' What's more, it appears that the man known for his one-liners failed to deliver any for his chief. It was Osborne who came up with the jokes, such as they were.

'Iain Duncan Smith told me that he thought neither of us was getting [Boris's] full attention and what were we going to do about it,' recalls Conrad Black. 'I replied that I was satisfied with what I was getting but that it couldn't go on forever.' Stuart Reid also seemed to be becoming increasingly unhappy as Boris's absences became ever longer and more frequent now that he was also an MP. He even wrote a cryptic piece in the *Telegraph* widely interpreted as relating to Boris. 'Now that Lent is here, one's thoughts turn to one's own failings, and, perhaps more keenly, to the failings of others,' he wrote '[I]t is apparently licit to enjoy high-wire acts, provided that part of your enjoyment does not lie in the possibility that one of the acrobats might fall and injure himself, or worse. Ergo: no normal human may watch a high-wire act without sinning. Something to consider when the circus next comes to town.'[8]

Nor did Boris's constituents feel at this point that they were getting a 'fair squeeze of the sauce bottle,' as Boris himself put it. His early coverage in the *Henley Standard* was minimal, particularly compared to local heroes such as the rowing champion Steve Redgrave. He did finally come to greater prominence in town nine months later, in March 2002, but for someone else's actions rather than his own: he was hit in the face by a bread roll as he addressed the Mayor of Henley's annual dinner one Friday evening. More than a hundred local dignitaries at the Henley Town Centre witnessed a Labour councillor, Eleanor Hards, throw a mini-baguette at him from her seat, three places down the table. For a while he was visibly shaken but later rallied with the quip: 'I am not upset. I'm flattered. It shows the Tories are on a roll!'[9] Councillor Hards explained that she had merely taken Boris 'at his word' when he had said in his speech: 'Many people ask me "what policies the Conservatives have to offer?" At the risk of being hit by a bread roll I shall tell you some of my ideas.' No one thought her joke very funny, though.

Indeed, the incident provided Boris with an opportunity: it attracted publicity, sympathy and admiration for him and marked the start of a new relationship between Henley and its MP. From then on, he courted the local paper and its readers more assiduously, flattering its young political reporter Tom Boyle by dubbing him the 'Woodward and Bernstein' of Henley. On another occasion, he ensured ever-greater loyalty from the paper by praising its 'attention to detail' and 'certain gentleness in outlook.'[10] He took care to refer to the *Henley Standard* supremo as 'my real editor' rather than the likes of Charles Moore on the *Telegraph*; he wrote a column for the paper too – although not as often as promised.

Boris learned how best to flatter not just local journalists – if courted correctly, often an MP's most devoted friends – but also his proud constituents. One of his best lines, confident that the *Telegraph* was perused avidly in Henley, was: 'If Amsterdam or Leningrad vie for the title of Venice of the North, then Venice – what compliment is high enough? Venice, with all her civilisation and ancient beauty, Venice with her addiction to curious aquatic means of transport, yes, my friends, Venice is the Henley of the South.'[11] The largely elderly Henley 'set' (in 2002, the town was dubbed the 'Costa Geriatrica' though not by Boris, it must be stressed) could not resist.

Michael Heseltine had not been particularly skilled at working the crowd at Henley's round of social events – or indeed eager to do so – but now every local socialite would try and lure Boris, the ultimate catch, to her salon. 'Michael didn't charm the Henley ladies, he was too much of a politician for them,' explains one senior Henley Tory. 'They wanted someone to grace their drinks parties – Boris made more of a fuss of them.' The schmoozing paid off, as did his relaxed attitude. 'We used to have a strawberry fair here at our house every summer,' recalls Peter Sutherland of the Henley Conservatives. 'Boris would come with his wife and family, and let himself in by the back gate without any fuss. We have a swimming pool, but his children would forget their swimming things. He didn't mind – he would always let them swim in their pants. He made the whole thing easy.'

Richard Reed, the *Henley Standard*'s news editor, remembers: 'There was more in the paper about Boris in a year than there ever was about

Heseltine. When people met him, they liked him and he put himself about.' Indeed, whatever his troubles in Westminster, Boris was proving a great support to local campaigns. Organising them might not have been his forte, but spearheading certainly was. He worked on keeping the local Townlands hospital open (leading a march of 6,000 local people), maintaining access to local courts (raising it in a Parliamentary committee), keeping Brakspear as an independent brewer and saving the air ambulance. It was just his persistent lateness for any meeting that rankled with the organisers. 'I once really had to tick him off,' recalls Brian Tiptree, a local activist. 'He arrived an hour and a half late at one meeting just as everyone was leaving.' On one occasion, he never turned up at all: a message came through to say that he had been test-driving a Ferrari and it had run out of petrol in the fast lane of the A40 in the rush-hour, causing tailbacks and confusion for miles. Two policemen had to push him out of the way.

When he did turn up to deliver speeches, he would often ostentatiously write a few notes on a serviette just minutes before he was due to stand and deliver (a performance reminiscent of writing his speech on a tree at the Eton debating society). This apparently off-the-cuff style went down brilliantly in an Oxfordshire sports club or Rotary dinner. His jokes were reverentially printed in the paper – one of the best being when bitten by an Alsatian while out canvassing. 'My thoughts are entirely with him and his family at this time,' he quipped about the dog. 'I have all manner of concern and sympathy for him and for anything he might have contracted from me, I apologise in advance.'[12]

On occasion he would send his *Spectator* colleague Petronella Wyatt – who would make remarkably similar speeches – to represent him. Other times he would turn up to fundraising lunches unprepared, on occasion giving an inappropriate talk such as decrying the trend to 'cotton wool' children to an audience of mothers who had paid handsomely to hear him and were not expecting to be lectured. He would also annoy people more than once (just as on *HIGNFY* and in the Commons chamber) by letting his mobile ring mid-flow. But Boris did not ignore his local responsibilities as MP – his constituency surgeries were popular and well regarded. He had hired the super-organised Wayne Lawley to handle the inevitable inquiries, complaints and pleas for help. Lawley ensured responses were prompt, letters answered and issues were raised. 'Boris did work his butt off for us while he was here,' says Brian Tiptree.

Yet Boris could never quite unite his constituency party behind him. A particular bone of contention – that led to at least one local resignation – was his changing position on Iraq. Boris set out his reasons for backing intervention cogently in the local paper in 2003 – and was also featured on the *Henley Standard* front page on a fact-finding trip to Baghdad. But he had previously given assurances that he would not be a supporter and there was a group of people who really minded the apparent change of heart.

Although Henley was relatively close to London, his visits put an even greater strain on his family life. Friday nights and some weekends were inevitably spent in the constituency. As yet Boris had rented only a fairly modest cottage in Swyncombe, which was too small for the whole family and he was regularly there without them. So in 2003 he bought a substantial Grade II-listed farmhouse just outside the affluent market town of Thame for £650,000. The Johnsons' occupancy started out typically chaotically: not all the kids had beds due to a miscalculation on the number needed and so spent the first few nights on mattresses on the floor.

Boris had long since longed for what he called a country schloss with tennis court and swimming pool. The pleasing house he bought is Georgian in period but a rambling T-shaped farmhouse in design rather than a grand, symmetrical 'gentleman's residence'. Tucked away at the end of a lane that peters out into a muddy track, it is solidly built of Flemish-bond red brick and backs onto an English vista of velvety green hills. An outhouse has been smartly renovated into guest accommodation and is also useful for changing for the outsize swimming pool the Johnsons have built next to it. There is also a swing in a tree, a trampoline tucked away on a side lawn, table tennis but as yet no tennis court.

Inside, the style is slightly cluttered comfort, with a classical bust standing guard in one window, various Indian artifacts contributed by

Marina and comfy, dark-coloured sofas encamped round an open log fire. Shelves are loaded with improving books such as *Rome: The Age of Augustus* and *The Origins of Freemasonry*. This is not the sort of weekend home where children become umbilically attached to a games console – or spellbound by a plasma TV – but where everyone is encouraged to exercise body and mind in equal measure. Nor is it the territory of Colefax & Fowler or indeed the minimalist brigade but something rather more down-to-earth and homely. Ceilings are low and the bedrooms romantically perched up in the old tiled roof.

Friends say Marina is always having 'things done' to the house and clearly, a great deal of effort – and money – have gone into improvements. Boris claimed from the tax payer interest payments of £85,000 in the years when he was an MP, so the taxpayer funded a good proportion of the cost until he resigned his seat in 2008. Mortgage brokers say such a sum would have sustained a loan of up to about £350,000 at the time, so Boris must also have invested some of his own cash. The large swimming pool, which could have easily cost £50,000, was installed before he left Parliament. 'They were all very excited when they put the pool in,' recalls journalist and friend Sarah Sands. The house has proved an excellent investment for the family and could be worth well over £1 million or more today.

However, guests at one January lunch at the Thame house found it slightly damp on arrival, with both Boris and Marina failing to get the fire lit for nearly an hour. Even when it finally got going, clouds of smoke chased into the sitting room. Perhaps it is fair to say that the couple do not make natural country folk, but the house provided Marina with a refuge from Boris's local political life. 'Marina didn't take to Henley at all,' said family friend Anthony Howard.

Marina herself has often talked of her concerns at the yawning political differences between them – a running theme in their marriage. She would even admit to some of Boris's more sympathetic Henley constituents that she did not always share her husband's political stance and sometimes found it difficult to defend. 'Marina didn't make it a secret that she was left of Boris,' recalls Maggie Pullen. 'I told her if you can live with it, Marina, then so can I.' She rarely accompanied Boris on official visits to the constituency, once asking Pullen exactly what functions she had to attend, and which she could skip. 'I don't think Marina has ever liked being an appendage,' observed Howard. Right from the start, she insisted on still being known as Marina Wheeler, a point of principle that seems to have annoyed Boris (who of course knew the importance of marital status in conservative Henley). He argued that her intransigence made it look as if he were just 'squiring some girlfriend around. I make a point, during my speech later on, of explaining her status.'[13]

Back in Westminster, though, there was real trouble. On 29 October 2003, the requisite 25 Conservative MPs forced a vote of no confidence in the hapless IDS. He lost by 90 votes to 75 and in just over a week, another right-winger, Michael Howard, was confirmed as the unopposed successor. This could have been bad news for Boris as a decade earlier he had written an unusually excoriating piece about the then Home Secretary in the *Spectator*, suggesting Howard's plans to 'sniff out illegal workers in the office and factory' would encourage a malicious Vichy society of curtain-twitchers.[14] It was one of his most personal attacks in print – perhaps he was not expecting Howard to rise further in the party – but that 'blessed sponge of amnesia' must have worked its magic yet again. As soon as Howard took over, in a brave move he rewarded Boris with his first proper job: vice-chairman of the Conservative party with special responsibility for campaigning.

'I thought he was a great asset to Parliament and to the Conservative party. We weren't over-endowed with popular Conservatives at the time – or even ones that everyone knew,' recalls Howard. 'The question was always how to channel this huge ability into something constructive and ensure that it was accompanied by a modicum of disciplined effort. Boris was doing all these other things and was distracted.' Indeed, Howard's attempts to 'channel' Boris were not universally popular with the party hierarchy, who thought them unwise. Many believed him too much of a lone player, a maverick and someone who could not be trusted; they urged Howard to avoid him: 'Boris was a nightmare for the whips who were against my giving him any job because he always missed votes with these ridiculous excuses that no one believed. They told me it would send a terrible signal to everyone else.'

Could the familiar-looking blond in this 1970s class photograph from Primrose Hill Primary School be the future Mayor of London?
Courtesy of Geoffrey Phillips

The playing fields of Eton: King's Scholars limbering up for the 'Wall Game' in front of 'College'. Boris, who left for Oxford University in 1983, was a notoriously aggressive player.
Press Association Images

No aristocrat himself, Boris's time at Eton and Oxford allowed him to mix in noble, and certainly very wealthy, circles. Here he is flanked by Allegra *(left)* and his sister Rachel *(right)* at the then Viscount Althorp's (Charles Spencer's) 21st birthday party. *Rex Features*

Allegra Mostyn-Owen, the Zuleika Dobson of her day, when going out with Boris at Oxford. As with so many women since, his ready wit helped win her over.

A young, slim Boris works his unforgettable charm on Greek Minister for Culture Melina Mercouri ahead of her speech to the Oxford Union on the Elgin Marbles. *Corbis*

TRINITY TERM 1986

Welcome back to Oxford and to the Summer term. You are reading a term card which has a lot in common with a Balliol salad. At first glance, it is a more or less anarchic collection of ingredients. After a few moments' mastication one becomes aware of several common themes, like onions, beetroot and bananas. So it is with the term card.

This term we will be talking about Rights – of blacks, women, embryos and animals. We will contrast Faith and facticity, from UFOs to the Empty Tomb to the Superpower conflict. We will look at our cultural influences: Dutch cheese, Indian curry, Japanese cars, West Indian poetry, American Humor and the marble sculptures of the Parthenon.

We will hear the controversies of modern Britain: crime, terrorism, AIDS, the future of the Unions and new technology, and the dangers and benefits of civilian Nuclear Power.

And by way of a sort of delicious creamy mayonnaise we have a rich stream of humour and shimmering social events.

But, as Aristotle said, all debate has a goal. At the risk of sounding pompous, the goal of these debates is your participation. What counts is your contribution and your decision. It's your Union. It's your salad. Tuck in.

BORIS JOHNSON

The term card for Boris's presidency of the Oxford Union. His mother Charlotte provided the cover illustration. Unsurprisingly, other members of the Johnson dynasty were also involved. *Author's Collection*

Darius Guppy and Charles Spencer at the latter's wedding, 16 September 1989. *Press Association Images*

Boris holding court at a private party in Brussels circa 1990. He hadn't started ruffling his hair yet. *Courtesy of Charles Grant*

A rare picture of Boris boogieing, from the same party. Note that, ever the Young Fogey, he didn't take off his tie. *Courtesy of Charles Grant*

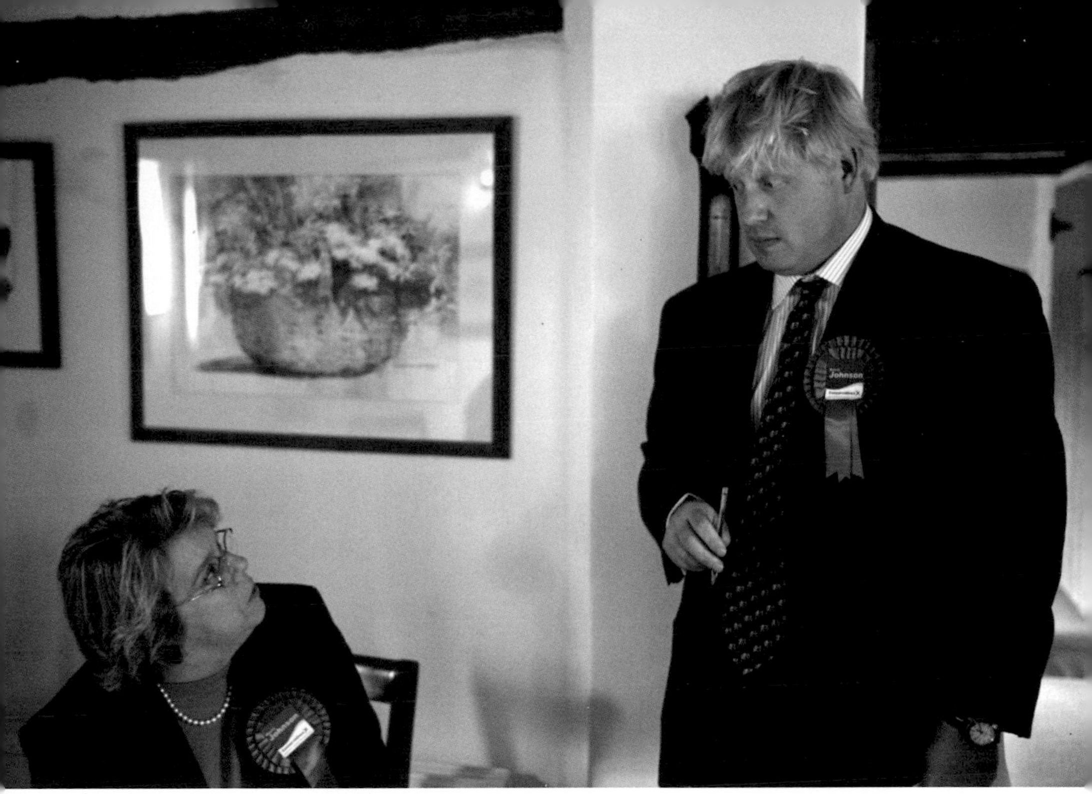

Boris with his constituency chairman Maggie Pullen in Henley. She was devastated when he won the selection for Conservative candidate in 2000. © *J. D. Perkins*

Boris sups a solitary pint in Henley. He has never been a pub or club man. *TopFoto*

Selection night at Benson Parish Hall in Henley: Marina supports her man but never really took to the life of a Tory MP's wife. *TopFoto*

A multitude of blond Johnsons, including Boris, Rachel and their children, in one boat in Henley. Marina is the only brunette. *Courtesy of the Henley Standard*

Boris cited Disraeli and Churchill in defence of his decision to remain editor of the *Spectator* whilst MP for Henley: both combined politics and journalism, both were outsiders variously ridiculed and written off, and both entered Downing Street. *Getty Images*

Boris's brand of high-wire bumbling on *Have I Got News for You* brought him national celebrity and rendered him untouchable. *© BBC*

Boris with Petronella Wyatt in June 2004. *Rex Features*

Boris's ribald regime at the 'Sextator' lent itself perfectly to Toby Young and Lloyd Evans' theatrical bonkathon *Who's the Daddy?*. *Getty Images*

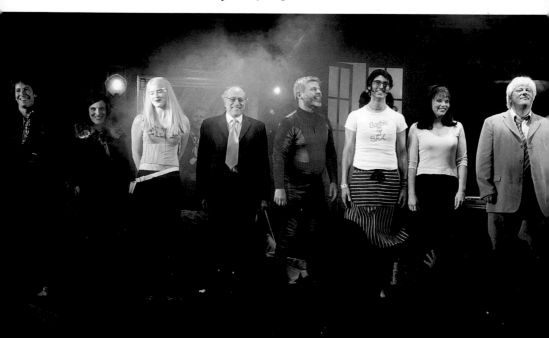

'Operation Scouse Grovel': A repentant Boris wins hearts, minds and media attention in Liverpool. *Rex Features*

Boris lends star quality to his father Stanley, the Conservative candidate for Teignbridge, during the 2005 general election. (Stanley lost, Boris retained his seat.) *Rex Features*

The News

THE MAN WHO STEALS BUSES PAGE 5

www.portsmouth.co.uk NEWSPAPER OF THE YEAR Tuesday, April 3, 2007 38p

All in LifeStyle – the section that gives your life a lift

WIN A LIFE-CHANGING £3,000 MAKEOVER

WIN beauty goodies

I was Kylie's dancer

LifeStyle Kylie, Robbie, Ronan and me

YOU TWIT!

Meet the big-mouth MP who says it's US who are overweight and hopeless

FULL STORY PAGE 3 COMMENT PAGE 6

Fears are voiced over building on beauty spot

BUILDING on a popular beauty spot cannot be ruled out, council bosses have admitted.

Havant Borough Council [illegible] future of the open green [illegible], which last year had been earmarked as the site for a major marina complex of luxury apartments, flats, shops and leisure facilities.

Those plans were thrown out but 12 months on residents and nature campaigners are still waiting in vain for assurances that Broadmarsh, off Harts Farm Way, Havant, will not be developed into a hotel, a housing estate or a marina.

The leader of the council, David Gillet, said: 'We have no plans at present but we need to keep our options open.

'There may be a need to use some of the area for some development in order to keep the rest of it sustainable.

'Our hand may be forced from forces outside of our control.'

Dog-walkers, birdwatchers and nature experts say it would be a disaster if the stretch of Langstone Harbour was lost.

Bosses at Havant Borough Council [illegible] what might become of the land, some of which is designated as a site of special scientific interest, and residents see their silence as an invitation to potential developers.

Late Night Opening

Late Night Opening Starts Wednesday 4th April
Wednesday and Thursday Open Until 8pm
Pick up Your Late Night Privilege Card

Spring Colour

Open seven days a week

Keydell Nurseries - More Than a Garden Centre

82149 Havant Road, Horndean • Tel : 023 9259 3839

Portsmouth is just one of several cities (and at least one country) that Boris has managed to insult. Unusually, the naval port didn't think him either funny or endearing. *The News, Portsmouth*

The battle for London: Ken Livingstone described Boris as 'the most formidable opponent I will face in my political career.' *Above: Getty Images; below: Rex Features*

Boris, Ken Livingstone and Liberal Democrat candidate Brian Paddick appear on ITV for a televised debate during the 2008 mayoral campaign. *Rex Features*

Victory night: A defeated Ken offers his hand in congratulations. Boris remains granite-faced. Later he promised to buy Ken a drink, but has never done so. *Rex Features*

The new Mayor of London has a clear desk – but problems quickly fill his in-tray.
Press Association Images

Boris at London's Gay Pride in July 2008 – he is a master of the photo opportunity. *Getty Images*

Rachel with her mother Charlotte in May 2008. Both women have been hugely influential and supportive in Boris's life. *Alamy*

Who cares (this much) wins! Boris takes 'whiff whaff' (table tennis to the rest of us) extremely seriously. *Getty Images*

Boris behind Sir Ian Blair, who believes he was the victim of the Mayor's political ambitions. *Press Association Images*

'Bonking Boris' has become a *Private Eye* favourite.

Reproduced by kind permission of PRIVATE EYE magazine

Helen Macintyre – 'the proverbial bloody good bloke with bosoms and a brain'. *London Media*

Boris launches the new Routemaster bus – it's all shine and voluptuous curves. *Getty Images*

Boris and Arnie at peace. The Hollywood actor and ex-California governor once accused Boris of 'fumbling'. Boris countered by dubbing Schwarzenegger a 'monosyllabic Austrian cyborg'. *Getty Images*

Boris and Marina attend the wedding of Prince William and Kate Middleton in April 2011. Marina has taken to wearing Indian dress more frequently in recent years. *Getty Images*

Boris and deputy mayor Kit Malthouse under pressure. Both show the strain when fielding persistent questions on the phone-hacking scandal at a rare City Hall press conference on 18 July 2011. *Getty Images*

Boris at the Conservative Party Conference in Manchester, 2010. Does he have what it takes to be Prime Minister? *Rex Features*

There were also rumours about Boris's sex life and a growing resentment at what was perceived as his lack of loyalty or Conservative team spirit. But Howard ploughed on against the advice with, at best, mixed results: 'Was he good at the vice-chairmanship? It could have been quite a big job. The fact is that he didn't put much in. With Boris, there is this issue with effort. I'm sure he did something. But if you asked me to identify what it was, I might be pretty pushed. Here was a Conservative who was much more popular than anyone else in the party and much better known. If he had contributed those attributes to campaigning for the Conservative party, you might assume that it would be successful. But he didn't, so it didn't really work.'

Howard also tried another tack. He kept on Duncan Smith's PMQ attack-team comprising Cameron, Osborne – and supposedly Boris. 'Boris certainly didn't turn up every week, but the other two did. He occasionally came up with a good idea. But I don't think his contribution was enormous,' continues Howard. 'David and George did most of the work – it was just something we all put up with. He has got great ability, great charm and he's very amusing. You'd sooner have him around than not, so you put up with things – up to a point.'

Indeed, on this unpromising foundation, Howard decided to promote Boris still further in his reshuffle of May 2004. Even with a new leader, the Conservatives continued to struggle to make inroads into New Labour territory and seemed as far away from returning to government as ever. In an attempt to win the arts vote from Labour – the party had cornered the market in luvvies – the Leader made him shadow arts minister. It was another colossal leap of faith. Howard appears to have been as powerlessly in thrall as Conrad Black, Boris's other employer. 'I thought that the job was tailor-made for him,' explains Howard. 'The arts community were notoriously unfriendly to the Conservative party. Who better to make friends with them than Boris? I think he did make friends a bit, I think he took it reasonably seriously but it didn't turn out quite right – he was always inhibited by all his other commitments. I thought that at some point he would have to choose and eventually he did, but it took him a long time and various events.'

It all started off with Boris at his best – or worst, depending on whether you were depending on him. Apparently surprised to be given the job, he told delighted journalists: 'Look, the point is . . . er, what is the point? It is a tough job but someone's got to do it,'[15] before launching into his manifesto as if he had not given it a moment's thought. 'I haven't cleared this with anybody, but here is what I think. On coming to power I am going to institute a Windows spell check in English so that schoolchildren in this country no longer feel they have got it wrong when they spell words correctly. The Greeks are going to be given an indistinguishable replica of all the Parthenon marbles, done in the most beautiful marble dust to end this acrimonious dispute between our great nations.

'I am going to open up the bandwidth, so there is much more freedom on the radio stations, [and] reduce some of the stuff allocated to the Pentagon, so you can get the Rolling Stones in Oxfordshire. I am fed up with just listening to treacly old Magic. Fourth? I can't remember what point four is. Ah, yes. We are going to convene a summit with Damien Hirst and the rest of the gang, at which they are going to explain to the nation what it all means. Let us have a national "mission to explain" by the Saatchi mob, which will be massively popular.'

Unsurprisingly, Boris captured the public's imagination with his brilliant off-the-cuff job description, although, like much of his extemporising, it is likely this had been meticulously rehearsed. In what was an artwork in itself, he consolidated his position as the humorous (and human) politician, who appeared to be on the public's side. 'Everything he did was laced with this same wry sardonic humour,' explains Toby Young, who has tracked Boris's career since Oxford. 'No one ever gets the impression that they are being talked down to by Boris – it's not like he's playing a role and expecting people to be taken in by it. Whenever he tries to fake sincerity, he's making it obvious that he's faking. He does it by eye-rolling or metaphorically forgetting the script he's supposed to be reciting, so he'll wander off-message or reverse what he started off saying. I don't think it is a straightforward case of pretending to be more befuddled than he really is in order to curry favour. I think he is genuinely a rather disorganised person, but he's made a virtue of that.'

Soon afterwards a marketing company called Superbrands placed Boris on a world 'cool list' alongside Johnny Depp, Bose stereos and Audi cars. It was a harmless bit of fun, but it reflected Boris's appeal even though he was now pushing 40 and neither sleek nor classically good-looking – and that supposed antithesis of cool, a Tory MP. But Boris zigged when everyone else zagged, Superbrands observed, and 'quite simply, there isn't anybody else quite like him and he's funny.' Boris was daring to be different, to make people laugh – and was loved for it.

While Boris was pronouncing on frock-wearing Turner Prize winners and fiddling at the edges of serious politics, however, David Cameron (who had been Howard's special adviser at the Home Office in the 1990s) was moving inexorably closer to the centre of Conservative power. In the summer of 2004, Howard made the 37-year-old Cameron head of policy co-ordination in what was clearly a pivotal role in the run-up to the next General Election, with a place in the shadow Cabinet. In September that year, at the age of just 33, George Osborne was parachuted into the key job of shadow chief secretary to the Treasury.

Meanwhile, 40-year-old Boris finally had to prove that he could fulfil his role, however second-tier it may have seemed. Julie Kirkbride had been his junior as a political journalist on the *Telegraph*, but now a Tory MP, she was Boris's boss during a brief stint as shadow Culture Secretary. She remembers him as very different from his public image, which she says he uses to 'make himself a more likeable, less feared character.'

'He organised himself extremely well,' she observes. 'He had a very good, assiduous researcher. And whatever needed doing was done. Boris is a very clever, classically educated guy who knows what he wants. While Boris is not quite the antithesis of his shambling appearance, he uses it as a smokescreen to disarm people.' The public act did not stop, however. 'When he was culture spokesman he made some minor gaffe and one journalist phoned him up and got the whole buffoon spiel,' remembers Andy McSmith. 'He printed it word for word in his newspaper. What so amused us was that another lobby [political] journalist had also phoned him up and got exactly the same bumbling routine, word for word, and had recorded it. The two routines were identical. Boris put in a very well rehearsed performance, both times – it shows it's all a construct.'

There was also plenty of clowning around over at the *Spectator*. In July 2004, Rod Liddle, the *Spectator*'s associate editor, was revealed to be having an affair with Alicia Munckton, the 22-year-old blonde on reception. In the laddish atmosphere that prevailed at the *Spectator* at the time, with its phwoaring, crude jokes and persistent ogling, Boris roared with laughter at the news. It was a jolly jape and one that apparently received his enthusiastic approval. Liddle's wife, whom he had married only six months previously after 12 years and two sons together, did not find it so amusing. Rachel Royce sought to expose not only her philandering husband but what she saw as Boris's licentious regime at the *Spectator* – one that not only seemed to condone such behaviour but even encouraged it. And she chose the perfect vehicle, the *Daily Mail*. The headline was: 'MY CHEATING HUSBAND ROD, TEN BAGS OF MANURE AND ME THE BUNNY BOILER. AS FOR THE SLAPPER . . . SHE'S WELCOME TO HIM.'[16]

'My impressions via my ex-husband were that my marriage collapsed after he started working at the *Spectator*,' says Royce several years later and now divorced. She was particularly concerned about goings-on at the magazine's notorious parties, which put together herds of powerful middle-aged men with gaggles of impressed – or perhaps that should be impressionable – young women, in a tightly-packed space. Flattery was traded, fuelled by the *Spectator*'s stocks of Ruinart champagne. Boris would invite beautiful young women – including, in 2004, 20-year old Ruzwana Bashir, the then President of the Oxford Union. With long, glossy dark hair and a good brain, she resembled a young Marina. A story in the *Mail on Sunday* suggested he 'had been all over her' at the party, but Bashir denied any impropriety, saying 'he's a really nice guy. But we have certainly not kissed.'

Royce became suspicious when she was invited to one such gathering a year earlier, but was barred by Liddle from attending any later events. 'Rod used to say that wives weren't invited,' says Royce. 'It might have been Rod making it up or the regime that Boris created at the *Spectator*. I felt it was Boris at the time – they were all at it.' The 2003 party worried her: she had arrived to find Marina and her father Charles Wheeler greeting guests at the door rather than Boris. 'Marina was as exhausted as I was – she'd been in Birmingham working. The party was heaving and where did I find my husband? He was on this little space outside a window that they were using as a roof terrace. He was agog at this blonde twenty-something. That was my impression of *Spectator* parties, full of young things in short dresses, high heels and lipstick, and the men flirting with them and ignoring their wives. I just felt that Boris was running the whole place like a knocking shop. It was a case of all being lads together, all girls in short skirts, and "phwooar, good on yer Rod." He was treated like a hero for having an affair, like a new Alan Clark figure.

'I probably blamed Boris more than I should, rather than my own husband, at the time. But why did he have to have young, gorgeous women on reception and not someone mature or even a man?'

Indeed, Marina is also thought to have disliked the parties – although she attended them out of loyalty. 'I remember coming to one very late and bumping into Marina standing in the street. She clearly was not looking forward to going at all,' recalled Anthony Howard.

The Liddle disclosures, however, were soon overtaken by a much bigger story. In August, the Home Secretary David Blunkett was revealed to be having an affair with the *Spectator*'s publisher Kimberly Fortier. Even though a giggling Fortier would steer Blunkett round *Spectator* parties like a living trophy, few if any had guessed exactly what the socialite had been doing with the socialist for the past three years. When news of the affair came out, another *Spectator* writer Petronella Wyatt described its origins: a dinner at Wheeler's restaurant in St James's back in 2001 that she had also attended. Fortier arrived at the restaurant and in her flirtatious manner, Wyatt recounted, told the defenceless Blunkett that she had always wondered what it was like to sleep with a blind man. She later found out. In perhaps her best line to date, Wyatt recalled: 'Mr Blunkett and

I ate Dover sole. Ms Fortier ate Mr Blunkett.'[17] Later, Fortier also gobbled up the *Spectator*'s wine correspondent, Simon Hoggart.

Blondes, blind men, champagne, American socialites, double affairs, government ministers and wiry lotharios – the *Spectator*, normally a minority-interest magazine, captured the entire nation's imagination. What fictional soap opera could possibly compete with the magazine they renamed the *Sextator*? Soon those US-based Boris-watching journalists were back to chronicle the goings-on. Some time later, *Vanity Fair* magazine expressed its admiration: 'Washington should steal a tabloid page from its closest and horniest ally, Great Britain. When it comes to whipping up a political sex scandal into a donnybrook, the Brits have us beat – they really know how to make the bedsheets billow.'[18]

Fortunately for the participants, it appears that Conrad Black and Dan Colson were similarly entertained by the goings-on. 'The whole tangle of relationships had their amusing aspects,' says Black. But they may also have influenced their decision not to offer Boris the editorship of the *Sunday Telegraph* in September 2003, as widely expected. 'We were a little worried that Boris was not quite mature and committed enough,' explains Colson. To be fair it is likely that Boris would not have accepted such an offer as it would have made continuing as an MP even more complicated. It was probably the last occasion, however, when Boris came near to pursuing a career as a national newspaper editor. The die was now cast.

Moreover, from late 2003, Black and Colson's influence was waning. Pressures were mounting on Black to step down from Hollinger, the parent company for both the *Spectator* and *Telegraph* titles. The other shareholders were concerned about Hollinger's performance and there were allegations about payments to Black from the company. As the row intensified, he put his 73 per cent voting stake in the company up for sale in November 2003. The following month the notoriously hard-line US Securities & Exchange Commission called Black in for questioning. On 18 January 2004, the Hollinger board mounted a $200 million lawsuit against Black over alleged financial irregularities and ousted him as chairman a day before he sold his shareholding to the Barclay brothers. The threat of criminal proceedings was also growing, with Black fighting for his survival.

In the next issue of the *Spectator*, Boris decided to run a two-page article on the man who had done so much to propel him into stardom and who was vigorously protesting his innocence. Entitled 'The ballad of Connie and Babs' and again written under the by-line of the political editor Peter Oborne, it accused Black of 'stolidity, clumsiness and provincialism' and having 'murky business origins.'[19] He had 'hairy knuckles and paddle-like hands' and a 'fondness for ceremony and dressing up [that] was pre-modern in its profound lack of irony and unabashed vulgarity.' He spoke very slowly, it went on, and his wife Barbara Amiel, although 'charming, clever and quite ravishingly beautiful,' was also 'capable of a definite grandeur of approach.' This was a breathtaking attack, even though balanced with kinder words such as 'Whatever sins he may have committed, he ran the *Telegraph* well.'[20]

Now that Black was no longer capable of helping Boris's career, his impersonations became even crueller. 'Boris took pleasure in mimicking Black's slow, deep transatlantic drawl and slightly laboured delivery, using clumsy grammatical devices such as "whereunto,"' recalls a *Spectator* staffer.

Boris, though, was riding high. His name was now regularly bandied about as a possible one-day contender for Downing Street – although each time he was posed the question about his ambitions for the top job, he disguised seriousness of purpose with a variation on the quip: 'My chances of being PM are about as good as the chances of finding Elvis on Mars, or of my being reincarnated as an olive.'

For the first time he also published a novel and when it was launched, Douglas Hurd said admiringly in a review that it read as if it were written in three days and nights 'flat out.'[21] *Seventy-Two Virgins: A Comedy of Errors* is actually a rollicking read for anyone with a modicum of interest in politics – or rather Boris. It centres on the figure of a middle-aged male Tory MP of such inept self-absorption that his bicycling becomes virtually his only appealing feature. Obsessed by fears that an embarrassing indiscretion is about to be exposed, Roger Barlow fails to notice a terrorist attack unfolding right in front of him. The similarities between Boris and Barlow are too numerous to dismiss. Other characters are also largely based on real figures. There are many in Boris's life, including Stuart Reid and most of the *Spectator* staff, who pored over the text in a bid to identify themselves. The names of the characters are instructive – the regally-mannered traffic warden, William Eric Kinloch Onyeama, shares his first three names with Boris's former Eton headmaster Sir (William) Eric Anderson. Barlow's beautiful and moralising (female) assistant is called Cameron, the woman police sniper is Nath, the surname of one of Boris's greatest rivals at Eton, while an ostrich bears the name of Kimberly.

Barlow groans and runs his hands through his hair in a familiar style and his most daring utterance echoes Boris's own support of any consenting union including that 'between three men and a dog.' He even sends Christmas cards to Justin and Nell, the names of Boris's closest friends. All in all, it's a breathtaking exercise in self-knowledge and/or self-parody. And as Hurd points out, the book even mocks in turn 'every possible attitude' to the Iraq War – 'which seems in harmony with the official *Spectator* line of supporting the war but impeaching the man who started it.'[22]

Given all the autobiographical teasing, one must assume Boris shares his character's rather hostile views on the Palace of Westminster. Barlow appears to despise some of the sacred Puginesque adornments – what he calls 'the whorls and volutes of the Pugin entablature' – branding them 'demented' and guilty of 'prinking pomposity.' And there is perhaps also a little Borissian self-congratulation. Cameron decides she wants an alpha male, an authority figure to supplant her father. She has a 'deep and sexist reverence for men who really knew stuff. It amazed her sometimes how little appearances mattered. He could be bald, he could be spindly or sweaty or tubby, but if that man's disquisition had enough interest, fluency and authority, it would speak directly to her groin.'[23]

Nineteenth-century commentators had scoured Disraeli's novels for clues as to the real nature of their author, finding in books such as *Sybil* and *Vivian Grey* 'the memoirs he never wrote.' Similarly, students of Boris should scrutinise *Seventy-Two Virgins*. They might well pause over the following two passages in particular for some useful insights into Boris's life philosophy. 'We all have in our lives someone who controls our emotional thermostat,' he writes. 'There is always someone whose function is to supply the pipette drops of praise, the intermittent goo'boy choc drops of external affirmation that gets us through the day. The story of our lives is essentially the rotation of that person's identity: mother, father, teacher, girlfriend, boyfriend, spouse and so on.' And later: 'To a man like Roger Barlow, the whole world just seemed to be a complicated joke, an accidental jumbling of ingredients on the cosmic stove, which had produced our selfish genes. For Barlow, everything was always up for grabs, capable of dispute; and religion, laws, principle, custom – these were nothing but sticks we plucked from the wayside to support our faltering steps.'[24]

There is also something eerily prescient about the book, a notion of life imitating art (not least because it features home-grown suicide bombers who try to blow up parts of London only a year before a similar atrocity takes place). But there is another strand. Here is Quentin Letts in a review in the *Evening Standard*: 'The Tory MP in the book is terrified that a sex-related indiscretion of his is about to be exposed in the *Daily Mirror*. It is interesting that Johnson should write so convincingly about a politician's fear of scandal.'[25] Indeed. And in so doing, Boris followed in the footsteps of another one-time Conservative party darling, Jeffrey Archer. Yet at this point it seemed for all the world as if scandal happened to other people, even if they were some of Boris's closest colleagues on the *Spectator*. In contrast, his own rise as a political celebrity appeared to be irresistible. One big-name American reporter enthused about the 'inspirational' Brit politician who was on the one hand 'arguably the English language's greatest pundit' and the natural heir to the charm and good humour of Ronald Reagan, and on the other suffering from a 'state of dishevelment as great [as any] seen in an employed person.'[26] The Boris brand was going global.

On Tuesday, 12 October 2004, Simon Heffer was showering at the

Garrick Club before dining with a Conservative politician. Heffer is one of that handful of journalists able to put together a cogent piece at breakneck speed and so it was not surprising that Boris phoned him in desperation when the *Spectator* was short of a leader at a late stage in its weekly editorial cycle. Off the cuff, Heffer suggested writing on the minute's silence requested (but largely ignored) at the England-Wales football match that week for Ken Bigley, a Liverpudlian contractor who had been murdered by terrorists in Iraq. He did not want to write it himself, having neither the time nor a computer. But Boris pleaded, and so early the next morning Heffer 'banged out' a piece first thing from the office and filed it. 'I didn't have time to check anything, such as the number of people who died at Hillsborough,' he told friends afterwards. 'Boris didn't check it, Stuart didn't check it and then things got a bit fruity.'

The article appeared on the Thursday and criticised 'the mawkish sentimentality of a society that has become hooked on grief and likes to wallow in a sense of vicarious victimhood.'[27] For good measure, it continued: 'The extreme reaction to Mr Bigley's murder is fed by the fact that he was a Liverpudlian. Liverpool is a handsome city with a tribal sense of community.'[28]

Stuart Reid took the piece in to Boris, suggesting '[it] was a bit rough on Bigley. We took out a few bits but it didn't occur to either of us that the stuff about Liverpool was a problem. We just thought it was common sense.' Possibly it is a reflection of the attention given to *Spectator* leaders that no one noticed the piece for 24 hours after it came out. It was not until Friday morning that a row started to brew, with calls for Boris to apologise for the remarks. At this point as the leader was unsigned, no one knew who had written it but as editor, the buck stopped with him. To his credit, he did not try to apportion the blame elsewhere. It was unfortunate in the extreme that the number of Hillsborough deaths was woefully understated at more than 50 (the real figure was 96) and that drunken fans were blamed when in fact this had been ruled out as a cause by an official inquiry.

While it was clear that Boris stood by the sentiment of the piece, the factual errors were not only embarrassing for him but even more so for his party leader, Michael Howard. Having cut his political teeth in the Edge Hill constituency in the 1966 General Election, when he fell in love with cheeky Scouse wit and the Beatles' music scene, Howard was indelibly linked with the city. The Tories were now also desperately trying to revive their fortunes in the Northwest and this sort of negative publicity could make their political situation there ever more hopeless. But most important of all was that Howard was a devoted supporter of Liverpool FC and, according to his closest aides, 'was driven by the intense fear that he would be booed at a match.' 'It was perceived as the first real Boris gaffe so it rapidly became a cause célèbre," recalls Guy Black, then Howard's press secretary. By Saturday, Howard was horrified at the row and publicly described the article as 'nonsense from beginning to end.'[29]

'Michael rang me up on Saturday morning and said this is completely unacceptable, Boris is going to have to go to Liverpool to apologise,' recalls Black. 'He had clearly made his mind up, although I did warn him that this will turn into a circus but he was coldly firm. He would not risk being booed.' Boris was duly ordered up to Liverpool to say sorry in what became widely known as 'Operation Scouse Grovel'. 'I don't think he put up much resistance,' says Guy Black. Conservative Central Office was put in charge of the trip, which began on Tuesday, with what was supposed to be a late-night flit up the motorway under cover of darkness. Before they set off, the minders even circled the block near Boris's house a few times to throw any pursuers off the scent.

It may be fair to say that this Hollywood movie approach was just one of a number of mistakes made in an exercise that quickly descended into farce. There were honourable reasons for trying to limit Boris's exposure to the regional press alone (it was supposed to be an apology to Liverpool, after all), but it was a hopelessly naïve strategy. The national newspapers and broadcasters sent armies of reporters and cameramen up North and they were not going to give up until they got their man. It was, after all, otherwise a slow news day and this story had a lot to offer: it pitched Etonian buffoon against outraged Scousers with the result entirely unpredictable. The fact that the Tories were sending up a team of supposedly beefy minders for Boris in a blacked out Range Rover just increased the media appeal –

although it annoyed Boris intensely to be 'handled' in this way rather than to be allowed to deal with it in his own style. He refused to refer to his leader as Michael, but repeatedly talked about him bitterly as 'Howard'.

Meanwhile, reporters staked out the stations and airports and as soon as Boris was spotted entering the Liverpool Institute for the Performing Arts, all hell let loose. One of the minders present described the scene as resembling Rorke's Drift with the Zulu impi pouring over the crest of the hill in the form of dozens of determined journalists and the British, represented by the Tory team, powerless to stop them.

There are not many who would deal with such bedlam; fewer still who would thrive in it. Boris began to enjoy himself and his minders soon realised their best ploy was to allow him to get on with it – even when that meant dictating his next *Spectator* column for him over the phone when the internet connection failed. Chased all over the city by a posse of reporters, his visit had all the anarchy of an Ealing comedy. He gave a dozen interviews to local papers and broadcasters, proffering words of apology to practically all and sundry but while there were plenty of smiles and jokes, there was also clearly underlying indignation. Boris infuriated the Tory handlers watching events unfold on television by insisting that Howard was 'completely wrong to say that the article was "nonsense from beginning to end." I don't think he can have read it properly.' They hissed back to the minders on the ground orders to get Boris back 'on message.' But while Boris admitted that the article presented an 'outdated stereotype' and apologised for inaccurate claims that drunken Liverpool fans contributed to the Hillsborough disaster, he said he could not retract 'the broad thrust of the article' about sentimentality and acceptance of risk in modern Britain: he was going to do it his way.

There was a sticky moment when Ken Bigley's brother Paul came on a BBC radio programme to tell Boris: 'You're a self-centred, pompous twit – even your body language on TV is wrong. You don't look right, never mind act right. Get out of public life!' It was a rare occasion when a member of the public has taken Boris on and for a moment he looked shaken by it. 'That was a difficult moment – it stripped a coat off him,' says Quentin Letts, one of the press pack following Boris. 'It hasn't happened much.'

He quickly escaped into the studio car park only to run straight into the clutches of a member of the Hillsborough families group. It was one of those days and by now no doubt Boris must have regretted agreeing to come in the first place. 'Are you trying to save your political career?' asked one journalist as he jumped into a car for the next stage of his tour of apology. 'I haven't got a political career,' responded Boris in return.

At the end of his day of repentance, the minders drove Boris back to Liverpool's Speke airport to fly home to London alone. By this time Boris was 'very grumpy.' He was most intent on persuading people that he had not been 'sent' up to Liverpool like some 'whipped cur' but had taken the decision to set the facts straight himself. 'He had started in fine form but got more and more frayed as the day went on, in private at least,' revealed one Tory insider. 'I am a squeezed lemon on this subject,' he admitted before climbing into the back of the car, an open packet of headache tablets clearly visible on the seat next to him. Boris told his minders that he had to leave immediately as he had an important event in London that he was speaking at that night and could not be late. His friend Susanna Gross has, however, subsequently said that he joined her and some other friends for dinner to 'unwind.'

Journalist, politician, celebrity, husband, father and apparently fall-guy too, it was now clear that Boris had much on his mind – and more than almost anyone else knew. For now he had saved his career. He had also made an initially unfortunate but ultimately definitive entrance on the national stage; his charm and apparent bonhomie defusing the immediate public row as it had so many times in private. 'Boris came out tops as he got publicity,' concludes Quentin Letts. 'Howard kept him on because he liked him and thought the trip had been both necessary and relatively successful.'

'Very few things in relation to Boris turn out exactly the way you expect and that is the nature of him,' observes Howard. 'Given that the article had appeared, I think that he and we came out of it as best we could. Bridges were repaired – sort of. We'd shown that we took it seriously, and that we very much regretted it.'

But the fact that Boris had once again 'got away with it' intensified the jealousies and resentments among his Parliamentary colleagues and there were now even louder questions about his ability to continue as both the editor of the *Spectator* and an MP. As Guy Black puts it: 'There was no question of sacking him over this as Michael wanted to keep him as part of the team but it stretched the string, as it were, and it was clear that if there were another incident, it would be more difficult.'

Boris was now instantly recognisable on any high street in Britain and his new notoriety in Liverpool actually increased *Spectator* sales in the city. The saga also rendered him a hero in parts of Liverpool's great rival, Manchester, where United football fans started chanting, 'There's only one Boris Johnson' to their Merseyside opponents and, 'You're just a self-pity city!' Michael Crick of BBC *Newsnight*, a lifelong United supporter, says he has attended at least 1,500 football matches and, 'this was the first and only time a politician has been celebrated in song – there were even Boris badges and leaflets at the ground.'

But while the kerfuffle might help sell copies of an irreverent magazine, the effect on his political career was not quite so benign: what he needed now was a period of reflective calm away from the headlines. But with Boris, was that actually possible?

Chapter Ten
'Busting with spunk'
The Sextator, 1999–2005

'She poured me out a glass of wine, went over to the chaise longue, kicked off her high heels and tucked her feet in under her bottom,' recalls Lloyd Evans, who was surprised to find Petronella Wyatt so comfortably ensconced in Boris's office at the *Spectator*. 'It was rather a *domestic* arrangement and it stuck in my mind. I should have twigged what was going on, but I didn't. I just remember thinking that she's a classic bit of fluff.'

Petronella, daughter of the much-married Labour MP turned royalist and columnist Woodrow Wyatt, is one of London society's better-known femmes fatales. She has written on gossip columns, such as the *Peterborough* diary on the *Telegraph* (where she was known for arriving spectacularly late and, on one memorable occasion, not at all because it was 'too windy.') However, she herself has just as often been a favoured subject of diarists. Some time after Evans witnessed Petronella acting the glamorous châtelaine in the early days of Boris's editorship, the *Daily Mail* started to drop heavy hints about a relationship between the two, whom, it observed: 'work closely together.' 'Boris,' it said, 'may be influenced unduly in his libertarian attitudes to sex by freethinking Petronella Wyatt.' On another occasion, the *Mail* ran a suggestive item noting, 'colleagues say Mr Johnson sometimes goes missing during the day to have one-to-one discussions about geopolitical matters with his colleague Petronella Wyatt.' Meanwhile, Boris dismissed the rumours as baseless – and he was believed. 'Dip [Marina's mother] was very loyal for a long time, saying this stuff being put about by Petronella is all lies,' recalled Anthony Howard. 'She tried to defend Boris.'

Wealthy Petronella owned her first Dior dressing gown at the age of three and had a good figure, which she habitually dressed to full advantage. On one occasion she posed for *Tatler* in satin baby-dolls and ostrich-feather mules. She was also impossibly well connected with the powerful and Conservative, once singing 'Lili Marlene' in husky Marlene Dietrich tones at the 50th birthday party of Norman Lamont when he was Chancellor of the Exchequer. Lamont's then wife Rosemary tried to match her up with David Cameron, who was at the time working for Lamont at the Treasury, although 'unaccountably' he chose to go out with Samantha Sheffield, now his wife. Petronella nevertheless exercised considerable power over men – and she knew it. One fellow journalist, Stephen Robinson, recalls her playfulness when he lent her his laptop in the US in the mid-1990s at a Republican convention in San Diego. He called her after breakfast to say he would be coming round to her hotel room to pick it up, giving her half an hour's notice. 'When I got there, she answered the door in a transparent negligee. It was a case of "take a look at this, mate". It was peculiar, a naked exercise of power – she was playing with me. Oh, and she'd broken the computer, not disastrously, but the screen was shattered.'

Petronella (widely known as 'Petsy') even had a brother called Pericles – after Boris's favourite historical figure – a fact that amused them both. That is not their only common reference point – in some ways Petronella is like a female Boris, but with only a fraction of his luck and resilience. Former colleagues say they share a similar sense of entitlement – and timekeeping. Like Boris, Petronella often drew on sex and her own private life in her work, even when interviewing politicians. One such interview with Denis Healey ended with the former chancellor complaining, 'Pity we've left no time for rumpy-pumpy.'

After an audience in November 2001 with Iain Duncan Smith, when he was Boris's political boss, Petronella gave him seven out of ten for sex appeal and mused on how 'these days' sexiness was a valuable attribute in a politician. She had been brought up with views on fidelity similarly continental to Boris's in their flexibility. Also in common with Boris she appears to have had problems in remembering to pay her bills – once being sent a summons by Westminster Council for non-payment of council tax. Talented and witty, she had risen at an early age to become deputy editor of the *Spectator* under Boris's predecessor Frank Johnson, but was removed from office when Boris came in. He gave her a column instead.

Over time, the fact that Boris was more than Petronella's editor became an open secret in journalistic circles. The pair liked to circle St John's Wood (where Petronella lived) in taxis, asking the driver to play a tape of her singing Puccini as they snogged away furiously on the back seat. As more than one wag has noted, it was hard luck on the driver as 'Boris doesn't tip much.'

What seems clear is that she wanted – and expected – Boris to leave Marina and marry her. And she was not averse to using her *Spectator* column 'Singular Life' to pursue this ambition. It may have been only Boris who realised the significance of her words, but in conjunction they read much like one side of an emotional, sometimes tender, often explicit and occasionally angry conversation between lovers. Early in 2000 she kicks off with word that she is setting up an erotic chocolate company and asks provocatively: 'Who is the greatest lover in England today?' It seems likely that it was Boris she was praising when she wrote that really nice people are 'without moral indignation but in possession of an all-embracing tolerance unlike those who put on niceness like a new frock.' No doubt she would also be aware of the likely impact on his sense of proprietorship by writing about receiving three marriage proposals in one day and of an 'irresistible urge' to go to bed. But then there is an intriguing mention in her column of February 2002, when she returns after an absence. She explains that she has spent the time in Florida 'recuperating after an illness.' We are not informed as to the nature of the condition, although it later becomes pretty clear.

On 9 February, she quickly bounces back with what sounds like another of a series of explicit invitations. 'Most women I know don't bother about orgasms at all. Well, sometimes we do and sometimes we don't. There is no mystery about it. It is like the weather.

Sometimes it rains and sometimes it doesn't. And if it doesn't, one gets a watering can and waters the flowers oneself.' Soon afterwards she launches into what is no doubt a well-targeted rebuke: 'If a man cannot organise his clothes it is often an indication that he cannot organise much else – either his life or the country. A man who cannot be bothered to take care of his clothes will often extend this cavalier attitude to his care of others.'

Later, in May 2002, we hear her pain in not having children: 'It is a truth universally acknowledged in the newspapers these days that a woman over 30 who has not yet had a child is in a very bad way indeed. Having limped over the age of 30 myself, this is all rather depressing stuff. Perhaps I should give up now and resign myself to a childless future or the lottery of adoption.' On another occasion, she writes about becoming unconscious after falling downstairs. In September, in what might be interpreted as a growing plea for help, she reveals that she has been mugged and notes: 'I am still nervous and emotional. I wished I had a man with me.' The following month she sounds even more desperate to retain both her man and her hopes of a family: 'There is no stigma attached to children born out of wedlock, indeed it has become the fashionable thing to do. Most Italians still cleave to the time-honoured tradition of keeping both a wife and a girlfriend.'

Perhaps just such a dual arrangement was still Boris's intention as he flew back from Liverpool to London a couple of years later in 2004, on the October evening of his apology tour to Merseyside. That night he was a major item on all the BBC bulletins and the next day the prospects for his future in politics were analysed in great detail in all the papers. The posse of Boris-watching journalists who now covered his every move in public did not yet know that his private life was also in turmoil. No wonder that he had been grumpy in the car to the airport. His affair with Petronella had continued for four years – sometimes brazenly, such as when he suggested she join a family holiday, and on another occasion when a snap of her somehow found its way into one of Stanley's family albums. Indeed, Marina had been aware of the relationship for some time but thought it not much more than an annoying distraction. Sometimes Petronella tried to end it, at one point becoming engaged to an American lawyer and living over in Rhode Island but clearly he was not a patch on the excitement that Boris offered. Petronella was to be one of the great loves of Boris's life and he wanted her back; she duly returned and the relationship resumed but just as his journalistic persona had crashed in on his political career, so too would his private life now dominate his public fate.

On 18 October, three days before Operation Scouse Grovel, Petronella booked into a private London hospital to abort the second child she had conceived by Boris. She was seven weeks into her pregnancy. It has been said that it was her idea and that she took the decision, even though Boris offered to support the child financially if she carried it to term. But other reports suggest Boris was keen on a termination and had claimed he was not in a position to support another child. 'Petronella said Boris kept changing his mind,' a friend of hers declared. 'She wanted to have the baby and at first he said she should have it, but said if she did, he wouldn't be able to support it. Then he said she should have an affair with someone else and say it was their child.' The same friend – later backed up publicly by Petronella's mother Lady Wyatt – also said Boris had refused to pay the £1,500 medical bills from the abortion, believing them to be too high.[1] It can only be guessed from her 'Singular Life' writings how painful these events must have been for Petronella, who was now 35 and after four years of the affair, seeing her hopes of marrying Boris fading fast. Whether or not he wanted the abortion to go ahead, the storm clouds of love and betrayal were now gathering.

Just a fortnight after the Merseyside farce, on 7 November 2004, the *Sunday Mirror* broke the story of the abortion although without naming either Petronella or Boris. On the same day, the *Sunday Express* reported that Boris was about to resign his post as shadow arts minister 'amid rumours of a crisis in his private life.' It also mentioned his 'close relationship' with Petronella, but went no further. Readers of both newspapers might just have been able to work out the full story – as did a lot of journalists – but most civilians would have been none the wiser. Both papers trod very carefully for good reason and the sequence of events is telling.

The *Sunday Mirror* had the full story about the affair, the pregnancy and the termination but was unable to contact Boris and so asked Guy Black, Howard's spokesman, about it instead. He in turn phoned Boris, who was with Marina at the time and reputedly spluttered: 'Outrageous tabloid! My poor wife, my poor wife, what on earth is she to make of all this? It's absolute nonsense, piffle, completely untrue!' Although offered the chance of another conversation when he was alone, Boris said it was not necessary and so an official denial was issued to the *Sunday Mirror.* Its editor Tina Weaver felt in the circumstances that she could not name the protagonists, however impeccable her sources.

Meanwhile, the *Mail on Sunday* had managed to contact Boris directly and although it did not run the abortion story, the paper still dealt the fatal blow. Boris gave the political editor Simon Walters a wonderful quote – and an unexploded bomb. 'I have not had an affair with Petronella,' he said. 'It is complete balderdash. It is an inverted pyramid of piffle. It is all completely untrue and ludicrous conjecture. I am amazed people can write this drivel.' Presumably Boris considered himself spared. His extraordinary 'pyramid of piffle' phrase – although not a new addition to his lexicon – was both eye-catching and definitive. Howard let it be known that he thought a politician's private life was just that – private. No further action was needed. On the Monday, Petronella's mother went along with Boris's denial, telling the *Daily Mail* that her daughter's liaison with Boris was nothing more than a 'close relationship.'

The story had broken just as Marina was setting off on a legal case at the high-security hospital at Broadmoor. Those present felt deeply for her. 'I kept thinking how lovely she was, and how desperately sorry I felt for her,' recalls one person on the same visit. 'But you soon realised that mentioning it or expressing sympathy would have been absolutely taboo – no matter what you read in the papers each day. She made it unthinkable to broach the subject. She was just focused on her work and you had to respect that.' Indeed, another former close friend found herself estranged when she contacted Marina again after reading about the Wyatt saga. It was as if she was offended that the friend had not only taken note but was now commenting on the story: 'When all the stuff came out, I hadn't seen her for a while but I sent her an email asking her whether she was OK. I never got a reply – and haven't heard from her since.' For a woman of such dignity, even expressions of sympathy must be torture.

While Boris was still denying the affair publicly, Marina obviously knew better and ordered him out of the family home. Because she had long since known about the relationship no doubt Boris thought she would now accept the media consequences too. But while she was angry at what she considered to be press exaggeration – although related to many journalists, Marina has a habit of not believing what she reads in the papers – she was also cross that it was now clear that Boris had continued to see Petronella when he had agreed to stop. In fact, the consensus is that Petronella became pregnant when Boris sought to rekindle the affair after a break over the summer holidays. Any hopes of Marina just accepting the situation – and the idea that Boris might be 'allowed' to have another family with Petronella – were seemingly dashed. Boris would have to choose.

With a single set of clothes – a grey tweed suit, white shirt and burgundy pullover – he retreated to the Camden home of Justin Rushbrooke, a friend from Balliol, and his wife Nell Butler, daughter of the former Cabinet Secretary, Lord Butler. Rushbrooke, who knew Marina before he met Boris, studied Classics at Balliol before returning to study Law. Nell, who works in television, is tactful and loyal. The couple, and particularly Nell, have taken on the role of supporters-in-chief in Johnsonian crises and crucially are not part of Petronella's circle. Boris is probably now closer to Rushbrooke – a witty cricket-mad Old Harrovian who regularly skis with him – than any other man outside his family. He finds a bond in fellow Classicists – even if Rushbrooke went on to pursue another degree and a career in another field. He and his wife, whose glittering circle of friends say they 'like to keep Boris to themselves,' are very discreet about the friendship. They have taken Boris in on more than one episode of marital discord and even tolerate his general messiness and predilection for leaving coffee cups around their house while in residence, despite the fact that they themselves are well-known for impeccable levels of tidiness.

Rushbrooke is said to enjoy the 'excitement' and 'unpredictability' of being friends with Boris – even when on occasion it leads to disappointment. At Rushbrooke's 40th birthday party in a London restaurant, Boris was designated to make the celebratory speech only to dry up in embarrassment. 'Boris fizzled out,' recalls another guest. 'He just made a very bad speech and ran out of things to say about the birthday man, which was surprising when Justin is supposedly his best friend. But Justin didn't mind, he just said that's what you get with Boris – you never know whether an idea he has will work out or not.' During the Petronella saga Rushbrooke put up Boris for a full week – even at one point smuggling him into a smart drinks party in Chester Square – in the same outfit, of course.

On the Thursday of that week Boris turned up again in the same garb at Claridge's for the *Spectator* Parliamentarian of the Year lunch. Held in the Art Deco ballroom, the event is well attended by media glitterati and the more interesting sort of politician. A place for Petronella was laid at one of the big round tables but she did not turn up. Someone removed her name from the guest list with a rubber. Nor did Marina appear. But invitees such as Jeremy Paxman, David Trimble, Sir David Frost and Lord Lawson all made an appearance. Over lunch of Filet d'Agneau and Mousseline of Soubise, there was quite a buzz about 'Boris's problem', with guests gossiping over the previous weekend's coverage. There was even more of a frisson of excitement when Boris and Michael Howard both mounted the stage just before coffee. Although Howard had stood by Boris, it was clear there was a tension between them – the fact that Marina had lost patience with her husband cannot have improved Howard's view. Boris opened with a remark about 'shrugging off the assaults of the press, which can be less than wholly helpful' before handing over to the Conservative Leader.

Howard, when relaxed, is quite a giggler in private but until that lunch he had not been widely known for a playful sense of humour and so it was all the more surprising when his address prompted an outbreak of mirth. For once, the crowd were laughing *at* Boris, rather than with him. 'The *Spectator* is an incomparable magazine,' Howard began. 'There is nothing like the *Spectator* for stirring up and stimulating political controversy. Indeed, in all senses of the word it could best be described as political Viagra. And I must take this opportunity of congratulating Boris on the tremendous enthusiasm with which you have approached your various front-bench duties. You were keen to make your mark with the City of Culture [Liverpool]. And you succeeded beyond my wildest dreams. All I can say is, Boris, keep it up!'

Cue unbounded hilarity from the audience who could not quite believe their ears. There was only one person in the room who was not creased up with laughter. According to Quentin Letts in the *Mail*, Boris's 'mouth assumed a fishy quality: gaping, rounded, assembled into an expression of hooked horror.' When he recovered slightly, those nearby could hear him muttering: 'He can't get away with this! Outrageous, outrageous!' Ever the joker, Boris does not care for the joke to be on him, but it was a joke rather than a dismissal, that much was clear.

On the Friday, he drove down to Henley – still in the same clothes – for a Golf Club dinner and returned home to his friends' house in Camden that night. When questioned about his failure to change his attire for nigh on a week, he shot back: 'I am a man of thrift and economy.' But he was also now a man of hope: there had been discreet talks with Marina and he was clearly hoping that a reconciliation might be on the cards.

On the Saturday, Guy Black's afternoon was disturbed again. Both Simon Walters of the *Mail on Sunday* and Andy Coulson of the *News of the World* (now David Cameron's notorious ex-spin doctor) rang as he ate lunch in a bistro on a weekend break to Paris. Now there was no way back. Petronella's 'friends' (who turned out to be her mother Verushka) had finally confirmed the whole story, from the affair to the abortion. She also revealed that Petronella was upset over Boris's denials of their relationship – almost certainly the reason why she had decided to speak out. Boris had told the most enormous whopper, not just to the press but also to Guy Black and Michael Howard. Moreover, Black had been made to look duplicitous. 'I think the indulgence of Boris had passed at that point but it was nothing to do with the way he conducted his private life,' says a well-placed source. 'The key here is that Michael couldn't bear any lying to the newspapers.'

At around 2 p.m., Howard, on his way to another football match, instructed Guy Black to inform Boris that he would have to resign from his position as shadow arts minister and party vice-chairman. His crime was not the affair or even the abortion but the fact that he had lied. But Boris refused to go, arguing he had a right to lie to the tabloid press, if he wanted.

By six that evening, the *Mail on Sunday* and *News of the World* were both requesting official statements. But however hard Guy Black argued, Boris refused to quit, insisting it was *acceptable* to lie. He had after all backed President Clinton in the Monica Lewinsky scandal, arguing then that it was not only sometimes justifiable but on occasion actually desirable to tell untruths about sex; he even took the view that Clinton had been Lewinsky's victim because she had hung around the outside of the Oval Office in a low-cut dress, 'transpiring at every pore with lust.'[2] Clinton continued to lead the Free World while conducting his fling, so Boris was unable to see why he should not continue as the Conservatives' man of the arts. Indeed, he argued whom he slept with had no bearing on his fitness for political office and he believed that revelations of his philandering, just as with Clinton, were motivated by 'snivelling and short-sighted' attitudes and jealousy. Perhaps the very fact that he appears to consider monogamy and constancy as pathetically suburban and bourgeois, contributes to his anarchic appeal. Many who know him expound the idea that Boris is the 'opposite of a little Englander' and that he despises anything bourgeois or petty-minded. Of course, such a lover of the ancient Greeks might well consider extra-marital sex as nothing more than a harmless pleasure. Boris does not preach to others, and certainly does not care to be preached at in turn. There was, in short, no persuading him to go.

With Howard's beloved Liverpool scraping a narrow 3-2 victory over comparative minnows Crystal Palace, Guy Black contacted him with the news that Boris was digging in his heels. Howard duly delivered the bullet himself by phone at 6.30 during a 'terse' conversation described at the time as one of the fastest political sackings in history. Boris's reaction was delivered through the letterbox of his friends' front door: 'I am sorry this decision has been taken in response to stories about my private life. I am looking forward to helping promote a new Conservative policy on the arts, and I will continue to do my utmost to serve the people of Henley and south Oxfordshire. I am now going to have a stiff drink.'

The next day the tabloids were awash with headlines. The *News of the World*'s front page screamed 'BONKING BORIS MADE ME PREGNANT' over pictures of 'mistress' Petronella opposite 'liar' and 'love cheat' Boris. A 'friend' was quoted in the paper as saying that Boris had agreed with Petronella's decision to terminate his child: 'and his reaction was of immense relief – just like any married man caught out by his infidelity.' The *Mail on Sunday*'s 'BORIS SACKED FOR LYING OVER AFFAIR' went on to reveal that Petronella had lost two babies, although one reportedly through a miscarriage (which appears to explain the recuperation in Florida).

Far from keeping it quiet, Boris's lies had ensured that details of his sex life were now plastered everywhere. He had made his party's top brass look like dupes. But while Howard – and perhaps Guy Black even more – were furious, Boris had in the interim managed to save his marriage. Marina's friends say the ferocity of the press coverage and Howard's decision to fire Boris actually helped him in his cause. Indeed, Boris put it about that he had asked to be dismissed. 'I'd recommend getting ignominiously sacked – and I want you to know that I insisted on my right to be sacked: "Sack me," I said, by way of an ultimatum because it is only by being sacked that you can truly engender sympathy. Nothing excites compassion, in friend and foe alike, as much as the sight of you ker-splonked on the Tarmac with your propeller buried six feet under.'[3] High risk maybe, this strategy certainly seems to have been effective. After a week in the doghouse, he was allowed back into the marital home, at first into a spare room but then eventually into his full conjugal status.

He celebrated with an early jog, leaving home at 7.30 on Monday, 15 November, just 24 hours after being dubbed the 'love rat' by the Sundays. Once again he used clothing to convey a message, in this case an outlandish get-up of floral board shorts and a skull and crossbones ski-hat belonging to one of his sons. It all spoke of a certain triumph and joy. He advised the astonished reporters waiting to interview to him to enjoy a 'beautiful day.' The jolly mood was rather deflated, however, when he returned home to find his front door locked. He had to wait to be allowed in (and later confessed to fantasies of 'mowing down' the journalists watching his discomfort 'like a scene in an old Sylvester Stallone film'.[4]) It was perhaps merely a defiant gesture, but as the seconds passed before he was admitted, Boris gave the press pack the Panglossian observation, 'all is for the best in the best of all possible worlds.'

This gnomic reference to Voltaire's famously optimistic character left most of those present baffled. Only with hindsight does it seem to imply that Boris may actually have been relieved at the outcome. His relationship with Howard was always going to be strained after Operation Scouse Grovel – and there were suggestions that he had planned to leave the front bench anyway of his own volition. The revelations about Petronella also forced him into making a once-and-for-all decision that by nature he was reluctant to take. But there was also a manic need for optimism in the face of adversity and he continued in the same relentlessly upbeat theme in the *Telegraph* with the comment: 'My friends, as I have discovered myself, there are no disasters, only opportunities. And, indeed, opportunities for fresh disasters.'

Marina's decision to take Boris back after such a public betrayal has puzzled many – and particularly women – ever since. Margaret Cook, whose husband Robin, the former Foreign Secretary, betrayed her with his secretary, was one such woman to vent her anger and dismay at the saga. 'The deference and privileges received in the Palace of Westminster,' she wrote, 'tend to inflate a man's idea of his own importance, and this particular man obviously feels above the rules that govern the plebs.'[5] She pointed to the contrasts between the pictures in the press of Petronella – 'frivolous party gear, all low necklines and stocking tops, fringes, flesh and fancy jewels' – with those of Marina – 'high-necked, cover-up, winter woollies.' But like many men – and a surprising number of women – she hinted that

Marina could barely have expected any other outcome: 'While feeling sorry for the wife, I cannot help remembering a time some eleven years ago when she performed the same trick on Allegra Mostyn-Owen. She became pregnant and got her man. Maybe that was what led Petronella to rate her chances highly of doing the same.'

If Cook's high-handed account sounded like the stuff of soap opera, the true picture was even more complicated. On 14 October Boris had defied a rare attack of flu not to attend either his pregnant mistress just four days before she had an abortion, or his wife and children at home, but an attractive young Oxford undergraduate. Boris explained that he was 'as sick as a dog and could barely speak. But I would be letting the side down if I hadn't attended.' The event in question was an Oxford Union debate – on the customary 'this House has no confidence in Her Majesty's Government' – with Lord Lamont and John Redwood. In the chair just happened to be one Ruzwana Bashir, with whom the papers said he had struck up 'a close relationship' (and who had attended that summer's *Spectator* party.)

Boris is nothing if not energetic and goes for a certain upmarket type. At any one time, there were usually at least one or two well-bred Oxbridge women in short skirts starting out in journalism – and quite a few found themselves invited to a *Spectator* lunch so that Boris could give them 'advice.' One such attractive, bright and well-heeled young woman – with the curtain of swishy straight hair he goes for – was targeted several times by Boris during this period and she spotted others of a similar style (he does not do cocktail waitresses) subjected to the same 'treatment'. She describes his technique: 'He invades your personal space, gets really close up to you, and then with those slightly popping blue eyes of his says intently in a deep voice: "You really must come and write for me at the *Spectator*."

'I can see why it would work with a particular sort of emotionally vulnerable young woman but it certainly didn't work with me. In the end he gave up and tried someone else,' she says.

Boris has an almost Clintonesque ability to make the person he is talking to at any one time – male or female – feel special. 'He makes the rest of the world disappear,' says one admirer. So while he was five foot ten inches of goosey flesh, overweight, sweaty and not classically handsome by any means, he was fast becoming one of Britain's most accomplished lotharios. It is, in any case, his brain that really attracts. Otherwise rational young women have even asked him to sign their underwear – knowing Boris, it is likely he obliged.

As so often in these situations, one or other of the women involved was attracting more of the blame than the culprit-in-chief himself. In Henley Marina's supposed failure as a wife was commonly held up as a reason for her husband's infidelity. 'We were having a Conservative ladies' luncheon when the Petronella story blew up,' recalls Maggie Pullen of the South Oxfordshire Conservatives. 'Some of them were quite elderly and I thought they're going to be horrified but they blamed Marina – it's all the wife's fault, they said. They all agreed that it was because she works and spends far too much time with the children.' But how Marina can be blamed for Boris's roving eye is far from clear. He once told another man that he had to have a lot of affairs because he was 'literally busting with spunk.' On another occasion, he is reputed to have asked a woman whether she would like to be Mistress 2009. 'Marrying Marina created a job vacancy for a mistress' became a common refrain among men who vicariously enjoyed his sexual adventures. The *Henley Standard* ran a banner headline over its front page: 'WE STAND BY BORIS'.

Not that Marina, who never really took to Henley anyway, would have taken much notice of the chatter: she is her own woman and would have taken the decision that best suited first, her children (her eldest had just started secondary school) and then her own needs. She handled it all with dignity, never succumbing to the temptation to vent her anger or frustration to a journalist – even though she personally knew dozens who would have lent a sympathetic ear. Like Boris, Marina seems particularly adept at compartmentalising her life. 'I had lunch with her at a time when she could easily have bawled him out about his behaviour,' says Sarah Sands. 'But she was very upbeat and loyal, calmly talking about plans for a family holiday.' And so she continued to focus on her work, enduring the stares and sotto voce comments of those she encountered, in and out of court.

In heart-breaking fashion, one of Marina's most protective friends explains her extraordinary fortitude: 'She copes because she knows he loves her. In any case, it is not so much the affair itself that hurts, it's the publicity and humiliation.' Robert Seabrook QC, the head of her chambers at One Crown Office Row, has observed her through many a crisis and marvels at Marina's ability to deal with Boris. 'Her self-containment is part of her charm,' he says. 'She must skip a beat but you never see her in tears.'

Whatever the appearances, their marriage is a union of equals. It is wrong to assume that Marina is the downtrodden wife who sticks by her errant husband because she has to. She has her own life, her own career, her own friends, her own beliefs – and, according to a couple of her friends, her own low-key flirtations including, it is said, a crush on the actor Neil Pearson. She expresses herself through a confident dress sense fortressed by a large collection of shoes and expensive hairdressing. Quieter and more reserved than Boris, in some ways Marina is tougher because she is not scared of confrontation – for example, in negotiations on house buying, she is plain speaking and forthright.

She also kept Boris on a long leash and the papers raised the suggestion that she might yet sue for divorce. She was, after all, an expert in that field of law and could have made it expensive. So concerned were the management at the *Spectator* that Dan Colson took Boris aside to give him a paternal word of advice. 'I said, "You know you're terrific, but I also think you must have a death wish,"' recalls Colson. "Because in case you've not noticed, you've got four kids, you're not rich and you're married to a fierce barrister, who is a divorce lawyer. You're going to be living on the bread line at this rate." He just did the normal Boris routine, "oh, aaarh, grrrr, of course, of course."'

Marina's parents – Charles and Dip Wheeler – had been so supportive of the marriage with Boris in its early days and continued to deny that he was guilty of any wrongdoing as long as they plausibly could. 'There was a great sense of embarrassment for them over the whole Boris thing,' says one prominent journalist and old friend of Charles. 'They were careful never to make disparaging remarks but the episode over Petronella was torture for them.' A couple of friends of the family suggest Marina's parents in part blamed Petronella's mother for pursuing the idea of her daughter marrying Boris. But in any case, it seems that Charles also took Boris aside for a talk – warning him to stop humiliating his daughter and the Wheelers as a whole. Boris respected and admired his father-in-law and no doubt took in his strong words on the subject.

Although never an establishment figure, Wheeler's reputation as a correspondent was such that ambassadors and Government ministers would rise deferentially when he entered a room and later, in 2006, he was granted a knighthood for Services to Journalism. In the presence of such a distinguished man, even Boris could appear uncharacteristically subdued. 'He was never the rumbustious figure with Charles that one knows publicly,' recalls the journalist Adam Raphael. Boris promised to behave and 'put on a good Christmas.' As part of the reconciliation process, he took the whole family away on a skiing holiday to St Anton.

While Marina grew in stature from the saga, Boris was undoubtedly chastened. His front-bench career seemed to be over, virtually before it had started. If, as Henry Kissinger once noted, 'power is the ultimate aphrodisiac,' then Boris perhaps found his sexual magnetism not quite 'weapons grade' any more. Michael Portillo led the growing chorus that Boris had proved himself a lightweight. 'When I first met Boris Johnson, I marked him down as unserious. He came to interview me as Defence Secretary and arrived forty-five minutes late. Apparently, experienced political journalist that he was, he had thought the ministry was in Victoria Street, not in Whitehall. He had the decency to look flushed and sweaty, but also gave the impression that I should find his shambolic performance endearing. I pretended to do so.'[6] Worse still, other Tories of his generation, such as David Cameron, George Osborne and Michael Gove, were winning glowing notices from Portillo and others. And they were all at least two years younger than him.

But that is not to say that there was not still some residual sympathy for Boris. Not a few (mostly male) commentators believed that Howard had done his own standing no good in being harsh with his far more popular subordinate. In the *Observer*, David Aaronovitch wrote that most voters were not nearly as 'narrow-minded as muck-raking Sunday tabloids or fear-scented politicians believe. They liked Boris and – my guess is – they will now like Michael Howard and his party less on account of his unnecessary departure.' And many years later – now retired from political life – even Howard has come to regret his decision, perhaps with the aid of that 'blessed sponge of amnesia' again.

'I should have been more relaxed,' he admits. 'We never knew whether the allegations were actually true. It was represented to me that he had lied to my press secretary and my press secretary took that very seriously. And that's why I didn't like it. But if I had my time again, I wouldn't sack him. Boris's view was that it would all have blown over. And I think it probably would.'

There were also a handful of senior Tories, even then, who still considered Boris destined for great things and believed his current troubles to be merely temporary distractions but at the tail end of 2004, the immediate outlook was not rosy. There were rumours again that his tenure at the *Spectator* was no longer secure. On the day of the famous jog, the magazine had passed from Conrad Black and, along with the *Telegraph* newspapers, into the less-indulgent hands of the Roman Catholic Barclay Brothers. The *Spectator*'s new chief executive was Andrew Neil, a grammar school boy from Paisley and former *Sunday Times* editor, who was not expected to take kindly to Boris's Etonian excesses. Boris's writ would never run so large again – there would be less laughter at the *Spectator* and perhaps rather less daytime sex, too. Harry, Ann Sindall's dog, was to be banned, as was ping pong in the garden. In fact, the whole magazine would eventually move out of the house of fun into rather less atmospheric accommodation.

Almost straightaway Neil told the Radio 4 *Today* programme – the message board for the chattering classes – that: 'We are looking forward to a period of quiet. I think the more time the editor spends in Doughty Street editing the magazine and the less we see of him in the newspapers, then the better for the editor and the better for the magazine.' The Barclay brothers were said to want a more serious and cerebral publication with fewer scandals (however good they might be for circulation, which was at a record high of nearly 70,000).

Mercifully for Boris, his 'period of quiet' came quickly. A week later, the *Sunday Telegraph* broke the story that 'open war' had broken out between Kimberly Fortier and David Blunkett. Their relationship had collapsed in acrimony when she returned to her husband Stephen Quinn. Blunkett also faced accusations that he had fast-tracked a visa for her Filipina nanny, and so began a series of events that finally led to the Labour Home Secretary's resignation on 15 December. The next day Kimberly was in hospital having her second child. Boris proposed a toast to 'absent friends now languishing in their beds. I miss her – this is not a popular view – I miss her dynamism.' It was classic two-edged Boris – giving something with one hand by saying he missed 'her dynamism' while taking it back with the other by saying, 'this is not a popular view.'

So at the end of a challenging year, Boris found himself on probation at home, considered an unreliable loose cannon by his own party and an attention-seeker by the *Spectator*'s new boss. At least the kerfuffle did nothing to dent his earnings, which were now mounting fast – one lucrative by-product of the *Sextator* saga was that he was in hot demand as an after-dinner speaker on some £10,000 a time. With his TV appearances, *Telegraph* column and other journalism, he was making £150,000 a year before either his undisclosed *Spectator* salary or the £59,000 MP's pay. But it meant that he ended the year having started (and finished) a frontbench career and with even more enemies in his own party's ranks.

Charles Moore, who continued to use him as a columnist, saw the funny side of the story. He started cracking the joke: 'I told Boris I don't care what he does in his private life and he told me, "Nor do I."' Others had a lot of fun with the 'pleasing similarity' of the word 'piffle' and Boris's third name 'de Pfeffel'. Even his old boss, Dan Colson, enjoyed the fun, noting: 'He always looked like he'd just got out of bed and apparently he had.' No doubt Boris hoped it would all die down into a longer period of what Andrew Neil called 'quiet' but alas, this was not to be. There was so much action in Boris's life that other people wanted a part of it.

The *Spectator Affair*, which was broadcast on BBC 2 in February 2005, had started off as a film portrait of Boris as much as his magazine. But in the event, there was surprise that Boris's 'shenaningans' were less prominent than those involving either Fortier or Rod Liddle. Boris, of course, was a national figure by this point. 'Boris emerged from the programme relatively unscathed,' the 'Londoner's Diary' in the *Evening Standard* reported. 'His affair with Petronella Wyatt was barely referred to – leading some to suggest a deal was done behind the scenes between Johnson and the BBC. "Boris had them over a barrel regarding interviews, filming in the *Spectator* offices and the *Spectator* archive," says an insider. However, the programme's producer, Patrick Forbes, denies accusations of a stitch-up.'[7]

In truth, Forbes – one of Britain's most experienced and respected documentary makers – had found Boris extremely difficult to work with. He recalls being shocked at his first meeting back in 2004, having known him previously only by reputation as a bumbling raconteur. An employee of Forbes' company, Oxford Film and Television, conducted the on-camera interview with Boris, 'but because we were more worried than usual about potential trouble, I went along as well. I have never seen anyone who is tougher behind the eyes than him in a billion years of interviewing. He is clearly a right piece of work. He's completely under control – except in one area, where women are concerned. He made no attempt to engage at all, and avoided answering all the questions. His bluster and wit serves to obscure his real politics, which are nasty. He is a charmingly evasive and ruthless customer.

'He gave the interview with eventual good grace after he realised that more of the other people involved were talking to us than he had expected. No fool he. We couldn't understand why he didn't want to do it, but then all the stuff about his private life exploded.'

The fly-on-the-wall concept was subsequently abandoned in favour of merely chronicling events – there were in any case a lot of them.

The *Spectator Affair* also featured an interview with a brooding Lord Black, now in the United States fighting criminal charges and multi-million dollar law suits. Perhaps understandably given the unflattering personal coverage Boris had run about his former patron, he hit out at him, dismissing his one-time protégé as treacherous. 'Boris has his charms,' he growled, 'but Boris is not Mr Loyalty.' It was a damaging, if justifiable, observation. But by July, there was a rapprochement and the pair lunched together in London on one of Black's last visits to Britain before his incarceration.

It appears that Boris had somehow avoided the blame for the 2004 *Spectator* article with its references to Black's hairy knuckles, murky business origins and provincialism. It had, after all, appeared under the political editor Peter Oborne's byline – like the earlier hazardous piece attacking the Conservative leader Iain Duncan Smith. Black's right-hand man and friend Dan Colson says: 'The Oborne piece was bitchy but I'm 99 per cent sure that Boris didn't read it before it went out. It's not OK, of course – it's Boris.' In turn, Black now comments: 'The Oborne piece was irritating but there were many worse at the time and (later) [Boris] wrote a nice letter to the trial judge in Chicago for me. I consider him a friendly acquaintance.'

Boris was now playing it safe at the *Spectator*, however, and the magazine no longer had the sparkle and irreverence of its recent past. But all these events were sideshows to the real political arena, where he was now a conspicuous absence. There were quite a few voices in the Conservative ranks – and elsewhere – who believed they were witnessing a sad squandering of talent. Even Guy Black began to feel some sympathy: 'Boris disappeared from view – you couldn't help feeling a bit sorry for him.' (In turn, Boris is said by colleagues of the time to have chiefly blamed Black for his downfall. His rage at him was 'scarcely containable,' one said.)

In the lead-up to the General Election of May 2005, however, Howard was intent on instilling discipline in the party as it prepared its latest attempt to dethrone Tony Blair. Conservative fixers were at pains to keep a tight leash on Boris – arguably still their greatest electoral asset. A senior member of the Conservative Central Office staff during that election recalls specifically being told to 'keep Boris out of the picture.' 'It was all very tightly controlled,' he recalls. 'Boris's quotes were kept to a minimum.' A very senior Tory (who now advises him) was just one who simply dismissed Boris at this point as an 'idiot.'

Even in Henley, Boris was comparatively little seen. Oliver Tickell, son of Sir Crispin and a family friend of the Johnsons, had stood for the Green Party against Boris in the 2001 election. Although he did not stand again in 2005, he watched the local campaigns closely and could not help noticing how rarely Boris was 'let out.'

Underemployed in Henley, Boris slipped away at one point to advance the Johnson dynasty as a whole by helping his father Stanley fight Teignbridge in South Devon – a rare example of a father attempting to follow his son into Parliament. Nevertheless, Boris increased his majority in Henley over the Liberal Democrats to 12,793. Stanley eventually lost to the Lib Dems by 6,215. Nationally, the Conservatives had lost for a third time to Tony Blair, winning only an extra 33 new seats and reducing Labour's majority from 167 to 66.

So Boris was returned to Henley, but some local Conservatives thought they detected a certain loss of fizz. 'I think he wanted something more,' recalls Maggie Pullen. Local campaigners working to save Townlands hospital also noticed a shift in his attitude and began to attack him publicly for failing in his support. Terry Buckett, chairman of the Save Townlands Action Group, told the *Henley Standard* how disappointed he was. 'I watched a House of Commons debate on the TV recently and Boris wasn't there,' he said. 'We want him to represent us at this level and he's not doing it.' A normally supportive councillor, Dianne Browne, complained: 'We've had no help from him recently.'[8]

Events in London would only make matters worse. In July 2005 the *Spectator*'s own theatre critics staged a play called *Who's the Daddy*? at the King's Head theatre in Islington. Toby Young and Lloyd Evans had decided to convert the *Sextator* 'bonkathon' into a stage farce with Boris as principal character. Many of those cackling in the audience at this spectacularly irreverent piece were *Spectator* staffers. They chortled at the actor playing Boris, who was wearing a pair of 'grotesque' tiger-print boxers over 'plump, margarine haunches glistening horridly' under the stage lights. One of them was Boris's assistant Ann Sindall, who claimed she had been driven by 'curiosity' to attend the riotous first night. Asked whether the on-stage version of the *Spectator* matched the real one, she refused to comment, although she did note, 'I think they've got Kimberly down to a tee.'[9]

It was also reported that a lawyer representing David Blunkett – now restored to the Cabinet in charge of Work and Pensions – was among those looking particularly amused. Actually Blunkett, who in real life had endured a painfully public spat over the paternity of Kimberly Fortier's second child plus a tearful resignation as Home Secretary, emerged as the play's most sympathetic character. Whereas Fortier was portrayed, according to the *Evening Standard*'s reviewer, as a 'heartless acquisitor of his powerful sexual scalp', who frequently scrapped with Petronella – typically clad in Chanel, glugging Krug and carrying dozens of upmarket shopping bags.

Boris utters a series of rugby cries as he seduces Petsy in a broom cupboard – 'Come on, Petsy, nothing like a good scrum after lunch!' He also boasts of having sired four children – or is it five, he affects not to remember – all the products of what he refers to as his 'weapons grade testosterone.' Asked if he was planning to watch the play too, Boris replied cuttingly: 'I don't know whether I'll have time to catch it before it closes.' But the publicity was such that after five days, the play sold out for the rest of its six-week run and was lined-up for a transfer to the West End.

Amid all the laughter was the home truth that actual events and real people with very real emotions were being portrayed. Indeed, at one point during the play, there is a sobering moment when Boris's character says: 'Fine – turn my life into farce, everyone else has.' A few days into the run, one couple in the audience (who do not wish to be identified) sat there stony-faced and miserable. 'We couldn't believe what this must be doing to Marina,' the husband said. 'We wished we hadn't gone.'

According to friends, Petronella was damaged by the affair and its aftermath. Her mother even claimed the *Spectator* had ruined her daughter's life. Certainly, despite a couple of near misses, Petronella was still single. Nor had she had the children she so fervently wished for by the time she was 43 – in 2011. Indeed, some believe she still holds a torch for Boris. 'The women in Boris's life never quite escape him,' notes one family friend.

But Boris did not sack the two members of staff who had retold his life as a comedy, a step he would have had every right to take. They had given him six weeks' warning of their intentions but decided against their original idea of inviting him to advise on the script, recognising this would more than test Boris's legendary sense of humour and might possibly bring the whole project to an abrupt halt. Instead they wrote to him in placatory terms:

> We were worried that having one of the key protagonists present during the creative process might skew our objectivity too heavily in your favour. Hope you'll come to the show. We're sure that everyone at the Spec will adore it . . .
> All the best
> Toby,
> Lloyd

In turn, he wrote them an equally flattering reply, part of which as seen above, was included in his character's lines. Just like Boris, Evans and Young are enthusiastic recyclers of life into art.

> Dear Lloyd and Toby,
> Thanks for your letter. I always had a feeling that my life would turn into a farce, and I am glad the script has been entrusted to 2 such distinguished men of letters.
> All the best, as ever
> Boris

Boris even allowed Young to go ahead with plans to edit a special issue of the magazine, declaring: 'I believe in spreading peace and love.'

'Unlike most ambitious politicians, Boris has worked out that it is much better that if someone has a go at you, to laugh it off,' explains an admirer. 'It is an extension of the never openly being rude thing that Boris has. It's very hard to do, but very effective in avoiding making enemies.' Indeed, Boris chose to underline his *sang froid* in one newspaper interview with a series of ostentatiously obscure words – as if his flexing his intellect publicly in this way gave him comfort or perhaps protection. Claiming to feel 'eirenic' (peace-seeking) and 'ataraxic' (serenely indiffererent) about Evans' and Young's act of perfidiousness, he declared: 'I'm certainly issuing no instructions to staff about it. It will not be deemed an act of disloyalty to go and see it.' Although when he added sarcastically, 'I'm sure it will be a thoroughly good lark. Ha, ha, ha,' the interviewer sensed Boris's ataraxia was not as 'complete and total' as he claimed.[10]

But Evans certainly admired how Boris continued to appear so calm, even forgiving in public, however angry it made him privately. 'Toby showed Boris the actual script of *Who's the Daddy?* before it went on stage and he found it utterly distressing,' he recalls of events just before opening night. 'He could only bring himself to read the first two or three pages but he played his hand very cleverly. He started off by indulging us, not sacking us, and sent us the note about turning his life into farce. But when it turned into a success and was going to transfer to the West End, he had moral leverage over us because he hadn't cut the rope before. At this point Toby, whom he knew would make the decision, was getting phone calls from Boris three times a day.'

Boris's moral leverage was of a heart-wrenching variety: the theatre was only a mile from the Johnsons' home in Furlong Road. Boris said his daughter passed it twice a day on her route to school. 'He told us that she was embarrassed answering questions about it from her friends,' says Evans. 'This way he persuaded us not to take the play to the West End, which was fair enough. But to blame us for the pain caused to Marina and the children is not fair. My theory is that we did Marina a favour. I imagine that some little part of Marina's mind would have said, "Well, this bloody serves Boris right!" From my point of view, yes, we were writing about this, but Boris initiated the pain. But I doubt she saw it like that – she has four children with Boris so she just has to get on with it.' (Later, Boris's mother Charlotte would admit her grandchildren had been 'through thick and thin' at this time but that fortunately they were 'survivors and sturdy.')

Publicly, Boris seemed to be rolling over and admitting mea culpa, even conceding, 'Yes, I was due for a good kicking.' When asked if he had begun to believe some of the fawning articles written about him before his fall from grace, he replied: 'I think we all construct a series of alternative illusions about ourselves,' and then after a long pause, 'verging from the modest and miserable to the really rather demented and grandiose. But there's no harm in allowing yourself, on a Wednesday evening, after you've drunk something and produced what you think is a particularly snorting column, to feel that you're quite good.'[11]

Marina, meanwhile, was indeed 'getting on with it.' At the *Spectator* annual summer party exactly a fortnight after the play opened, she turned up as usual in a heroic display of marital loyalty. A protective knot formed round her as Toby Young also showed and pressed past her through the crowd into the garden. Relations between the Johnson camp and the playwrights were undoubtedly cool. In solidarity, Rachel Johnson disinvited Young to her birthday celebrations. And according to a senior Henley Tory, the local agent Wayne Lawley now started acting as Boris's 'minder.' 'After the Petronella story, Wayne was always there with Boris to keep him roped in,' he said.

But no one could claim the past nine months had been anything short of disastrous for Boris. What's more, Guy Black would now be a colleague – he was about to join the *Telegraph* group as director of communications. The rumours continued about Boris's editorship at the *Spectator*. Even one of his own contributors – his predecessor as editor, Frank Johnson – regularly wrote about him in 'unflattering' terms. While Boris affected ignorance of the speculation on his future and batted away criticisms with his usual brand of humour, the strains must have told. 'There will come an evening or a morning or a noon day when I will be gathered to the Valhalla of ex-*Spectator* editors, but I haven't yet,' he quipped to the *Independent*. Even under stress, he could still turn a pretty phrase. No doubt that was why the criticism of him was less severe than it might otherwise have been and his popularity nationally showed few signs of abating. He chose not to react by becoming more serious and pompous – as his fellow politicians would have him do – but persisted in the reverse.

In one of the most revealing interviews in this period of his life, he was asked whether the Barclay Brothers continued to support him. He told the *Independent*: 'Oh, they've been absolutely fine. I know that highly misleading newspaper reports may have given another impression but we live a life of almost embarrassingly monastic seclusion and contemplation. It is no exaggeration to say that we are capable of arguing for three hours about Anselm's ontological argument. There is a *Name of the Rose* kind of atmosphere here. You know, monks bent over . . .' (He drifts off for a moment, leaving open just what the monks are up to while 'bent over'.) 'I can't quite remember what happens in *The Name of the Rose*. Oh, it gets rather racy, doesn't it? OK, forget it!' He continued to insist humour should not hold him back in politics, whatever the sages might warn of its effect on his career. 'I mean, I find I don't have much difficulty getting people to listen to me seriously when I want to. And I'm not going to produce a series of spine-crackingly tedious pamphlets for the sake of gravitas. I think it's important to remember that most people find politics unbelievably dull, so I don't see any particular vice in trying to sugar the pill with a few jokes.'

But if the sagas of the previous months had taught him anything, it was surely a recognition that he must eventually choose between journalism and politics. At the age of 41, with a future at the *Spectator* no longer realistically a long-term option, with his failure to land the *Sunday Telegraph* editorship, perhaps it was no wonder he was leaning towards politics. 'It's a great privilege to run the *Spectator*,' he said, 'but I'm also a Member of Parliament. There must come a point when the two horses start to diverge. I think it would be pretty rotten to keep asking the people of Henley to return me to Westminster and not give it a really good kick of the can.'[12]

And yet his party was little nearer to returning to government and he was arguably further than ever from returning to the front benches: it was Boris who had been given a good kicking.

Chapter Eleven
'Cynical self-interest'

2005–2007

Boris might be down, but a man of such determined optimism should rarely be considered out. The disappointing Conservative showing in the May 2005 General Election gave him just the opportunity he needed to re-enter the fray. The next day, Michael Howard announced that he would be resigning, prompting the fourth change of Tory Leader in eight years. Not that Boris was intending to stand, of course, at least not yet; he was far too canny not to appreciate that such a short, junior and accident-prone stint on the front benches was hardly a fitting qualification for throwing his own headwear into the ring. 'My hat is firmly in my sock drawer, where it will remain,' he quipped.

Howard said he wanted to make way for a younger man. His decision to delay the contest until the autumn – to allow the party to consider whether to change the rules for electing a successor – played into the hands of a very young contender indeed. David Davis, a 56-year-old south London grammar school boy from the Right of the party, was the initial favourite. But Davis's brand of populist working-class Toryism – he had been brought up by a single mother on a council estate – had never been to Boris's taste. Boris had already recognised the electoral potential of the rapidly rising 38-year-old fellow Old Etonian, David Cameron.

Months before Cameron became a serious runner with an official campaign launch in September, Boris decided to back the man who had been two years his junior at school (and unlike him, certainly not a star). As early as June, he was one of a 'gaggle' of 14 mostly blue-blooded MPs, who came to pledge loyalty in a secret meeting in Portcullis House, a smart new annexe to the Palace of Westminster. The meeting was not a success – Cameron still seemed to be dithering about whether or not to stand – but Tory sources say Boris was one of those 'pressing hardest' on Cameron, right through his early 'wobble'.

News of Cameron's ambitions, and the fact that they were attracting support such as Boris's, soon emerged and by mid-June, bookmakers were placing Cameron second favourite behind Davis on odds of 5:1. Even so, backing Cameron had its risks for Boris and his hopes of returning to the front bench. Going into September 2005, the Cameroon 'compassionate Conservatism' campaign looked to be in trouble. It had so far failed to attract much Parliamentary support; there were even suggestions from some MPs that he should 'go away.' But Cameron's official launch on 29 September highlighted the contrast between his modernising style (chill-out music and strawberry smoothies in a circular white space) and the tired, retread feel of Davis's event in a stuffy oak-panelled room. Sensing the tide turning towards his man, Boris told the *Independent*: 'I am backing David Cameron's campaign out of pure, cynical self-interest.' And his gamble looked as if it just might pay off.

Fortunately, Cameron was able to repay Boris's confidence a few days later at the Party Conference. At the Leadership candidates' beauty parade in Blackpool's Winter Gardens on 4 October, he delivered a career-changing performance that would define his image as a modern Conservative. Speaking without notes in the verb-light oratorical style developed by Tony Blair, he gave a rousing speech on bringing in a new generation to change the party and the country. When his pregnant wife Samantha joined him on stage, he patted her stomach and the wild applause continued for several extra minutes. In contrast, Davis's speech, although good in parts, received a negative press reaction. Boris had backed the right horse: Cameron had converted many doubters (despite his ill-advised quip at a private dinner that he was the 'heir to Blair.')

But Cameron's triumph was not an unalloyed joy for Boris – who had hitherto always been so much better known, and had also already passed the landmark age of 40. Boris was more experienced as a public performer, particularly on television where his cross-party popularity with the under-35s exceeded even the wildest Central Office fantasy. The unfortunate situation was made even worse by the fact that it was another *Etonian* laying claim to the great prize, and one who had also scooped a First-class Oxford degree compared to Boris's 2:1. Neither had Boris abandoned his own hopes entirely: for one thing, he had been assiduous in wooing his own constituency association with flattery and bonhomie but also many others with speeches to Tory activists all over the country. He had become a beloved figure in the national party – and outside it.

Boris's evident frustration at Cameron's success boiled over in a *Telegraph* piece at the beginning of October, which on closer reading portrayed the younger man as an over-praised unknown, who had stolen ideas from the far more deserving Boris – as well as his rightful job. He opens with the observation that 'over the past few months I have lost count of the number of people who have asked me – satirically – why I am not standing in the current Tory leadership contest.' (The clever deployment of 'satirically' here is a common Boris-ism used to leaven a very serious point with jokey self-deprecation.) He writes that he 'bumbles' out some reply on such occasions, and then says he is backing David Cameron instead. 'For the most part, this answer has so far drawn a look of anxious blankness, the look you see when people are sure that they ought to have read some classic work, and are in two minds whether to bluff it out or admit ignorance,' continues Boris in withering style. '"Oh yes," they say, mentally noting they ought to get to grips with the subject of David Cameron, Stephen Hawking's *Brief History of Time* and *Midnight's Children* by Salman Rushdie.' Ouch!

And while Boris concedes Cameron has some nice lines – not least his constant repetition of 'we're all in this together' – he continues, 'I have a feeling he nicked it from me.' He then takes the mockery to yet another level by citing a piece in that week's *Spectator* by Bruce Anderson (which he himself had commissioned), which he brands a 'kind of tear-sodden *nunc dimittis*. Like old Simeon in the temple, Brucie has seen our salvation . . . Cameron is our saviour and a light to lighten the gentiles.' However, even Boris is forced to admit that 'it has been the 38-year-old's week.'

Anderson was furious that his piece was thus portrayed as a drooling eulogy to Cameron and used as a stick with which to beat them both. But as usual, Boris had skilfully made his point without actually appearing to be nasty. It was a masterpiece in subtle sabotage – where a piece affects to conclude one thing when the balance of its arguments is very much in favour of the other. He covers his tracks beautifully by rounding off with the empty flourish that reform of both Toryism and the country was 'the job for Cameron, and Cameron is the man for the job' entirely against the tenor of the rest of the article.[1]

'Boris is brilliant at this subtle and cunning way of delivering a message while apparently saying the reverse,' notes Paul Goodman, his former comment editor at the *Telegraph*. It is indeed Boris's ingenious way of avoiding the full-on confrontation he fears; but in reality the article said more about his own anxieties than it did about Cameron's qualifications for the job.

It was time, though, for Boris to reposition himself as a serious politician. He had to convince Cameron during the final stages of the leadership race that despite these exercises in subtle sabotage, he was ready, willing and able to come back to frontbench politics. Indeed, surely it would be his just desserts. As usual, Boris chose an inventive route – an appearance on BBC Radio 4's *Desert Island Discs* with Sue Lawley. But far from the friendly chat he might have expected to be able to control, he was subjected to quite an interrogation by an interviewer he seems to have under-estimated. Now that he was re-branding himself as 'serious,' radio no longer permitted him many of the evasive tactics available in interviews past – jokes, Latin tags, flights of fantasy, strange gutteral noises (aaaaghs, grrrrrrs, mwahs, etc.). So, when Lawley confronted him on the choice that he had avoided ever since he was elected as an MP, he had no option but to answer.

Lawley: If you had to choose between journalism and politics, and you might, who knows, one day, have to do so, you'd choose politics, would you?

Boris: Yes, of course. But I don't think I would abandon journalism.

Lawley: But you'd have to. I mean, people have told you time and again: you can't ride two horses. You've probably proved you can't ride two horses.

Boris: I think I have successfully ridden two horses for quite a long time, but I have to admit there have been moments when the distance between the two horses has grown terrifyingly wide.

Lawley: Split you right down the middle.

Boris: And I did momentarily come off.

Lawley: But if you had to choose, you would choose, would you, politics?

Boris: Yes, of course. I always wanted to do it. I always knew I was going to be an MP. I didn't read *Hansard* as a pre-pubescent but I had the sense that this was the single most interesting job you can do, the job that involved testing you to the greatest extent and it involves the broadest possible canvas.

So, rather in the manner of the Petronella saga, extraneous events and other people were cornering Boris into making a decision. Where others including Conrad Black had failed, Lawley had in effect forced Boris to commit to leaving the *Spectator* to focus on his ambitions in politics. He even dropped a hint that a job in the unlikely-sounding agriculture or world trade would be an appropriate reward. Lawley then probed him about the extent of his political sights, and particularly whether they included becoming Prime Minister. His former mother-in-law Gaia, she said, had revealed that he always expressed from a young age a determination to become PM. When pressed, he feigned laughter but conceded publicly for the first time that he did have his eyes on the top job: 'I suppose all politicians in the end are like crazed wasps in a jam jar, each individually convinced that they're going to make it. My ambition silicon chip has been programmed to try to scrabble my way up this ladder.' When Lawley suggested he was a risk-taker, fond of 'playing with fire,' he concurred, 'I suppose there is an element of truth in that.'

At least his choice of records was carefully uncontroversial. In fact, it had been the subject of nearly a decade of planning. Boris knew that when the call finally came his selection would be subjected to forensic examination for clues on character, popular appeal and seriousness of purpose. Indeed, he admitted with the sort of candour second nature to a journalist – although perhaps not an ambitious minister-in-waiting – that even the programme producer had suspected him of making 'political' choices. 'It's like you're kind of trying to appeal to everyone, a bit of Stones, a bit of Bach, you know. I mean, Nigella Lawson chose Eminem!' the producer had said. 'I was shattered, and insulted to the core,' noted Boris, before replying, 'But I love this music. And, much as I like him, I don't want Eminem on a desert island.' 'She then tried to reassure me about my taste, and what exquisite choices they were, but I couldn't help feeling, as she left, that I had failed one of life's great tests.'[2] (Interestingly, exactly 12 months previously, he *had* chosen Eminem as one of his four all-time favourite CDs but that was for an interview with the laddish *Esquire* magazine under the headline 'Bo'selecta' and some time before he felt the need to be quite so seriously safe. Another case of chameleon Boris, perhaps.)

For the record the tracks he chose were: 'Here Comes the Sun' by the Beatles; 'Soul Limbo' by Booker T and the MGs, better known as the theme tune to *Test Match Special*; 'Here Would I stand Beside Thee' from Bach's 'St Matthew's Passion'; 'Start Me Up' by The Rolling Stones; 'Finale of Brahms' Variations on a Theme' by Haydn; Van Morrison's Brown Eyed Girl; 'Pressure Drop' by The Clash and finally, the opening of the last movement of Beethoven's Symphony No. 5. There were no contemporary choices at all – the most recent piece of music on his list was 'Start Me Up', which was released in 1981 but actually dated from much further back. It was all very Radio 4. Boris also asked for a copy of Homer to translate, and a large pot of French mustard.

Frank Johnson, like many others, realised exactly what had taken place. In the *Spectator* on 5 November 2005, he wrote up an imaginary conversation between Cameron and close political ally George Osborne (and Boris allowed him to do so).

Mr Cameron: 'Anything else we need worry about, George?'

Mr Osborne: 'Well, yeah. Boris has just announced on *Desert Island Discs* that he's going into politics.'

Mr Cameron: 'What? Why isn't he content to be MP for Henley?'
Mr Osborne: 'He said he thought it will soon be time for him to choose. So if we win, he says he'd like to be a front-bench spokesman for agriculture or trade or something like that.'
Mr Cameron: 'You mean, he intends to join our front bench?'
Mr Osborne: 'Looks like it. What are we gonna do?'

In fact, when Cameron became Party Leader on 4 December, he did not do much. Or rather, he announced the names of the shadow cabinet and Boris was not among them. The next day, though, he was appointed shadow higher education minister – a relatively lowly position, if one that aimed at exploiting his popularity with students. It hardly compensated, though, for having to resign immediately from the *Spectator* editorship. There were no longer any choices. It was the end of an era in British journalism but there was little doubt the fun had already gone out of it.

'Andrew Neil was the man who changed everything,' recalls Stuart Reid, Boris's deputy, 'he was the Barclay Brothers' man. We'd had a pretty good relationship with Conrad Black – he loved Boris. Once he'd gone we all realised how much we loved Conrad.' Indeed, so regretful was Boris about the 'good old days' under Black – and perhaps his cavalier treatment of someone who had been such an indulgent boss – that as he left the *Spectator*, he suggested to Reid that they visit him in jail in Florida. 'It seemed like a good idea,' Reid says. 'Boris didn't go, but the idea was more than a joke – I think he thought it would be appropriate in an ideal world.'

There was undoubtedly a certain misty-eyed wistfulness for Conrad's regime in the last days of Boris's editorship at the *Spectator*. Andrew Neil, the new chief executive, was inevitably going to be more hands-on than his predecessors. He had made it clear as soon as he took over in November 2004 that 'things' could not go on in the same way, that even the *Spectator* had to be 'managed' and its people made to 'report.' 'We all have bosses in this world and that's true of the *Spectator* too,' he had announced.[3] But it was not welcome news to the *Spectator* staff and Boris in particular, who was disturbed by the fact that Neil (who had started to wear an old-fogey fob watch) seemed quite so happy. 'Boris just expressed amused scepticism about Andrew,' says Reid. 'He noticed early on that Andrew was going out of his way to smile a lot. It is said that Andrew didn't like Boris and I'm more than happy to believe that. There was no sense that Andrew made Boris's life unpleasant, but equally there was an inevitability that Boris would go. The jig was up; it had been for some time – The Andrew and Boris Show was never going to work.'

Not since Charlie Wilson (another tough Scot) at *The Times* had Boris encountered a less accommodating boss when it came to his personal whims. Reid has referred to a certain 'abrasive management style.' With a physical presence to match Boris's, Neil had made it clear early on that his editor could not hold a front-bench position and continue at the *Spectator*. Boris was overheard in the office complaining 'Neil is trying push me out' and there were whispers that he had been offered a different, but lesser, job. For the first year of Neil's tenure, these were merely rumblings as Boris was languishing out of favour on the backbenches and so the conflicts of interest were less acute. But with the job offer from Cameron on the table in December 2005, Boris's departure could be delayed no longer – neither Neil nor the Tories were prepared to risk another Liverpool. After six and a half years at the helm, Boris was out – taking his bust of Pericles with him – and Neil could finally bring in the more 'serious' editor he had long wanted.

And Boris had quite a serious new job, too – definitely a step up from the arts portfolio. It suggested that his past misdemeanours had been forgotten, or at least forgiven. He did not try to entertain with a spoof manifesto this time, but was almost unnaturally careful about what he said, and to whom he said it. His appointment was widely welcomed, as it seemed to suggest the Conservatives wanted to give the important question of higher education more prominence than it had previously warranted.

Indeed, the leading trade journal, *Times Higher Education*, was enthusiastic. Its newly appointed twenty-something political reporter, the super-confident Anna Fazackerley, wrote of him as the Conservatives' 'most popular and irrepressible' politician. Under another headline, 'RUMPLED AND READY TO RUMBLE', she later wrote: 'Mr Johnson is not known for his discretion,' before excitedly noting, 'He reels off exact numbers of universities, courses and students in the UK at high speed. "I am going to paralyse you with statistics!" he cries.' And finally, she decides: 'It is clear that those expecting controversy will not have long to wait. Mr Johnson has arrived. Let the show begin.'

Her editor, John O'Leary, was less excited, but still pleased that Boris did not continue with his predecessor's policy of cutting university places, 'when the Tory Party was supposed to stand for equal opportunities.' Boris stepped back from his comments during the 2005 election, when he had dismissed 'loony degrees in windsurfing from Bangor University' (prompting arguably Stanley's best-ever quip that, 'they also surf who only stand and wait'). In contrast, Boris now declared: 'My instincts are not to go around trying to exterminate Mickey Mouse courses. One man's Mickey Mouse course is another man's *literae humaniores*.'

A close aide to Boris at the time explains his change of position: 'Boris realised that a lot of people working on these courses wouldn't like him if he attacked them. And Boris likes to be liked.' But Boris did broadly share Labour's less popular views on the need for top-up fees. 'Most of the vice-chancellors who met Boris were reasonably impressed,' says O'Leary. 'He was quite interested in the subject. But it was all very much through the prism of Oxbridge; that was clearly his number one priority.'

Outside Oxbridge, Boris appeared to take the greatest interest in Edinburgh University, where in early 2006 he stood in the election for the vacant rectorship (a job once held by his hero Winston Churchill). He canvassed quite actively, attracted 200 nominations and signed a female student's bare chest. No doubt he felt in with a strong chance against the two other journalist candidates – Magnus Linklater, former editor of the *Scotsman*, and the campaigning documentary-maker, John Pilger. But his support for top-up fees prompted an energetic 'Anyone but Boris' campaign, with its 'Bog Off Boris, you Top-up Tory' and 'Don't Wake up With a Dumb Blond' slogans. More than once protestors threw beer over him, but on each occasion he remembered to thank the culprit for 'refreshing' him.

'I made a beeline to the oppo, swaying and chanting under banners saying "Bog off Boris!" and put on my best Cecil Parkinson beam,' Boris wrote afterwards. '"Hell-air!" I said, thrusting out my hand to the nearest Left-wing agitator; and to my amazement it was taken, and shaken warmly.'[4]

But while he clearly enjoyed the attention and described the position of rector as 'a fantastic opportunity to be an ambassador for a world-class university,' it was still an odd decision to stand. Perhaps it reflected a restlessness, an unsatisfied hunger, even with his return to front bench politics. Or was it a practice-run for something bigger? In any case, his charm and fame – combined with a New Boris seriousness of tone – were simply unable to swing him the vote. He came third to Mark Ballard, a 34-year-old Green member of the Scottish Parliament and former student. Linklater, a fellow Old Etonian, came second. It was a lesson in how an unpopular policy can derail a popular politician's best efforts. Most London commentators, his team – and perhaps most particularly Boris himself – had been certain he would win.

He had better luck with his other pet project of the time. In fact, the timing, though accidental, could not have been better. In January 2006, his two-part series, *Dream of Rome* (shown on BBC 2) and followed by an accompanying book in February, displayed Boris at his best. Enthusiastic, funny and inspiring, he used all the senses, startling comparisons between ancient and modern – and of course, sex – to educate through entertainment.

So, the baritus noise made by Barbarians in victory against the Romans was a giant roar 'like a chorus of Rolf Harris didgeridoos.' We also learned, 'it was standard for the [Barbarian] wives to bare their breasts in a kind of *Sun* Page 3 exhortation to the troops.' Indeed, these sexy Barbarians were 'clad in nothing but the kind of fur accessories you might find in a fetish shop.'

He drew beguiling comparisons between the Roman Empire and the EU – people who rejected toga-wearing as a revolt against control from Rome, for instance, were ancient versions of today's Euro-sceptics. But whatever the flashes of fun and ingenuity, there was also a flick of laziness, a sense that the book at least had been rushed.

There are key details missing, arguments not fully backed up with facts. A colleague from the *Telegraph* remembers Boris grumbling that it was 'bloody hard work, this book thing.' Asked how long it had taken, Boris replied: 'Bloody hell, two weeks!' At the launch in Daunt Books in Marylebone High Street, he revealed a similar impatience with politics: 'I occasionally wonder what people like me are doing in public life. It is because we hope to become shadow spokesman for higher education!'[5]

The experience had, however, given him a taste for television presenting – and not just the knock-about style of *HIGNFY*. He quickly realised that it was almost certainly the most lucrative way of flexing the Boris brand – and would provide an escape route from politics, if necessary. Charles Brand, director of history at Tiger Aspect (the TV company that made *Dream of Rome*) remembers Boris as an onscreen 'natural.' But it was Tiger Aspect who came up with the arresting idea of comparing ancient Rome to the modern EU.

Next, Brand wanted David Jeffcock to come on board as director. 'David had recently worked on the *Spectator* programme and he also loved that period of history,' remembers Brand. 'He is an old school, died-in-the-wool Leftie, who is very principled and extremely hard working. [But] he was very sniffy, saying he didn't want anything to do with Boris. We tried very hard to persuade him to do it but clearly something had happened on the *Spectator* film.' Fortunately, at the last minute Jeffcock changed his mind and then worked flat out, 'which was very important indeed as Boris is not an old-school grafter.'

Boris could provide something invaluable, though – a certain wit and sheen to 'give the prose a real lift.' Jeffcock would complain about his lack of preparation and getting him to turn up for filming was arduous in the extreme. 'I would be told I had to shout at him, but he would always be unbelievably apologetic,' remembers Brand. 'He would roll over just like a puppy, saying it was his fault, how he would never do it again – until the next time. He got away with it because he was good at what he did – eventually. But what Boris was not doing was the source stuff [the research] – although he would, on occasion, question it. Boris hadn't done anything about Rome for 20 years: he would start reading like mad about it, but never before he got on the plane to where we were filming. It was David who would sit until four in the morning writing the script and Boris would then spend half an hour adding a few words and making it great.'

Despite the tribulations, *Dream of Rome* was well received. Brand began searching around for another project. But Boris had other ideas. In the greatest of secrecy, he lured the hard-working Jeffcock away to help him set up a rival production company to make a follow-up series. The idea was specifically to cut out Tiger Aspect so that Boris could make a bigger profit. 'When David told me, he was very embarrassed,' remembers Brand. 'Nine months earlier, we'd had to beg him to work with this "charlatan," and it was irritating as *Dream of Rome* had been our idea and our hard graft.' Perhaps Boris felt some guilt. Not frequently one for buying lunch, he took Brand to the Cinnamon Club, an upmarket Indian restaurant in Westminster, and played on his sympathy. 'He wanted to keep the bridges open between us,' says Brand. 'He confided in me that he thought he had gone down the political pecking order since the Liverpool saga and other "events." He said he was not sure he had a future career in Parliament, so to provide for his family he needed to get into TV and make more money from it. He flattered and charmed me into not thinking ill of him, but the result was we were cut out of the follow-up to our own series. It was annoying in the extreme, but what could we do?'

About a year later, Boris's new company – Finland Station – duly made the less successful follow-up *After Rome: Holy Wars and Conquests* on the rise of Islam up to the time of Crusades. Boris was later found guilty by the Parliamentary authorities of failing to register his shareholding.

Charles Brand need not have felt too sorry for Boris or overly concerned about his bank balance. He might have given up the *Spectator* and the editor's considerable salary and stock options, but Boris had certainly not given up journalism. It was during these early weeks of 2006 that he was able to take advantage of turmoil at the *Telegraph* to negotiate a pay increase for his column – which he had refused to surrender. As one of its biggest stars, Boris persuaded the acting editor John Bryant to raise his yearly fee from £200,000 to

£250,000 on the understanding that he would also write a column for the *Sunday Telegraph*. That has never happened – Boris has claimed to be too busy to honour the deal or to be ignorant of it – and the £5,000-a-piece rate has remained. (Indeed, according to figures lodged with the Parliamentary authorities he brought in up to £540,000, or nine times an MP's salary, over the following year, making him the third highest-paid MP after William Hague and David Blunkett.)

The rate of £5,000 a column in particular is a hefty sum, even for someone of Boris's journalistic stature. Over the years, he has become proficient at writing his column at a speed that would leave others gasping. Typically, he would ask one of his brightest members of staff to do the homework. 'He used to want a maximum of three facts for his column,' recalls a former Boris staffer. 'The researcher would find some good ones and then he would bash it all out in an hour and a half.' Boris's greatest challenge, though has often been finding the right subject. In those days, the column appeared on Thursdays. On Wednesday afternoons he would typically seek inspiration by visiting his Westminster staff in the annexe room, where he would play a game to find the best idea. On occasion this would descend into a competition to suggest the theme most likely to produce catastrophic consequences for his career. One of Boris's favourites was: 'Why David Cameron is a complete c**t' – indeed, he was so enthused, he even started to compose an introduction beginning: 'One thing that has become apparent to me in my years of Parliamentary service is that David Cameron is a complete c**t'. Another time, it was, 'Why I believe in a European superstate'.

From the way he talked during the fun and games, it was clear that Boris preferred the views and company of those inhabiting the more pro-European and Left-leaning reaches of Toryism rather than the ones at the opposite end of the spectrum. 'Boris and I got on because we have similar dislike of most members of the Conservative party,' explains Chris Cook – one of David Willetts' aides, also based in the annexe room. 'He's clearly not on the Right wing, but actually quite Europhile in Tory terms. He liked to come into our office to gossip and bitch about the Right-wingers, particularly

Liam Fox, or indeed anyone else he thought had screwed up the party that week.'

He also came across as being genuinely proud of being, as he called it, a 'mongrel.' At several universities he visited, while working on his yet-to-be-published book on Britain, he talked to groups of Muslim students. 'He told them that we should just all marry each other [as in his own family] and then all our problems would go away,' recalls one astonished onlooker. 'I'm not sure they really appreciated that idea.' But those who worked with him thought Boris genuinely liberal and by no means a racist. 'He's unbelievably tolerant, both on an individual level and on a macro level,' said one. 'He's very liberal on the way that people personally lead their lives, as well as being very liberal in policy terms.' Boris was friendly with his staff and could be great fun, but he did not become friends with them: he remained a detached figure who never quite relaxed or let himself go.

Meanwhile, things were looking up, the disappointments and disasters of 2004 and early 2005 now behind him. True, he had insulted another city – this time Portsmouth – as 'full of drugs, obesity, underachievement and Labour MPs' but no Operation Pompey Grovel was really thought necessary. (Later in the year, he offered to go on an 'apology world tour', when he upset an entire country by comparing the leadership crisis in the Labour party with 'Papua New Guinea-style orgies of cannibalism and chief-killing', but he similarly got away with it.) Otherwise in his new higher education capacity, he was making well-received speeches in favour of the study of Latin and Greek, and Ancient and Medieval History. He was earning a lot of money, too – through journalism, books, after-dinner speeches and TV.

Somehow though, it is never enough. Boris's old friend the 'death wish' made a return. On 2 April 2006, the *News of the World* splashed its front page with the headline 'BORIS CHEATS WITH A BLONDE – MARRIED TORY HAS AFFAIR NO. 2'. The piece continued: 'We caught the shadow minister enjoying a series of secret trysts with blonde beauty Anna Fazackerley, 29, at her London flat.' Inside, under the banner: 'Oh Boris. Not again,' were some familiar and lurid details. Three times in ten days, Boris had been spotted visiting

Fazackerley's King's Road, Chelsea flat. On one occasion he was seen discreetly walking yards behind her, a beanie hat pulled down over his conspicuous blond hair, but then he was photographed furtively nipping through her front door as she held it open for him.

Two hours later, he emerged, hailed a cab and headed off to see Petronella Wyatt at her St John's Wood home for the next couple of hours (before going home to Marina). On another occasion, he was photographed waving to Fazackerley's taxi and on another day, she gave a 'satisfied smile' as he wheeled his bicycle away from her doorstep. He was also seen dining with her at a Knightsbridge restaurant called Racine – a traditional French eaterie that does Boris's favourite uncooked steak tartare. Once again, he was spotted getting frisky in the back of a black cab. Plans to take her on his official fact-finding trip to China had been quietly dropped, we were told, because they were too risky – she was instead intending to accompany him on visits to British universities. Anna, it was reported, was 'smitten' and Boris found her 'irresistible.' Together, they were supposedly 'head over heels in lust.' But when the paper approached both for a comment, they separately refused to comply. Boris had learned his lesson – this was not the time for colourful phrases but something plain, blunt and not open to challenge. 'You're very kind, but no thank you. Absolutely not! No comment whatsoever. Thanks a lot, bye,' was what he said. Fazackerley was even briefer: 'Absolutely not.'

This smart move allowed doubts to creep in that this was not an affair but merely a series of meetings to discuss higher education policy. After all, it was a patch they both patrolled, in their different ways. No doubt Boris, now a master manipulator of the media, was hoping this would be the general conclusion when presented with what was only, after all, circumstantial evidence. When the *News of the World* followed up its revelations with a further piece the following Sunday, there were suggestions that the woman photographed coming out of his room at the Pershing Hall Hotel in Paris (he had booked under his brother's name on his way back from China) was actually Marina. And after catching the Eurostar back to London, he then spent the next day in Henley, innocently opening a public footpath. So, was Boris having an affair with Anna or not?

While Boris was thousands of miles away on his trip to China, Marina had the press camped outside the family's Islington home again, trying to find out the answer to that very question. She was grilled on the street by reporters in front of her children and always eager to protect them, lodged a complaint with the Press Complaints Commission. The four children were later driven away from the press scrum to an undisclosed house in the country. Back in London, it was yet another torrid time for Marina, who was seen to have moved her wedding ring to her middle finger. Her father Charles did what he could by arriving to tell the press that the story was 'rubbish.' The newspapers began asking whether it was the 'last hurrah for hanky panky Boris.' But Boris acted publicly as if everything were normal – and two days later, whisked his wife and family off on a foreign holiday. Press coverage soon dried up – although the questions persisted. When asked about the latest stories by colleagues at the BBC where she worked, Marina's sister Shirin would frequently shrug her shoulders with apparent resignation and reply: 'He's just Boris, what can I say?'

But there were two other parties also upset by the coverage. Petronella Wyatt was said to feel 'heartbroken and betrayed' by the news that Boris was allegedly having another affair. At the time she worked for Peter McKay, editor of the waspish diary column on the *Daily Mail* called 'Ephraim Hardcastle'. The diary began running almost daily items on Boris, accusing him of suffering from satyrism or 'unusually strong sexual desires' and suggesting he seek treatment for sex addiction like Hollywood filmstar Michael Douglas. Meanwhile, there were other newspaper reports from 'friends' of Petronella's that Boris had made a 'lunge' for her the evening he had visited her after leaving Fazackerley – 'Boris is so driven by sex he's quite capable of going from one girl to another in the space of one evening,' the 'pals' declared in more than one newspaper.

There were a few half-hearted calls for Boris's dismissal from the frontbench but Cameron chose to ignore them and he was allowed to continue in his post. However, sources close to David Willetts, shadow education secretary and then Boris's boss, said he was privately 'narked' with him as he felt that he had been lied to about the affair.

And while there were few immediate repercussions, the story undoubtedly added to Tory fears that Boris was a loose cannon and a lightweight. On his website, Boris took his normal light-hearted view of events with the comment: 'Heads down and tin hats on while news stories fly.' It was followed by the message written by his secretary Melissa Crawshay-Williams: 'We, in the Boris Johnson MP office, have every confidence that Boris's talent and ability can weather any storm.' After all, he was used to this sort of attention.

As for Anna Fazackerley, the stories were to have more painful consequences. No one should doubt that there are casualties in a jolly Johnson jape – and they are usually women (or children). When Fazackerley joined the *Times Higher Ed* – as it is commonly known – she made an immediate mark and not just because of her short skirts and brightly coloured tops. With a first-class degree from Manchester University (after rejecting a place at Cambridge), she was undoubtedly intellectually impressive. 'Anna's mistake was that she just took the concept of having contacts too literally,' says a somewhat acerbic former colleague. And this was not an atypical comment from both male and female journalists. 'She was very bright and outgoing, an unusually confident person,' is how her then editor John O'Leary puts it. 'She was a go-getter, someone who shook things up a bit. She liked to shock – we had to ask her to tone her language down a bit after a member of staff complained. Like Boris, she came over as very posh, very blonde and very ambitious. I might not, though, have realised how ambitious she was.'

Anna's evident charms worked well with university vice-chancellors, typically middle-aged men older than Boris – 'They were flattered by her and gave her stories.' After she had interviewed Boris in January 2006, she began meeting him for lunch. 'But then we noticed that the lunches were becoming longer and longer,' recalls O'Leary, 'but we still didn't know exactly what was going on. Then her mobile phone went mysteriously missing and two weeks later the *News of the World* came out with their story. By that stage we were not surprised.'

O'Leary took a more hardline view than Cameron: he quickly realised the news coverage would be seen to be compromising

Fazackerley's perceived impartiality as a reporter, so on Monday morning he called her in.

'She denied the affair and continues to deny it. She was very upset when I took her off the politics beat. But whether or not she's had an affair, the other political parties would not talk to her if she were seen just to be rewriting Tory policy. She took it badly, starting off with tears and moving onto anger. She never gave a full explanation of what Boris was doing in her flat, just that the story was wrong. She was advised to take some time off – and I think she took a week.' It was then that Boris became directly involved. He asked O'Leary out to lunch – an invitation that confirmed it was a crisis – and 'slipped into the conversation' that reports of the affair were 'nonsense.' O'Leary told colleagues that he had quickly realised that Boris was pleading Fazackerley's case and that she should be allowed to continue in her role as politics reporter. But the paper's management felt she had lost the confidence of her readership. Shortly afterwards, Fazackerley resigned, but her new notoriety made it difficult to find work.

'Anna freelanced for a bit, but found it hard-going because she had been effectively blacklisted by the *Times Higher Ed*,' recalls a close friend, who consoled her in the aftermath. 'She found that as an education journalist if you can't write for the specialist press, there is not enough regular work. She also fell out with a lot of her friends, who were very insensitive about what they had been reading. One "friend" was even quoted in the papers as saying: "I stopped respecting her when she did this [the alleged affair.] Partly because she had been so damn self-righteous and judgemental before, but also because I know what divorce can do to people, especially children, and she was smart enough to know that too."'[6] Her genuine friend was much more sympathetic, though: 'It was grim. She got lots of nonsense written about her, such as how she was an heiress. It was all rubbish, because the papers didn't know that her mother had changed her name to the district of Liverpool, where she lived – they had followed the wrong family tree. Her mother was very upset, too. Anna is just a very nice standard middle-class girl who got caught up in a storm.'

Finally, in September 2006, Fazackerley secured a job as director – and sole employee – of a new think tank called Agora, set up to support Boris and his successors as Tory higher education spokesman, on a salary of £27,250. Agora (Greek for open place of assembly) was later taken over by Policy Exchange, a favourite with both Boris and Cameron. Fazackerley moved with it. Her first Agora project was the publication in May 2007 of a book, *Can the Prizes Still Glitter: The Future of British Universities in a Changing World* (Boris was a contributor).

Fazackerley's friend, who is well connected in Tory circles, is in no doubt that Boris was also behind her appointment: 'I think Boris felt he owed her one – he did screw up her life. There has also been the issue that she was forever going to be Anna Fazackerley, the girl who had an affair with Boris. It made it very difficult to meet anyone else or sustain a relationship if she did. She died her hair darker and would just call herself Anna, anything to get away from it. When she eventually met her husband-to-be on a blind date, the Boris stuff was virtually the first thing she said. She wanted to get it out of the way and avoid damaging the relationship later on when he inevitably found out.' As for the question, why don't any of the women linked to Boris ever do a 'kiss and tell'? Fazackerley's experience suggests they ask themselves who would fare worst if they did. The answer to that question is not Boris.

Boris's popularity seemed higher than ever. Indeed, the more he philandered, the more of a hero he became and the more the women got the blame. Soon after the Fazackerley stories, his status as untouchable folk hero became clear when he was invited to play in a charity football match against Germany. As he ran onto the pitch in an England red shirt at the Madejski stadium in Reading, the crowd of 15,000 chanted, 'We want Boris!'

Despite all the distractions, he was also making an impact on his shadow education brief, outside Westminster at least. 'I think he is a serious figure,' said Professor Steve Smith, vice-chancellor of Exeter University. 'I am a Boris Johnson fan,' declared Bahram Bekhradnia, director of the Higher Education Policy Institute. 'He has some interesting ideas about higher education.'[7] Here at last was the beginning of what looked like a genuine political career – that involved, well, policies.

Boris worked quite hard on the brief, attending meetings and dinners at universities around the country. He was still *GQ* motoring correspondent, so he would sometimes arrive in an often impossibly flashy car. At Portsmouth University, for instance, he was chauffeur driven in a Russian mafia-style limousine fitted with stainless steel champagne flutes. But the fun did not stop him slogging hard on his speeches. 'The whole premise of him being unprepared is completely wrong,' says a well-placed source. 'He is last-minutish, but never unprepared. He wrote out every single word of those speeches on higher education, including the gaps, tone, everything, taking an hour or two in the process. That rambling delivery was planned exactly in the writing. It is true that the more comic stuff gets written on the back of a napkin, but there is always a great deal of thought beforehand.'

Boris was working extremely long hours on all his different interests – and expected his staff to do the same; staying on until nine or ten at night and working over the weekend was commonplace. There were tensions and mistakes made but he was both fun and pleasant to work for. 'He's incredibly nice, unbelievably nice,' says one former employee. 'He's the sort of person who, at least verbally, will blame himself if you mess up. But one of the disadvantages of working for him is that he can never say "no" to anyone and when anyone's in the room, he desperately wants that person to like him. He's not like any other boss in that you'd have to tell *him* to tell you what to do – he wasn't an employer in any classic sense. I was able to be sarcastic and tell him off. It wouldn't be something that most people would put up with.'

His main policy interest was how to streamline university funding – not then a populist subject and consequently not much covered outside the specialist journals and the *Financial Times*. And yet, admirably, Boris persisted. He also dutifully attended the Tory education team's meetings held by David Willetts. The relationship was workmanlike, although one of Willetts' aides notes with some understatement, 'it is never easy for someone to have Boris as a junior on his team.'

'Their styles are very different,' recalls another aide. 'David is incredibly bright but he probably slightly resented the fact that Boris was more famous. He had been one of the massive rising stars under Thatcher but it never quite came off for him. He's a phenomenal policy-maker but not a superb politician – whereas in many ways, Boris is instinctively a brilliant politician but not so much a policy guy.' On one issue in particular, though, Boris held strong views that were diametrically opposed to Willetts'. 'Boris was furious about the grammar school speech [on 19 May 2007, Willetts prompted a furore when he defended the existing Conservative Party policy of not reintroducing grammar schools].Willetts hadn't consulted the team and Boris was, at least then, fervently pro-selection.' Their opposing approaches to life were also demonstrated on the ice-rink at Christmas 2006, when Willetts held his annual skating party at Somerset House. Willetts is an accomplished and skilled master of the ice, while Boris gave an amusing performance in which he managed to stay more or less upright through, according to one fellow guest, a mixture of 'sheer aggression and lack of fear.'

In the autumn of 2006, Boris hired Frances Banks, another reliable supporter, being Charles Moore's former secretary at the *Telegraph*. Both she, and her predecessor, Crawshay-Williams, would try to mother Boris, by 'tidying him up' with a hairbrush. 'But Boris doesn't like feeling hemmed in,' says an observer, 'so he would disappear for hours at a time. He didn't like being followed around.'

When he took the education job, an anonymous Henley donor provided the funds for him to hire a researcher. But Boris did not raid the usual ranks of obsessive politics graduates. Instead he asked applicants to write two 500-word essays – one on universities and the other on either 'My trip on a Spaceship', 'A Country Ramble' or the "Taj Mahal'. Those short-listed after this Eton scholarship-style paper were called for interview during which he spouted out phrases such as 'throwing the baby out with the bathwater' and challenged them to 'translate them into common English.' Clearly this was a test of facility with language and also how applicants thought on their feet.

The somewhat eccentric selection process proved highly effective as it produced Rachel Wolf, a highly intelligent natural sciences graduate from Cambridge, and daughter of the *FT* commentator, Martin Wolf. She had never been involved in politics before but was many cuts above the typical researcher and rose to the considerable challenge of working with Boris. One day a week she helped him with his journalism – doing the research, even structuring his pieces so that he could spend the minimum of time, 'turning them into Boris.'

On 3 October 2006, at the Conservative Party Conference in Bournemouth, Boris was bashing out a 'particularly tricky passage' of one of these pieces (for the *Times Higher Ed*) when he heard an Apache-style 'whooping' and the drumming of feet of a mob outside. It was the eve of Cameron's first Party Conference speech as Leader, in which he was to deliver the crucial message that the NHS was 'safe' in Conservative hands and the party was 'getting ready to serve again.' It was imperative the media were keyed up to cover this pivotal moment as the Tory top brass planned. But instead of focussing on Cameron's bid to win the next election, dozens of journalists and photographers were encamped in a car-park, trying to spy on Boris.

'To the sound of rhythmic chanting, a ladder appeared over the top of the wall and the red eye of a TV news camera was trained on us,' he recalls. Boris's minders in the Tory press office (where he had gone to borrow a computer) urged him to hurry up and finish the piece, 'because the whole thing was getting a bit Gordon at Khartoum.'[8] In fact, he was trapped inside for more than an hour before managing to escape.

So, why was Boris attracting all this attention and not Cameron? Boris had attacked Jamie Oliver and his campaign for healthier school dinners! And only days after Cameron had (again) made a point of lauding Oliver's campaign to improve school food – saying he had done more than any government minister for this undeniably worthy cause. But at a conference fringe meeting, Boris had not only called for Oliver to be sacked but even offered support to some much-derided Yorkshire mothers, who had passed burgers and chips through the fence so that their children could avoid what they regarded as Jamie's 'over-priced, low-fat rubbish' in the school canteen. Boris had said: 'I say, let people eat what they like! Why shouldn't they push pies through the railings? If I was in charge, I would get rid of Jamie Oliver.'

Now under massive pressure from the Tory leadership, as well as the media itself, he called an impromptu press conference and trotted out the tired old politico line that he had been 'misquoted.' But the BBC, who broke the story, stood by it. So, Boris – who coincidentally now weighed in at 17 stone – quickly backtracked and in a humiliating climb-down, declared Oliver variously a 'national saint' and a 'messiah.' He also went on to say that junk food should be banned from schools. At least he deftly ducked questions about whether he was going to apologise or resign before asking, 'What is the story? Don't you think you might be over-egging this?' Excessive egg or not, the truth was that top Tories were furious that Boris's remarks were overshadowing his leader's carefully crafted speech. He had created a good deal of resentment and anger, but for what?

'It was a perfect storm,' recalls Matthew Parris, one of the journalists covering the fray that day, 'but he didn't entirely like it. This view of Boris as a kind of bouncy, "golly gosh, what have I done, isn't this appalling, never mind" person isn't quite right. Like lots of us, he has a trouble-making demon, a demon that *enjoys* the trouble, so he plays it up but then he worries he's gone too far. And so when I came across him in a car park later, he was looking genuinely downcast. The two halves of his character are more pronounced, more exotic and more obviously in warfare against each other than with most of us.'

The following day, 4 October, Cameron joked about Boris in his speech, saying he had 'put his foot in it' but insisting that he did not mind him going 'off message.' Joking apart, the Tory leader was obviously infuriated because he had not been given the clear media run he wanted. So, was this just another Boris death wish or an explosion of frustration and envy? And what good did it do him except place him at the centre of a media firestorm for 24 hours? What was clear was that with only a narrow lead over Labour, it was the last thing the Tories had planned or wanted (but being Boris, there was little they could do about it).

'There have been specific occasions when I have been there when

David has had to ring Boris and reprimand him,' says Andrew Mackay, then Cameron's senior parliamentary and political adviser. 'Any leader with a colleague who does something that brings the party into disrepute, or confuses the message, or causes unreasonable controversy will be cross. And Boris was always mea culpa about it; he'd be theatrical, like a child. Having said that, I always felt that rightly there was a "Boris is Boris" element. The leader gave him more licence than he would to others.'

By this point Simon Heffer, a fellow columnist on Boris's own newspaper, the *Telegraph*, was no longer in the mood for 'giving licence.' Although claiming to harbour 'some affection' for Boris after working alongside him for nearly 20 years, he declared: 'A man blessed with high intelligence and great abilities has, through moral failure and self-indulgence, now largely ceased to be taken seriously in public life.'[9]

And yet Boris seemed not to be able to resist pressing yet more thorns into the leadership's side. Only a week later, his *Telegraph* column laid out a case – apparently in all seriousness – for giving the Iranians the nuclear bomb. They would eventually acquire one any way, the argument went, so better for the Americans to lend them assistance with the technology in exchange for extracting agreements on being nicer to the Israelis and accelerating the move towards genuine democracy. It was one of those moments when a Boris-watcher gasps and asks: Is this for real?

'The column absolutely enraged [shadow foreign secretary] William Hague,' a source close to Boris recalls. 'The word around Parliament was that he had been about to be moved to shadow minister for Europe and that he wasn't as a direct result. The problem is that he's much more extreme in print than he is in person – he's a showman. When he's writing columns he's thinking what will be amusing or controversial to say rather than what it is that he actually thinks. His column is a weekly Oxbridge entrance essay. Just like in the film *The History Boys*, he is taking something and then turning it on its head in order to show how clever he is.' Boris may have relinquished the *Spectator* but he was clearly still driven by journalistic rather than political imperatives, by his love of a clever argument well constructed over a viable, if duller policy.

'The trouble was also that Boris never played the game that shadow ministers play,' the source continues. 'For a start, most ambitious politicians who are trying to be promoted are obsessed with getting their researchers to table Parliamentary Questions trying to get statistics to turn into stories – it's their way of doing their bit for the party and getting noticed at the same time. But Boris wasn't interested in playing that game and certainly never asked his researchers to play it for him.'

After 16 months of thankless toiling away on university campuses, Boris was paying the price for not 'playing the game'. An original Cameron supporter, he must have felt that he had hardly received the payback he naïvely expected – particularly from a fellow Etonian. Around March 2007, he started talking to a few confidants about a new idea. 'I remember him saying that becoming Mayor of London would be a fun job to do,' says one insider. 'He would mention it every couple of weeks or so.'

Ironically, the idea had a close Henley connection: elected mayors in Britain were first mooted in the 1980s by Boris's Henley successor, Michael Heseltine. Word got round the party, but nothing came of it. Yet the situation of Conservative mayoral candidate for the forthcoming 2008 election was certainly vacant. In 2006, Cameron had decided on a new-fangled US-style primary election to find a candidate in which non-Tories could also vote. The original thought was that a big name from outside politics would enter the fray but it never happened. In fact, the whole exercise had had to be embarrassingly postponed in August 2006 when it failed to produce a candidate with even a residue of star quality. Meanwhile, an unofficial candidate from the modernising wing of the party – and a friend of Cameron's – had been enthusiastically working on his campaign. Nick Boles had even given up the security and salary of his job as director of Policy Exchange, the Cameroon think-tank, to do so. But although thoughtful, clever, metropolitan and gay, he was not the high-profile figure that the Tory leadership believed could win against the wily Labour incumbent, Ken Livingstone.

An increasingly desperate Cameron decided to take personal control of the search. Figures approached or under consideration included (Lord) Sebastian Coe, Lord Stevens of Kirkwhelpington (formerly Sir John Stevens, head of the Metropolitan Police), the former ambassador to the US Sir Christopher Meyer, TV presenters Anne Robinson and Andrew Neil, the ex-army chief General Sir Mike Jackson, Nick Ferrari of LBC and Sir John Major. For one reason or another, they all faded away.

Veronica Wadley, editor of the *Evening Standard*, had been persistently pushing Boris's name to Cameron (and anyone else who would listen) as the obvious candidate since at least Christmas 2005, when Cameron had invited her to a roast chicken dinner at his house in North Kensington. But Boris, despite his popularity, was just not considered seriously. Some months later, the idea was raised again at a lunch at the newspaper's Kensington offices when Cameron was 'pleasantly dismissive.' 'He wasn't nasty about Boris,' recalls a fellow guest, 'but he just smiled and said, "Yes, that's an interesting idea isn't it?" and immediately changed the subject.'

By spring 2007, the whole process of choosing a candidate was a year behind schedule and in danger of descending into farce. Cameron then humiliated both himself – and more particularly, Boles – by approaching the Liberal Democrat leader Sir Menzies Campbell to discuss the idea of a joint Lib Dem-Conservative candidate, Greg Dyke (an interesting fore-runner of the 2010 coalition). Back then, the idea of such a pact between the two parties was considered so outlandish it was quickly dismissed – but not before it had caused considerable personal damage to Boles. Boles (and not Charles Moore, as widely rumoured at the time) leaked news of the discussions to the *Standard*, knowing the publicity would definitively kill them off. Dyke, by inclination a Lib-Dem and formerly a Labour supporter, went on to deny any plans to run for the Mayorship, later saying his mother would never have forgiven him had he stood on a Tory ticket. (Later, he actually came out in support for Ken Livingstone.)

In February 2007, Boles had discovered a lump on his neck and at the end of June, was informed that he would need six months of treatment for cancer. He called Cameron to say he was pulling out on

Monday, 2 July, the very day that the Tory leader was to announce his shadow cabinet reshuffle. Now Cameron did not even have a fallback candidate for an election he knew the Conservatives needed to win. It looked as though, by default, the businessman Steve Norris would step in. Though likeable and competent, he had already lost the mayoral election twice, however, and what was needed now was someone new who could win it.

In the reshuffle Cameron promoted three MPs from the 2005 intake to the top table, including Michael Gove. One of Boris's 'stooges' at Oxford and three years younger, Gove now professionally leap-frogged the senior man. Boris's age was beginning to trouble him: he was older than all of the shadow cabinet's key players (Cameron, Osborne, Gove) and by the time they had finished their political careers and moved on, he would be too old to replace them. They were effectively blocking him out from any of the top spots. Some Tories tried to placate Boris by attributing the decision to not being able to promote another Etonian but the idea did not really hold water and in any case, it was not as if Boris had been offered any advancement, however minimal. A close Cameron associate explains: 'Generally, there was a feeling of do we really *need* to promote Boris?'

So, Boris's hopes of immediate advance within Westminster were dashed. With Nick Boles out of the running, the job that had tickled his fancy back in March now seemed even more appetising. 'The shadow cabinet reshuffle unquestionably pushed him,' recalls a close associate. 'He didn't *expect* to be promoted by Cameron, but he had *hoped* to be.' But he would not want to run if the inevitable result would be a crushing defeat to Ken Livingstone in a city where the Left had long predominated. National polls in July showed the Tories narrowly ahead, but London would always be a harder nut to crack.

Still Cameron could not face approaching the man who now seemed the obvious choice and understandably, Boris did not want to seem too eager – or desperate – to ask. But Cameron did dispatch his spin doctor Andy Coulson to sound him out. And then Nick Boles' campaign manager, Dan Ritterband (who had also worked as a special adviser to Cameron) cornered Boris at a *Spectator* party with some enticing news. Polling data proved for the first time that Ken was beatable and for all its Left-leaning tendencies, London could be secured. The whole 'optic had changed,' is how one senior Tory has put it.

In the absence of anyone else, Cameron finally put his support behind the idea, texting Boris with the message 'Don't go wobbly on me now.'[10] Word began to seep out that Cameron had changed tack, but understandably Boris did not want to make it too easy for him. 'Boris really didn't want to do it,' claims a well-placed Cameron source. 'We – George Osborne, Dave himself, Andy Coulson, Steve Hilton – endlessly had to go on about the fact he could win. One of the big factors in persuading him was being able to say that we knew from Veronica [Wadley] that the *Standard* would be completely behind him. There were a lot of meetings and calls, and Dave would keep asking, "Is he there yet?"'

With the news of the *Standard*'s full-square commitment, Boris took a couple of days to discuss the idea with his family. But it was clear that the job was now more enticing. 'Boris saw that only by making a power base for himself in London could he ever now hope to make his way to the top,' says a former colleague. By Wednesday the news was out, but in characteristic chaotic style. Boris bumped into Nick Robinson, the BBC political editor who lived near him in north London, early that morning on the tube. 'Boris clung onto me throughout the journey to stop members of the public mobbing him,' he recalls. Robinson had heard the rumours of Cameron's newfound enthusiasm for Boris, yet considered them 'so implausible' that he did not even raise them with the very man standing beside him. It was only when they were riding up the escalators at Westminster station that finally Robinson joked: 'I had this call yesterday and – you'll never believe it – someone said you were going to run for Mayor of London!' Instead of the horrified guffaw Robinson was expecting, 'Boris did that classic Boris thing of "Oh god! Oh right! Aaagh! Oh!" and instead of denying it, which I would have believed, said, "Do me a favour and don't reveal it for a couple of hours." I said: "You're bloody doing it! I don't believe it!"' Yet Robinson could not bring himself to believe it" 'I still regarded it as faintly preposterous – which I suppose is the product of having gone to university with him.'

Armed with this first-hand admission, Robinson wrote about the candidacy on his blog and mentioned it on the BBC's *Daily Politics* show but only 'as a jokey "you'll never guess what" line with Andrew Neil.' Steve Norris was brought on the phone to condemn it as a ridiculous idea. The story didn't make the *Six* or *Ten O'Clock News* at all. 'I just couldn't see it as real,' explains Robinson. He suggested that it was down to a change of heart on Cameron's part that Boris was entering the race, but in a statement swiftly issued by Central Office Boris said: 'I want to stress that this idea did not come from David Cameron, or from anyone in his office.' It was a declaration of independence from the centre that Boris has sustained – and repeated – ever since. Understandably, he never wanted to be painted as the Tories' 'last chance man', the desperate solution sought only after all else had failed. And perhaps as a result, still Boris did not actually commit himself completely, citing the obvious impediment that he represented a Parliamentary constituency some 40 miles outside London.

His remarks to that week's *Henley Standard* are classic bet-hedging Boris. At first, he told reporters that he was flattered to be considered for the mayoral race but that there were 'overwhelming logistical difficulties' and it was 'not really a goer.' Just hours later, the message changed to 'I am ruling nothing out. Being Mayor of London would be a fantastic job. I have, of course, been struck by the number of people who have been urging me to run.'

There were still moments of doubt, however, on both sides. Henley was a sticking point. The Cameron supporters wanted him to give up his seat to focus on fighting for London but Boris was understandably not keen to surrender his Parliamentary fallback. 'Boris never wants to deny himself the right to have his cake, eat it and then have a bun,' notes one senior Tory involved in the talks. (Precedent supported him, however: Ken Livingstone had kept on his Parliamentary constituency of Brent East for a year after he first became mayor in 2000 until the next general election.) A compromise was eventually reached with Boris able to keep Henley until the mayoral election of May 2008 (saving him some £80,000 in income and mortgage expenses) – but if he won, he would then surrender it more or less immediately.

He would also step down from the unpaid higher education brief at once.

On his blog of Friday the 13th, Boris announced his intention to stand – although the post was quickly taken down again on the grounds that it was not an 'official' statement. But just a couple of hours before the noon deadline for nominations on 16 July, Boris did finally go live. The campaign soon descended into pandemonium as he weaved his bicycle into the waiting media scrum outside the Mayor's HQ at City Hall. Repeatedly telling journalists and photographers jostling against him to 'get back,' he promised to be 'frank and candid,' to 'put a smile on people's faces' and declared himself 'thrilled and excited' about running for mayor.

Boris had chosen to ignore advice from a raft of people that he would be variously bored, excluded from real power or crushed by Ken Livingstone but the Leadership was less able to bat away rumbling concerns that he would prove a 'disaster waiting to happen', both as a candidate and then mayor – someone who would make their return to government less rather than more likely. George Osborne, who was in charge of the campaign, told friends that he (perhaps more than Cameron) was agonising over Boris's candidacy and whether the Leadership should 'block or back it.' But it was too late for cold feet – no other viable candidate had come forward and now they were left with someone who did not actually need their support to win the candidacy for he had his own powerbase, popular support and genius for publicity.

The very quality that gave the Tories palpitations – his comic dilettante reputation – was the one that made Boris so popular with the people. If control is power in politics, by turning to him for the mayoral elections, the Cameroons had just lost it. Cameron knew that he needed someone above or separate from his party – and he had found the very person who fitted the bill. Clearly, he did not come without risks, though. And his application for the candidacy – scrawled in messy handwriting and bursting with sarcasm and jokes – did little to assuage the fears. He listed his political and employment history but when it came to the section 'challenges faced', Boris could not help but raise a smile: '1. Trying to help raise 4 children in inner

London. Outcome: too early to call, but looking promising. 2. Taking on Blair and Campbell in the battle of Black Rod's Memorandum on the Queen Mother's lying-in-state. Outcome: Total victory. 3. Negotiating Hyde Park Corner by bicycle. Outcome: survival.' He left the section marked 'personal character' blank. (Polly Toynbee of the *Guardian* tried to fill it in for him with an extraordinary piece the next day, calling him a 'jester, toff, self-absorbed sociopath and serial liar.')

Nor was the word out of Henley particularly encouraging. Peter Sutherland of the Henley Conservatives, normally an ardent Boris supporter, publicly doubted his mayoral credentials. 'It is very easy to question whether he is up to the job,' he told the *Henley Standard*. Henley's own mayor Terry Buckett said he believed Boris was too inexperienced – 'If I lived in London, I would be concerned.' And he was also angry at the way the decision had been made. 'He should have sought approval from his constituents before declaring to run,' he said.[11] Other Henley voters were more succinct: 'Traitor!' declared one woman, coming up to him at a Conservative gathering.

With Boris in a different league from the rest of the Conservative candidates still in the race, some thought there would be a coronation rather than the originally planned primary. But in the end, it went ahead with Boris standing against Andrew Boff (runner-up to Steve Norris in 2000) and two councillors from Kensington & Chelsea: Warwick Lightfoot and Victoria Borwick.

During the lead-up, a YouGov poll indicated that, if chosen for the Tories, Boris would lead Ken by 46 to 40 per cent. The result made the contest even more of a foregone conclusion. And Boris did indeed triumph with 79 per cent of the primary vote. Admittedly, the sample was tiny – fewer than 20,000 Londoners bothered to participate. But now, at last, the real contest could begin. It was one for which Boris's entire life now seemed to have been in preparation: Boris versus Ken.

Chapter Twelve
Too Funny to be Mayor?
2007–2008

'He is the most formidable opponent I will face in my political career.' So pronounced Ken Livingstone in early August 2007 on BBC Radio 4's *Today* programme. Unlike many of his Conservative opponents, *he* did not doubt Boris's electoral firepower as a 'charming and engaging rogue.' Ken instinctively scented trouble in the personality contest and so he insisted: 'I want to get onto the policy: this is not a sort of "Celebrity Big Mayor" – it's a serious issue about how you run the city.'

But there was no disguising the fact that Ken vs. Boris was developing nicely into Britain's first celebrity election. Political parties barely seemed to matter, it was not even a contest between Left and Right: it was more a question of whether Londoners preferred blond, bumbling Boris (who promised something new and somehow cheerier) or wily old Ken (who had arguably run out of steam after eight eventful years). If Ken was aware of Boris's electoral appeal, then the Tories were equally cognisant of Ken's track record. 'He is the only truly successful Left-wing British politician of modern times,' had been Charles Moore's assessment.[1]

Not only was he a brilliant strategist, but Ken, now 62, could claim to have improved London's buses, as well as introducing the Congestion Charge and Oyster travel pass. Indeed, he had presided over the transformation from a capital slammed by travel guides in the late-90s to one of the hippest tourist destinations in the world. On his watch, London had overtaken New York as the globe's leading financial centre. He had also brought the Olympics to the capital and been a calm and unifying force after the 7/7 suicide bombings of 2005.

Forty-three-year-old Boris, meanwhile, had a rocky Parliamentary career and a couple of sex scandals on his slate and had not shown much noticeable interest in London before. But he had also made a lot of people laugh, featured on various 'cool' lists, got into plenty of entertaining scrapes and run a notorious magazine. Ken knew he had to take the battle to Boris, so while publicly talking policy, he was actually busy trying to chip away at Boris's likeability. He and his staff had been combing through newspapers and books for ammunition against the Cult of Boris and they first alighted on some of his writings on the subject of race.

Boris's damning comments on the Macpherson report, which had uncovered 'institutional racism' in the Metropolitan Police's handling of the 1993 murder of the black teenager Stephen Lawrence, were widely circulated. As we have seen, he had branded it 'hysterical' and 'weird', and its suggestions for new race crimes likely to intrude further into private life than anything under Ceausescu's Romania. Doreen Lawrence, Stephen's mother, declared Boris to be 'not an appropriate person to run a multicultural city like London – those people that think he is a lovable rogue need to take a good look at themselves and look at him. I think once people read his views, there is no way he is going to get the support of any people in the black community.'

A spokesman for Boris insisted that he 'loathed racism' and pointed to the undeniable fact that his later articles were more sympathetic to Macpherson but the accusations began to hit target. Team Ken went on to release snippets of Boris's (now fairly aged) articles that supported the Iraq War or could potentially cause offence to homosexuals, women or people on the minimum wage. The aim was to portray him as a Right-wing bigot, with no love for multi-cultural London.

As if this were not bad enough, Gordon Brown had been enjoying a political honeymoon since he became Prime Minister in June, with Labour several points ahead in the polls. Voters liked the fact that, unlike Blair, Brown did not holiday with Berlusconi, brought in Tories and Lib Dems to serve in his administration (as GOATs, or Government Of All the Talents) and handled the Glasgow airport bombing with firmness and tact.

Boris deserves credit for standing firm under fire at this seemingly hopeless point – although critics claim he just did not notice the woeful position he was in. To the sounds of 'London Calling' by the Clash, he launched his 'Back Boris' campaign in early September, warning that he reserved the right to continue to make jokes but that he was also 'deadly serious' in his bid to become mayor. That latter aim was not advanced by a series of technical failures, a lightness of policy (beyond a promise to bring back the beloved Routemaster bus in modern form) and his fondness for quips. It was not long afterwards that a journalist from the *Wall Street Journal*, who had been trailing Boris with increasing fascination, inquired: 'Are you too funny to be mayor?'

But none of this stopped him from receiving a hero's welcome at the Conservative Party conference in Blackpool later that month. Two years after Cameron had walked the stage of the Winter Gardens in the leadership contest, Boris was busy wooing the audience into believing that he too was really a serious player. 'When people ask me, "Are you serious about this?" I can tell them that I can think of nothing more serious than the security and prosperity of the powerhouse of the British economy, whose booming service industries are the best possible vindication of the revolutions brought in by Conservative governments.' The speech was delivered in classic Boris rambling style – one familiar to his immediate audience but not to the Governor of California, Arnold Schwarzenegger, who was waiting to broadcast a message by satellite link from the United States. 'He's fumbling all over the place,' Schwarzenegger observed to aides on footage that quickly found its way onto the Internet but the legendary 'Fumbulator' attack played to Boris's hand. Not only was it free publicity, it also served to highlight the contrast between his amusing, if stylised eloquence and the stilted delivery of a man he later branded a 'monosyllabic Austrian cyborg.'

The 2007 Conservative conference went well for Boris and the party – peaking when the shadow chancellor George Osborne stole a march on Labour by announcing a policy to take all but millionaires out of the inheritance tax trap. Hitherto widely expected to announce a snap election, Brown now 'bottled it'. On 6 October, he made it clear that he would not be going to the country and fortuitously Boris was spared the embarrassment of trying to keep Henley – which he had admitted was his intention – and simultaneously fighting for London.

Now it was finally time to get down to work. To demonstrate his commitment, Boris made two announcements. He was to give up alcohol for the duration of the campaign – and in the process went on to lose a stone and a half. And he would withdraw into a self-imposed purdah so that, he said, he could work on policies and read into the role. Indeed, he was extremely busy during this period – albeit away from the campaign working on no fewer than three different television projects filmed in six different countries, including another episode of *Have I Got News For You*. And until February, he was still writing his weekly column for the *Telegraph*, promoting his new book of verse, *The Perils of the Pushy Parents*, and throughout this time fulfilling at least some of his duties as a constituency MP. It was almost as if he could not quite believe that he was running for mayor, or that it was worth his complete and serious attention. Quite likely he subscribed to the widely held opinion that it was impossible that he could win, but had gambled that a narrow, yet glorious defeat might be just the career booster needed. Ken certainly believed it was a case of Boris seeking to reposition himself: 'I think he just thought this will let me back in the game,' he says. Indeed, when an associate Boris knew from Brussels bumped into him at the House of Commons he cheeped, 'Have you heard what I'm up to?' like an excitable schoolboy who had just worked out how to escape a detention.

Boris inherited a youthful campaign team created by Boles and led by 32-year-old ex-Saatchi executive Dan Ritterband. It came with £60,000 of funding and a suite of rooms in Centre Point, a design guru's dream overlooking the fleshpots of Soho, but crucially, a 35-minute walk from Tory HQ. The capable, but inexperienced Rachel Wolf had moved over in July (but left in dismay, months later). Tom Dyke, a former law student who had only recently been an intern at the Policy Exchange, was in charge of environmental policy.

Ritterband also brought in Alex Crowley, a film studies graduate in his early twenties, who had worked for the London Assembly Tories, as chief of research. Katie Perrior and Jo Tanner, former middle-ranking members of the Central Office press team, were in charge of media. Although undoubtedly talented and eager, none had run a campaign of this magnitude before and it was a tall order keeping tabs on Boris. Many of the old hands outside the team felt that invaluable time was being lost: Ken was already popping shots at Boris, but the fire was not being returned. Those inside recall feeling swamped – they were, after all, far outnumbered by Ken's entourage, which was said to have the use of 70 press officers to their two.

Boris did make the odd public appearance towards the end of the year – such as in late November, when he announced that he would create a Mayor's Fund to raise millions for youth charities. True, he wrote a piece in the *Evening Standard* on knife crime and praised the work done by Ray Lewis with black boys from disadvantaged backgrounds at the Eastside Young Leaders Academy. But Boris's near-invisibility allowed Ken to quip: 'I've sent the police out to look for him – I'm afraid he might have been kidnapped.'

The Tory feeling was also that his appearances such as they were, were sporadic and poorly planned, and that Boris was relying on his fame and charisma to wing him through. While these attributes had served him extraordinarily well so far, they were hardly a match for beating the formidable Ken and his Labour Party machine. George Osborne, who was in overall charge, started briefing the Tory activist website *ConservativeHome* that he was concerned at the campaign's 'worrying drift' and that there was 'disappointment that the Henley MP is not yet firing on all cylinders.' It was part of a concerted effort to corner a reluctant Boris into accepting outside help. The Leadership was right to be worried – 'The team needed some grown-ups, they were out of their depth,' said one person who was closely involved. 'The whole thing was a peculiar shambles.'

Still apparently semi-detached, Boris was nevertheless trying to bolster his office off his own back. In November, David Willetts lent him his young assistant Chris Cook for six weeks (Boris trusted Cook from when he worked from his staff annexe in Westminster and fortunately, he was also rated by Central Office). However talented, it was nevertheless the case that he had been working for the Tories for just two-and-a-half years and while that made him a veteran compared to some of the campaign team, it was hardly the sort of battle-hardened experience Boris needed. 'It was unbearable when I arrived,' Cook recalls. In the absence of proper direction, at least one team-member resorted to seeking help from what Cook dubs, 'a trendy American political pot-boiler.'

'The big problem was that the disorganisation led to some real on-the-hoof decision-making,' recalls Cook. One such issue was the third runway at Heathrow. Boris and his team 'were of a view' that he was going to come out against it, but no final decision had been made about the call or when it would be made. But somehow, in a blunder symptomatic of the lack of discipline, the policy slipped out without any strategic planning. 'When it started going wrong, he came to me, with his head in his hands, saying, "I don't think they know what they are doing."'

Cook set to work on deciding the attack lines against Ken, but found he was working virtually alone. 'There was no political leadership and no discipline,' he recalls. 'People would just get distracted with ephemera and leave important things like media planning much too late. No one was checking that Ken's claims on various things were actually true, breaking the first rule of political campaigns.' Nor would Boris take the lead himself. 'Boris wanted to be liked, he wanted to outsource responsibility for getting it going,' explains Cook. 'He wasn't going to go in and do the shouting; he was looking for someone to sort it out. But he did not want to bring in people from Central Office – he wanted only people who were loyal to him.'

Boris was also reluctant to let anyone else write his speeches or monitor the ones he had written, but this led to an inevitable logjam. 'I told him that you actually want people to say, "oh, one of those boring political speeches!" We had to make him sound like an administrator, a mayor. But he would always bugger around with everything. It led to things not being ready for print runs or briefings.'

With just six months to go until the election, time – and patience – was running out. It was not so much Ken as the Liberal Democrat candidate Brian Paddick (who had recently left the police after 30 years), who brought the matter to a head for, as a former deputy assistant commissioner, he knew his subject well. And as another populist maverick, Paddick was swift to call for the resignation of his former boss, the Metropolitan Police Commissioner Sir Ian Blair, over the fatal police shooting of an innocent Brazilian, Jean Charles de Menezes, on 22 July 2005 in the aftermath of the London bombings. It was an opportunistic move by Paddick, on the very day of his nomination, against an increasingly vulnerable Commissioner (who had long been a major Tory target for what was perceived to be his politically-motivated style of policing). The Met had been found guilty of 'corporate failure' and a series of errors that had endangered the public. Boris had given a quote claiming the Commissioner's position was 'untenable,' but had failed to go further, leaving the way clear for Paddick to reap the political capital. Senior Tories thought Boris had been left looking strangely passive and underpowered.

Boris's admittedly feeble defence was that he had agreed to leave the field to his colleague, the shadow home secretary David Davis. But the affair – a mayoral issue par excellence – alarmed the Leadership. Although Cameron made fun of him by saying: 'Inside Boris there is a serious, ambitious politician fighting to get out,' the seemingly affectionate joke veiled a distinct threat. It was accompanied by a summons from George Osborne for a meeting at which he pressed Boris to 'engage' with the fight and accept a forthright Australian Central Office staffer called James McGrath to instill the missing discipline and urgency. But Boris, fearing a Cameroon 'spy in the cab', fought hard against it.

Even his staunchest supporters were telling him to 'get a grip'. Veronica Wadley, who had done more than anyone to make him the Conservative candidate for mayor, publicly attacked Boris in November 2007 for being 'pathetic.' In front of a crowd at the *Spectator* Parliamentary awards lunch, she icily declared: 'You need to get your finger out!'

In December, one of Wadley's senior reporters, Andrew Gilligan (who had worked for Boris on the *Spectator* and whom Boris had staunchly defended in print as a journalistic hero[2]) started writing about Lee Jasper, a long-term friend of Ken's and his director of equalities and policing. Gilligan reported that Jasper was being investigated for channelling £2.5 million from the Mayor's Office and the London Development Agency to organisations 'controlled by himself, his friends and his business associates' that appeared 'to do little or no work in return.' More accusations and disturbing material followed and kept on coming, and the Met police were called in to investigate. Ken continued to denounce them as 'tissues of lies' and attacked Gilligan for waging a 'dirty and mendacious campaign.' But Wadley, a formidable if unemotional figure, stood by Gilligan as an 'outstanding and fearless' journalist pursuing investigations 'in the public interest.' Nothing would deter her from what she started calling 'the campaign.'

'Veronica put her entire being into it, frequently coming in at 4 a.m. to prepare that day's Gilligan coverage and never later than six. Overall, she worked round the clock, seven days a week,' recalls a close colleague. Indeed, Wadley might have added that she and Gilligan were doing more to further the 'Back Boris' bid than the man himself. Gilligan's investigations were at the very least tarnishing Ken with the jaded air of *fin de regime* (and possibly much worse). In the process they were also directing the spotlight away from Boris's faltering performance.

But while the outside world may not yet have been looking closely at Boris, Osborne and Cameron feared his campaign was quietly heading for disaster – with all this would entail for Tory national ambitions. The mayoral was seen as Cameron's first big electoral test as Leader and if London were to be won by the Tories, the benefits in terms of morale would be incalculable. A crushing defeat, however, could damage the whole Cameroon project and the pair were no longer of a mind to cut Boris any slack. The last straw was his failure to deal with, let alone pre-empt, the embarrassing disinterment of his 2002 article, in which he used the words 'piccaninnies' and 'watermelon smiles.' Initially, he seemed unrepentant, defiant even – once again banging the table in fury at a private dinner over what he dismissed as 'dirty tricks' against him. It was a naïve, even foolish outburst, particularly from a Conservative politician, and it played directly into Ken's hands.

Boris's campaign office was now moved from Centre Point to County Hall – Ken's former HQ when he had run the GLC – directly across the river from the Houses of Parliament and within easy striking distance of Conservative HQ. Cameron himself brought in a crucial new recruit, Lord Marland, a wealthy businessman who, when previously treasurer of the Conservative Party, had raised £75 million. Now he set about creating a campaign chest of £1.5 million for Boris – dwarfing the £80,000 or so previously built up. And the cash poured in: one dinner alone raised £250,000, with high-profile donors including Sir Tim Rice and Sir Cameron Mackintosh.

This was the sort of money needed to employ professional campaigners to do a professional job. Osborne and Marland knew exactly whom they wanted and they swiftly set about persuading him to come. Marland had known Lynton Crosby, the Australian political strategist nicknamed the 'Wizard of Oz', since the pair worked together on the 2005 General Election campaign. He had become a controversial figure not only because of his abrasive plain-speaking style, but because some blamed him for Michael Howard's much-criticised so-called 'dog-whistle' emphasis on immigration. But Crosby's organisational skills had won him many plaudits too. Even though the Tories lost that election, Crosby had masterminded four consecutive election victories in Australia for John Howard, the country's second-longest serving prime minister.

Now Marland worked on persuading the Australian, who had been watching Boris's campaign from afar with increasing concern, to weave his magic in London – but at a massive discount. He told Crosby that the normal funding available in a General Election was not possible for the mayorals but taking on Boris would be an opportunity to resurrect his reputation in Britain and prove his worth to any Crosby sceptics still critical of his work.

In December, Crosby took a call from Osborne while he was 'winding down' on summer holiday at his in-laws' house in South Australia. Crosby told him that he believed that Boris was 'the right sort of candidate' for the mayoralty. But after all he had seen and heard – Crosby had been highly critical of Boris during the 2005 election and thought him at best 'unhelpful' – the Australian said he wanted proof that Boris was genuinely committed. Boris himself rang him soon afterwards to try to persuade him. 'Our conversation led me to conclude he was serious,' recalls Crosby, 'but that he needed to change his approach. Talking to Boris gave me the confidence to work with him. It became clear that he knew there were issues to resolve and that he needed to put structure and process into the campaign. Someone told me that the Eton headmaster said he was the smartest boy he had ever come across but Boris had realised that that was not enough.'

With Crosby on board, Boris's bid to become mayor, as Wadley puts it, 'ceased to be just a very serious job application. He realised he had a chance of winning and therefore had to apply himself.' Officials at City Hall also recognised that Crosby's appointment meant that Boris was an even more 'formidable' contender. The chief executive Anthony Mayer (a Whitehall veteran who had also headed up the Mayoralty's permanent staff since it started in 2000) took the unprecedented step in January of contacting Boris's office to arrange a series of private briefings on 'how to be mayor'.

Crosby – known back home variously as 'grubby', 'brilliant' and 'ruthless' – does not come cheap, even on the 30 to 60 per cent discount negotiated by Marland. His four months working in London on Boris's campaign cost the Conservatives around £140,000. To save money, Crosby took up residence in Marland's smart London townhouse in Knightsbridge. But he was an inspired choice: he is both workaholic and election addict – once joking when asked if he had met HM the Queen that there was 'no point' as she 'doesn't vote and doesn't live in one of our target seats.' After Christmas, Crosby flew over to London to meet Boris at his headquarters and set the right tone from the start. After years of indulgence and special treatment, Boris did not know what had hit him: he was informed that he had to 'lift his game' to avoid 'letting down his team.'

Working in tandem on forcing home the message, Crosby and Marland took Boris out to dinner at Quirinale, a smart modern Italian restaurant in Westminster. Boris arrived with the words: 'I've already done it!' Done *what*? was the reply. 'I've already booked a haircut – I'm going tomorrow.' His new chiefs realised that Boris was trying to show willing but it was an all-too rare flash of humour that night. Marland and Crosby had decided not only did they have to take control of Boris for the duration of the campaign, but that he needed an immediate 'awakening' to some bitter home truths. Talking softly but bluntly across the white linen tablecloth, the pair delivered a sobering message: he had to show commitment to winning. Losing, even by a tiny margin, was not an option.

'Boris had been able to wing it all his life through charm, intelligence and bashfulness,' says Marland, 'and so he had really believed until then that just saying, "I'm Boris Johnson" and playing "London Calling" would do the job. We had to awaken in him the realisation that it wasn't, and if he carried on the same way, he really could lose. We even asked him, "Do you want to win?" Because if you do, we told him, you need to focus on the fact that losing would be disastrous for you. You would be the one who couldn't win London for the Conservatives against the backdrop of the most unpopular Labour government ever. You will give all your enemies the chance to crucify you.' He was also warned that there would be 'a lot of grunt work' and that the tightest self-discipline would be required – and that specifically included his 'personal life.' It was made perfectly clear that the new regime would not tolerate any further unexpected revelations of philandering and they asked him to list any past misdemeanours that might still come out. Any eventuality was meticulously prepared for. As Marland puts it: 'The known unknowns you can deal with, it's the unknown unknowns that kill you.'

Boris was also instructed if he were a minute late for a quickly arranged breakfast meeting of hedge-funders and other potential donors then Marland, for one, would immediately pull out. Lastly, he was told in no uncertain terms: 'If you let us down, we'll cut your fucking knees off!'

That first week, Crosby also quickly dealt with the issue of the team. 'Boris's people were a good bunch, but many hadn't had the experience,' he says. 'So they often responded to the wrong things.

Candidates need confidence in order to perform, they can't be worrying about things getting done right.' Dan Ritterband was assigned to marketing – a position better suited to his undoubted creative talents. Two tough, bluff and gruff Australians, who would brook no nonsense from Boris, would now orchestrate every minute of his day. At Crosby's insistence, James McGrath – another galvanising force from Down Under who had been advising Osborne – finally came from Central Office to work alongside him. 'He was very hands-on,' recalls one observer. 'He was very good at what matters, deciding what doesn't, and cutting through the crap. He drove things forward with his strength of will. He's quite aggressive and would bark at people, if he had to. Somehow as an Australian it was easier for him to do the necessary shouting.'

Boris HQ subsequently became more boot camp than bohemian hangout – a bugle was even sounded to call the troops to a daily morning meeting also attended by the Opposition Chief Whip, Patrick McLoughlin, or one of his colleagues, who ensured lines remained open within the Parliamentary party. There was to be no more Rhodesia-style UDI. Work started at eight at the latest, seven days a week. The same rules applied to the 20 paid staff and the 20 unpaid volunteers. It could not have been less like Boris's regime at the *Spectator*, with sofas provided for 'fits of the vapours' and long, drunken lunches. Those who failed to perform were bawled out, the successful lavishly praised and asked to take a bow.

Even Boris did not escape the military-style discipline. Designated a punishing regime of appearances and speeches, he would receive an admonishing text from Crosby if he stepped out of line by being late, off-message or scruffy. The running joke on the campaign team was that Crosby kept Boris squarely in the cross hairs of a sniper rifle, ready to bring him down the second his mouth ran away with him. To his credit, Boris submitted himself to Crosby's strictures but it cannot have been easy. 'He was neither petulant nor precious about it,' recalls Crosby.

Boris's hair was cut and combed, his suit, shirt and tie collection refreshed. And despite his energetic resistance, he was sent for media training with another bull-like Antipodean, Scott Chisholm – an ex-

Sky News anchorman originally from New Zealand but who started his working life in Australia. With a big physical presence and nice line in put-downs, he is not one to be impressed by Old Etonian bumbling.

Initially, Boris could not see the need for media training – after all, he had conquered the airwaves with his buffoonery on *Have I Got News for You*. He was also a journalist with a proven way with words. But Crosby knew that Boris had to change his style for the quick-fire demands of a political campaign, particularly the forthcoming televised debates against Ken and Paddick. It was yet another battle that Boris could not win – but one he was glad in the end to have lost for Chisholm is a master at helping people hone their thoughts into television-friendly sound-bites lasting barely a couple of seconds or a handful of words. Accustomed to the luxury of being allowed to ramble at will, Boris admitted to his team afterwards that he had 'needed' it. For a man so eloquent in print, Boris can be strikingly inarticulate in speech.

Intent on keeping Boris in check and on message, Crosby continued to attend his more important media appearances, calmly coaching him on the spot just before the cameras started rolling. He knew that Boris had to prove he was both serious and competent – smirking was specifically banned – and only the slickest of performances would do the job. So, to avoid mishaps, access to Boris was tightly controlled and most journalists, even those who waited months for an interview, never got near him. Boris insisted it was 'absolute bollocks' that he had been gagged, but he did once let slip that he considered his new handlers 'scary.'

Crosby's most important task now was to devise a strategy that would persuade people to turn out and vote for Boris. Early on, he was given an intriguing piece of research. People were asked to look at pictures of Ken's, Boris's and the other candidates' faces and to say which ones made them happy. The results were encouraging as not only did Boris score much higher than Ken and the others, but his face also triggered feelings of affection, even if people did not always agree with his political views. He had, in short, a likeability factor that put him above and beyond the normal bounds of politics. Crosby himself noticed that people smiled when they saw him in the street; somehow they picked up that 'with the ego comes a sensitivity, a real desire to make people like him.' Paddick and his team also found that the 'most common response we got on the doorstep was, "I'm voting for Boris because he is a laugh." It's a sad reflection in terms of interest in politics. People now judge their politicians not on their policies, but in the same way as they judge other celebrities.'

Not that this news permitted any complacency. Crosby believes that the message is the most important element in politics. Boris's needed 'some refinement' and to be delivered 'to the right people.' The themes were to be simple but emotive: getting rid of bendy buses, reducing youth crime and making public transport safer. They were to be delivered in ways that would suppress Ken's votes – by attacking his record on all three – and ensuring that Conservative voters were encouraged to turn out and make change happen. Ken was to be portrayed as a Zone One and Two man – an ideologue not interested in the millions who come from the 'outer rim' of London and more interested in pet causes and 'playing politics' than in the realities of life for Londoners.

Boris's general strengths as a 'non-politician,' celebrated optimist and raconteur were similarly to be emphasised. And any negative assaults from the other side on issues such as race, homophobia or simply being too posh were to be systematically dealt with, the rebuttal lines carefully prepared. Crosby felt that overall Labour had, in any case, underestimated the power of Boris' personality and, relying on the shambles of his early campaign, had fought a poor fight with contradictory messages. Labour ministers such as Harriet Harman, Ed Balls or Hazel Blears would either dismiss Boris as a 'clown' on the one hand or an 'evil, nasty, elitist, racist, Thatcherite Tory' on the other. But as it was difficult to be both, he believed neither tag would really stick in the end. Tony Travers, the London politics expert at the London School of Economics, talks about Labour tactics directly boosting Boris's vote. 'Johnson and his entourage should give Ken and chums daily thanks,' he observes. 'They built up Boris to such a monster that it has helped him ever since. They said he was stupid – wrong; nasty – wrong; a clown – less easy to say wrong. It's the opposite of President Obama, who was built up as the saviour of the world and the best hope for liberals anywhere. So when the love actually clicked into power, he was bound to fail. By contrast, Boris could only exceed expectations.'

But Crosby's strategy went far further than that. He identified three key reasons why people would not vote Boris: that he wasn't up to it (solution: Crosby's unforgiving regime of discipline and preparation); that people hadn't heard of him (solution: a relentless round of micro-targeted appearances and interviews) and lastly, that he wasn't going to make a difference (solution: the now-infamous 'doughnut' strategy targeting likely Tory supporters in outer London, who had not previously bothered to vote in mayoral elections, and demonstrating what a good mayor could do for them by improving transport, cleaning up parks, reducing congestion and planting trees). Crosby believed a high turnout might well increase Ken's support, but it would boost the Conservative vote even more. The team was instructed 'to lock in the base' first before going for the 'swing.' 'Like an exam paper, tackle the easy questions that you know first,' he would say.

So the campaign focused in turn on five goals: first, persuading voters outside central London who had not voted in previous mayoral elections to vote for Boris now; then motivating existing Tories to vote for Boris (a significant group of so-called 'Livingstone Tories' had voted for Ken because Steve Norris was perceived to lack star quality); then persuading non-Tories in inner London to vote for Boris (by trading on his personality and promoting his liberal credentials); followed by suppressing Labour's vote, particularly in its strongest areas (by attacking Ken's record, above all on crime); and finally, going after Liberal Democrat voters on the basis that their candidate could not win and Boris was worth at least a second preference vote.

Crosby's research told him that the 'most significant issue' in influencing Liberal Democrats (for both their first and second preference votes) was the environment. But while this could have been tricky for Boris, who had until recently been a critic of what he thought was the cult of climate change and its deluded disciples, focus in the mayoral campaign was local rather than planetary. Voters wanted to know who would clear rubbish in the streets, stop the building on green spaces and soften the hard edges of living in London. With judicious and well targeted leafleting and announcements – including that the £1 million saved by abolishing Ken's free-sheet newspaper would be spent on more trees – Team Boris were able to convince many that their man was stronger on the *local* environment. It was yet another example of Crosby's micro-management of voter concerns with matching policies, a strategy that saw his team write and distribute no fewer than 397 different pieces of campaigning literature. It was, in effect, much of a re-run of Boris's Oxford chameleon strategy of being 'something for everyone' when running for President of the Union, but played out on a massive and grown-up stage.

Meanwhile, that new ultra-disciplined regime was proving effective in cutting down on gaffes, improving punctuality and making sure Boris knew his brief. Indeed, the more Ken and Labour still tried to portray him as a bumbling toff, the more voters took the attacks as proof of his authenticity as a man of the people. The more the ruling elite attacked Boris as incompetent, disastrous and lightweight, the more he was willed to succeed and forgiven the odd lapse. As the cliché goes, the British love no one more than an underdog – particularly one with a cracking self-deprecatory wit.

In January 2008, Nick Cohen summed up the view of many a pundit in an article in the *Evening Standard*: 'My dilemma: Ken is past it and Boris hasn't a clue.' Ian Hislop, editor of the satirical magazine *Private Eye*, liked to quip: 'People always ask me the same question, they say, "Is Boris a very, very clever man pretending to be an idiot?" And I always say, "No."' But Crosby revelled in the pundits' hostility – he thought it actually beneficial to be attacked by what he sneeringly dubbed 'Zone One' commentators – as it consolidated Boris's links with ordinary Londoners in the 'burbs. And indeed, the voters started showing signs that they shared none of the reservations about Boris that even his own side could not shake off. A poll in January put Boris on 44 per cent, just a point behind Ken and leagues ahead of Paddick on 7 per cent: it was the first concrete indication that he really could win.

Crucially, Marina also got involved. Rarely seen in Henley, she was inspired by the fight for London, which she saw far more in personal terms for Boris than the Conservative party. It was the first time she had had to vote for Boris – she had not registered on the electoral roll in Henley – and according to his closest aides, the first time she had voted Conservative. She now appeared on walkabouts, such as a tour round Billingsgate Market with Boris, and David and Samantha Cameron; attended hustings and having her ear to the liberal metropolitan heartbeat, advised Boris on how he could woo over non-Tory voters like her to his cause. She, in effect, joined his kitchen cabinet and earned Crosby's respect for 'being emotionally on board.' 'Marina got increasingly involved,' recalls a key aide. 'The Mayorship is a very personal thing, and success or failure is very personal too so she became more protective of him. She was seen with him, which she rarely was in Henley. For the spouses, it's often about how their partner is seen – and it was for her.' Her reassuring presence also helped to contain awkward questions about Boris's sex life now and his affairs in the past.

Not that it was all plain sailing – Boris was still Boris, after all. At a demonstration against aircraft-noise in west London, he watched the planes passing overhead only to remark, 'That's bad, but it's not wrist-slittingly bad, it is?' Then another plane flew over, lower and noisier than before, and with evident relief Boris was able to say: 'Yes, that's *very* bad. Very bad indeed!' Then, when climbing onto a wall to deliver an address, he narrowly missed kicking Cameron in the head (the Leader was in the middle of a television interview in support of him at the time).

On other occasions, Boris's careful preparation, on-message delivery and determination to present himself as a serious man of policy first baffled audiences, who had come expecting laughs, and then, frankly, bored them. The struggle to contain the comic within was clearly exhausting and his face certainly started to show the strain. 'I simply cannot afford to give the media any sign that I'm not taking it seriously,' he told the *Standard*. 'This is by far the best thing I've ever tried to do.' After all, it was only three years since suicide bombers had killed 52 innocent people in the capital – an atrocity that Ken was widely perceived to have dealt with well. Even Boris's supporters wondered aloud whether he had the necessary gravitas and leadership skills to pull London through another outrage. 'I kept thinking if something horrible happens in London,' said one, 'will Bertie Wooster be able to deal with it?'

Occasionally there would be a reversion to type – the suit would be creased, the hair ruffled, the delivery more bumbling and the odd statistic or fact forgotten. His first face-to-face television encounter with Ken and Paddick – on ITV's *London Talking* programme – was a case in point. Boris showed a new forcefulness when he tackled Ken on rising crime and the spate of teenage murders. The first week of January 2008 alone had seen two deaths and Boris scored a hit when he said the Mayor, 'must get a grip on this problem, it breaks my heart to see so many kids growing up scared, and so many adults scared of kids.' Boris was also witty, though clearly still not fully on top of his brief: he fluffed answers on questions about bus conductors and flannelled when asked why he had not previously shown much interest in London before (before his mayoral campaign began, Boris had mentioned London in Parliament just 15 times in six years as an MP).[3]

Not normally an orator, Paddick was nervous up against two men he called 'heavyweights,' but came across well as both serious and prepared. Ken was considered to have had the best line, opening with: 'If you don't believe that London's improved over the past eight years, then don't vote for me.' That said, it was widely considered to have been Boris's night. He had waffled too much and forgotten a couple of answers, but he had surprised his audience with his passion and seriousness of purpose.

Throughout January, the *Standard* continued its series of stories about Ken and his staff – joined by further disclosures from Channel 4 *Dispatches* and BBC London. They ranged from freebie holidays for a deputy to using GLA funds to pay for a character assassination – all were damaging for Ken. On one night, though, the spotlight moved onto Boris's turf at one of the *Standard*'s 'Influentials' debates. Michael Eboda, the former editor of the black newspaper *One Nation*, warned Boris that in a multicultural city like London the piccanniny references would come back again and again to haunt him. Boris now knew better how to handle such an attack and wasted no time in giving his rehearsed apology for any offence his words may have caused, while insisting they had been taken out of context. 'If you look at the article as written, they really do not bear the construction you're putting on them,' he said. 'I'm absolutely 100 per cent anti-racist: I despise and loathe racism.'

But soon afterwards, and despite all the revelations, another poll showed the Mayor with an increased lead of four points. Ken's advantage was then helped by the news that Boris had accepted his office space in County Hall from Shirayama Europe, a company previously in dispute with the Mayor. Boris was swift to deny any wrongdoing: 'This is a donation and has been registered as such. This type of story from Ken's campaign goes to show how low they are prepared to go.' Indeed, Boris was making a virtue of fighting a clean war. The fact was, though, that Team Boris did not need to do much digging on Ken – Gilligan and others were more than prepared to do it for him.

For Boris, the next poll proved a mixed blessing and suggested that there was still more rebranding to do. A ComRes survey of business leaders for the *Independent* found that they still thought of Boris as a 'buffoon.' Nevertheless they preferred him to Ken, whom they considered divisive and too Left-wing.

February saw Boris placing crime at the top of the agenda, where Crosby would work hard to keep it until polling day in May. The much-publicised killings of teenagers on the capital's streets were dominating the news – on what Ken contemptuously calls the grounds of 'if it bleeds, it leads.' It was no accident that this subject had been chosen for Boris's first policy manifesto or that while launching it, he was flanked by David Davis, the shadow home secretary, whose presence was also intended to dispel growing and persistent reports that the Leadership did not really want Boris to win. Boris's, or rather Crosby's, choice of battleground was now clear: crime, and particularly youth killings. Some working on the team felt concerned that the crime emphasis risked making it a 'nasty' campaign but Crosby clearly had no such qualms.

By the end of the month, the polls were mixed. A YouGov poll now showed Boris with a five-point lead over Ken and another, a private poll for the Labour party, put Ken ahead by nine points. These conflicting messages from different pollsters continued throughout the campaign, but it was clear that Boris was very much in the race. But so – notwithstanding all the allegations – was Ken.

On 27 February, Boris came up with a statistic that would turn out to be false and a gift to his opponent. In an interview on BBC London radio, he said that the cost of employing conductors to work on his proposed new fleet of Routemasters would be just £8 million a year. It soon became clear this figure was erroneous because more new Routemasters would be needed than the number of bendy buses they replaced. Unaccountably, Boris stuck with it.

On firmer ground, he returned to his old opportunistic self with news that the Met was investigating him for purloining the cigar case of Tariq Aziz, the former Deputy Prime Minister of Iraq. The incident had taken place a full five years earlier and he had even written about it in the *Telegraph* at the time. Yet, bizarrely, now Scotland Yard was pursuing the case – and during an election campaign increasingly dominated by stories of teenagers dying on London's streets. It was another electoral gift. Boris allowed himself to be described as 'fuming.' 'There were over 18,000 crimes in London last month and yet the police write to me about this!' he exclaimed. As so often in his life, his salvation yet again came by way of his opponents.

Ken played his part, too. Tuesday, 4 March was a turning point in the election and it was another Andrew Gilligan story that made it so. The *Standard* splashed with the revelation that £100,000 of public money had gone to projects run by Karen Chouhan, to whom the controversial Lee Jasper had written a number of sexually charged emails. One from Jasper's City Hall email address ran: 'Happy Birthday my gorgeous, wonderful, sexy Kazzi. I want to wisk (sic) you away to a deserted island beach, honey-glase (sic) you, let you cook slowly before a torrid and passionate embrace.' Jasper had not declared any relationship with Chouhan, and she in turn denied any sexual liaison between them. But Jasper now had to go, although not before blaming, 'the racist nature of a relentless media campaign.'

Incredibly, Ken continued to back him, saying: 'I would bet my own life that [the police] will clear Lee Jasper and I will reappoint him when they do.' It was surely a blind spot not to see the damage being done to his campaign. Indeed, some of his most loyal advisers such as John Ross, his economics guru, appeared to break ranks at this point to criticise Jasper. It did not help that a couple of arrests of Jasper 'associates' soon followed and more came later.

Boris's Aussie-powered campaign machine seized its chance. Boris exploited the Mayor's troubles by announcing plans the very next day to make City Hall more transparent and accountable. If elected, Boris said he would publish on the City Hall website the biographies, responsibilities, register of interests and contact details of all mayoral advisers for the public to inspect, along with a code of conduct. Once dubbed the evil racist, Boris was now occupying the moral high ground and it was a good place to be. He then attacked Ken for making London an even more expensive place to live through increases in tube fares and the GLA council tax precept (effectively the Mayor's levy), plus what he described as his 'vainglorious foreign policy ventures' (the so-called 'Kenbassies' set up abroad in countries like China to attract inward investment) and lastly the *Londoner*, which he branded 'the Mayor's ludicrous Pyongyang-style newspaper.'

Then came the news in a report leaked to *The Times* that Ken was 'secretly planning' a large-scale expansion of his congestion charging zone. A delighted Crosby, now working a regular 18-hour day, immediately put out attack leaflets to all nine areas the newspaper said were under consideration. Ken, whom Boris began to dub 'Ken Leaving-soon', was feeling Crosby's heat. In a reference to his opponent's Australian nationality, he was overheard saying: 'For the first time in my life, I can actually see the benefits of a rigorous deportation policy.'

Ken's celebrity friends – including Kevin Spacey, director of the Old Vic theatre – continued to support him but others in the normally reliably Labour-supporting arts world, such as Tracy Emin and Dinos Chapman, distanced themselves. They were both signatories to an open letter attacking Ken's love of tall buildings in the East End, which they said were 'destroying what makes London special.' But much worse was to come the next day from another so-called friend – the

Chancellor of the Exchequer, Alistair Darling – who was delivering his first budget on 12 March. There was little good news – increased borrowings, lower than expected growth rates, higher taxes on alcohol and family cars. Worst of all was that he confirmed that the hugely unpopular planned abolition of the 10p starting tax rate would go ahead – leaving some five million low-paid taxpayers worse off (not a few of them living in London). The electoral ripples were immediate and disastrous for Labour – whose support fell to a 25-year low – and especially for Ken. In London, Labour was now trailing the Conservatives by a massive 24 points compared to 16 points nationally. Labour was hugely unpopular but incredibly Ken (who had for so long outperformed his party) was more unpopular still.

It was at this point that Ken first scented defeat. Seemingly the worst he could pin on Boris was that he had under-costed his Routemaster bus policy by £100 million. It was a subject that Andrew Neil also pursued when he interviewed his former employee on the BBC *Daily Politics* show. Under persistent questioning from the Scot, Boris finally admitted that he did not know the exact cost after all. But although it was embarrassing, set against a collapsing Labour vote and the still-rumbling Jasper saga, 'bus-gate' was a sparrow among hawks. On 27 March, *The Times* reported that Gordon Brown had 'all but written off' Ken's chances of winning and was seeking consolation in the fact that a Boris victory would be a 'disaster' for David Cameron. Downing Street rejected the story as 'utter garbage' but it was clear that Labour was now rattled.

Although just named Britain's fourteenth-worst dressed man by his old employers at *GQ*, Boris looked very smart for his official campaign launch at a community hall in Edmonton (a location chosen by Crosby because three teenagers had been murdered in the area in recent weeks). Both Ray Lewis – the black youth leader now regularly seen with Boris – and David Cameron joined him. Cameron made the introductions, dubbing his fellow Etonian 'twice as charismatic' and 'twice as energetic' as Ken. 'I don't always agree with him,' he conceded, 'but I respect the fact that he's absolutely his own man.' (Soon afterwards, Cameron would give an even clearer sanction to Boris's departures from the national line with: 'It's very important that it's his manifesto, his proposals and his mayoralty.') Meanwhile, Boris offered a choice between his own 'fresh approach' and what he colourfully called his opposition – 'a superannuated Marxist cabal.' On 17 March, A *Standard* YouGov poll – which had been first to put Boris in the lead on 26 February – found him in first position once again, with a 10-point advantage over Ken.

That night the three contenders clashed in another *Standard* debate. With Paddick looking increasingly irrelevant, Ken and Boris were now settling into a nicely matched routine of point-scoring repartee in what felt more and more like a mayoral edition of *The X Factor*. Ken had brazenly adopted one of Boris's policies – on obliging miscreant youths to earn back their right to free travel – but when its original owner pointed this out, retorted: 'What sort of idiot, when they hear a good idea, wouldn't take it on board?' He then invited Boris to make a return raid on one of his own policies – a curious deal swapping cheap Venezuelan oil for London's buses for advice on transport, waste and tourism – offering: 'Would you like to meet President Chavez?' When they disagreed on whether London had become safer under Ken, Boris pointed out that the Home Secretary Jacqui Smith had recently declared that she was frightened to go out for a kebab in her neighbourhood of Peckham. 'That's because she doesn't know what is in it,' quipped Ken. 'I want a London where the most dangerous thing in Peckham is the kebab,' Boris shot right back.

With a month to go until the election, April Fools' Day was a difficult one for both main candidates. First, Labour's deputy leader Harriet Harman inflicted further damage on Ken's claims to have made the capital safer when she was filmed walking round her south London constituency in broad daylight in a stab-proof vest. Then the far-right BNP endorsed Boris on its website on the grounds that 'the Tory clown Johnson is a lesser evil than the Marxist crank Livingstone.' The posting coincided with the re-release of yet more apparently racist articles in the *Spectator* while Boris was editor. Boris apologised again 'for what was previously written, as it does not reflect what is in my heart' and attacked Ken for peddling personal slurs.

Yet even within City Hall itself, word was being put about that a

Boris Mayorship would make life difficult for black staffers. Such was the fear generated by the rumour mongering about Boris's views on race that several organised themselves into a 'Don't Let Boris In' caucus. 'They were led to believe that Boris was some sort of Right-wing Neanderthal and several black City Hall workers came to us to see how we could help them,' recalls Steve Pope of the black newspaper, the *Voice*. 'What was interesting was that they were genuinely afraid of what would happen to them.'

Outside the febrile atmosphere of Ken's lair at City Hall, though, Crosby's view was most voters were not interested in what he said, or allowed to be said, in years gone by. The point was Boris was no longer saying anything even potentially offensive now – and indeed was going out of his way to win over minority groups. And Ken's determination to push this issue was also beginning to backfire in some quarters as people struggled to equate the monster his team said would want to ban the Koran with the *HIGNFY* figure now going round London spreading bonhomie in a smart-ish suit.

Two days later, Gilligan – who had by now become a key figure in the election – made what some thought to be his first mistake in an otherwise meticulous coverage of Ken. Straying away from hard facts on the news pages, he wrote a savage opinion piece on the Mayor in the *Standard* under the headline, 'NOW WE'RE ALL COUNTING THE REAL COST OF KEN'. Soon afterwards, he won the prestigious Journalist of the Year award at the British Press Awards for what the judges described as 'relentless investigative journalism at its best.' But even some of his colleagues on the *Standard* felt that Gilligan would have been better advised not to display his personal views in this way – and that the newspaper was straying dangerously close to becoming the *Evening Boris*. Even a key member of the Boris campaign team fretted the *Standard*'s unrelenting championship of their man might prove counter-productive. 'Support from a newspaper is obviously always very helpful,' he concurs, 'but it would probably have been even more powerful if they had said something more along the lines of, "on the one hand this and the other that" and then allowed readers to choose.'

Ken also had other concerns. BBC London now revealed that he had five children by three women, rather than the two previously known about with his current partner. He said the matter had not been 'secret', merely 'private' and that all the children and their mothers were known to each other and that he was an 'involved' father with them all. 'I don't think anybody in this city is shocked about what consenting adults do,' he said, after what was widely thought to be a planned leak. The disclosure came just ahead of Andrew Hosken's forthcoming biography, which would have revealed the children for the first time in a *Daily Mail* serialisation (at least this way, Ken got his comments in first).

The usual pundits tried to make much of his complex family arrangements, but in truth as Ken said, it was not a big deal in a city as liberal as London. What is likely, though, is that his private life would have made it more difficult for him to make much of Boris's sexual history. And indeed – although Crosby was ready to deal with any trouble on that front – the spectre of 'bonking Boris' barely featured in the entire campaign. Boris himself knew better than to make trouble for Ken on this issue: both men wanted cloaks drawn over their history of begetting.

And in any case, Boris was simultaneously dealing with the fall-out from a *Marie Claire* interview with Janet Street-Porter in which he had admitted to smoking dope before going to university and an admission that he *might* have taken cocaine while at Oxford. There followed an outburst of synthetic outrage from predictable quarters – but it was brief.

By mid-April, word was coming out that the Conservatives believed they were now in with a real chance of winning – and that coming close was no longer 'good enough.' It was a seismic shift of thought and expectation, not least for Boris himself. Until then, senior figures had only dared hope for a narrow, but glorious defeat. Yet with the polls turning against them, Labour's sole solution seemed to be London minister Tessa Jowell threatening to fine ministers £5 for referring to Boris from now on as anything but 'Boris Johnson' or the 'Conservative candidate'. The public reason given was that first names reduced a very important contest to the status of a 'joke.' Privately, officials were admitting a flash of panic brought on by the belated realisation that the fact that their opponent was known as 'just Boris' reflected just how fond people were of him. (Incidentally, it seems that Boris may have received a similar briefing as he also stopped calling his opponent 'Ken' around this time, starting to refer to him in formal tones as the 'Labour Mayor'.)

Not all Conservatives looked forward to a Boris triumph, however. George Walden, the former Tory MP once attacked by Boris for being a member of the 'liberal elite', chose the morning of 9 April and the pages of *The Times* to urge Londoners not to vote for any of the candidates, whom he spit-roasted in turn for their failings. But he saved the real heat for Boris, or as he called him, 'Johnson': 'The gaiety of nations I understand, but the most entertaining thing about Johnson is when he puts on his serious, solicitous look. Like David Cameron, he is coming to believe in his own sincerity. Servility to celebrity has partially replaced class deference and the adoring polls suggest that Johnson benefits from both. A Greek grocer I knew put his finger on it. Musing about how Alan Clark imagined relieving himself on the public from his ministerial balcony, he concluded: "The English don't mind being pissed on, so long as it's from a great height." It is not Johnson one should feel embarrassed for, as he clowns around, it is the country.'

That night, the candidates met again, this time under the chairmanship of Jeremy Paxman on the BBC's *Newsnight*. The highlight was a tug of wills between a Paxman and Boris over the recurring issue of the cost of his Routemaster policy. Boris now appeared to be backtracking from the £8 million figure, but did not seem to have another more realistic one in its place. Or if he did, he did not want to reveal what it was. Sensing blood, Paxman kept returning to the point, asking no fewer than 13 times for a costing: 'Give us a figure, come on!' Throughout, Boris kept flannelling and in the end, Paxman theatrically declared: 'A figure! A figure! I despair!' Boris had scored a spectacular own goal. At one point he even appealed to Ken for help by asking him for a figure on what he intended to spend on 500 new bendy-buses.

Crosby thought the debate to be the low point of the campaign –

Boris had stopped clowning around but still couldn't be trusted with figures (although Boris's minders believe this was his only lapse in self-discipline in what was otherwise a focused and commendable effort). But even now many viewers thought that Boris's desperation in the line of fire had somehow made him still more 'endearing.' There was something of the naughty but charismatic schoolboy being slapped down and shown up by a heartless and insistent master – although Paxman noticeably did not press Boris with the cold determination he has inflicted on other politicians. It proved just how effective Boris's politics of personality could be – even Ken was seen laughing at his jokes and straightening his collar in a fatherly gesture. (Boris was later caught on a Labour supporter's mobile phone admitting the new Routemasters would indeed cost £100 million. Undoubtedly the fiasco over bus figures was his weakest point in the campaign, however forgiving some of the public might be.)

That same evening at yet another hustings, the London Citizens' Convention in Westminster's Methodist Central Hall, Boris's performance was much more politically assured. He showed just how far he was prepared to stray into liberal territory and take advantage of Cameron's licence to differ. The audience was composed of church members, trade unionists and school children. It was perhaps not a naturally sympathetic collection of people for an Etonian member of the Bullingdon Club (especially compared to many other hustings, where Paddick says he repeatedly spotted a 'very vocal Boris supporting group ready to shout everyone else down and led by a thick-set Mediterranean-looking guy in his 50s in a Boris T-shirt'). All the candidates were asked the same politically tricky question on whether they agreed with an earned amnesty for illegal immigrants. Having now been Crosby-ed for several months, Boris knew his audience, both within and outside the hall. So (incorrectly) describing himself as the grandson of a Muslim immigrant from Turkey, he theatrically (and in direct contravention of his own party's policy) declared his support. He even went on to emphasise the point by imagining the pride that he believed his grandfather would have had in him for adopting such a platform – he knew he needed one 'brave' policy, some eye-catching initiative to set him apart from his party and avoid the dangers of 'boring.' It also served as a brilliant antidote to all the 'racist' chatter about him.

This was not the performance of an out-of-touch heartless toff, but a politician who had read his electorate accurately and responded to them. It will never be possible to apportion the credit between Boris and Crosby, but what was clear by now was that they made a formidable team. And while they were reaching out to the Left, the *Sun* was meanwhile also preparing to come out in support.

Indeed, such was the interest in every aspect of Boris's life by now that the media had started to focus on his family. Marina has always sought to provide them with as normal a childhood as possible, though, and decided to use the provisions of privacy law she knew so well to protect the children. With Boris, she lodged a successful complaint to the Press Complaints Commission against a newspaper that had published photographs of his children on holiday in Turkey. 'The London Mayor considers those photos an unwarranted intrusion into the private lives of his children,' his spokesman said. 'It is clear from one photo that this intrusion has caused some distress to one of his daughters. Another seems to mock his youngest son by inviting comparisons with his father.' The move paid off and the Johnson kids have been allowed to grow up out of the public spotlight, with at least one newspaper since then deciding against naming them in a potentially embarrassing story.

Back on the campaign, Ken was catching up in the polls. Meanwhile, Boris was coming under mounting pressure to name his chief players in London if he were elected. He seemed strangely reluctant to do so – claiming that he did not want to prejudice the outcome of the election or his proposed staff and advisers by naming them. He had just one name to give out – but it was a big one. Bob Diamond, the American-born president of Barclays, was to help set up the Mayor's Fund.

Race was to prove an issue one more time for Boris when he appeared on a live on-air hustings on BBC Asian Network. Ken was late – pleading he had stayed behind to see his children because they 'don't understand why Daddy spends more time with Boris than with them.' Maybe this unsettled Boris, but he started to sound uncomfortable when asked by the presenter Nihal Arthanayake whether he had met his Turkish relatives or kept up any part of his Turkish heritage. Boris evaded the question by announcing that he had Turkish cousins living in London and denied that he had only recently uncovered them to help him win the ethnic vote. 'Lots of Turkish relations have been coming and going in our family for a long time,' he countered. But when Arthanayake asked him: 'Are you down with the ethnics?' Boris replied: 'I'm down with the ethnics. You can't out-ethnic me, Nihal,' before later adding, 'My children are a quarter Indian, so put that in your pipe and smoke it!' Arthanayake ended the exchange by saying: 'OK, let's not try to out-brown each other.'

Of course, there was one other minority group that Boris had also annoyed in the past with his support for Section 28 and for having once compared civil partnerships to 'three men and a dog' getting married. For him, this was yet another vulnerable territory as Ken had traditionally been very strong on gay issues (although more recently he had lost support over his links with a Muslim cleric who had called for homosexuals to be killed). Nevertheless, on 19 April at one of the last hustings before the poll – this time organised by the gay rights group, Stonewall – Boris knew he had work to do. He wasted no opportunity to make up lost ground in declaring 'half' his campaign group was gay. But then there were loud theatrical 'oooohs!' from the audience when he thumped the table in angry response to a hostile question on his one-time support for Section 28. He hastily pointed out that he had more recently been supportive of its repeal against the Tory party line at the time. The flash of temper passed and he regained his composure when Andrew Pierce of the *Telegraph* asked a helpful question. Recalling the 'out-ethnicking the ethnics' comments, Pierce invited him to 'out-gay the gays and reveal whether, perhaps while at Eton, he had had a gay sexual experience.' 'The answer is . . .' Boris replied, and then after a dramatic pause, 'not so far!' The exchange demonstrated just how far he had travelled, while Ken remained the same old Ken.

By this time, though, the pressure of the relentless hustings, press conferences and interviews was telling. In yet another meeting with his two opponents the next day on BBC One's *Politics Show*, it was Paddick who demonstrated the quickest wit. Asked to describe each other in one word, both Ken and Boris broke the rules with long and pedestrian responses. When it came to the Liberal Democrat's turn, he came up with the simple, but devastating: 'Tragedy; comedy.'

With a week to go, some thought the result too close to call. But the Tory Leadership was waking up to the realities of quite possibly being only a week away from a Boris Mayorship. It had taken them a long time to realise the very qualities that would be deadly to 'normal' politicians were still working very well for Boris. A well-sourced piece in the *Telegraph* on 24 April reported Cameron's team had spent a 'significant amount of time' discussing what kind of relationship it would have with Boris, should he become mayor. According to the piece, the top priority was, 'to find ways of insulating' the leadership 'from the fallout if Boris hits trouble of any sort once in office. A degree of distance will be required between the Westminster front bench and Boris.' So, although it was widely believed among top Tories that Boris could now win, there were deep fears about the consequences for the Party at large and its hopes for the General Election if it proved to be the case. The fear that there would be another Boris scandal after he was elected now became intense. It was not exactly a ringing endorsement from his own side as he entered the final days of the fray.

That same day, on the *Standard*'s front page, Ken publicly contemplated defeat for the first time. Under the headline, 'MAYOR ADMITS THAT JOHNSON COULD WIN', he even advised Boris to oversee a 'graduated transition' if he were to be elected to City Hall in a week's time. Playing on the heart-strings – and once again mentioning his children – he said, 'If I don't win, come 6 May, I will be taking the kids to school and starting a book on my last eight years as Mayor.' In the evening, there was yet another television debate, this time on a special edition of the BBC's *Question Time* chaired by David Dimbleby. Perhaps mindful of what the Shadow Cabinet had been discussing, Boris emphasised his independence with the declaration: 'I would gladly embarrass any Government that is in power, if it was in the interests of Londoners.'

More difficult to deal with was a question from the audience about morality. Dimbleby and then Paddick pressed him on his affairs as Marina and her mother, Dip, and ailing father, Charles – who would die just a few weeks later from lung cancer – sat watching in the audience. After the recording finished, Boris went straight up to his wife but a few moments later, she seemed more intent on dealing with someone else. She stormed over to Paddick's Green Room behind stage, where he was celebrating his birthday with a friend. Quivering with anger, she shouted: 'Don't you *dare* bring my family into this!' It was a bravura performance that both impressed – and saddened – everyone who witnessed it. A contrite Paddick, unaware Marina had been in the audience, apologised to Boris the following morning when the pair met at the BBC offices for a radio show. 'He just said, "Don't worry about it, ol' boy – it's just one of those things,"' recalls the former senior police officer. Marina's obvious hurt had shaken everyone, though. 'It was a very tense evening indeed,' one of Boris's minders recalls.

Interestingly, this was the only major occasion when the subject of Boris's philandering was raised. Crosby believes that Boris benefited from the 'Clinton effect' – during the Monica Lewinsky saga, the US president's ratings actually went up. In neither case, in Crosby's view, were the sex stories seen by voters as 'consequential' to political performance and in London, with Boris he detected that voters quite often thought 'good on him.'

In the final hours of the campaign, Boris taunted Ken with his words of 1998, about how a mayor should serve only two terms because otherwise the office would inevitably, 'become corrupt or corrupted.' It was a good point – and perhaps appreciated more by the voters than the commentariat, who held quite different views from many of their readers by this time. Although by no means a supporter of Ken, one of Boris's own colleagues on the *Telegraph*, Simon Heffer, wrote: 'Mr Johnson is not a politician. He is an act. For some of us the joke has worn not thin, but out. Yet many less cynical than I am find it appealing. It conceals two things: a blinding lack of attention to detail and a ruthless ambition. He is pushy, he is thoughtless, he is indiscreet about his private life; none of this matters much to anyone these days, which is why he has gone so far in spite of them, and tomorrow may go further still.'

Then, on Thursday, 1st May – polling day itself – the *Guardian*, which had attacked the *Standard* for its perceived bias during the campaign, printed one of the most bizarre sections on politics ever seen in a national newspaper (in spite of the gravest of reservations of several senior staff). Under a screaming headline: 'BE AFRAID. BE VERY AFRAID', the paper ran five whole pages of personal attacks on Boris, beginning: 'Unbelievable as it may seem, Boris Johnson has a real chance of being elected London mayor today. A number of *Guardian* writers and other Londoners imagine what it would be like if this bigoted, lying, Old Etonian buffoon got his hands on our diverse and liberal capital.' Inside was an astonishing catalogue of insults – from 'moneyed creep' to 'flagrant and flamboyant liar' to Alan Rickman's: 'If Boris gets elected, it would be a case of the lunatic having no clue how to run the asylum' and Charlie Brooker's: 'I'd sooner vote for a dog than Boris Johnson. Cartoon characters should only run cartoon cities.'

The columnist Zoe Williams kicked off the section with: 'Ach. That flopping hair, and that sodding bicycle. Has any man ever before managed to persuade such a huge number of people that he was a decent chap on two such flimsy, trivial, irrelevant, modish pieces of ephemera? He has all the mendacity, the slyness, the patronising sleight of hand that the *Daily Mail* spews out, only he doesn't seem so outright unpleasant, because of that sodding hair and that poxing bicycle. Let's just concentrate on this myth of his being a nice guy. He is not a nice guy.' At the same time, the *Voice*, reflecting those fears of black City Hall workers, also came out strongly against Boris, devoting an entire front page to telling readers to vote Ken. Once again, Boris was polarising opinions to the extreme.

But voters had their own ideas on who the nice guy was. The *Standard*'s first edition reported: 'Boris ahead in polls, but it's so close.' YouGov put him on 43 per cent of first-preference votes to Ken's 36 per cent, predicting Boris to win in the run-off, 53 to 47 per cent. Boris was out canvassing with his team that day from dawn until the polling stations shut at 10 p.m. That night, results from local elections around the country gave Labour its worst showing for 40 years and BBC analysis put the Tories on 44 per cent nationally with Labour in third place overall on just 24 per cent. The figures were excellent news for Boris but he would have to wait another 24 hours to find out his own fate. The London result would not be announced until the following evening, giving all three candidates a night of torrid suspense. Boris certainly felt the strain and, according to a family friend, was saying in a tone of dismay: 'Crikey! It looks like I'm going to win.'

That Friday, Marina once again demonstrated her support by going for an early-morning jog with her husband – a rare sight as he usually runs alone. In newsrooms around London, meanwhile, there were earnest discussions on how early it would be safe to call the result in favour of Boris. The original estimated declaration time of 8.30 p.m. looked optimistic as a higher-than-expected turnout of around 45 per cent meant there were simply more votes than usual (at nearly 5.5 million including second preferences) to count.

Over at the *Standard*, Veronica Wadley was booked on a late flight out to the South of France for a holiday she had no intention of missing. She pleaded with management to hold the presses for an extra half-hour, but at around 6 p.m. decided that she was prepared to gamble her job on calling it right and getting it out in what was probably the latest-ever planned edition of London's paper. Admittedly, this was by now a negligible risk, but some six hours before the official result she decided to go ahead and print a special late edition under the headline 'BORIS IS THE MAYOR'. 'By 4 p.m. I had confirmation from both parties that Boris had won. But I also knew that if they were wrong and Ken kept his job, I would lose mine,' she concedes.

Marina brought in all four children to sit with her in the front row of the Assembly Chamber gallery for the result when it finally came. The original declaration time was supposed to have been 8.30, but in the event the first GLA seat was not declared before 9 and the mayoral result took much longer still. Broadcasters were scrambling pundits and even impersonators to fill time. The morning newspapers were still on tenterhooks. Tessa Jowell for the first time admitted the possibility that Ken might not have won. But not until 11.30 were the candidates finally invited to join the rowdy throng in Committee Room One for an announcement that was to change the lives of the Johnsons for ever.

Chapter Thirteen
Sense of Wonderment
First Days at City Hall, 2008

At 11.54 p.m. precisely, the Returning Officer Anthony Mayer walked into Committee Room One at City Hall. It was packed, noisy and expectant. As they stood up to hear the result, many of the dozens of candidates and advisers present suspected that Ken already knew he had lost. Still more caught Boris looking as if *surely* he could not have won, whatever the *Standard* had screamed on its front page earlier that evening.

Mayer cleared his throat and, 40 long hours after polling began, delivered the final results. On the first count Boris had secured more than a million votes – 1,043,761 – compared to Ken's 893,877. Paddick was left trailing a poor third. But with Boris and Ken on 43.2 and 37.0 per cent respectively, second preference votes would have to be taken into consideration. What Veronica Wadley over at the *Standard* had counted on in her calculation – that second preferences would divide almost equally between the two main candidates – turned out to be about right. Despite polling some 350,000 more votes than when he won in 2004, Ken was out. Overall, Boris had won by a relatively narrow margin of 1,168,738 to Ken's 1,028,966 but he had scooped up more votes than his predecessor Steve Norris in the preceding two mayoral elections put together: Boris had got the voters out, *and* he had got them out for him.

There was, however, no outbreak of triumphant cheering from the Boris corner – it seemed inappropriate when the far-right BNP had also just grabbed its first GLA seat. Ken, who felt shell-shocked and emotional, just remembers 'Boris bouncing over to me and saying, "This is all Gordon Brown's fault!"'

Mayer led the candidates down to the Assembly Chamber, where the news was to be announced publicly. Each candidate was then called in and climbed a slope to stand at their allotted place on a podium. Marina, dressed in a matching denim skirt and shirt, sat smiling with her equally happy-looking children in the public gallery. Lara, the eldest, leant over to her younger siblings and told them to keep their fingers crossed 'for Daddy.'

At just gone midnight Mayer pronounced Boris the Mayor-Elect of London and Marina clapped her hands in delight. Another unknown woman in the audience also shrieked with joy. As Simon Jenkins noted at the time, people from all walks of life simply liked Boris more than they liked Ken. 'The campaign that brought this [victory] to pass has shown that British politics can, when allowed, shift gear from party cabalism to American-style personality projection. It can galvanise interest, activity and turnout.'

Looking shattered, Boris gave a gracious speech – the unique composition of emotion, wit and politics presenting him at his best. No doubt it puzzled those who had bought the 'Boris is a monster' line with its playfulness and lack of triumphalism. First, he thanked the candidates from the smaller parties, though specifically not the BNP candidate. He then went on: 'But mainly, I want to thank my two colleagues [Ken and Paddick] in the strange triumvirate who have been trundling around London's church halls and TV studios violently disputing the meaning of multiculturalism and the exact cost of conductors. On which point I think I'm going to declare victory. And I want to congratulate you, Brian, on your great common sense and decency with which you put your case and I do hope that it is not the end of our discussions about the Police.

'And as for Ken, Mayor Livingstone, I think you have been a very considerable public servant and a distinguished leader of this city. You shaped the office of mayor, you gave it national prominence and when London was attacked on 7 July 2005, you spoke for London. And I can tell you that your courage and the sheer exuberant nerve with which you stuck it to your enemies, especially in New Labour, have thereby earned you the thanks and admiration of millions of Londoners, even if you think that they have a funny way of showing it today.

'And when we have that drink together which we both so richly deserve, I hope we can discover a way in which the mayoralty can continue to benefit from your transparent love of London, a city whose energy conquered the world and which now brings the world together in one city. And that brings me to my final thank you, which is of course to the people of London. I would like to thank first the vast multitudes who voted against me – and I have met quite a few in the last nine months, not all of them entirely polite. I will work flat out to dispel some of the myths that have been created about me. And as for those who voted for me, I know there will be many whose pencils hovered for an instant before putting an X in my box and I will work flat out to repay and to justify your confidence.

'We have a new team ready to go in to City Hall,' he added, and then in a passage echoing the St Francis of Assisi prayer style used by Margaret Thatcher on her election victory in 1979, he continued: 'Where there have been mistakes, we will rectify them. Where there are achievements, we will build on them. Where there are neglected opportunities, we will seize on them and we will focus on the priorities of the people of London. Let's get cracking tomorrow and let's have a drink tonight.'

The moment also brought the best out in Ken – who might have blamed the *Standard* or the failings of the Labour Government, or both, for his defeat but instead conceded that the fault was entirely his own. 'I accept that responsibility,' he said.

After they left the podium, Ken took Boris to a private room for a quick chat. 'I advised him to take his time before doing too much and to keep Mark Watts on Environment (which he didn't) and Peter Hendy at Transport (which he did),' recalls Ken. 'He offered me lunch – but he does that to everybody. He must have said that at least a dozen times but we never have, not even the drink he mentioned. I knew even then that that was the last time I'd be able to get to him.'

On several occasions since, Boris has publicly made a point of claiming that he and Ken were due to have variously lunch, dinner or a drink together soon, but at no time has this actually even gone so far as even a date in the diary. It sounds friendly enough, but in fact at least for the first three years after the election there was no contact between the two men except for bumping into each other at the odd function. Boris has never followed up his pronouncements with an actual invitation – and indeed rarely 'goes for a drink' with anyone, let alone a political opponent. However, he continues to praise Ken privately – while occasionally jabbing at him in print – but Ken can be withering in private about his successor's integrity.

Meanwhile, David Cameron hailed Boris's victory and he in turn signalled his intention to stand down as MP for Henley, 'as soon as possible.' He told waiting journalists that he was still the same man as the bumbling habitué of *HIGNFY*, even though he was now the first Conservative to hold executive power in Britain for 11 years and had the biggest personal political mandate of anyone in this country, not to mention the third biggest in Europe after the Presidents of Russia and France. Indeed, he could not resist the temptation for a bit of Old Boris parody with a play on Tony Blair's famous New Labour declaration: 'I was elected as new Boris and I will govern as new Boris.' Nevertheless, even he seemed a little confused by his newfound Manichean identity. 'This is the existential question that everyone keeps posing and it is driving me slightly nuts,' he said later, while scratching his head. 'There is no discontinuity between old Boris and new Boris.'

Following this, he headed off for the victory party then in full swing at the Tories' head office in Millbank Tower, upriver at Westminster. By the time he got there, the Altitude bar on the 29th floor was packed with guests including Sir Tim Rice, Lord Marland, and his parents, Stanley and Charlotte. Champagne had been served since 6 p.m., there were unlimited oysters and caviar. An all-blonde girl band in black ball gowns struck up 'Jerusalem' when Boris finally made his entrance shortly before one. Cameron held up Boris's hand in victory – making the new Mayor look distinctly uncomfortable – and both men acknowledged the other's contribution to the win. Boris, sipping his first glass of champagne since Christmas, also took a call of congratulations from the Mayor of New York, Michael Bloomberg, but was mainly closeted away with advisers.

The following day, a Saturday, Boris allowed Ken and his staff time to pack up their belongings and leave before laying claim to his new office on the eighth floor. He did, however, return to City Hall for the signing-in ceremony in London's Living Room, the events space with commanding views of the capital from the ninth floor. Boris arrived looking uncharacteristically smart – tidy hair, smart indigo tie and the classic statesmanlike combination of white shirt, plain dark suit. With Marina in his wake, he was swept upstairs to be greeted by 400 vocal supporters football chanting, 'Bor-iss! Bor-iss!' 'What am I supposed to be doing?' he whispered to Anthony Mayer and was told, equally discreetly: 'Don't worry, I'm in charge of this one! Sit down next to me and you'll get a nice pen to sign a book. Don't do anything until I say, "Now I want to present the Mayor of London, Boris Johnson."'

Typically, Boris did not follow instructions and stood up when he was supposed to be sitting down, and then when he was required to stand up and follow Mayer to the podium, he promptly tripped. But this is the sort of challenge at which he excels, and he duly made a joke about the stage being 'booby-trapped,' recovered well and was officially sworn in. It was not all laughter, though. He reasserted his manifesto pledge to put crime at the top of his priorities – not least because a 15-year-old boy from Peckham had been stabbed to death in a stairwell in the early hours of Saturday just as the Tories were downing champagne at the victory party, a few miles away. Boris talked of 'this problem of kids growing up without boundaries and getting lost in tragic and self-destructive choices [being] the number one issue we face in this city.'

No doubt in a reference to those staff in the building who had openly campaigned against him during the election, he served warning against anyone who did not co-operate with his new regime. 'If there are any dogs in the manger, I will have those dogs humanely euthanased,' he cautioned menacingly. Boris was not due to receive the Seals of Office until the following night, so he quipped that, 'Until that time, I imagine there are shredding machines quietly puffing and panting away in various parts of the building, and quite right too. Heaven knows what we shall uncover in the course of the next few days!'

He was then whisked off to his first mayoral meeting with his four executive chiefs – Ron Dobson (head of the Fire Brigade), Transport chief Peter Hendy (who had watched Boris win on Friday night in the same row of seats as Marina), Metropolitan Police Commissioner Sir Ian Blair and Manny Lewis, head of the London Development Agency. Blair and Dobson turned up in their uniforms. Boris is reputed to have thought Blair 'pompous' and Dobson matter-of-fact – 'I just put out fires,' he explained. Hendy had worked out some material on transport policies in the manifesto – including revoking the western extension to the Congestion Charge – and Lewis had a flipchart presentation on the organisation of the LDA that quickly looked as if it was testing Boris's patience. And indeed within days, Lewis was out of a job and within months, so too was Blair.

Meanwhile, Anthony Mayer busied himself with preparing Boris's entry pass and helping to ready his office once Ken had cleared it of the accumulation of eight years in power. There is no Mayoral car, Chain of Office or official accommodation to hand over, merely a set of cheap-looking office furniture, Venetian blinds and a phone. At Boris's request, he also gave orders for inner walls and doorways to be dismantled to make the offices open-plan – apart from the Mayor's own eighth-floor inner-sanctum.

On the Sunday, Boris and Marina attended his first official engagement in Trafalgar Square: an event celebrating the Sikh festival of Vaisakhi. Marina wore a crimson-coloured *kameez* with matching *dupatta* (a long tunic and scarf) from her collection of traditional Indian dress – not something seen much in Henley – and looked more at home than Boris did when he donned a policeman's hat. 'The last few days have been very, very exciting and very, very exhausting, but this is the single most wonderful job in British politics,' he declared. Amid a great deal of newspaper speculation about his possible early moves, he was about to find out whether this was true.

Monday saw him taking the time to be introduced to the 600 City Hall staff and to shake their hands. Most people were impressed by his easy sociability as he addressed each floor of the building in turn, including the ground-floor canteen. But what shocked many was that he had arrived without his own staff: Ken had come into City Hall with a group of five or six people whom he had known and worked with for some 15 years. Intensely loyal, they were known as 'Ken's cadre' and enforced his will throughout the building, working entirely in his name. Albeit on a much smaller scale, they operated much as the President's minders do in the US, over and above the mostly relatively junior permanent staff members. Although Boris had said in his acceptance speech on Friday night that he had a new team ready and waiting to take over, this was not actually the case.

That Monday morning, Boris arrived virtually alone. Over the next few days, some would start their new posts but it would take six months for a final team to emerge. Not until Friday of that week did he unveil one of his earliest appointments: Guto Harri, a Welsh-speaking rugby fan, as his director of communications. The pair had been at Oxford together but suggestions that this was Boris bringing in a crony were wide of the mark. They had never been particular friends and had barely seen each other socially since university. Indeed, it is not clear why Boris chose Harri, who had no previous experience in political spinning; it may just have been pure opportunism.

Harri, who had just left journalism to join a London-based public relations agency a few weeks before, had called Boris on the Tuesday before the Thursday election because he had to write an assessment for clients on Boris's electoral chances. The conversation was interrupted when Boris suddenly exclaimed: 'I've been trying to get hold of you. Come and work for me if I win!' 'It sounded like the idea had just popped into his head right then, rather than anything premeditated,' recalls Harri. And it almost certainly had, but it may also have been an exercise in point scoring: Harri had been sounded out by Cameron in the summer of 2006 for a job, but it came to nothing because he had at that point only just moved to New York to report for the BBC and felt he could not uproot his young family again. Now Boris had the man that had once interested his great rival and warned of a 'Stalingrad-like resistance' to attempts from Tory high command to poach him or other members of his team.

No need – working for Boris is widely considered in Tory circles to be considerably better paid, less of a grinding, all-hours prospect and more fun than a job working for David Cameron, even since he has been in Number Ten. Five out of the six best-paid political advisers in

Britain work for Boris, including Harri on £127,784 (2010). As this book goes to press, Munira Mirza, the 33-year-old arts adviser, has just received a 55 per cent increase to take her pay from £82,200 to £127,874. Boris is also, at £143,911, paid more than the Prime Minister (£142,500 in 2010). The other point of interest is that despite the ill-disguised ambitions of a handful in City Hall, Cameron consistently failed to show interest in Boris's staff, even after the General Election. This was despite the fact they were the only Tories around with recent experience of executive government. 'We have not even thought of making an approach,' sniffs a highly-placed Downing Street source.

Harri's previous experience on the BBC's Westminster staff followed by a stint in New York – where he observed how the Mayor, Michael Bloomberg, kept potentially hostile press at bay – has, in any case, obviously come in useful. It has proved an astute appointment, with both men enjoying ribald humour. They also share a rigid distrust of 'unhelpful' journalists who seek to scrutinise Boris more than they would like. James Landale, who replaced Harri at the BBC, understands his predecessor's appeal: 'He's a player, a gossip, all that Welsh passion; he's a schemer, lively, fun. He's quite like Boris in many ways.' Boris would also bring over Ann Sindall, his loyal secretary from the *Spectator*, as his executive assistant. Once again, Sindall has become indispensable to him, well beyond her nominal pay grade, and even the biggest hitters in City Hall understand her importance. 'I wouldn't fall out with Ann,' shudders one very senior official.

There was, however, certainly no Ken-style 'cadre'. Nick Boles, the early contender for mayor and seen as ultra-loyal to Cameron, was therefore sent in by Central Office as acting chief of staff. But the two men had never been close and the strain of the two months to come – with Boris resenting what he saw as interference from the Leadership – would certainly drive them further apart. Despite Boles' best efforts, Boris's 'early doors' as mayor would demonstrate all too publicly his woeful lack of preparation for the job – or understanding of it. It was as if he were playing in *Richard III* all over again, only this time he could not hope to paste up crib-sheets behind pillars when he did not know his lines. He was now presiding over a £12 billion administration covering issues from race to the environment through the economy and transport. His seat-of-the-pants approach was in danger of ripping apart but the origins of Boris's near-destruction as mayor during the summer of 2008 dated back to the campaign itself.

Boles had made good progress in overcoming Hodgkin's disease the previous autumn and in January had talked to Cameron and Osborne about building up a mayoral implementation team. But there remained little enthusiasm while victory still seemed a distant dream. By March – as some polls began putting Boris ahead of Ken – there was a wider understanding that should the Conservatives win the Mayoralty but surrender the advantage through poor planning, then it could well derail their chances of winning the next General Election. And yet, incredibly, there was still next to no preparation until the very last. Perhaps the disbelief that Boris could win was too firmly entrenched. It was, of course, a difficult job in part because the Mayoralty is so different from Whitehall government and the Parliamentary system – there is no shadow mayor with a shadow cabinet ready and waiting. Indeed, there was very little precedent at all as Ken had been Mayor of London since its inception in 2000 and largely crafted the role in his own image. But if Boris won, there would also be no transition period between the two mayoralties – to brief, let alone *create* a team – beyond the 48 hours needed to complete the statutory formalities.

'There were no obvious people you can slot into obvious jobs as you have with a shadow government,' recalls Boles. 'Boris is a curious guy. One of the things that he doesn't have is a political clique – there are no Johnsonites. This created a source of tension during the campaign, as Lynton [Crosby], reasonably enough, was furious at the idea that any minute of the day should be devoted to thinking about after the election, rather than how to win it. He was also concerned that it would look incredibly bad if the public thought Boris was already counting his chickens. I was prepared to do the work, but I did need to speak to Boris about what he wanted.'

Eventually, there were several arguments – or a 'tussle' as Boles puts it – with Crosby's team determined not to let Boris become distracted. But in the end Boles was allowed a brief meeting, although it did nothing to solve the problem as Boris had yet to come up with names for his team, or indeed a vision as to how he wanted to run the Mayoralty, if he won it. 'It was much too little, much too late,' recalls Boles, 'but we did what we could in the time available.'

In the increasingly frantic final lead-up to polling day, Lord Marland, one of the campaign chiefs, came up with the idea of making Boris a 'chairman mayor' backed up by 'an absolutely top-flight chief operating officer.' Boris, not known for his administrative abilities or even interest, would be the public face of the mayoralty – putting the 'bubbles in the champagne' was one phrase used – but there would be someone else who 'would actually run the mayoralty and City Hall.' Boris immediately seized hold of the plan.

'Not unreasonably, Boris thought the idea was a great one,' says Boles. 'This was the way he had run the *Spectator* – with Boris providing leadership and Stuart Reid [his deputy] making the trains run on time.' Indeed, so taken with the idea was Boris that he would exclaim with joy at the thought: 'Yes, I need a Stuart Reid! I need a Stuart Reid!' Some of the old hands were troubled by his reaction to the idea of offloading many of the Mayoral responsibilities, however. 'It looked like Boris wasn't running for mayor because he actually wanted to run the thing,' adds one. 'He seemed just to want to be mayor because it's a big job and it was there for him.'

Feelers were swiftly put out to find a tough, energetic businessman with superb management skills to do the bits that Boris couldn't – or wouldn't – do. The leading name to come out of the hat was Richard Bowker of the train company GNER, who was well-known to some of Boris's financial backers. There were numerous 'back channel' conversations and he 'seemed to be in,' says one campaign insider. 'Everyone was very excited.' But there were still other jobs with no names attached to them at all. In fact, pretty much all the situations were still vacant. Finally, Boles was permitted to have a proper meeting with Boris about his chosen advisers but incredibly not until the day of the actual poll itself, on 1 May. Another insider remembers feeling 'shocked' that such an important discussion had been left so late. For the first time that morning, in Boris's sitting room in Furlong Road, the pair went through a list of policy areas and tried to 'staple together' names to match. Many – such as Kit Malthouse as deputy mayor for Policing – were former colleagues of Boles' from Westminster Council. Some, such as Munira Mirza on Arts (an appointment seen as bolstering Boris's non-racist credentials), Boles knew from his days at Policy Exchange. He persuaded Boris to take Dan Ritterband from the campaign team as marketing manager and Kulveer Ranger, whom he also knew, on Transport. 'Boris's ideas by then were Ray Lewis on Youth – whom I wholly endorsed – and Ian Clement as deputy mayor for Government Relations. Boris insisted on making a place for Clement: he had been a loyal campaigner and the first London council leader to row in behind Boris as a candidate. A former postman who had become Leader of Bexley Council, he also had a lot of charm. Boris saw him as someone with his feet on the ground and found him very appealing as a result. But by far and away his best idea was Guto Harri on Media.

'So, on the day of the poll we stitched together Boris's team in what was really a chaotic way. We certainly didn't have time even to *think* of vetting! We came up with the names on Thursday morning and after winning the election started offering the jobs on Saturday morning.' But this by no means meant that Boris had a proper functioning team in place. On the point of signing, Bowker added to the sense of disarray by dramatically pulling out. Another sympathetic, but hard-nosed businessman was swiftly approached. And fortunately, Tim Parker agreed to take up the challenge – and for a nominal salary of £1 a year. Meanwhile, another Boles' idea was inviting in Simon Milton, leader of Westminster Council, who became adviser on Housing and Planning. James McGrath, the 34-year-old Australian who, as Crosby's number two during the election campaign had done so much to get Boris elected, was to come in as Boris's director of strategy.

Meanwhile, the tricky question of Boris's family had to be tactfully dealt with. 'They all wanted jobs in City Hall afterwards,' fumes a very senior Tory. 'The other Johnsons are like baggage who come with Boris everywhere. They were all around us all the time; they turned up at all the parties. Stanley wanted the Environment job, for instance, and was really pressing for it. Can you imagine what it must be like round the Johnson family dinner table, all of them giving their views over each other's voices?' There were even rumours that Boris's younger brother Jo would be pitching up as the mayor's head of strategy before McGrath was shoehorned into the job.

A week after Boris's election as mayor in 2008, Rachel advanced the dynastic feel still further when she appeared on BBC1's *Question Time* as her elder brother's most devoted and determined cheerleader, promising viewers many years of 'Boris-induced sunshine.' In answer to virtually any question, Rachel claimed his victory had brought the Tory party to 'a collective orgasm.' In a flash she brushed away an off-piste inquiry about Scottish devolution with the comment: 'I'm not sure I will be physically able to answer a question that's not about my brother.'

But this time it was made clear that Boris would not be allowed to hire his family and turn City Hall into a mayoral version of the *Spectator* – or *Johnsonator*, as it was known at one point when so many Johnsons were writing for it.

Despite – or rather because of – all this furious below-water paddling, Boris wanted to make a quick and eye-catching announcement on his team. The one he *could* make that Monday was the appointment of Ray Lewis (director of EastSide Young Leaders Academy and an increasingly frequent presence during Boris's electoral appearances) as Deputy Mayor for Young People. Billed as a former prison governor and pastor, Lewis was credited with inspirational work on keeping disenchanted young men out of gangs and out of trouble. Black himself and respected within his community, his inclusion fitted nicely with Boris's stated themes of a multi-ethnic team at City Hall and tackling crime and anti-social behaviour through self-respect, hard work and aspiration. He was certainly an interesting foil for an Old Etonian member of the Bullingdon – and Boris's supporters pointed to this as evidence of a changed perception of social problems. They argue that campaigning for mayor had extended his sights beyond his own privileged lifestyle for the first time.

Marina, too is credited with helping to instill in him more of a social conscience – and in part backed his mayoral ambitions as a means for

Boris to make a difference in the way that being MP for Henley could not. He also made his own comparisons between his former, mostly well-heeled constituency of Henley and the far more socially diverse city he was about to represent. 'People's preoccupations are very similar in Henley and parts of inner London,' he said, but, 'the scale of the problem is much bigger,' he now realised. Being an MP for a comfortable Oxfordshire seat, he went on, had protected him from 'really having to deal with issues that relate to modern Britain.'

If that last comment sounded slightly wistful, then perhaps it was. At this time he wrote a farewell letter to his Henley constituents betraying his surprise at having become mayor, seemingly tinged with certain sadness. A week after his victory, it appeared in the *Henley Standard*:

> Dear all – When I set out on my mission to unseat Ken Livingstone more than nine months ago I knew there were to be all kinds of risks. There was a considerable risk that I would be thrashed by the Great Newt. And then there was a risk I would win – and therefore lose Henley, just about the loveliest seat in the House of Commons. At the time, I have to admit, it seemed a pretty small risk.

There had been one very good personal reason why Boris really did not want to give up his old life and become mayor. Just days before the election when victory seemed ever more likely, he had been unusually candid with Brian Paddick as the pair waited alone to go into a BBC radio studio. 'I don't know how I'm going to manage financially,' he confessed. Boris was 'very concerned that he was going to win,' recalls Paddick, 'because of the money.' No doubt he would not like the thought of possibly earning less than Marina, but there was also the issue of being able to continue paying his children's school fees (which must come to nearly £100,000 a year) and maintain two large houses on the then mayoral salary of around £140,000.

What also seems clear is that the old Johnson 'tramp dread' fear of descending into poverty had made an unwelcome return, however ludicrous. As a successful barrister, Marina's earnings alone would sustain most families in considerable style and despite his endless quest to make his fortune Boris is hardly the master of bling. Although he spends on hand-made shoes (from Tricker's of Jermyn Street), when asked the name of his tailor, he likes to reply Boden – the mid-market mail-order business run by fellow Old Etonian Johnnie Boden, rather than an establishment in Savile Row. He also has a reputation for not putting his hand in his pocket for staff drinks. In fact, those around Boris constantly wonder what it is that he does spend all his money on.

Wherever the money goes, Boris thought it unlikely he would be able to keep on his £250,000-a-year *Telegraph* column, considering what trouble journalism had inflicted in the past on his political sights. When elected, the problem no doubt gnawed away at him until salvation arrived in the form of the editor of the *Daily Telegraph*, Will Lewis. Having been informed by the *Telegraph* number crunchers that Boris's column added 15,000 sales on its weekly Monday slot, within a couple of weeks of the election he visited the new mayor at City Hall to persuade him to stay on. He had, in any case, failed to find a suitable replacement during the four months Boris had taken off during the mayoral campaign. Lewis was also worried in case Boris signed up with the *Standard* after the paper had backed him so strongly in the election – although it is unlikely the London paper would ever be able to match the *Telegraph*'s fee. Boris was delighted at the approach – even more so when the City Hall authorities gave him permission to accept it as there was deemed to be 'no conflict of interest.'

But while keeping the column meant the school fees were more than covered, Nick Boles was appalled that Boris was still trying to keep hold of his journalistic career. 'I was furious,' recalls Boles. 'In a classic Boris way, he didn't mention it. But when I found out, I told him, "Look, you've just got one of the greatest jobs in British public life – you're the Mayor of London – and now you're saying you're going to take a half-day or so a week to be a part-time columnist!"' After a great deal of 'discussion', Boris was persuaded to hold off another week before he restarted the column on 17 June with a rather half-baked piece about cycling without a helmet. But his minders also extracted another far bigger concession from Boris that led to him squealing with fury: 'It's outrageous! I've been raped! I've been raped!'

In fact, Boles 'ganged up' with Guto Harri to extract a promise from Boris that he would give a fifth of his £250,000 *Telegraph* fee to charity as a means of quelling any criticism. It was decided that half was to go to a 'Boris bursary' for students of journalism at the London College of Communications and the rest in support of the teaching of Classics at state schools in the capital. Boris was forced to agree, but he continues to feel resentment at being strong-armed into the commitment through what he refers to as the punitively high 'Boles tax.' 'I feel a bit guilty about the column hoo-ha,' Boles commented later, after the bid to re-elect Boris in 2012 had begun. 'It hasn't harmed his work as mayor and it has helped him maintain his national profile.'

Boris does not appear to have given away the full 20 per cent, however, which by the end of his third year in office should have amounted to £150,000. He told the *Evening Standard* on 14 May 2008 that he would give £25,000 a year to the journalism bursaries and the same amount to Classics in state schools projects, but even his office put the total donation figure in June 2011 as 'more than £50,000' rather than the £150,000 pledged up to that point. Aides in part blamed tax and national insurance for the shortfall, but much of that should be reclaimable. City Hall is not forthcoming with complete figures but what is known is that by June 2011, he had so far donated only a total of £20,000 over three years (compared to the £75,000 pledged) to fund six bursaries for a sports journalism course at the College of Communications, with another final sum of £10,000 expected. He had also not given 'nearly as much' as £75,000 to a new charity set up by Friends of Classics to support Latin and Greek teaching in state schools, although according to co-founder Dr Peter Jones, he had donated 'a good whack.' Undoubtedly, Boris has given a tidy sum but it appears a long way short of what was publicly promised in return for resuming his column. There is also no future commitment for his second term, should he win. Once again Boris seems to have been reluctant to part with his cash, whatever his moral if not legal obligations.

It was not only Boris's colleagues, however, who had severe misgivings about him resuming regular journalism. Anthony Howard, a friend of his parents', was just one of several political commentators who deemed it 'an absolute scandal,' declaring: 'It may be true that he bashes it out on a Sunday morning – it reads like it. But the Mayor of London should have better things to do and not allow himself to be distracted. It's totally inappropriate.' But the fact is that many well-placed Tories believe that Boris may well have decided not to stand for a second term as mayor without the column. Politically, of course, it would have been unacceptable to ask for a large mayoral pay rise, particularly during a downturn. 'You cannot stand up to Londoners and say you cannot live on the salary of the Mayor because it is a bloody good salary,' says one Conservative close to Boris. 'But actually he can't live on the salary he has – or at least not the way he lives. After he became mayor, Boris bought a posher London house and has also done up the old constituency house in Thame. I can well understand why it was non-negotiable for him.'

Nevertheless, Boris is sensitive to public criticism about being both a highly paid mayor of London and one of Britain's best-remunerated journalists. In July 2009, in an attempt to play down his dual role on the BBC's *HARDTalk* programme, he unwisely prompted another burst of outrage from public sector unions and others when he dismissed his *Telegraph* contract as 'chicken feed.' Realising his mistake, he tried unsuccessfully to turn the tables on his interviewer, Stephen Sackur, by asking about his own BBC salary. It is an offence/defence tactic he has used frequently since – but it failed on that occasion.

From the start, Boris was also concerned that his natural writing exuberance would once again land him in trouble politically but he was given undertakings by the *Telegraph* that senior editors would 'baby-sit' his column and guide him away from any potentially incendiary ideas. As one very senior *Telegraph* executive puts it: 'We consider it our duty to nurture and protect him – sometimes from himself. His copy is painstakingly checked every week for any unexploded political devices likely to damage him. That protection service is part of the deal and on more than one occasion, Boris has been steered off subjects or views that would have got him in trouble. We are effectively starfuckers. Boris is the Wayne Rooney of the *Telegraph* and we do everything in our power to make him feel wanted.'

While the editorial staff have long been indulgent of their star, the commercial side of the *Telegraph* has from time to time been rather less enamoured. Particularly annoying was an occasion when Boris put up a newsworthy column on his personal website in apparent contravention of copyright. The early release of his column on strike-busting laws ahead of the Tory Party Conference of 2010 allowed the *Telegraph*'s rivals access to his thoughts even before they were printed. This rather impudent move, which benefited Boris with a great deal of extra media coverage, prompted an outburst from one executive: 'Just who does he think pays his fucking wages?'

Just after the election, July 2008 also saw the death of Marina's father Charles and a thanksgiving service in Westminster Abbey attended by large numbers of the BBC's top brass and other distinguished mourners from the media, military and Foreign Service. Boris was the only senior politician to attend, but Dip was too distressed to go. Charles had known for some time that he was fighting a losing battle against his cancer and before he died, he made it perfectly clear how angry and distressed he was over Boris's infidelities and the humiliation and pain they brought on his family as a whole, not just his daughter. 'Boris would listen to Charles more than almost anyone,' says a family friend. 'But who knows what good it did.'

Meanwhile, back at City Hall, Boris was still shoring up his own side. Kate Hoey, the Labour MP, was a good catch and agreed to come in as sports commissioner while David Ross, the co-founder of Carphone Warehouse, was hired as Olympic adviser. So, with a hastily arranged team stitched together in this way, Boris at last appeared to have the nucleus of his own mini-government in City Hall. Flanked by Tower Bridge on one side and HMS *Belfast* on the other, his Praetorian Guard could focus on trailblazing a new form of Conservative rule while David Cameron could still only dream of making policies and seeing them put into action.

On Wednesday, 7 May 2008, Boris announced a ban on drinking alcohol on public transport. It was a curious decision because temperamentally he does not like banning things but the idea is said to have come from Lynton Crosby's disgust at the behaviour of his compatriots on the tube. It also met the need – in the absence of anything else – for a decisive, populist and eye-catching initiative for his first week. Even more curious, though was that he was photographed that same evening sipping Pol Roger champagne at the *Spectator*'s 180th birthday party at the Hyatt Regency Hotel in Mayfair – an event his presence completely overshadowed.

'I saw how much Boris was enjoying being the star,' remembers one guest. 'Every camera was trained on him and Cameron, who looked really annoyed, was just ignored in the scrum – it was like a coronation.' It was only when someone asked him 'Are you giddy on power?' that Boris began to look nervous. He stopped drinking the champagne, stuffed his hands into his pockets and left before 10 p.m. That incident, and his continued resemblance to a 'human laundry basket,' did not stop him from becoming London's most sought-after guest, with *Tatler* magazine hailing 'the priapic Bozza [as] pure party Viagra.'

By the end of the week he had launched an investigation into hundreds of projects funded by the London Development Agency to be led by Patience Wheatcroft, a former financial journalist and ex-*Telegraph* colleague who would go on to become a Tory peer (but did not find the dirt on Ken, Lee Jasper and others that had been expected). He had also drunk tea with fire-fighters in Dagenham, called the Transport Commissioner Peter Hendy 'mate', invited an all-women group of Guinean soldiers to Trafalgar Square for an Africa Day festival, mocked 'crazed Thatcherite neo-cons' and cycled to work; he had also instructed staff that they could call him just Boris, without fear of being fined £5 by Tessa Jowell.

On his first Friday he played the international statesman when he received the billionaire mayor of New York, Michael Bloomberg. Together with the Ray Lewis appointment, this was not a bad week for a man denounced by the *Guardian* and others as variously evil, a clown, a racist and a bigot. Boris even began telling friends how much he was enjoying having 'real power.' He told the *Guardian*: 'Every day I wake up in a state of wonderment that I have been elected – obviously knowing that millions of other people wake up in a state of wonderment that I have been elected too!'

There was also a little wonderment in some quarters at his unexpected ruthlessness. Boris set about dispatching people he presumably thought were those 'dogs in the manger' mentioned in his speech. Members of the old guard who were paid off included five of City Hall's most senior women, such as Ken's partner Emma Beal, who had been his administration manager. That left only two influential women on a staff of nearly 800. The most important was the young, highly competent Roisha Hughes, Boris's private secretary and a former aide to Labour minister Tessa Jowell, credited by many as being 'the toughest person in the building.' One senior insider notes that Boris 'quickly became very dependent on Roisha to hold the whole thing together.' Although Hughes, like Ann Sindall, is once again not thought to share Boris's political views, she is known to have 'become extremely committed to his personal wellbeing – he is able to attract that kind of loyalty.' The other woman is Munira Mirza on the relatively junior portfolio of arts. On the whole, Boris does not gravitate towards women of power but prefers them in an assisting, non-competive, role.

It all added up to an initial impression of pace and energy, one that Boris was intent on creating against the continuing private fears of senior Tories that a series of mayoral gaffes would scupper the Party's chances at the next General Election. But it did not help that Boris was characteristically late for two official functions in his first week. These included a meeting with Prince Charles, when Boris arrived drenched in sweat and over half an hour late after boarding a tube travelling in the wrong direction whilst being mobbed by a group of middle-aged London-Chinese women (and not noticing for several stops). Nor the fact that after only three weeks in the job – and promising to work 'flat out' – he went on a week's family sailing holiday on the Dalaman coast of Turkey.

Further cracks soon appeared. First, *Private Eye* started questioning the veracity of Ray Lewis's CV, pointing out that he had not actually been a prison governor but a member of the bottom management grade in prisons, known as governor grade 5. A further blow came when Bob Diamond, Boris's very first appointment, resigned from the Mayor's Fund after just six weeks, pleading lack of time. But then came Boris's first real test on what he knew to be his most vulnerable ground – race.

Just weeks into his administration he fired one of his own appointees – James McGrath – over a comment he had made before the election that was now published and denounced as racist. McGrath had been responding to a claim that some black people might leave Britain if Boris became mayor, saying: 'Let them go if they don't like it here.' In turn, he said that he had been quoted out of context and although clearly an ill-advised response, Boris might have left it at that. But knowing that he needed to prove his credentials on race, Boris first admitted that McGrath was 'not a racist,' but then decreed the remarks made it 'impossible' for him to keep his job.

It was a ruthless and perhaps necessary decision – and was immediately backed by Cameron, who was similarly seeking to decontaminate the Tory brand. But it was not universally welcomed. McGrath, who with Crosby had done so much to get Boris elected, resisted it for as long as possible. Iain Dale, the Conservative blogger, spoke for many Tories when he wrote about what he saw as Boris's disloyalty and hypocrisy: 'James McGrath is a no-nonsense Aussie. These remarks could have been made about any group who "don't like it here" – white, black, whatever. What [Boris] should have done is stand by the man who has stood by him through thick and thin over the last eight months. Instead, Boris has hung James McGrath out to dry in the most despicable and cowardly manner possible. Having defended Boris over his "piccaninny" and "watermelon" comments I am now wondering why we all bothered. It may be a good thing that Boris has made a rod for his own back. It can go where his backbone should be.'

It was an unusually savage attack, but only the start of Boris's trial by fire. Less than a fortnight later, on Wednesday, 2 July, Boris's bêtes noires at the *Guardian* approached him with questions about Ray Lewis' past – in particular, sexual and financial allegations concerning his time as a Church of England clergyman. On the Thursday, Boris declared he had 'every confidence' in his 'tremendous deputy.' But by Friday night, following a day of frantic talks between Tory Central Office and City Hall, Boris seemingly changed his mind and accepted Lewis's resignation, 'with regret'. In the interval, it had emerged that Lewis had been investigated three times by the Metropolitan Police over allegations of blackmail, theft and deception. No action was taken in any case – although he was in his absence barred by the Church. *Private Eye*'s revelations on Lewis not having been prison governor were also confirmed. But the final blow had been when it was discovered that he had never practised or even been formally appointed as a magistrate. Boris had used the fact that he was a Justice of the Peace to vouch for his integrity at a crisis press conference (an event universally derided as a 'shambles' and 'farce'). Not only had Boris lost his perfect answer to questions about his views on race, once again he also looked like someone who was pathologically incapable of doing his homework. Significantly, he has hardly held any press conferences since.

Boris had now lost two key aides in less than two weeks. Now all the fears about him being a loose cannon resurfaced with a vengeance. There was talk about him going up in flames and the conflagration burning the entire Conservative party. Interestingly, the former leader Iain Duncan Smith – to whom Boris had shown precious little loyalty – was one of the few to come out and attack the media for 'crushing' Lewis, whom he branded a 'good man.' But most others in the Party rapidly distanced themselves from the whole affair, and particularly Boris. Inside City Hall, Boris started to admit to those staff he trusted most that he did not 'have the faintest clue' and began quietly to seek advice.

An exhausted Boles – now the brunt of much of Boris's frustration – was only too glad to be leaving City Hall that weekend as the flak intensified. 'Boris was vituperative about Boles,' recalls one senior official, as the Mayor tried to offload the blame. Boles was replaced by Tim Parker, who joined at the end of June, taking on the title of first deputy mayor and the chief executive role Marland had envisaged. It had been announced majestically at the end of May that he would implement Boris's vision efficiently and effectively.

Parker is said to exude ruthless competence and Boris and his backers obviously hoped that he would streamline City Hall in the same way, with perhaps similar techniques to those he had used on companies. But it was not the best of starts with the City Hall staff. Indeed, Parker's job-slashing reputation from his time at Clarks, Kwik-Fit and the AA earned him the soubriquet among the unions of 'Prince of Darkness'. That did not stop him from getting on with his job, though. And what a job it was – chief executive of the entire GLA Group (comprising the Greater London Authority, Transport for London, the Metropolitan Police Authority, the London Development Agency and the London Fire and Emergency Planning Authority) and chairman of Transport for London. That left little mayoral for Mayor Boris to do beyond Planning – and in any case, the highly effective Milton was already dealing with that.

Parker took the office next to Boris's on the east side of the building that the Mayor liked to call the 'onion.' He had to share it, though, with Milton – who by now had left Westminster Council to become another of Boris's deputy mayors. Milton was a legend in Tory circles for a 20-year career of presiding over highly rated local services and low council taxes while, as a modern Tory who was openly gay, avoiding the tag of 'hatchet-man'. Although physically weakened by cancer and the gruelling treatment for his illness, his brain and talent for administration were as sharp as ever. Even so, in what was perhaps always destined to be one of London's greatest-ever bureaucratic turf wars, the smart money was on the curly-headed Parker to win.

Parker began by describing London's voters as 'shareholders' and public services such as the Police and the Tube as the city's 'core products.' He had a natural distrust of the public sector and those steeped in its culture but most importantly of all, since he was chief executive and first deputy mayor, Parker insisted that everyone including the appalled Milton should report to him. He had been led to believe that he would run London while Boris served as a figurehead.

'Parker had been a chief executive of huge organisations and like all chief execs, in a way he was a bit of a control freak,' recalls a key City Hall official. 'But then Boris realised *he* had to make the decisions, if politically he was going to have to defend them.' And there were some decisions that the chief executive wanted to make – such as his idea of abolishing free travel for children – that were not politically viable. Boris saw the pure financial argument, of course, but to back such a policy would scupper his chances of being re-elected.

By now Parker had alienated most of Boris's other key aides, including Guto Harri, the colleague closest to Boris. He and others began to warn Boris that Parker was 'exceeding his brief' and acting as if he were mayor himself. Incredibly, Boris still failed to take charge and avoided the obviously necessary showdown. In desperation, Anthony Mayer – who was about to retire – decided to take Boris out to dinner and hold a 'very serious chat about how things were going.' He chose a deliberately dark corner in Joe Allen's, a relaxed Covent Garden basement restaurant favoured by politicians and the theatre crowd; somewhere they would not be interrupted by star-struck diners. Mayer, who had not only served Ken for eight years but had been principal private secretary to three ministers in Whitehall (including Heseltine) ordered a couple of bottles of his favourite Zinfandel Californian wine – most of which he drank, as Boris barely sipped from his glass. Finally, after exchanging the usual pleasantries, Mayer dabbed his lips with a napkin and delivered a forceful message: 'Boris, you've got to start being *mayor*. Go out there and be in charge! It always takes a few months to get the hang of it but now you have really got to get a grip!'

To his credit, Boris took the exhortation from the old hand 'extremely well.' He seemed to lap up the advice that Mayer could offer and the pair parted later on good terms. It had been made crystal clear that City Hall was not just a larger version of the *Spectator* – even with the best 'Stuart Reid' character in the world, Boris could not afford to be semi-permanently out to lunch. He had to get down and get dirty, to run things himself. Mayer noticed an immediate change in his approach after that momentous evening but was in no doubt as to where the problem originated. Boris lacked his version of Ken's 'cadre' and when he unexpectedly won the mayoralty, he was consequently isolated and vulnerable to panicky – and arguably, disastrous –appointments, such as Lewis and now Parker. After 40 years in national and London government, Mayer knew all too well that the idea of a symbolic mayor was never going to work: Boris did indeed need to 'get a grip' and Parker had to go. There was room for only one mayor.

Parker was to become the third of Boris's advisers to depart within as many months. Days later, the two men met for the 'divorce' lunch to hammer out the details at a South Bank restaurant overlooking the river, near City Hall. The atmosphere was not exactly amicable, but not overtly unpleasant either. Perhaps with Mayer's words ringing in his ears, Boris said he had now realised that he wanted to be a 'real' mayor and Parker returned that if he could not make the decisions, he could not do the job. Both men were astute enough to realise they had not only misunderstood their respective roles and how they could be divided up, but also themselves and their own drives.

'The background to my role was that Boris needed someone who would be his right-hand man in charge of running things,' recalls Parker. 'But when I arrived at City Hall, I found that although I was the first deputy mayor, I was not the head deputy mayor. It was clear that the other deputies did not see themselves as reporting through me. It was also apparent that Boris, and not myself, should really be chairing Transport for London as this was by far his biggest budget and he was the elected people's representative. I concluded that if Boris needed anyone, it was a chief of staff political fixer, which he duly got in Simon Milton.' Parker says he enjoyed working with Boris, but he departed hastily back to business after he left City Hall.

The problem now was how to explain to the outside world that within little more than 100 days of the election, he had lost his second deputy mayor and his third key adviser. The answer lay not in apology but in defiance. Boris would now present himself as a ruthless operator in defence of his power base and his beliefs. Parker's departure also marked the exit of Boris the Bumbler and the arrival of Mayor Boris.

Boris was due to leave almost immediately for Beijing and the closing ceremony of the Olympics, where he was to wave the Olympic flag to signal the games were coming to London next. He had originally questioned the need to go – suggesting a deputy mayor represent him. Post-Parker, he now realised that it was a job that the mayor had to do himself and in any case, there was a certain cachet in strutting around a stage in front of an estimated 1.6 billion viewers.

Lord (Sebastian) Coe, who had led the London bid, had said: 'Let's hope he doesn't drop it,' but bumbling Boris was already moving on. On the very day that Parker had resigned, Boris chose to silence his detractors with what looked like a direct swipe at David Cameron and the start of an alternative Tory philosophy. He used his *Telegraph* column to argue that British sporting triumphs in Beijing had shown that it was 'piffle' to suggest, as the Tory leader had just done, that Britain was a 'broken society in which the courage and morals of young people have been sapped by welfarism and political correctness.'

How many politicians, one commentator asked, call their leader's oft-repeated views 'piffle' in public? Far from the Parker saga sapping Boris's strength, the grit that the Mayor had now shown under pressure portrayed him as an alternative Tory chieftain who would not be dominated by anybody or play by their rules. It immediately gave rise to new suggestions that he might well one day challenge for the Leadership himself – suggestions he did little or nothing to quell. As if to demonstrate how long a week is in politics, Boris had travelled in days from the shambolic nadir just before Parker's departure to serious speculation that City Hall was the natural springboard to Downing Street.

His new focus also saw the return of an old opportunism. He let it be known that in keeping with his drive to cut waste, his team was switching to a cheaper hotel than the one originally booked by Ken when he was mayor for their trip to Beijing and would also be flying economy. The effect was spoilt, however, by the revelation that his aides had unsuccessfully tried to get Boris an upgrade. And there was also another side to Boris that had still to be reformed: his failure to button up his jacket while waving the flag in Beijing caused a mini diplomatic incident – offending his Chinese hosts and many other older viewers, who thought him scruffy and disrespectful. Crucially, though, back home the row was swiftly filed under the 'Boris will be Boris' category and was soon forgotten. After all Boris was now basking in the reflected glories of being officially in charge of the preparations for the next Olympic Games in 2012.

Boris had also moved quickly from wanting to keep Henley to wanting to be shot of it as soon as possible. Central Office, though, was keen closely to control the by-election and pushed the date back to allow time for meticulous planning. The Leadership wanted to block any chance whatsoever of another egocentric MP springing up from this idyllic corner of Oxfordshire with big ambitions for the Leadership and/or explosive media headlines. Cameron particularly did not want a dynastic takeover. Stanley's vigorous campaign to inherit Henley from Boris – launched within hours of the mayoral victory – was therefore quietly but ruthlessly quashed. Unusually, Central Office produced a shortlist of three local councillors – all 'sound' names not known nationally or frankly, ever likely to be. No other candidate was to be considered – and certainly not one called Johnson. To drive home the message, just three weeks after Boris became mayor, Cameron himself travelled out to Henley to oversee the process. 'The whole episode made Cameron look frightened of Boris,' one local Tory complained. When the by-election was held on 26 June, the Conservatives won more than comfortably on a 10,000 majority.

Downriver at City Hall, Boris was dismantling some of Ken's old regime. Out was the oil-for-advice deal with Venezuela – to be replaced by the rather more nebulous 'partnership and exchange' programme with New York. The *Londoner* newspaper was abolished, as promised – and new trees planted with some of the money saved. He also fulfilled his pledge to axe six-monthly black-cab inspections: it had proved, as expected, a keen recruiter of the taxi driver vote (although nearly three years later, they would be reinstated). However, Boris's pledge to abolish the Kenbassies was soon kicked into the long grass via the time-honoured means of a 'review' – in fact, all but one have been retained. Indeed, whatever the rhetoric, Boris's whole approach was largely 'leave well alone.'

'Boris certainly did not destroy the architecture that Ken had built,' says one City Hall insider. 'He trimmed at the edges, but he largely ignored the Tory warnings that the place was inhabited by a bunch of Marxists. If they were good, like Hendy at Transport, he mostly kept people on. And once the initial departures were over, the atmosphere really improved.' 'City Hall has become a nicer place to work under Boris, with less politicking than there was under Ken,' says another. 'There is less unpleasantness.' Even officials previously seen as natural Ken supporters gush about how 'nice' Boris is to work for. 'Personally, he is extremely good to me,' notes one. 'And Boris is brighter than Ken. With the odd permissible exception on technical matters, you never need to explain things to Boris more than once. He immediately gets things.' Indeed, one of few personal complaints is that the Mayor does not shower after a typically thigh-pumping cycle into work – and the windows at City Hall are not designed to open. 'We wish the Mayor would use deodorant,' says one colleague.

A more serious charge that crops up repeatedly is that with greater leeway given to staff by Boris – notorious for his dislike of rigid structure – comes a lack of direction. 'Under Ken there was a weekly meeting of the mayoral management board, where everything was thrashed out for the week ahead,' says one senior official. 'Boris abolished that meeting and others and there is a consequent lack of coherence – people don't always know what they should be doing. I would go in to see Ken and know exactly what his view would be about something. With Boris, it's impossible to predict and he likes to keep everything close to his chest.' 'I imagine it's rather like the *Spectator*,' notes another old hand. 'Boris is surrounded by people who are seeking to advance their own careers rather than his vision but he doesn't seem to mind and we're not clear what his vision is anyway. After a load of shouting they get down to things, but no one knows what.'

In Boris's City Hall, there are not many senior women but the gay community is well represented in the upper ranks. 'Our chief of staff is gay, our director of marketing is gay, four out of the ten top people are gay,' notes Guto Harri. 'We are the most gay administration in British history.' Steve Pope of the *Voice* had led the campaign to keep Boris out because of the fears of black voters, including City Hall staff, but even he has become a Boris convert. 'He is the best thing that could have happened,' says Pope, speaking 18 months into the new mayoralty. 'You have a reputation, but once you arrive it's all down to how you treat people.' He confirms Boris's reputation as a 'listener' to Ken's 'dictator' tendencies and concludes: 'Boris has woven a magic spell over us – he's not harboured any grudges. His press team have been noticeably more welcoming to a black newspaper like ours than Ken's ever were.'

It's an astonishing change of view from Pope and his newspaper – and all the more so given that in July 2008, Boris brought in 'to help promote the Mayor's diversity policies' a man who once wrote that third-world immigrants brought 'too many germs into the country.'[1] Anthony Browne, whom Boris hired as policy director on a salary of £124,000 a year, was previously director of the Cameroon think-tank Policy Exchange (having replaced Boles). His most infamous political pamphlet – 'Do We Need Mass Immigration?' – was a 150-page tract against large-scale immigration on the grounds that British people did not want to be 'culturally enriched' by immigrants, most immigrants 'do not pay their way', Britain is already overcrowded, immigrants lower wages for indigenous workers, cause social fragmentation and also housing shortages.

When the book was spotted in the BNP online gift shop, Browne was forced to apologise for his comments – which he had also rehearsed in the *Spectator* under Boris's editorship – saying they were not a fair reflection of his real views. This time, though, Boris knew better than to sack him at the first hint of 'incoming' as his detractors accused him of doing with James McGrath. 'I do very much regret any offence caused,' announced Browne. 'It really never was my intention to cause offence, but to provoke debate. I want to make clear that I am emphatically not anti-immigration.' Browne's supporters, some of them eminent Lefties, defended him as anxious to ask difficult questions rather than peddle any racist agenda. Indeed, by now the two men were spearheading a debate on an amnesty for an estimated 400,000 long-standing illegal immigrants residing in London somewhat undercutting the anti-immigrant charge. Nevertheless, this was another high-risk appointment that did not last the full mayoral term, although Browne is working on his re-election campaign.

Despite his record in print and the hostile attention this has attracted, Boris has been phenomenally successful in batting away questions over race. It is testament to his extraordinary power to charm different people with different views and convince them simultaneously of his sincerity. He does this by performing a political and personal seduction on practically every interest group, even if they might seem to hold opposing positions. What's more, he knows the importance of gestures – whether it's riding a bike to work (great with the Greens) or ensuring that ethnic minority newspapers are treated the same as the mainstream press. So, what's to stop Boris donning a pink Stetson as he did to attend a Gay Pride rally, for instance, or waving the flag of St George to celebrate the ancient heritage of England? It is more astonishing that other politicians seem to think that you have to choose one over the other, when Boris's highly effective policy on cake, as we already know, is both having and eating it.

Boris found no problems with the 'soft power' issues of wooing different interest groups but after nearly six months' baptism of fire at the beginning of his mayorship, he was still struggling to exert any 'hard power.' Parker might be gone but what he really needed to establish himself as a serious player was a glorious victory over someone – or something – more significant. As usual, luck provided him with the perfect opportunity.

Chapter Fourteen

The Politics of Power

As Mayor, 2008–2011

On Wednesday, 1 October 2008, Sir Ian Blair hurried into Boris's office overlooking Tower Bridge. He was a few minutes' late for a meeting with the Mayor, scheduled for noon. As Metropolitan Police Commissioner for four years, Blair had long served as a whipping boy for the Tory right who saw him as a New Labour stooge but as he took his seat to Boris's left, he was confident that he had built a good working relationship with a Conservative mayor whom he considered witty and likeable. 'Ian thought Boris was leaving all the political vitriol behind him,' observes a source close to Blair.

Following the exit of Tim Parker in August, however, Boris had decided to exert more control over his fiefdom by becoming chairman of the Metropolitan Police Authority, the body designated to hold the Commissioner to account. It was in this new capacity that after a few minutes, according to Blair's account, Boris declared: 'There's no easy way to say this, Ian . . .' The Mayor then pronounced that a change of leadership at the Met was vital; that Blair could not continue in the post with 'distractions' such as inquiries into his alleged involvement in awarding Met contracts to his own friends and the continuing fallout from the police shooting of the innocent Brazilian Jean Charles de Menezes.

Boris conceded that he did not have the power to fire him but looking across at his beefy deputy mayor for policing, Kit Malthouse, as if for reassurance, said he would prompt a vote of no confidence at the next full Police Authority meeting. Describing Boris's manner as 'pleasant but determined,' Blair recalls: 'that was the moment when the first intimation came to me that I might have to go.'[1] At this now notorious meeting, however, he merely agreed to consider his position.

The next morning there were exquisitely timed allegations in the *Daily Mail* that Blair had paid a friend's PR company £15,000 of Met money to sharpen up his image under a 'vanity contract.' The Commissioner denied any impropriety, even that the contract had anything to do with boosting his image, but still felt cornered and subsequently resigned his post.

Blair's allies claim that persistent charges of impropriety against him in the media – which were later to be disproved – had come from rivals within Scotland Yard, a notorious cauldron of jealousy and political intrigue. A few of the most senior officers are known to have regularly gathered at The Tapster, a wine bar in Caxton Street across the road from Scotland Yard, where they would complain about Blair, sometimes in the company of a select group of journalists. At least three of the coppers involved were known to have had close links to News International titles in particular. 'There was an element of disloyalty involved but also ambition,' recalls one very senior officer who felt uncomfortable about the plotting. 'They were busy chopping Blair's legs away.' Met sources also claim a very senior City Hall official dined with at least one of the officers involved.

Boris has declined to give his own version of events, preferring to dodge questions. However, the balance of probabilities suggests the Mayor opportunistically nudged Blair towards the door, but was astonished when he took the matter into his own hands and resigned the very next day. Freedom of Information[2] inquiries reveal that Boris had taken no legal advice on removing Blair – an odd omission for anyone actively contemplating such a radical step. It is also believed no one at Conservative HQ (including David Cameron) had been forewarned either. One senior City Hall official says that although the Mayor was certainly hoping that Blair would eventually go, with his well-known dislike of open confrontation, 'I'm not sure Boris actually *expected* to get rid of Ian Blair himself. When Blair went, he looked shell-shocked.' Indeed, a well-placed Tory source is privately clear about who was really responsible for the departure: 'Kit [Malthouse] took the lead in manoeuvring Boris and Blair into positions where there was no alternative. It was a clever way of dealing with both of them, not least because we all thought it would be an absolute case of "Boris blinking."'

At this point Boris refused to say that he had sacked Blair, insisting instead that it had been the Commissoner's own decision to go. Indeed, at the full Metropolitan Police Authority meeting on the Monday, an uncomfortable-looking mayor was ostentatiously apologetic; he even seemed to support a motion accusing him of usurping his powers in Blair's dismissal, saying disarmingly: 'Thank you very much. I don't disagree with your motion at all.'[3]

Crucially, however, the *external* perception that Assassin Boris had dispatched Blair with cool efficiency transformed the Mayor's reputation outside City Hall. 'Firing' a commissioner for the first time in the post's 180-year history silenced the "Boris is a bumbler" mob overnight; and so it was not long before Boris's office also referred openly to the 'sacking of Ian Blair.' Polls of party members found them ecstatic at this dazzling display of muscular Conservatism. Tory HQ's initial fears that Boris was a 'disaster in slow motion' were swiftly replaced within 48 hours by a new appraisal that he was a steely and focused threat to Labour ministers – and potentially to the Tory leadership too.

Observing how the 'Boris as Brutus' tale served him well, the Mayor has remained unforthcoming about the real story. When it was suggested in an interview eight months later that Blair's departure had been decided on the spur of the moment, rather than as a calculated move, Boris replied with unusual brevity: 'That supposition is not correct.' A question on why he had omitted to forewarn Cameron was met with the similarly terse: 'I don't want to go back into the details of all that.'[4] Amid this uncertainty, Blair ironically served Boris's cause within the Tory party by consistently portraying himself as a victim of the Mayor's political ruthlessness. Blair also suggests, however, that Boris was prepared to trample over the constitutional niceties (under which the hiring and firing of the Commissioner were the prerogative of the Home Secretary, Jacqui

Smith) and to endanger the independence of the police, all to help him win a 'private tussle' with Cameron.[5]

He is correct that – by accident or design – Boris had indeed upstaged Cameron who was at the time still marooned in the impotence of Opposition, but it also appears to be the case that Boris had once again benefited from other's misfortunes (or misadventures). As Blair ruefully noted, Boris had now been seen to 'stamp his authority on the mayoralty'[6] but it is equally apparent that someone else almost certainly did the stamping.

Boris now had strategic control of policing in the capital but it was only a matter of weeks before his crime-fighting credibility – and even more, the Police's political independence under his regime – would be tested to the maximum.

Still under Labour's stewardship, the Home Office was suffering regular leaks of confidential documents with the culprit obviously enjoying access to the Home Secretary's private safe. The fact that even a draft letter to Prime Minister Gordon Brown had been intercepted was considered a major security risk. Some of the material was appearing in newspapers with apparent close links to the Conservatives' immigration spokesman Damian Green. After some 30 incidents over two years, the Civil Service called for an investigation. A mid-ranking civil servant, Christopher Galley, was arrested and admitted that he was connected to prominent Tories, including Green, whom he claimed had asked him to 'get dirt and damage on Labour' in the same conversation as job opportunities in the Tory party were discussed (although both men agree that Green never actively encouraged Galley to leak documents).

A Gold Group of eight senior policemen met to decide the highly sensitive question of whether to arrest the MP and legal advice was taken from the Met's own lawyers. Initially, the group favoured arrest by appointment, but Galley claimed that after he had been released on bail, Green had asked him not to mention the name of another prominent MP involved in the affair: David Davis. With evidence suggesting that Green was attempting to hide his or another's liaison with Galley the group therefore unanimously voted in favour of a raid. The Crown Prosecution Service also backed the move. 'It's a decision I will defend until the day I die,' insists Bob Quick, the senior officer in charge. 'We were in a horrible situation. I wished it would go away, but it wouldn't, and we were not going to bend the rules either.'

Approval was also sought from Sir Paul Stephenson, the acting commissioner who had replaced Blair, and who, according to Quick, (equally reluctantly) gave it. At 9.55 a.m. on 27 November, Stephenson informed Boris (in his capacity as MPA chair) that an unnamed politician was to be raided that day as part of a major leak inquiry. At 1.19 p.m. Stephenson told Boris who it was, but because Green could not initially be located the arrest did not take place for another 18 minutes. Despite his role as chairman of the MPA and his subsequent denials, according to at least one police officer working on the case the Mayor then attempted to speak to his political colleague, Green.

'I was told that Boris had phoned Green near the time of the arrest and remain puzzled that this alleged call was not the subject of a subsequent investigation, as it could potentially be a criminal offence,' confirms Bob Quick, the Commanding Officer. Whether the suspected call came in during or just after the arrest rather than before, Quick is insistent the Mayor could not have known for sure that he was not pre-empting police action or making it possible for evidence to be concealed or destroyed. If Boris did try to call Green soon after learning of the planned raid this could constitute, according to Quick, attempting to assist an offender or impede an arrest under the 1977 Criminal Justice Act. However, the matter was allowed to slip away in the ensuing Conservative party-fuelled furore and during a six-week hiatus called after Damian Green cited Parliamentary privilege, which effectively halted all enquiries.

Indeed, it was not Boris who was the subject of an outburst of public indignation and concern about the conduct of a publicly elected mayor with responsibility for, and powers over, the Met. The flak was directed entirely at the Police for proceeding with Green's arrest in what has since been described by Quick as, 'a shitstorm, with the Conservative machinery claiming it was all politically motivated.' One senior Tory even told the *Guardian*, 'Bob Quick is behind this.

I'm going to fucking get him.'[7] Former shadow home secretary David Davis, whom Galley had been instructed not to identify, claimed the officers' actions smacked of a 'police state.'[8]

Green was detained for nine hours on suspicion of misconduct in public office and his computer hard drive, documents and phone were all seized in searches of his Parliamentary office as well as his Kent home. Allegations were made that the Police had acted in a 'heavy-handed' manner. Boris himself geared up the resultant Tory furore (thus helping to direct the spotlight away from him) by putting out a press statement later that night, carried in the *Times*, outlining in 'trenchant terms' his 'grave concern' as to whether the arrest had been a 'proportionate' response. 'I was surprised Boris used the "proportionate" term,' recalls Quick. 'How could he make the calculation if he didn't know the detail of the evidence?' Stories now began to appear in certain newspapers distancing the Acting Commissioner, Stephenson (City Hall's favourite to succeed Blair) from the Green arrest – the saga was becoming toxic for anyone involved.

Boris has conceded only that two days after the arrest his spokesman Guto Harri texted Green with the words 'Can you talk?' and that on the following day, despite Green's continuing status as a potential suspect in a major criminal inquiry, Boris spoke by telephone to the MP himself. Interestingly, he took the precaution of doing so in the company of two of his aides no doubt aware that a call that long after the arrest would not be taken so seriously as one on the day of the arrest itself.

Two police inquiries were duly launched into the handling of the affair. One by the Inspectorate of Constabulary decreed that the use of police resources in this way had been 'debatable' while an internal police review concluded Green's arrest was lawful though 'not proportionate' – although Quick insists the review 'airbrushed out' key facts reinforcing that the arrest was both proper and proportionate; facts that did not fit the 'disproportionate' line initiated by Boris. Considered by many to be one of the finest coppers of his generation and an ex-chief constable of Surrey police, Quick saw this as 'nothing short of a capitulation by the Met in the face of an aggressive and unpleasant Tory response; at best, a sop to the Tories and at worst, the result of political pressure to influence the outcome of the investigation.' In the event neither Green nor the civil servant who admitted handing him the material was charged.

Boris's intervention was still highly controversial, however, and Len Duvall, former chairman of the MPA, demanded an official Standards Board inquiry into his actions. Curiously, this too made no mention of any call on the day of the arrest. Indeed, the inquiry was not even made aware of the allegations of an earlier call. It did find that Boris, while not guilty of breaching the mayoral codes of conduct, should not have contacted Green at all while the police inquiry was still underway and that to have done so was 'extraordinary and unwise.'[9]

Boris, meanwhile, was being investigated by a second body – the House of Commons' Home Affairs Select Committee chaired by the Labour MP Keith Vaz – as part of its inquiry into government leaks. Originally, he had been called to give evidence on 3 February 2009, but on the day itself committee members were not expecting him because of an understanding that he would be too busy dealing with transport chaos caused by heavy snowfall. They were caught on the hoof – and were therefore somewhat under-prepared – when with only a few minutes' notice Boris came bounding into the room after all. Perhaps as a result he was able to butterfly-dance his way round the MPs' line of questioning.

Labour's David Winnick, while objecting to Green's arrest, was nonetheless aghast that 'one politician [Boris] had been warned in advance by the Police that another politician was to be arrested.' Winnick claims to have heard 'rumours' and 'suspicions' that Boris had made use of the intelligence on the planned raid to contact Green beforehand and therefore asked Boris: 'When you learned what was going to happen . . . you contacted him? Boris replied: 'No. Certainly not before his arrest' but said nothing about whether he had made any calls on that day, merely adding that he had had a 'conversation' with Green on the Monday, as was well known. He also insisted that he had not talked to David Cameron on the day of the arrest, but then changed his evidence and admitted he *had* spoken 'briefly' to the

Conservative Leader at 3 p.m. at a memorial service at Southwark Cathedral for the schoolboy Damilola Taylor who was killed in 2000. Just when the net appeared to be closing in, he quickly claimed the conversation with Cameron had been cut short because of 'the sensitivities of our great leader' Gordon Brown. The Prime Minister, he told the committee, had been 'appalled' at the idea of sitting next to the Mayor of London and insisted he was moved further away. Downing Street denied any such objection but the tale (whether true or not) provided a colourful distraction from what had been discussed with Cameron and once again allowed Boris to fly out of trouble.

Adding to the confusion, Boris remembered (but only once safely outside the committee) that he had also called Cameron about the Green affair shortly after the arrest itself. But by then, of course, it was too late for him to be questioned about it. Altogether, it was a bravura performance. As sketchwriters and supporters alike noticed at the time, these 'lapses' mattered not one jot. 'Boris had got away without even a scratch. He was so relaxed, he didn't even feel the need to muss up his hair,' wrote Simon Hoggart in the *Guardian*. Paul Goodman noted on *ConservativeHome* that the 'Damian Green imbroglio,' was another instance of 'Boris chalk[ing] up' one of his 'many Houdini-like feats.'

However, it was not to be quite so easy even for a latterday master of political escapology. Vaz described the 'four different accounts' in Boris's testimony as a 'very serious matter' and the Mayor was then asked for clarification. There followed a soon-to-be notorious telephone conversation on 4 February between Vaz and Boris, during which the Mayor exploded with anger that the matter of his conflicting evidence was being pursued. Minutes of the call were later passed on to the press and the result was a banner headline 'MAYOR BORIS IN F-WORD TIRADE' across the front page of the *Evening Standard*.

To those who have worked with Boris, and seen him react to anyone who has crossed him, this aggressive language came as no surprise but it was certainly a departure from the genial joker image still entertained by the majority of voters. Yet Vaz recalls that 'F-gate' actually turned out to be useful to Boris. 'All the screaming and shouting became the story,' he notes, 'so I do wonder whether it was a diversion tactic.' Meanwhile, devoted fans argued the affair merely served to enhance Boris's loveable rogue persona. And once again, of course, the squalls subsided. Vaz was not the sort of public figure who commanded national outpourings of sympathy and Boris's tantrum was soon seen as merely providing colour (in stark contrast to public horror at Gordon Brown's reported outbursts). The Home Affairs Committee's report barely mentioned Boris's role and reserved most of its criticism for other parties to the story, attacking what it deemed to be heavy-handed policing and the civil servants who it said had exaggerated the damage caused by the leaks: the butterfly had fluttered away.

While Boris had emerged unscathed, his adversaries were not quite so lucky. Quick was the first casualty. A week before the select committee report left Boris in the clear, the policeman had already been skewered; a fate hastened though not orchestrated by the Mayor. On 8 April, Quick – who was Scotland Yard's counter-terrorism chief and widely seen in Tory circles as an ally of Sir Ian Blair's – was photographed outside Number Ten holding secret briefing notes on an imminent undercover operation. The security breach meant that raids in the North of England had to be brought forward by several hours and were, according to senior sources at the time, 'compromised'. Quick made it clear to the new Commissioner, Sir Paul Stephenson, that he was considering resigning. Not until the next day at 7.30 a.m. was Boris informed that Quick was expected to quit but just 40 minutes later (while the raids were still in progress), Boris phoned BBC Radio 4's *Today* programme to announce Quick's departure. 'In the end,' he told listeners, 'Bob Quick decided it was the best thing to do. It's a matter of sadness as he had a very, very distinguished career in counter-terrorism.'

In doing so Boris not only pre-empted a public statement from Scotland Yard but once again stole the thunder from the hapless Home Secretary Jacqui Smith. In a pre-emptive swoop that left senior Met figures gasping with fury he even announced Quick's replacement, John Yates. However, Quick was perhaps most astonished of all, not least because he had not yet actually tendered his resignation.

'I had told an MPA representative that I intended to resign but I had not yet done so,' he recalls. 'I hadn't even spoken to Boris.'

Of course, Quick was now left with no choice. In any case, he viewed resignation in large part as a protest at what he considered an invidious politicisation of the Met: 'It was actually more about the Green affair than the bit of paper in Downing Street. I could have withstood that on the day, admitting to a split-second mistake and turning the spotlight on the photographer who had appeared mercenary and unpatriotic, but I felt that the tide was against me because of Green and the political levers now being used on the Met. I had spoken out in December [2008] about the corruption I was witnessing around me [but] I was simply attacked by the Tories, the tabloids and one or two colleagues I felt were trying to derail the investigation. And so it was hopeless.' Quick's convictions commanded some outside support. Martin Kettle, for instance, wrote in the *Guardian*: 'Quick lost his job for 100 per cent political reasons.' And five months later, the smouldering row over political interference reignited in public when Kit Malthouse declared that he and Boris had their 'hands on the tiller' at the Met and had 'seized control' of its senior officers, prompting an explosion of outrage from Stephenson and the head of the Association of Chief Police Officers Sir Hugh Orde, not to mention a growing sense of unease in the ranks over at Scotland Yard.

Boris would have to wait to exact his revenge on Keith Vaz but in an article entitled 'Limo-Loving Politicians' in the *Daily Telegraph* the following May, he lambasted Vaz's 'rear end' as the 'symbol of everything wrong with British politics.' It was, he said, 'cupped, cosseted, cocooned on the velour upholstery of a government car' and, as the vehicle passed Boris on a Whitehall street, 'Vaz hauled down the window to hail me. Actually, I can't be sure that it was Vaz who pressed the button. It might have been him, or the driver, or the bodyguard.' Vaz then offered him a lift, he continued, 'in the kindly tones of Louis XIV leaning from his carriage to comfort a poor peasant woman struggling along in the mud.' Boris wrote that he refused this offer – '"No, it's OK, thanks, Keith," I said, slapping the battered old handlebars of my machine. "I've got my bike."' – and then decried the cost to the taxpayer of Vaz's grandiose entourage, complaining, 'He didn't face the slightest threat to his security, except possibly from people like me, and here he was cruising around London as though he was Charles blooming de Gaulle.'

Vaz wearily points out that (as Boris would know) a mere select committee chairman does not have a government car, still less a chauffeur or bodyguard. It was, he says, his assistant at the wheel of his own family Prius and that it was 'all a nonsense.' But Vaz knows as well as anyone that there is no point in trying to hold Houdini to account.

Back in April 2009, though, events at the Met looked set to engulf Boris yet again. A bystander had died after being struck and pushed over by a policeman on the fringes of the demonstrations against the G20 gathering of world leaders. Pictures of the incident handed to the *Guardian* a week later show Ian Tomlinson, a homeless newspaper seller, was walking away with his hands in his pockets when the officer assaulted him. His death consequently struck at the heart of police accountability and the rights of the individual – both themes that Boris had enthusiastically expounded, before and since becoming mayor. This time, though, he chose to keep surprisingly quiet beyond describing the pictures as 'disturbing' and saying that his deputy on the MPA would be meeting the police complaints body. He even complained about what he called 'a very unbalanced orgy of cop bashing.'

In an interview with Jon Gaunt on SunTalk radio, Boris said: 'It is wildly overdone – everybody understands that there are serious questions to answer about what happened to some of the protesters at the G20, and particularly Ian Tomlinson, and thoughts are with his family, but you have to get it into proportion.' Boris's ideas on proportion are instructive: his comments on police conduct at the G20 – which led to a newspaper seller's death and a verdict of 'unlawful killing' followed by a charge of manslaughter against the policeman in question – compare interestingly with his outrage over the raid on a frontbench Tory MP suspected of receiving leaked information potentially damaging to national security.

Questions over policing in London continued to dominate Boris's mayorship, but after previous dramas he was muted in his criticism of the force. And yet his mayorship has seen some of the Met's most turbulent years with controversies raging over its crowd-control techniques and the catalogue of errors in the case of multiple rapist John Worboys that allowed him to continue to attack women for years after he might have been caught. Arguments over whether he has raised or reduced the overall numbers of officers have also swirled over a jumble of confusing figures – leading to Boris being dubbed a 'liar' on the subject by at least one Labour member of the London Assembly. It is therefore perhaps no surprise that in due course he recognised that continuing as chairman of the MPA was adding more to the debit than the credit side of his mayoral balance sheet. On 26 January 2010, he resigned and no doubt with some relief handed over the reins to Kit Malthouse. It was another electoral promise broken – a key plank of his manifesto had been that he would chair the MPA to hold the Police to account. But if he thought that in doing so he would be able to file away the Met as someone else's problem, he would be proven much mistaken.

Boris's decision to step down from the MPA coincided with an escalation of the row over the Met's failure to investigate phone-hacking allegations against the *News of the World*, the paper that had revealed two of his own affairs. On this subject Boris appeared to be almost unquestioningly on the side of the Police and indeed, the newspaper itself, denouncing the allegations of illegal hacking as 'codswallop' and a 'politically motivated put-up job by the Labour party.'[10] It was a surprising stance because the Police had warned him that his own phone had been targetted around the time that news of his liaison with Anna Fazackerley broke in the paper. Later he changed his line to suggesting the paper should not be singled out as the practice of phone-hacking was widespread in journalism and celebrities actively liked being hacked.[11]

Like other senior Tories, Boris seemed unwilling to confront the *News of the World* or more particularly its bosses at News International (with its stable of electorally influential papers such as the *Sun* and *The Times*) despite mounting evidence against them.

Only when it emerged in July 2011 that the *News of the World* may have been hacking phones belonging to murdered schoolgirl Milly Dowler and the relatives of dead servicemen and terrorist victims, together with compelling evidence that the Police were either complicit or at best disinterested in the offences – leading to an outbreak of public revulsion and the dramatic closure of the *News of the World* – did Boris finally call for a 'ruthless' investigation. Yet he still praised Rupert Murdoch's 'very considerable' contribution[12] to the British media, adding that he did not subscribe to the line that the media tycoon had in any way 'corrupted or corroded our political debate.'

Although media attention focused on David Cameron's relationship with News International, after becoming mayor Boris had also cultivated relationships with both James Murdoch, chairman of News International's European parent company, and UK chief executive Rebekah Brooks, who resigned and was then arrested over the affair. Boris was at Eton with Brooks' husband Charlie, and has lunched and dined with both Brooks and Murdoch (on one occasion with Marina) and has also been taken out to dinner by James' father, Rupert Murdoch. The links do not end there – Sky sponsored Boris's cycling events (Skyrides), News International was planning to sponsor a mayoral academy and has considered plans for investing in other Boris projects while backing many of his policies in print.

When the phone hacking scandal claimed the two most senior Police appointments made under his mayoralty – Sir Paul Stephenson who resigned as Commissioner in July 2011 followed swiftly by John Yates as head of Counter Terrorism – Boris reluctantly accepted their resignations. At a very rare press conference on 18 July, under intense questioning by journalists he now admitted he had 'misunderstood the severity of the [phone hacking] allegations.' Although he also claimed, that he had always said he would 'look again' at the affair if new evidence came to light. It was an extremely rare case of Boris submitting himself to some of journalism's most dogged questioners, and he looked particularly flushed as some present began to ask if he had considered his own position. Downing Street also slapped him down after he seemed not fully to have backed

David Cameron over the scandal. Unusually, Boris looked neither confident not comfortable.

Back in April 2009, though, Boris was coming up to his anniversary in power and his first annual appraisal. The one from the voters was effusive – a poll in the *Standard* had him trouncing Ken on a massive 49 per cent of the vote. Despite the early chaos, resignations, rows with Commons committees and skirmishes with the Police, Boris's mayorship was proving one of breezy survival: London had not collapsed into farce or been taken over by jack-booted racists. Although a Tory, he had moved to the Left in various ways – supporting the London living wage and an amnesty for illegal immigrants (although the *Guardian* compared this stance to 'someone's social conscience coming out of a coma'[13]) – just as Ken shifted rightwards with his enthusiastic adoption of the City (leading one independent commentator to brand him 'a curious mix of Trotsky and Thatcher').

Indeed, there were remarkably few changes considering Boris's electoral mandate: his regime had not become the laboratory for Conservative policy wonkery many had expected. 'Boris is a captive of City Hall,' observes one former colleague. 'The place is a monument to Ken Livingstone. The meetings are like some 1970s throwback to municipal socialism. It's a nightmare for anyone instinctively Conservative.' 'It's just the world's biggest think-tank,' complains another Tory. 'The Police and Transport run themselves and it produces a lot of reports that are largely ignored.' Even Boris admitted much of City Hall's output has to be 'filed vertically.'

Boris won acres of favourable coverage, however, by making speeches in Latin or cracking a good joke after falling in a river; he did what good entertainers do and cheered people up. Voters, it seemed, enjoyed having a mayor who might not know every detail of the Circle Line, but swore like a celebrity chef when cornered and claimed to identify with the Incredible Hulk, since 'the madder Hulk gets, the stronger Hulk gets.'[14]

So, Boris was saying all the right things – but was he actually doing them? 'It may be that a bold personality and cautious policies is the right mix for a London mayor,' suggested the *Economist*. Maybe so, but the lack of an answer to Ken's 'big picture' achievements – the

Oyster Card or the Congestion Charge, both of which may be said to have improved London life – was worrying. Media outings were consequently meticulously orchestrated to project the 'big personality' and avoid questions about the lack of grand ideas. Such control meant journalists considered more probing or knowledgeable were regularly refused interviews. Nor would Boris be likely to bestride the airwaves whenever thornier issues such as Tube breakdowns, strikes or London's streets being seized up with roadworks were high on the agenda. As one of his aides put it: 'Boris does not do bad news.'

His good fortune was that although ostensibly a small-state Tory, he was reaping the political rewards from big-spending projects such as Crossrail, a new railway traversing London, and the 2012 Olympics. And yet in reality he could justifiably claim little credit for either – both had been won on Ken's watch.

His own initiatives were on a smaller scale. They included the fact that, as promised, he was getting rid of the hated bendy buses – albeit slowly. He had also cut costs at City Hall and frozen the precept (the Mayor's share of the council tax take, thus saving the average household a notional and not life-changing £8 in his first year). More divisive was his decision to abolish plans to impose a high-rate Congestion Charge on gas-guzzling 4x4s (just one of many measures that angered the Greens). And although the effects were not yet visible, he also seemed to have gone back on his word to stop seemingly randomly scattered skyscrapers from trashing the city's skyline. 'Erectile disorder seems the occupational disease of London mayors,' railed the commentator Simon Jenkins about Boris's new-found enthusiasm for towers.[15] As soon as Boris had taken occupancy of 'the testicle' (his nickname for elliptical City Hall), he 'craved a phallus.'

He was even dragging his feet on removing the western extension to the Congestion Charge – perhaps the most important of several election pledges made in haste that he was now repenting in leisure – no doubt largely because of the lost revenue, in this case amounting to £55 million a year (a shortfall he was effectively forced to make up through higher bus fares). Yet another pledge that quickly looked less appealing from his new vantage point in City Hall was to keep tube station ticket offices open – a folly he quickly tried to abandon after realising the phenomenal success of the Oyster card meant some offices were selling as few as 16 tickets a day.

If concrete achievements were thin, as if to compensate announcements out of City Hall came thick and fast, ranging from a wheeze to build another airport on an island in the Thames estuary, or opening up company lavatories for public use, to planting potatoes on roofs. In truth, his greatest achievement this far seemed to be the simple avoidance of disaster. After a year in office Boris' hopes for London were still not clear – whereas Ken, for all his faults, had always been certain.

The *Guardian* now adopted a new line of attack, Describing his style as government by columnist, the paper decreed: 'You can tell there are no think-tanks or academics behind any of this. This is just Boris in the bath.'[16] Across the Atlantic, even *Newsweek* magazine was commenting that 'the sole connective tissue providing coherence to Johnson's ideas sometimes seem to be that they happen to be Johnson's ideas.'[17] Meanwhile, at home one respected City Hall blogger branded him 'Boris the Boring'.[18] And it was not only his detractors asking whether Boris was an ambitious mayor without a discernible ambition. Even his closest aides conceded the Mayor himself was concerned about what he personally dubbed the 'vision problem.' 'We're all working on it,' said one. 'We know it's the weakness.'

No big deal – for now at least. Boris the brand was still in hot demand and could afford to ignore the nit-picking commentariat. *Time* magazine had just hailed him one of the hundred most influential people in the world (party boss Cameron did not feature). This in turn led him to once again play intriguing mind games as to his hopes for the future. He intimated to the *Evening Standard*, for instance, that he might stay only one term as mayor and would afterwards be ready to serve as prime minister. But then he told a political website that the mayorship was, by contrast, 'almost certainly' his 'last big job in politics.' And while he was liberal Boris as London mayor, he used his *Telegraph* column to flaunt a more traditional Boris to right-wing Tories across the country, uneasy about Cameroonian soft-soap Conservatism, by repeating his calls for the abolition of the 50p tax rate on the rich and the return of the grammar schools. Later, on the thirtieth anniversary of her becoming prime minister, he whipped his readers up still further with an ecstatic appraisal of Margaret Thatcher (something Cameron would have never have dared do). Indeed, far from continuing to dread Boris messing up his mayorship, Cameron might have been forgiven at this point for thinking it would have been better if he had.

In May 2009 a news story broke that truly traumatised British politics. Records of expenses claims passed to the *Daily Telegraph* by a disgruntled Parliamentary employee were published to reveal an orgy of trough snuffling by MPs and members of the House of Lords. Every day over many weeks, the newspaper exposed claims for phantom mortgages, moat cleaning, duck houses, £8,000 television sets, horse manure, bath plugs, wisteria pruning and even porn videos, as well as the names of politicians engaging in so-called 'flipping' – the practice of swapping properties designated primary or secondary residences to avoid capital gains tax. All parties, and all ranks of Parliamentarians were seen to be 'at it', with even the then Prime Minister Gordon Brown ordered to repay £12,400 claimed for cleaning and gardening bills. The revelations led to a rash of resignations, 'retirements', sackings and even criminal prosecutions, but most of all they provoked public disgust at politicians' evident sense of entitlement to taxpayers' hard-earned money.

No longer an MP, of course, Boris reacted to the exposé with an air of saintly bafflement. Explaining that his own Parliamentary expenses had been only for above-board mortgage payments and utility bills for his old Henley constituency home and insisting he had nothing to fear from public scrutiny as any concerns would 'probably have come out by now', he said that he was 'almost embarrassed' not to have claimed more. He also made great play of travelling to engagements by bicycle because 'unless you're completely insane or devious or a Liberal Democrat then there is no way you can fiddle your bike expenses.'[19]

It is instructive how frequently Boris's bike takes centre-stage whenever questions of integrity or likeability are at stake. His spokesman also put it around that in contrast to his former colleagues Boris led a life of carbolic-clean abstinence and economy. 'He got all that big spending, big dinner stuff out of his system at the Bullingdon,' he said. 'Boris barely claims expenses at all.' While privately bombarding the *Telegraph* editor Will Lewis (who was also his employer) with enquiries as to what the newspaper intended to run about him, in public Boris could adopt the stance of a morally superior spectator.

On 2 June, the media finally switched its attention to another political drama after five Labour Cabinet ministers resigned from Gordon Brown's government within a week, leaving the Prime Minister's authority in tatters. As the chatterati entered a frenzied discussion over whether Brown could possibly survive, Boris's Parliamentary expenses were finally published on a corner of page nine of the *Telegraph*. And indeed they showed that Boris had, as he said, claimed for mortgage payments on his constituency home of £85,299 over the four years of his time as MP – the last two at the maximum rate. But he had also claimed £16.50 for a Remembrance Sunday wreath – a detail that risked casting the Mayor in a damningly ungenerous light. Boris quickly explained that the wreath had been 'mistakenly added' to his claim and he had 'happily' paid for it out of his own pocket when asked to do so.[20]

Just two days later, however, public unrest over politicians' expenses threatened to cross the Thames when it emerged that one of Boris's deputy mayors, Ian Clement, had been using his City Hall credit card for personal use, including the purchase of an upmarket car stereo system. It was subsequently announced that Boris had confiscated the card and 'bollocked' Clement, who had repaid the money. 'Transparency and taxpayer value are at the heart of my administration,' Boris crowed. But more details began to seep out, including the fact that there had been concerns about Clement's spending since the previous year and that Boris had reprimanded him as early as August 2008 for using the card to upgrade his flight to the Beijing Olympics. Assembly members were told the Mayor had assumed that Clement had subsequently given up his card, but as recently as April 2009 Boris had still been signing off Clement's expenses personally, including claims for a list of disallowed items.

Although further damaging evidence came to light throughout June 2009 Boris maintained, despite his 'deep sense of fury', that Clement's mistakes had merely been 'crass' rather than dishonest. Then the *Evening Standard* and other newspapers began to publish stories about how Clement had used the card to entertain his young mistress when claiming to be dining with council leaders. After facing accusations of turning a blind eye to his deputy's wrongdoing, Boris finally summoned Clement and he was forced to resign.

In just over a year, Boris had now lost his third deputy mayor – and in circumstances suggesting he was not wholly in control of his kingdom or its coffers. Two days later, Scotland Yard launched an investigation and in the October, Clement pleaded guilty to fraud and was sentenced to a suspended prison sentence, community service and a curfew. In total, it transpired he had run up a credit card bill of £7,000 over ten months without any apparent checks and in breach of Inland Revenue rules and the GLA's own regulations.

Boris had once been fond of comparing trying to skewer 'Teflon' Tony Blair to 'nailing jelly to a wall.' Arguably, his own non-stick coating at this point was even more effective. Beyond the odd grumble on the blogosphere, the Clement episode barely registered with the public or dented the Mayor's popularity. Boris's escape from public censure is all the more extraordinary when compared to Ken's patent – and justified – electoral damage as a result of revelations on Lee Jasper's conduct during the 2008 campaign. Shortly after Clement left City Hall in disgrace, an Inquiry by the District Auditor cleared Jasper of claims that he had fraudulently given public funds to friends and associates (although there had been 'sloppy' monitoring). And although four arrests were linked to the affair, unlike with Clement no police charges have been brought, let alone convictions.

There was still very little fuss even when Boris was found to have made some questionable withdrawals from the public purse of his own. The cycling mayor had spent £4,698 on taxis during his first year in office, far more than previously acknowledged. One journey alone cost taxpayers £237. In total there were 13 receipts for fares over £100 and yet all of them were for journeys of a few miles around London.

Some claims amounted to as much as £33 per mile, such as a £99.50 return taxi from City Hall to Elephant and Castle, less than 1.5 miles away. A large number of the fares were either to or from his home in Furlong Road, Islington, in apparent contravention of City Hall rules stating journeys to or from home should not generally be claimed. As a blogosphere wag – a rare dissenting voice – put it: 'Where exactly does Boris cycle to? Is it just to and from photo shoots?'

Certainly there were soon to be plenty of cycling photo opportunities. On 9 June, the RMT transport union called a 48-hour tube driver's strike over job cuts, pay and working conditions. Boris made great play of defiantly getting round town on his bike – no taxis now – with the cameras in tow. The industrial action pitched two wily, driven and strategic men against each other, even if they did not come directly face-to-face. (Old Etonian roué Boris refused to meet Bob Crow, the implacable class warrior at the head of one of Britain's most militant unions.) Few, though, were putting money on the blond to win such a contest. And yet somehow Boris's bike symbolised – and perhaps inspired – the determination of almost all Londoners to circumvent the strike themselves by walking, scootering, taking the bus or – like the Mayor – cycling. Drivers from other unions continued to work and there were claims some RMT members also turned up for duty, so that two lines worked normally and all ran at least some services. Crow's belligerence garnered little public support. In contrast Boris was seen to be a rallying figure for everyday Londoners, who felt they were being put to a great deal of inconvenience by strikers who, on £40,000 for a 35-hour week, were paid £10,000 a year more than nurses. Paradoxically it was to be the toff who emerged as a man of the people and the union leader supposedly against them, with the saga of the taxi fares soon forgotten.

It was perhaps surprising that it was at this early high point that a flash of discontent broke out about the 'do-little' mayor. Stephan Shakespeare, founder of the YouGov pollsters (the ones who had so accurately predicted Boris's triumph) wrote of his disappointment on *ConservativeHome*, the website he also co-owned. Boris, he said, provided 'welcome amusement' and had been a 'jolly decent mayor.' But he added that he had, however, delivered 'no notable achievement, no sense that anything important will change, no grip. Real problems are not solved – in fact, there's not even a discernible attempt to solve them.'[21]

Of course there were voices who came to Boris's defence, such as Sir Simon Milton, now his official chief of staff. But there was still a feeling that despite his popularity, he had yet to prove himself as mayor. A farcical incident in August involving a shed and a set of irate neighbours did not exactly advance Boris's campaign to be taken seriously. A year after becoming mayor, Boris and his family moved from Furlong Road to Colebrooke Row, a more solidly upmarket Islington street beloved of the highest ranks of the media and legal professions. The latest Johnson residence, an imposing Georgian townhouse purchased for £2.3 million, has an air of orderly elegance only families with the means to keep staff can maintain. 'It's a flash, very expensive and nice house,' notes one regular visitor, who was impressed by the 'nice bits of furniture', the back garden overlooking the Regent's Canal and invaluable off-street parking for two cars at the side. Even for the Johnsons, this was a major investment and Boris frequently asks colleagues whether he made a sound financial decision. (In further evidence of her formidable toughness, Marina reportedly knocked £600,000 off the original asking price of £2.9 million, which suggests they probably did.)

Boris managed to alienate his smart new neighbours just four months after moving in, however, by putting up a 'monstrosity' on the back balcony. The Mayor of London had apparently flouted his own planning rules by failing to apply for permission for what looked suspiciously like a B&Q shed. Neighbours, who accused the Mayor of acting without 'any thought' for them, informed the local council who instructed him to remove it immediately. That night, dressed in floral swimming trunks, he was seen with several members of staff taking it apart. It was an embarrassing incident – and a bizarre one, too. Either the Mayor, who is responsible for setting London's planning policies, was ignorant of his own planning rules or he simply chose to ignore them. He dealt with the episode with characteristic evasion, urging one radio interviewer not to 'intrude in the private grief' of a fellow man's 'ex-shed.'

When public life resumed after the summer break, it was another scion of the Johnson clan who was attracting comment. Rachel had been appointed editor of the *Lady*, a venerable women's magazine that had lost its way. Her imperious sexy manner – which has cast a spell over so many men over the years – certainly entranced Ben Budworth, the son of the magazine's owner, who appointed her in favour of twenty rival candidates in a 'beauty contest.' There followed a flurry of media interest, and even a fly-on-the-wall documentary, *The Lady and the Revamp*, that chronicled Rachel's ball-breaking blonde ambition and talent for humiliating staff.

A slew of racy and graphic articles – including one by Stanley on his gall bladder operation (yes, up he crops again) and another by Charles Glass on how to bed the nanny – kept the enchanted Ben happy but not his feisty septuagenarian mother. Mrs Budworth publicly called for Rachel to be sacked, accusing her of being vain, mad, obsessed with penises and 'a [social] climber, like the other Johnsons.' Above all, said Mrs Budworth, Rachel was using the magazine to promote herself. 'It's all about her. I suppose it's the same with Boris and we should have spotted that. But nobody told us.'[22] 'That's a fair cop,' Rachel responded with engaging candour, '[but] who was talking about the *Lady* before?'

While his sister was busy losing friends and alienating people, Boris embarked on a series of profile-boosting stunts aimed at quite the opposite. First, he jetted off on a trip to New York ostensibly to promote London and meet up again with the New York Mayor, Michael Bloomberg. He was particularly smitten with being driven round protected by Bloomberg's security detail – which he breathlessly described as a 'very detailed detail' involving 30 terrifyingly enormous cops.[23] After he criticised the release of the Lockerbie bomber, Abdelbaset Ali al-Megrahi, in the US media, describing the decision as 'mysterious' and 'crazy,' he was gratified when Americans lined up to shake his hand in Times Square. Whether he achieved much during that four-day trip beyond advancing his own personal fame – and persuading Bloomberg to grow rhubarb on his roof – is debatable but Boris's absence nicely set up yet another media triumph on his return. The *Standard* was running a series about how Transport for London had dropped the river from Tube maps to simplify them. Sensing an easy populist hit, Boris quickly let it be known that he had 'hit the roof' at such stupidity and ordered Transport for London to reinstate the Thames forthwith.

Next came a cameo in the BBC soap *EastEnders*, in which he plays himself in the unlikely plotline of an Old Etonian mayor of London wandering into an East End pub and softening the supposed battleaxe landlady (played by Barbara Windsor) into a state of adulation with the words, 'Please, call me Boris.' Depending on taste he beams like a simpleton or an endearing little boy lost – the artful hopelessness of his acting, it was said, befitting a man whose entire life is an act. Whatever the reviews, the slot rammed home the message of man of the people – or rather toff gets down with the lower orders and likes it!

Yet despite these heroic efforts, it was still David Cameron, who as Leader of the Opposition garnered the headlines that mattered. It was Cameron who dominated the media as the Conservatives prepared for the 2010 General Election with a 15 to 17 point lead in the polls, which put him on track to become the youngest prime minister since Lord Liverpool. Not to be outdone, Boris fought back at the Tory Party Conference in Manchester later that month, whipping the party faithful into a frenzy of excitement with incendiary comments on Europe and the Lisbon Treaty on a new EU constitution. Throwing buckets of salt into old Tory wounds, Boris said that British voters deserved a referendum on the Treaty – even if it was already ratified (as seemed almost certain) by the time the Conservatives came into government. The call was a direct contradiction of Cameron's refusal to promise a post-ratification vote and threatened to reignite old divisions over Europe that had helped lose the Tories three previous General Elections. Team Cameron scrambled to limit the damage but Boris was once again dominating a conference meticulously and expensively planned to project the leadership and their policies rather than his. He protested innocence, claiming he had never intended to upstage Cameron or his shadow foreign secretary William Hague, but that – as he must have been able to predict – was exactly what he had done.

Publicly senior Tories were claiming that Boris had merely 'got carried away' or 'wired up' by the sense of occasion but privately, Team Cameron smouldered with rage. Rumours abounded of an abusive text having been sent to the Mayor from one particularly incandescent Cameroon. Later Nick Boles identified himself as the author of this threatening mafia-style message to the man he had helped into City Hall stating: '*La vendetta è un piatto che va mangiato freddo*' (revenge is a dish best eaten cold). Cameron's means of exacting revenge on his unbiddable mayor were, however, severely limited. As usual, Boris charmed the conference into rhapsodic ecstasy – playing the *EastEnders*' theme tune as he took to the stage and opening by saying how pleased he was to be in Manchester, 'one of the few great British cities I have yet to insult.' Cameron could only look on with furrowed brow while Boris confirmed his status as party darling.

Boris's seduction of the conference crowd yielded another dividend – it allowed him to peddle his most unpopular view with comparative impunity. There remains one area where he is startlingly at odds with many (even most) voters, a subject on which he seems uniquely prepared to risk surrendering all that populist bonhomie he has created over the years. This speech was just one of many occasions since 2008 when he saved his most powerful rhetoric to attack the 50p tax rate for higher earners and the deluded 'banker bashers' who support it as payback time for plunging the economy into chaos. On that occasion, he warned the audience not to forget how much Britain relies on what he described as the 'leper colony' in the City of London.

On other occasions, Boris has sought to sugar the pill with crowd-pleasing references to bankers variously as 'scum' and 'tossers'; he has also touched on the 'deep public rage' at their actions that have left the majority so much poorer, but their own bonuses seemingly generous as ever. But he has warned repeatedly that manufacturing cannot be boosted or the economy re-balanced by 'machine-gunning' financiers, predicting an unwelcoming tax regime would drive thousands of them out of the City and into the eager hands of rival financial centres such as Zurich or Hong Kong.

It's a subject on which he has commented probably more than any other and City Hall sources confirm that he spends much of his time schmoozing bankers in person or on the phone. Of course, the City is key to London's and Britain's economy – providing some 350,000 jobs and billions of tax revenues. But victims of knife crime or police brutality, commuters trapped in tunnels by tube breakdowns, the homeless, the vast numbers who have lost their jobs, prospects or pension rights in the downturn have not earned such energetic and persistent support from Boris as these 'masters of the universe.' He has also directed a lot of his comments on the folly of the 50p tax rate, personally and publicly to George Osborne. By implication, he has criticised both Osborne and Cameron for failing to be sufficiently accommodating to bankers – though surely recognising the political impossibility of granting them favours while the poor and middle-earners find themselves squeezed by both higher taxes and the higher cost of living. Since his first months in office, Boris's attitude towards the City and the super-rich has been at odds with his 'mayor of the people' persona. As Simon Jenkins of the *Standard* put it: 'His defence of bankers' greed is Bullingdon morality, pure and simple.'[24]

So what lies behind this persistent and puzzling trend of banker-backing? Well, only a cynic (or Ken Livingstone) would look at who backed Boris's well-funded 2008 campaign. But those who examined the Electoral Commission records would find an impressive list of hedge funders (such as Hugh Sloane, Stanley Fink and John Tilney), financiers (Simon Keswick), private equity experts (Edmund Lazarus), investment boutiques (ECM), financial services houses (Dawnay Day), insurers (Patrick Snowball), and multi-millionaire businessmen (Frank Brake and Lord Irvine Laidlaw). According to Livingstone: 'Looking at who our respective backers are gives the clearest possible indication of where we stand. Eighty per cent of my backing comes from trade unions and almost as much of Boris's stems from the financial sector. He will defend them, as unions will expect to be broadly defended by me. We shouldn't be shocked by this.'

The 2009 conference speech was significant for another reason, not least because he had pulled off a similar stunt back at Cameron's first conference as Leader in 2006 with his attack on Jamie Oliver. It bore the hallmarks of a systematic campaign to undermine Cameron. But if it is – and Boris would be the first to deny any such objective – it is not one that he formulates with his team. 'No one at City Hall knew that Boris was about to do that,' says a senior insider, who recalls astonishment in the mayoral office. 'Or what he meant to achieve by it. He's very difficult to read. When you see him every day, he's open about some relatively unimportant things, but on the big stuff he's completely closed.'

Back in London, trouble was brewing. During his electoral campaign, Boris had promised to root cronyism out of City Hall but now he himself was accused of giving preferential treatment to Veronica Wadley, who as editor of the *Standard* had championed his candidacy and attacked Ken for indulging his friends. She had since been removed from the paper by its new owners and so Boris put her up for the job of chairing London's Arts Council.

After advice that Wadley had not been the best-qualified candidate, however, the Labour Culture Secretary Ben Bradshaw refused to rubber stamp her appointment. The move led to a bitter row on both sides about political partisanship. Boris tried various ways to circumvent Bradshaw's ban, prompting a rash of pieces in the Left-leaning press in which his motives were questioned. 'Boris feared that if he failed to get her the job, Veronica would go on the warpath saying, "But I created you!"' explains a former colleague. 'The sense of payback had become acute. He was a little scared of her and even thought she had a crush on him – cracking jokes about her being Mrs Robinson in *The Graduate*. He was panicking when she got turned down.' It was no doubt a relief for Boris when this embarrassing episode was finally brought to an end in June 2010 when the incoming Conservative Culture Secretary Jeremy Hunt at last appointed Wadley.

Niggles over his support for Wadley aside, the media continued to indulge the Mayor. Most journalists were interested in only two sorts of story: the Boris gaffe or the Boris row with Dave. Few, with honourable exceptions, bothered to track his performance at City Hall on the important work of making tubes and buses run on time, easing congestion, cutting crime and improving housing. Privately, City Hall insiders reported a sense of almost total lack of scrutiny. 'No one's really watching if we cock things up,' said one. 'People like Paxman or Andrew Neil just ask him about the Bullingdon Club or what he thinks of Cameron. He knows they won't press him on the real stuff such as spending cuts or U-turns.'

There is also no shadow mayor – and virtually no open press conferences (beyond the rare exception mentioned above). And just as Boris had earned a reputation for treating committees in the House of Commons with contempt so did he frequently trade insults rather than information with the 25 London Assembly members elected to hold him to account. Anyone attending Mayor's Question Time at City Hall would not be wholly surprised to learn that Boris's favourite film is *Dodgeball*, with its running motto of 'dodge, dip, duck, dive and dodge'. Knowing that each member is limited to a six-minute slot in which to ask him questions, he filibusters, goes off on tangents, asks for the question to be repeated, answers a totally different question, constantly shouts over questions, and employs each and every tactic to avoid answering, to the continual annoyance of successive assembly chairmen. And when that is not enough, he does what they do in *Dodgeball* and throws the ball right back at his opponents in the form of personal insults such as accusing Opposition members of needing 'care in the community' or 'suffering from Tourette's Syndrome' and patronising female members by addressing them as 'my dear'. Indeed, so practiced is he at fancy footwork from his days at the Eton Debating Society that he barely breaks a sweat – although his eyes roam the room like a Great White Shark sizing up some goldfish, while he strokes his upper lip. Unsurprisingly these one-sided sessions lack the crackle and drama of the best of the Commons' committees and are rarely covered by the media. Not all of the Assembly Members can claim to have first-class forensic brains and few, if any, have become household names. Moreover City Hall is an oddly deadening building, its lighting poor and the air quality heavy.

Many Boris observers in early 2010 started to speculate that the

Mayor was also looking heavy – not only physically but emotionally too. 'I think he's bored,' offered one former Parliamentary assistant. 'I can see the signs – he's put on weight and looks tired.' It did not help that attention was on events at Westminster, as preparations geared up for the General Election and the Conservative assault on Downing Street. In the first months of 2010, Boris struggled to find airspace. 'His people were always coming to us with pitches for stories,' recalls one senior BBC political journalist, 'but we just weren't taking anything that wasn't national and about the election.'

After the election was finally called by Gordon Brown on 6 April, Boris forecast a 'solid' overall majority for Cameron of 40 seats – when the polls indicated such an outcome was virtually impossible. Was this just another of his outbursts of almost hysterical optimism or a bid to cast Cameron's inevitable failure to win such a mandate into even greater contrast? Boris appeared with him on the campaign trail merely a handful of times and overshadowed him when he did (such as his irreverent larking about on a visit to Chelsea Pensioners at the Royal Hospital). On the one hand, there was a widespread feeling that campaign supremo George Osborne had woefully underplayed the Party's prize electoral asset, but other Tories detected an unwillingness on the Mayor's part to 'waste' any of his personal magic on his great rival's account.

Boris did help his brother Jo to win his first attempt at a Parliamentary seat, however, and in the process launch a new political dynasty. (One senior Tory present recalls the 'feeling that Jo's selection in Orpington was the start of a Johnson takeover.' During the campaign, Rachel even made the offices of the *Lady* available to Jo's supporters for telephone canvassing . She explained the offer as 'fealty' to her family rather than the Conservatives – although this did not entirely protect her from criticism – the magazine had not once been overtly political in its 125-year history.)

Boris cast some personal insults in the direction of the Liberal Democrat leader Nick Clegg describing him as a 'cutprice edition of David Cameron hastily knocked off by a Shanghai sweatshop to satisfy unexpected market demand' and naturally Gordon Brown, of whom he asked voters, 'Do we really want another five years of holepunchhurling horror?' But there was no doubting that this campaign was the Cameron and Osborne show, with Boris playing the role of occasional jester.

When Labour performed better in London than elsewhere it was proof, if any were needed, that Cameron had not played well with the capital. The Leadership also failed by a long chalk to gain the 116 seats it needed for an overall Commons majority – one that had for so long looked as if it was in the bag.

As it became clear that Cameron would not be passing through the door of Number Ten the next day – and possibly never – Rachel was quick to tweet: 'It's all gone tits up. Time to call for Boris.' But after five days of horse trading, Cameron and Clegg formed a coalition government and Boris found himself no longer the most powerful Conservative in the land. Cameron was in Number Ten with his finger on the nuclear button, while Boris was, well – Boris was cycling home as normal. It is hard not to feel some sympathy for a man with reason to believe, whatever his faults, that he might well have been able to deliver his party a more satisfactory result – and without the help of the Lib Dems.

Cameron, the less charismatic of the two leaders, was forming a new Government. Boris, two years older – and said to think himself 'the cleverest man in the world' – was still judging 'busker of the year' competitions. And just as Boris appeared to be mastering his brief, the initial excitement of the job was no doubt draining away. Perhaps this feeling of drift was not helped by the sight of Jo so readily adapting to the ways of Westminster, rapidly acquiring a reputation as an expert on both the economy and India It will no doubt have served to remind him that Jo scooped the First Class Oxford degree that he himself had so fervently wanted. Indeed, Rachel (also a 2:1) had phoned her elder brother at the time with some trepidation to break the 'terrible news.'

The sheer grind of being an executive mayor with no cabinet as supporters or scapegoats is enough to wear down someone with even Boris's stamina. But now that there was a new prime minister in Downing Street, Boris's other options were no longer obvious. There is compelling evidence that originally he never intended to stay more than one term as mayor, hoping for a higher calling back in Westminster thereafter. One of his closest aides let slip in his first year in City Hall that Boris was 'disappointed' that he would miss the Olympics, which take place three months after the 2012 mayoral elections. Tory insiders suggest Boris had supported Ken's campaign before the 2008 election for a one-off one-year extension of the Mayoral term so that the sitting mayor could preside over the Games and leave in 2013. However, the then Labour government had rejected the idea as it would require legislation.

Cameron's victory, however partial, changed everything. No doubt when Boris boarded a flight to the football World Cup in South Africa six weeks after the election – to promote England's bid to host the tournament in 2018 – he had resigned himself to making the most of being mayor (and that meant going for another term). But, as always with Boris, there was something else on his mind. Although no great football fan himself – he is more of a rugby man – Marina is keen and accompanied him on the trip to watch England play. The couple looked relaxed as he larked around with a vuvuzela for the cameras and she watched the matches. 'There was no sign of tension between them,' says a close observer, 'quite the reverse. Marina can't have known what was about to come out.'

Perhaps the pair took the time together to plan out his future – Marina's ambitions for her husband were now firmly in tune with his; she even began to champion his cause within the Tory party. As one friend notes: 'Marina can be a bit wicked at times.' At a dinner in a private dining room at Wiltons restaurant shortly after their return from the World Cup, attended by the Education Secretary Michael Gove and other prominent Conservatives, there had been much anguished discussion of a bad week for the coalition. Observing their collective dismay, Marina asked waspishly: 'Is it just an accident that seven things have gone wrong this week? Or are you, by any chance, doing something wrong?' There was no mistaking her message: if only my husband were leader, he would do better than you.

Boris followed this display of wifely loyalty by teaming up with another guest – Oxford contemporary Radek Sikorski, now the foreign minister of Poland. The two proud former members of the

Bullingdon Club decided to celebrate old times by repeatedly banging on the table and chanting at top voice: 'Buller! Buller! Buller!' There are no reports of smashed crockery or flying glasses like the good old college days but for some present, at least, it was a surprise to see London's 46-year-old mayor re-enact his controversial past.

Meanwhile, City Hall was briefing the media that Boris was about to launch his bid for re-election in 2012 and then suddenly, with only hours to go, the announcement at a State of London debate was cancelled. The public explanation – that lawyers had warned him that he would be breaching rules by using a statutory event for political purposes – failed to convince. Now the fog thickened with talk that he would wait to see whether his proposed bike hire scheme succeeded or how London fared in the spending cuts before making up his mind. Speculation was rife, but Boris merely hedged or teased. On the executive eighth floor of City Hall, however, the real story was already well known, although it would take nearly another three weeks for Boris's 'problem' to emerge, by which time the Mayor suspected he might be in serious trouble.

Suspicions about another affair were first aired publicly in the *Daily Mirror*, but it was not until 18 July that pictures finally appeared in the *Mail on Sunday* of a young woman with an eight-month-old, blue-eyed, fair-haired daughter who looked uncannily like Boris. The child's mother was 36-year-old Helen Macintyre, a Belgravia-based art consultant brought in to City Hall by the Mayor without announcement as an unpaid adviser. (Indeed, her appointment, made in May 2009, led to yet more accusations of cronyism and even another inquiry into Boris's conduct.) Invitations to senior staff to visit Boris and Marina's country home near Thame for a swim and barbecue on the same day the pictures ran were hastily withdrawn.

Unnamed 'friends' of Macintyre were quoted in the press saying she was in no doubt that Boris was the father of her baby (although he had not taken a DNA test to prove it). Her live-in boyfriend was a wealthy dark-haired Canadian financier called Pierre Rolin (who Macintyre had persuaded to donate £80,000 to Boris's so-called 'Olympian Erection' – the 400ft-high red metal tower commissioned as a landmark sculpture for the 2012 Games). Rolin initially believed the child was his and spent £30,000 on private care for mother and daughter, during and after the birth. But when the baby was born in November 2009 she was physically so unlike him that he took a paternity test and this proved that he could not have been the father. Shortly afterwards, he split up with Macintyre, publicly blaming Boris for the breakdown of his three-year relationship. He had long since become jealous and suspicious when she started coming home late after meetings with the Mayor.

Perhaps wise from the furore that followed his colourful denial of the affair with Petronella Wyatt, Boris refused to confirm or deny paternity. At work, he tried to laugh it off by pointing out to staff that the baby had gingery hair, but it was clear there was little to be gained from attempting to deny a relationship. When pressed by journalists, he dodgeballed his way out of trouble, on at least one occasion displaying a flash of temper towards persistent questioners. Privately, Boris contacted newspaper editors to remind them that he had 'never set out to preach about the private lives of others' and now had 'no intention of talking about his own.'

Macintyre, meanwhile, declined to talk to the media at all. But a visit by Boris to the home she shared with Rolin in South Eaton Place when Rolin was away on business had been caught on security camera. A close associate of Rolin's also describes feeling uncomfortable when lunching with Macintyre at Franco's restaurant in Knightsbridge when Macintyre was pregnant. She recalls that Boris would call Macintyre repeatedly during the meal, making her giggle and even blush. 'I thought then that Helen was speaking like she had a crush,' the associate says. 'I asked her who she was speaking to, and she said Boris.'

Boris had first met Macintyre 15 years previously at Edinburgh University, where she enjoyed a reputation as a party girl with rich boyfriends. She has just the sort of upmarket appearance, with a good bust and legs and swishy shoulder-length hair that appeals to him. What's more, she dresses well, speaks well with a voice slightly husky from smoking and is supremely ambitious. Her friend Annabel Rivkin describes her as 'the proverbial bloody good bloke with bosoms and a brain'.

Macintyre and Boris met again at the economic forum at Davos in January 2009, when the Mayor was staying in the same chic Swiss-chalet-style Morosani Posthotel, right on the Promenade. She had long been interested in Boris, keeping a pile of books by or about him by her bed. 'She would say all the time, "Boris is so brilliant, so smart, he'll be Prime Minister one day,"' says Rolin. 'She'd make me read his columns.' Macintyre had also pressed Rolin to take her with him to Davos, where, he claims, she behaved oddly whenever she encountered the Mayor. 'I remember Helen running after Boris several times wanting to advise him on art, or at least that is what I thought she wanted. And then I saw him in the hotel lift,' recalls Rolin. 'He knew who I was and he suddenly got really nervous, his eyes shifting all over the place.'

In early March, Macintyre told Rolin, who was by this time engrossed in a business crisis, that she was pregnant. 'My first comment was, "Are you sure?" I had been travelling quite a bit. When I did the maths, the dates seemed out by a fortnight.' He says he was persuaded the baby was his and when she was born on 14 November, paid for a private room on the VIP floor of the private Portland Hospital (where coincidentally Petronella Wyatt had had her abortion). Two weeks after she left hospital and following several rows, Macintyre moved out of their joint home and Rolin rented a nearby flat for her and the baby. Soon afterwards, she admitted the child might not be his, and in April a paternity test proved this to be the case. To say Rolin was angry about what happened is an understatement. 'How could Boris take £80,000 off a Tory donor after sleeping with his live-in partner of three years and possibly father[ing] her child?' he rants. 'He has no moral compass whatsoever! Despite my donation, I have not been asked to any Olympic event under Boris's instructions but he has also never returned the money.'

While Rolin has been left picking up the pieces of his life, Macintyre has disappeared from public view. Like other women with whom Boris has been linked romantically, she has not spoken about him and the paternity of her daughter has never been declared. Indeed, the child's birth certificate does not name the father. Nonetheless the suspicions of infidelity raised by the press had left Marina faced with yet another intolerable situation. Shortly after the story broke she was seen without her wedding ring and once again she ordered Boris out of the marital home, this time to take up residence in a rented one-bedroom flat on the same road. Marina's housekeeper was spotted carrying clean laundry to Boris's modest two-roomed place of exile – a bolthole plagued by unreliable plumbing that on occasion made its presence felt in the apartment below. Finally, Boris had used up his nine marital lives, or so it seemed. It was becoming impossible to ignore the damage inflicted on those closest to him by such a buccaneering approach to life. His children, ranging in age from 11 to 17, could no longer be fully protected. Boris too seemed unusually stressed. Colleagues noticed that the Mayor was more than usually concerned with his finances – perhaps paying for the country home, four children in private school and now two London residences and the staff to run them was putting a strain on even *his* considerable earnings.

But then Boris and Marina were spotted playing tennis together apparently amicably – if ultra-competitively – on a north London court. Yet another rapprochement seemed to be on the cards. It may be going slightly too far to compare the two with Bill and Hillary Clinton – although Boris has more than once poured praise on the former presidential couple – but Boris, like Bill, certainly holds his wife's respect and tenacity dear. And despite all her suffering at his hands, Marina shares Hillary's one-time tigress determination to further her husband's career. She puts up with his temper and apparent selfishness – and the peremptory way in which he sometimes addresses her in private.

According to her close friends, she takes the old upper-class view that the family should be put first. For her, the publicity is almost always worse than the affair itself because of the harm it might do to her children but she also simply disbelieves a lot of the worst that is said about her husband and feels anger and sympathy on his behalf when his ambitions are thwarted. Despite all his straying, those who know her well say she still casts her life in terms of 'Boris and Marina against the rest of the world.'

*

In August 2010 Boris repeated his usual habit after stories about an affair of taking his family on a lavish holiday. This time they stayed for two weeks in Tanzania, enjoying a retreat at the Lazy Lagoon in the Zanzibar channel – at least until Boris was swept away by powerful currents on his morning dip and had to be rescued by staff in a boat! Together the Johnsons went diving and also spent time on safari (thrillingly, their Land Rover broke down next to a pride of lions and their headwaiter had bite marks on his forehead). And at Christmas, the Mayor and his family shipped off to India on yet another enviable vacation. Boris, who made a public point that he was paying his own expenses, attributed the trip to an ambition to promote London's interests in one of the world's most dynamic economies but those close to the couple recognised that the jaunt was the latest phase in Boris's marital repair campaign – not least because it gave Marina the chance to revisit her beloved India. Just before Christmas, he had surrendered the lease on his flat and moved back into the marital home.

As usual, Boris had read the emotional runes cleverly. He perfectly judged the resonance a trip to India would have for his wife and deftly avoided criticism of such lavish expense. The Johnsons spent New Year's Eve at Serai, a luxury camp of tented villas in the Thar desert, Rajasthan, that has sent all the glossy travel magazines into a frenzy. *Conde Nast Traveller* observed the 24 'tents' around a pool (in a desert!) inspired by a traditional Indian step-well represented 'a new level of luxury.' 'If you want to know the state of Boris's marriage,' says a source close to him, 'just look at the holidays. When he thinks he's on the road to redemption, he'll pull out all the stops!'

True to form, no one else noticed Boris's extravagance – suites for two cost up to £716 for bed and breakfast per night – because all eyes were on George Osborne. The 'age of austerity' Chancellor of the Exchequer had fallen foul of the press by reportedly splashing out £11,000 on a skiing trip to the fashionable resort of Klosters. And it must have been even more galling for David Cameron, who had to cancel his own long-planned Christmas holiday in Thailand – the first long-haul family holiday since the death of his disabled son Ivan – amid fears as to how this would play with the public. But Boris's man of the people credentials remained untarnished after yet another super-luxury vacation.

Marina's dignified silence has helped Boris to sail through each new set of revelations virtually unscathed – both must know that if she turned against him in public or divorced him, his career might never recover. He has also been fortunate in his mistresses – none has yet denounced him. 'He's got that shameless charm and it obviously works in keeping them onside,' says one male admirer. His lack of hypocrisy also helps to keep the commentariat onside – allegations of fathering a lovechild with an adviser would almost certainly have meant curtains for virtually any other politician in Britain with, ironically, the possible exception of his opponent Ken (in many ways, the two are uncannily alike). Any fears on his part that the news would damage him politically proved totally unfounded though. Dominic Lawson explains Boris's success as the Great Survivor through the fact that 'unlike a lot of Tories – or indeed politicians in general – he does not strike high moral attitudes about other people or himself.'

Of course, his luck may yet run out. As he nears his late 40s, it might sometimes seem as if his interest in other women remains undiminished. One female associate, whom he once targeted unsuccessfully, has seen him lunch over the years with a series of different women at Magdalen, a French restaurant near City Hall. With dark red walls and thick curtains, the intimate venue serves the hearty Gallic fare favoured by the Mayor. He likes to sit in a corner with his back to the rest of the room 'facing these women in their twenties or thirties who are never stunning exactly but hearty, posh women with character and always full-breasted'. As she observes, 'his kingdom is built on women but his relationships with them are not ones of respect.'

Back at City Hall, Boris's kingdom was now part of a new blue geopolitical map. But he soon discovered how a Conservative government could be just as eager to clip his wings as a Labour one. In July, it was also the fifth anniversary of the 7/7 attacks in which 52 innocent people were killed by suicide bombers in the worst terrorist atrocity London has seen. Ken, who had been mayor at the time, was judged to have risen to the occasion with inspiring messages of defiance and unity. Now London expected its current mayor to prove himself statesman as well as entertainer.

The Culture Department, headed by Boris's potential future leadership rival Jeremy Hunt, had different ideas, however. Hunt had inherited formal responsibility for care of the victims' families and he decreed that the majority of them did not want the commemoration to be a formal event or for Boris to attend. 'City Hall was very anxious,' recalls one close observer. 'They were worried that the *Standard* would run a front page branding him the non-caring mayor when in fact his choice would have been to be there.' The fact that the paper relegated the story to an inside page was surprising (and yet again fortunate) given some families attacked the Mayor for 'forgetting' the dead. Although Boris was able to send a wreath and a handwritten card to a memorial site in Hyde Park, he had for once been comprehensively outgunned by the Cameroons on his own patch.

Boris did not lose the advantage for long, however. The unplanned uncertainty over whether he would stand again as mayor was yet another occasion when events played into his hands. He was now in the throes of negotiations with George Osborne at the Treasury over his future budget. Osborne was intent on cutting £81 billion from the Government's total expenditure to bring the country's economy back from the 'brink' and like every other area, Boris's spending in London faced cuts of up to 40 per cent – or so he would have us believe. Brilliantly timed comments played up the threat to Crossrail here and the vital upgrade work on the Tube there. There was even a story in the *Sunday Times* suggesting Boris had threatened to quit as mayor over cuts and seek a Parliamentary seat at the first possible by-election.[25]

Such talk was swiftly denied by City Hall, who stated tantalisingly that he would '*almost* certainly [my italics]' stand again in 2012. 'George [Osborne] knew exactly what Boris was up to,' says a senior Downing Street source. 'He's too much of a politician himself not to understand.' But it was clear that Boris had seized the propaganda initiative from the Cameroons in what he likes to call the 'air war.'

The fact was that Boris was ostentatiously campaigning to save Crossrail – when Cameron had been telling him for the past 12 months that it was already safe. London's transport budget was never one of the main targets for Osborne's axe but that did not stop Boris from rejoining the battle in his *Telegraph* column in which he upped the pressure on Osborne by questioning the speed and depth of the cuts. 'The consensus around drastic and immediate deficit reduction is in danger of breaking down,' Boris wrote, before highlighting how the slower, softer approach advocated by Labour heavyweight Ed Balls was 'finding an audience, even among those who might normally be counted as state-shrinking free-marketeers.'[26]

What we were witnessing was the posturing and brinkmanship of an intricate power-dance in which Boris ran rings around his opponents. This was an intoxicating taste of what he is capable of achieving when fired up with a purpose beyond mere self-advancement. He even did his homework for crux meetings with Cameron, Osborne and the Treasury Chief Secretary, Danny Alexander. 'He knew the detail, he was purposeful, he knew exactly what he wanted and he pretty much got it,' observes one official present. 'People just weren't expecting Boris to be such a master of his brief.' 'He played an absolute blinder for us in the talks,' confirms Peter Hendy, London's transport commissioner. 'He held out when some people around him wanted to settle early and extracted an extra £700 million out of the Government as a result.'

It was a worthy victory, but one that in truth merely safeguarded projects that were Ken's in origin. Boris still needed something eye-catching of his own to symbolise the fun and freedom of his mayorship. Ironically, once again he raided Ken's idea-bank for a solution. A cycle hire scheme based on the Vélib bikes of Paris had been in the planning stages under the previous mayor – although City Hall staff have since been instructed 'not to mention that it had come from Ken'. That said, Boris picked up the notion and gave it the pedal power that only he could provide. Even the alliterative 'Boris Bikes' nickname worked in his favour – somehow Ken's Bikes fails to trip off the tongue so easily.

But the £140 million scheme was not the easy run it may have at first appeared. One of the problems was the sheer speed at which the scheme travelled from drawing board to completion. No-one working on it was in any doubt of its political significance for Boris and the need for the scheme to be firmly established well ahead of the next mayoral election in 2012. 'We had to do three years' work on it in two,' explains one official. Another City Hall insider, who recalls problems with payment arrangements, computer systems, docking the bikes, siting the docking stations and even physically delivering the bikes at all recalls: 'We were seconds away from being a catastrophe. There were frenzied discussions right up to the wire; it was badly managed and rushed.' And yet, when the first bikes finally hit the streets in July 2010, they were hailed as a delightful addition to a city in search of novelty. 'The Boris bikes have had an amazing cultural effect on London,' remarks journalist Sarah Sands, just one of many fans. 'They are fun. Every time you see one, it's a little bit of Boris.' Indeed, a cartoon character resembling Boris was even designed to promote the bikes (although that was a step too far for commentators such as BBC *Newsnight*'s Michael Crick, who mischievously suggested that the cost of developing the drawing should count as electoral expenditure).

The bikes – originally a subtle blue-green in colour – were painted the strident blue of Barclays Bank, which had emerged as the key sponsor to the tune of up to £25 million over five years. However, although the bank's branding and livery was plastered over the bikes, its contribution covered less than a fifth of their projected cost and despite Boris's pledge that they would not be a drain on the public purse, the bikes are proving to be a hugely expensive 'rich boy's toy' – one largely for the benefit of a central London elite. During their first three months they generated on average £3,370 a day (equivalent to £1.23 million a year) compared to the £114 million over five years they will cost *after* the Barclays sponsorship. The middle-aged, affluent white men found to be the greatest users of Boris bikes cleverly avoided paying for them (beyond the £1 access fee) by returning them within the 30-minute period granted for free.

Senior sources involved in the scheme, while pointing out its popular success, concede it has proved a financial swamp. Latest internal estimates within Transport for London suggest the much-trumpeted Boris Bikes could cost taxpayers no less than £100 million over his first mayoral term. And critics have begun to question whether giving well-off professional types living in zone one (where the first tranche of bikes were based) a highly subsidised commute to work at such enormous cost to the rest of London is justifiable in an age of austerity. A poll commissioned by Boris,found that those living in poorer outer boroughs had barely registered their existence. Yet clever marketing of their undoubted qualities has ensured the eloquent squeals of the pinstriped Boris biker drown out the worries of the number-crunchers. 'The bikes will be enough to get Boris re-elected,' is a common Tory view.

With the bikes finally up and running and the money for Crossrail and the tube in the bag, Boris turned his attention to a much more serious matter: taunting Cameron's government. Indeed, he was developing a considerable track record of attacks but arguably one that owed more to his libertarian instincts than any ideological consistency. His most serious and perhaps surprising assault on official Tory policy was on its proposed cap on housing benefit. The Government was introducing a highly controversial £400-a-week maximum spend on housing benefit applications, a limit that would have greatest impact on claimants living in central London. Some might be obliged to move as they would no longer be able to afford market rents in the centre of the city. With his eye firmly on re-election in 2012, Boris summed up the case against with these explosive words. 'What we will not accept,' he told BBC Radio London in October 2010, 'is any kind of Kosovo-style social cleansing of London.' The result was a gratifying commotion – and a multitude of new fans from the Left, who suddenly saw him as a champion against the Conservative government's cuts.

'That's the first thing Boris has said that would make me vote for him,' was a typical response from Ken's traditional support base. Indeed, Boris had cunningly invaded Livingstone's natural territory leaving little room for his Labour opponent – who had previously identified the Coalition's hard-line welfare policies as his greatest electoral weapon.

As might be expected, the response was not so warm from the Cameroons. The Prime Minister was reported to have decided at the last minute to avoid a full public confrontation with Boris, but it was made very clear that Number Ten (and its Liberal Democrat allies) were thoroughly displeased. Downing Street will always be restrained in its criticism of Boris: in reality, it prefers him to be in City Hall over Ken. In any case, once the point had been emphatically made – Boris is far too astute a wordsmith not to have chosen his words very carefully for maximum impact – he resorted to the time-honoured politician get-out clause of claiming he had been taken out of context. 'I do not agree,' he shuffled, 'with the wild accusations from defenders of the current system that reform will lead to social cleansing.' But no one took much notice of this fancy footwork – it was just more of what his *Telegraph* colleague Benedict Brogan calls Boris's 'drive-by' style of politics in which he knocks on Number Ten's door and then runs away.[27]

Other populist interventions included accusing the Government of not standing up for the British company BP in the oil spillage saga in the US (on BBC Radio 4's *Today* programme), through calling for a rethink of the abolition of the Education Maintenance Allowance for 16- to 19-year-olds (BBC TV's *Question Time*) to warning against sabre-rattling over the crisis in Libya and bailing out Greece for a second time (both in his *Telegraph* column). As a journalist and Mayor Boris had no need of the floor of the House of Commons – he was making increasingly expert use of his privileged access to, and command of, the media to make his voice heard.

When he also attacked Ken Clarke, the Conservative justice secretary (and a man he himself once backed for leader) over plans to halve jail terms in return for early guilty pleas, there were more than stirrings of interest on his party's back benches. His comments in the *Sun* newspaper in June 2011 that 'soft is the perfect way to enjoy French cheese, but not how we should approach punishing criminals' not only signified his close relationship with the paper, it also earned him a loud cheer for supporting 'Conservative values' from MPs alarmed at what they perceived to be the touchy-feely influences of their Lib-Dem partners. The response will have been exactly as Boris hoped. Just as his predecessor Ken had marketed a 'real Labour' vision in defiance of 'phony' Tony Blair, he himself was on track to become the 'real Tory' full-blooded alternative to coalition Cameron.

Yet for all Boris's clever posturing, the fact remains that while he is still in Downing Street, David Cameron holds all the aces in terms of real power. In the lead-up to the mayoral elections of May 2012, Boris will in any case eventually have to re-focus his attacks on his old Labour adversary, the wily old King Newt himself, Ken Livingstone. Will Boris be able to sustain his sparkling electoral record in London? And, even more interestingly, will he want to?

Epilogue

The mayoral election of May 2012 will again pitch into the ring two of Britain's most charismatic political showmen – and mark yet another turning point in Boris Johnson's extraordinary career. The first Boris v. Ken contest in 2008 made great theatre, proving that personality politics could rival *The X Factor* for drama, entertainment and even voter participation. But as the opposing teams limbered up for the 2012 rematch there was just a faint whiff of a foregone conclusion; a sense that the task of extracting a popular celebrity from his perch in City Hall might prove too exacting for a figure in his late sixties with the air of yesterday's man. There were some around Ken Livingstone who sensed that he was not 'really up for it this time,' that an apparent 'grumpiness' and media invisibility early in the contest reflected a lack of real hunger for his old crown. Even when Ken *was* talking publicly about Boris's faults or failings, it was not altogether clear that he was being heard. In the Labour camp, the growing fear during the turbulent summer months of 2011 was that, barring disaster, Boris would walk it.

That is not to say that Ken does not remain a formidable operator, who will inevitably sniff out chinks in Boris's armour as the election draws closer. Or that the unpredictable fall-out from the phone-hacking scandal and the resulting upheavals at Scotland Yard will not in some way affect the mayoral contest, possibly to Ken's advantage. But Tory thinkers believe that Boris has once again struck lucky; that Labour, distracted by the 2010 leadership race, made a fatal error in selecting as its candidate a politician with his own questions to answer. Ken, who for years outperformed his party in London, was by June 2011 trailing it by 10 points. In fact, a YouGov/*New Statesman* poll that month found that one in five *Labour* voters in the capital planned to vote for Boris.[1] Overall, the Mayor was polling at 48 per cent, seven points ahead of Ken and 16 points over his own party. Once again Boris was proving his invaluable – and possibly unique – cross-party appeal in Left-leaning London.

Yet this cheering endorsement came at a time when the Mayor seemed to have outgrown his political playpen, with his attention more focussed on events national and international rather than London local. In one of those sporadic outbursts of Boris-mania, he was once again being tipped by serious commentators to become the next prime minister. Indeed, there seemed to be a growing possibility that an election that neither party leader could afford to lose would be fought by two candidates whose hearts were not entirely in it.

It was therefore significant that Boris and Marina were invited to dinner with David and Samantha Cameron in their Downing Street flat, with its chic, sleek new kitchen and the yellow velour sofa on which Sam Cam and Michelle Obama were famously photographed, one spring evening in May 2011. The event was arranged in part to emphasise Cameron and Boris's 'easy relationship' after years of speculation about serious friction (although Boris continues to be somewhat dismissive of Cameron's deputy prime minister, Nick Clegg, and according to senior Tories, Samantha Cameron is said to disapprove of Boris because of his philandering). In some ways the two men *are* close: they text each other frequently and Boris often breaks off in City Hall meetings to declare, 'Wait! I'm going to text Dave about this!' They meet, but not on a formally regular basis, and Cameron is said merely to shrug his shoulders at news of Boris's latest antics with a rhetorical 'oh, has he?' One Downing Street source claims Cameron is so relaxed about the Mayor, that 'in fact he rarely mentions him. Contrary to popular perception, the Prime Minister is not obsessed with Boris.'

Even so, Cameron's people concede that media reports on the rivalry have 'amplified' any real-life tensions by making their respective entourages suspicious of each other. Although nothing on the scale of Blair and Brown, insiders say papers are not always distributed between the two, information is sometimes held back and the atmosphere permeated by a certain distrust. So, with a year to go until the next mayoral elections, the word was out that the Downing Street dinner reflected the Prime Minister's full square support of Boris's bid for a second term in office.

For Cameron, a Boris victory in 2012 would be a double prize. It would, of course, be a huge boost to his party in that difficult mid-term period but perhaps equally important, it would effectively box in the country's most popular Tory until the next mayoral election in 2016. Jumping ship before then to fight a Commons seat would trigger a mid-term mayoral race, costing taxpayers around £12 million; an extra burden difficult for Boris to justify in times of austerity when the sole purpose would so clearly be the advancement of his own national ambitions. In any case, in this age of younger, healthier MPs by-elections come up less often. Perhaps Boris's younger brother Jo might be persuaded to give up his seat in Orpington for the Johnson dynasty's greater good. On current form, though, this seems unlikely. And so to the question, 'how do you solve a problem like Boris?', the Prime Minister had, it seems, found the perfect answer – unlike previous party leaders. It's conceivable, even likely, that Cameron wants a Boris victory in 2012 more than the man himself.

And it's largely for these reasons that, as a source close to the Prime Minister puts it, 'Boris is always treated as a very privileged person.' As we have already seen, he did well out of George Osborne's 2010 spending review when other departments suffered budgetary slash and burn. Extra powers have also been given to the mayoralty – although not yet as many as Boris would like. (Cameron likes to tell a story about one meeting on this subject when Boris launched himself over the table to try and grab the Prime Minister's briefing papers, which he refused to let him have, leading to an undignified, albeit somewhat symbolic tug o'war.)

Boris is also afforded leeway in other areas – to keep him both tolerably happy and, of course, electable. 'Like Ken with Labour, Boris comes out against the government from time to time,' says a senior

Downing Street source with knowing understatement. 'But it's part of his *job* to be distinct; it's no use if mayors are automatons.' Indeed, it seems Downing Street almost actively encourages such public disagreements, regarding them as electoral bling useful for winning over metropolitan voters. The Cameroons, like so many others in Boris's life, appear prepared to go to extraordinary lengths to accommodate his whims.

In contrast, he rarely returns that loyalty. When Sir Paul Stephenson and John Yates resigned from the Met in July 2011 over allegations about their links to News International, the circumstances prompted comparisons with the Prime Minister's decision to hire Andy Coulson as his Director of Communications, but Boris was noticeably unforthcoming in his support for Cameron. Indeed, although Downing Street announced that Boris would be putting out a formally supportive statement for the Prime Minister (who was away in Africa at the time) it failed to materialise. His spokesman said merely that the Mayor thought the Prime Minister a 'top guy who has to make some very difficult decisions. It is totally mischievous to suggest that he doesn't fully support him.'[2]

Earlier, Boris had dismayed those campaigning – like Cameron – against the Alternative Vote electoral system in the April 2011 referendum by refusing to take a more active role. 'We pleaded with him to do some high-profile events because we knew it would make a difference,' recalls one senior Tory official. 'But our pleas fell on deaf ears – he didn't see it as in his own interests.' There were even suggestions that Boris had toyed with the potentially explosive idea of coming out for the other side in support of AV before he was firmly reined in by Cameron's people on the No Campaign.

As always, there is also the question of trust – a perception that he does not 'bat for the team'. In another incident, a private conversation between Boris and senior Tory Oliver Letwin – in which the Cabinet minister suggested he did not wish to see more people from Sheffield flying away on 'cheap holidays' – somehow ended up splashed all over the newspapers. It caused huge embarrassment for Letwin and damaged the Government's efforts to be seen to be 'all in this together.'

Meanwhile, Boris – who had declared himself 'scandalised' by the sentiments – once again managed to present himself as the champion of the Ryanair classes, if not the most loyal of colleagues. 'That is what Boris is like,' explains the same Downing Street source. 'I don't think he's malicious, or that it's part of a concerted plan – he's created that environment round himself in which different rules apply from the rest of us. People tend to like maverick politicians, like Ken or Boris. Before the mayorship, there was no outlet for them but now, at last, there is.'

The relief in that last sentence is palpable. Some in Downing Street say it is now accepted that – unless Cameron falls victim to events – Boris will not get a chance to challenge for the Leadership until after the Prime Minister *wants* to move on. Downing Street sources say they are not giving a 'moment's thought' to Boris not serving a second term as mayor: 'We just believe he will win.' In the Tory high command minds are already turning to a potential Boris v. George Osborne contest *after* 2016, when it is thought likely that Cameron will step down to 'pursue other interests'. But as the architect of the Cameron government's divisive austerity plan, Osborne may find himself ruled out of the running and in any case, chancellors rarely go on to make a success of the top slot.

At the time of writing, with the phone hacking scandal still raging, it is still difficult to predict whose reputations will emerge unscathed and whose will be irreparably damaged. It has already been suggested that Boris should consider his own position for not having taken the scandal seriously enough, or ensuring that it was properly investigated by the Metropolitan Police, over whom he presides as mayor. Moreover it is far too early to predict who else will pitch in for the Leadership, whenever the vacancy arises. After a faltering performance over News Corporation's increasingly controversial bid to take full control of BSkyB, shares in rising star Jeremy Hunt are now being sold by political commentators, whereas Osborne has remained conspicuously distant and the previously unfancied Philip Hammond and Theresa May have won new fans. But they might all struggle to appeal to enough northern or Scottish voters to seal a definitive Conservative majority. There is the very real possibility that the next

Tory leadership election will be won by someone still shrouded in obscurity but already hatching his (or her) master plan for glory.

If Boris does stay in City Hall until 2016 – when he will be pushing 52 – his age but more importantly, his familiarity, might also begin to count against him. All politicians have their shelf life and after eight years as London mayor, he may well start to look like a throwback to another age. Boris could fall victim, like a whole generation of Labour politicians born between 1955 and 1964, to a party deciding to skip a generation in its search for freshness and new direction (possibly plumping for a leader who has never supped with the Murdochs.) Indeed, if Boris is stuck in the political long-term car park of a second mayoral term, that will suit his rivals and the current occupants of Downing Street just fine. Insiders ill-disguise their satisfaction that it will be 'a long road' from City Hall for Boris to realise 'the ambitions we know he has in national government.' But then, as we have seen over and over, it is perilous to underestimate his ability to spring a surprise or recover miraculously from what looks like a hopeless situation. No doubt he himself is wondering if it would not be better to go down to a heroic and stylish defeat in the 2012 mayorals to give himself more options.

Worryingly for his prime ministerial ambitions, though, was that while the June 2011 poll (conducted before the phone hacking scandal really took off) found that 50 per cent of voters thought Boris 'charismatic', only 13 per cent deemed him a 'natural leader'. Just 18 per cent saw Ken as charismatic, but a slightly higher 19 per cent per cent regarded him as a 'natural leader'. Twice as many also believed Ken would be good in a crisis compared to Boris (23 per cent to 12). These apparently conflicting views strengthen the widespread perception that voters back Boris for the mayorship largely on personality as opposed to policy. Perhaps they would feel differently if he was pitching himself as a future prime minister with the altogether more serious job of pursuing the national interest. No doubt this is something that troubles a man who has always struggled to be taken seriously: it poses the question that while a Boris premiership would undoubtedly be fun and possibly exciting, what would it achieve?

On the surface most senior Tories have been glowing about Boris's track record as mayor. After all, the return of Ken is a far worse prospect for them than Boris's re-election. 'Boris has shown himself a serious political leader and executive – we're impressed,' says the Downing Street source on cue. 'He's filled the shoes of Livingstone, and that was always going to be difficult. Before the election, people were saying Boris was a bit of a joke, but not any more.'

Pushed on the detail of real achievements, however and the tone is immediately more hesitant. As usual, the 'sacking' of Ian Blair is wheeled out as the significant victory (although that 'victory' has begun to look distinctly hollow after Boris's chosen replacement at the top of the Met resigned after just three years in his post, leaving behind him a force facing its biggest crisis for four decades). 'Otherwise, he's doing loads of stuff under the radar,' observes the Downing Street man. 'But we would concede that there's no big-ticket achievement and we're surprised that after three years in power, there are *still* calls for him to take an axe to City Hall.'

A leading backbench Tory MP (and one of the first to come out in support of Boris as mayoral candidate) is more direct: 'He has been showman rather than politician – he's a disappointment.' Leaders of the outer boroughs have also started to privately grumble that Boris has reneged on his promise to look after the suburban 'doughnut'. Most schemes emanating from City Hall benefit Zone One areas, such as the smart part of Islington where he lives. His appointment in February 2011 of Teresa O'Neill, Tory leader of Bexley, as his new Outer London Adviser – and borrowing £40 million towards an outer London fund – were attempts to bring his natural allies back on side. Even so, the 'doughnut' Tories complain this amounts to too little, too late.

Some activists also report feeling disappointed. 'I campaigned for him as President of the Union at Oxford and I campaigned for him in 2008,' says one former supporter. 'I know lots of Tories who said in the first mayoral election that they wouldn't vote for "that clown." And now they think he's not been so bad as they expected. But those of us who expected more, feel let down – he's done nothing for the doughnut areas and I think he almost deserves to lose next time.'

The hope is that 'noticeable' additions to London life in the pipeline will dazzle the detractors and provide Boris with the bragging rights he needs for a second term and beyond. As he entered the fourth year of his mayoralty, City Hall staff noticed he was devoting a 'huge' proportion of his time in trying to extract funds from private donors, often bankers and, yes, sometimes his friends at News International, but also little-known overseas companies for a range of increasingly bizarre, even panicky 'legacy' projects. 'Subjects such as crime and transport are now much further down the agenda,' says one despairing aide.

Boris had kicked off with the laudable Mayor's Fund – a much-trumpeted charity intended to help the disadvantaged youth of London – with donations from the City's hugely advantaged bankers. It did not start well, with Bob Diamond – the £7 million-a-year man from Barclays – saying that he didn't have the time after all and bailing out after just six weeks. And despite the Mayor's commendable efforts to invite bankers to 'palliate their guilt' by siphoning off the small change from their bonuses, the sums since raised have proved a humiliating fraction of the many millions he had promised (and expected). A sheepish Boris admitted in March 2009 that 'there's not an awful lot there yet.'[3]

By 2010 the Fund was still spending less than £1.5 million a year across the whole of London. Even one of Boris's chief supporters, Lord Marland, admits the Fund is 'stuck in process and is sluggish. It has not had the significant impact that was hoped and needs a game change.' In the event, Boris had discovered that extracting money from bankers is not so easy as it should be.

Of course the 'Boris bikes' are the largest, most expensive and popular project and he has brought in up to £25 million from Barclays for that. But only in return for colossal brand exposure – and as we know, the taxpayer is still expected to have to fork out another £100 million or so over the 2008–2012 mayoralty, too. Yet despite the enormous cost, beyond the bikes are at least four other grandiose schemes that the Mayor is enthusiastically pursuing.

'Money is no object when it comes to making these prestige projects happen,' observes one senior City Hall official. Despite the excitable puffs from City Hall, these are not free gifts to the metropolis as many assume. In fact, the total bill for all the Mayor's 'vanity projects' (as they are nicknamed privately, even by his staff) could run into hundreds of millions of pounds. With Boris tightly constrained on how he can raise revenues, the ever-rising costs could well push up transport fares, which have already risen by up to 44 per cent under his reign, even further.

The first is the officially titled ArcelorMittal Orbit after its sponsor – a global steel company – which Boris hopes will be London's answer to the Statue of Liberty or the Eiffel Tower. A £24 million (initially, £19 million) 115-metre red-metal tower next to the Olympic park in east London, it resembles either a hookah pipe or a demented treble clef, but is, apparently, 'an electron cloud moving' to City Hall. Nicknamed the 'Olympic Erection' or 'Piffle Tower', it was branded by the *Observer*'s architecture critic Rowan Moore 'the most extravagant example of the idea that a huge, strange object can affect tens of thousands'. But describing it as 'ponderous and confused', he concluded: 'This could be the point at which the idea stops working.'[4] Taxpayers will nevertheless be paying at least £3 million towards it, and more to visit. Furthermore, it is not widely known that profits from visitors will not go back to the public purse but instead to ArcelorMittal: the company has donated £10 million in cash towards the project and lent the money for most of the rest, but in return will benefit from enormous publicity and naming rights in perpetuity, as well as the visitor income stream.

Another much-touted wheeze is the new Routemaster bus – an emotionally resonant but, according to its detractors, financially nonsensical investment of £8 million for a first batch of just five buses (or £1.6 million each) loosely based on the old hop-on, hop-off double-deckers. The first few were scheduled to appear on London's streets by the end of 2011 and should cut quite a dash, with their rounded behinds and glazed-over staircases. Later models are expected to be cheaper as development costs are absorbed but eventually the cost of extra conductors alone is expected to top £20 million a year.

Next, Boris wants to build a ski-lift style cable car from the O2 Arena on the Greenwich Peninsula south across the river to the Royal

Docks and the ExCeL London exhibition centre. Elegant, certainly, its route has nevertheless puzzled locals, who are unlikely to make that particular journey often after the Olympics are over, and links with other public transport routes are questionable. Boris promised the original £25 million cost – now slated at up to £57 million – would be paid for by the private sector but by June 2011 he was furiously back-pedalling and said he could no longer 'guarantee' the taxpayer would not have to foot the bill.[5] Meanwhile, he has been making his usual round of calls to drum up cash from advertisers or sponsors, persistently pressing James Murdoch of News International for one to cough up. (There were suggestions that the defunct *News of the World* might be a sponsor.) The quest for backers has been made more difficult by the financial uncertainty, however, as well as concerns over safety issues surrounding the 300ft support towers. Together they mean that the cable car may well not be ready in time for the Games – its principal raison d'être. No matter, work has begun, so the taxpayer is already committed.

Finally, Boris was able to claim in the spring of 2011 that he had secured up to £60 million for a futuristic kilometre-long floating pontoon along the Thames shoreline from Blackfriars to the Tower of London, yet another planned attraction for the Olympics, as well as the Queen's Diamond Jubilee celebrations. According to City Hall, the principal backers for this addition to a World Heritage Site were to be the Singapore-based Venus Group. In fact, the company's real name is Venus Asset Management, a little-known outfit whose website has neither a postal address nor telephone number, and which comprises a lot of subsidiaries called Guru. A director of one of these companies, Guru Fund Management, is the signatory to the agreement with Boris. There are even fewer details about Guru Fund Management except that its UK registered office is located in a brick-built block of modest flats in Stratford, east London, and its director, Sri Nadarajah, lives in the same block, where homes typically sell for an average of around £150,000. (Attemps to contact Nadarajah at this address have met with scant success, repeated phone calls going unanswered before defaulting to a fax machine.)

To date, the origins of the promised £60 million have not been disclosed and the deal has provoked questions at City Hall. Boris's incoming chief of staff, Sir Eddie Lister, handwrote along the bottom of official documents that he would not agree to the deal without due diligence conducted on Guru and a guarantee no public funds would be committed. City Hall claims due diligence has since been done but has declined to provide further details on Venus Group, or the money, on grounds of commercial confidentiality. Privately, officials remain 'concerned.' 'We have no real idea who these people are or where their money is coming from,' says one. 'It is not the sort of agreement that the Mayor of London should be entering, but Boris would not be dissuaded.'

Meanwhile, many of Boris's aides have tried to re-focus his attention on the all-important, if comparatively dreary issues of transport and crime. It appears that he is often too taken with his bold schemes to be dragged down to earth, though: it's as if he fears nothing more than having his mayoralty described as dull. As one observer put it: why is it that politicians prefer to leave a legacy in the shape of a towering folly rather than an efficiently-running transport system? It's not as if Boris is short of media attention – he still has an instinctive feel for a photo opportunity. When he and a camera crew accompanied police on a drugs raid in the summer of 2011, when he saw the Mayor, the astonished suspect exclaimed: 'What the fuck are *you* doing here?' Fame indeed.

Boris is an assiduous caller of newspaper editors – and enjoys almost unparalleled access, helped by the fact that he has worked for them (such as Tony Gallagher, editor at the *Telegraph*), gone to university with them (Ian Katz, deputy editor at the *Guardian*), lived nearby (Katz again), attended the same school (fellow Old Etonian Geordie Greig at the *Standard*) or worked opposite them (Lionel Barber at the *Financial Times*, who was in Brussels at the same time). He is also in regular contact with James Murdoch of News International, and before she resigned, Rebekah Brooks, and is given top billing when he writes for the *Sun*. He has even attended a News International board meeting, and been wined and dined by the company at least six times. *The Times* has been vociferous in support of his 'Boris Island' airport in the

Thames estuary idea, when most other news organisations (like the airlines) have discounted it. Jeremy Paxman on *Newsnight* is a family friend, David Dimbleby on *Question Time* is a fellow ex-Bullingdonian – so many BBC interviewers are part of the greater Johnson diaspora. Curiously, the BBC decided not to run with the Helen Macintyre story – ensuring a débâcle that might have been a difficult issue for the Mayor fizzled out within days. 'There was a feeling that it wasn't a story, it was just Boris,' explains a BBC executive. (It is also interesting that it was not his tormentor of old, the *News of the World*, but the *Daily Mirror* that broke the story.) It's a cosy world – and Boris, Rachel and Stanley occupy some of its sunniest spots.

Seriously critical coverage – bar the occasional outburst in the *Guardian* or *Daily Mail* – is rare. Boris charms and he cajoles and is often treated indulgently in return. He has a reputation for not behaving like a normal politician and so he is not judged like one; to date, at least, he has been forgiven where others are simply forgotten. Although, of course, if in the future he does go for Downing Street, he might well find that his indiscretions with women suddenly become a political issue, where for so long – since his sacking over Petronella Wyatt – they have been overlooked. Almost certainly, it would be calamitous should Marina ever leave or denounce him.

Older Tories – and even some of his one-time staunchest supporters, such as Sir Max Hastings – shake their heads with dismay whenever Boris is cited as a plausible candidate for Number Ten. 'Cameron is taking a huge political risk in the national interest,' writes Hastings in the *Daily Mail*, 'while London's Mayor seeks to advance, or at least protect, his own career. I know which of the two I want to run Britain, and it is not Boris.' Despite this (and as even his critics concede) as a celebrity toff, Boris embodies two of the great trends of our age. 'Servility to celebrity has partially replaced class deference,' notes George Walden, the former Tory MP, 'and the adoring polls suggest that Johnson benefits from both.'[6]

Indeed, who would have thought a mere decade ago, that politics in the twenty-first century would be dominated by two Old Etonian ex-members of the Bullingdon Club? For most of the latter half of the twentieth century it was the meritocratic grammar schools that held sway. Their products occupied Number Ten for 33 years from when Harold Wilson ousted the aristocratic Alec Douglas-Home in 1964 through the Heath and Thatcher years to John Major's departure in 1997. And yet in the new millennium, Cameron and Boris preside over a political elite once again drawn from a tiny, privileged social caste. It is as if in some ways, Margaret Thatcher – daughter of a Grantham grocer – never existed. True, if Ed Miliband makes it into Number Ten he will be the first premier to emerge from an English comprehensive but the last electorally successful Labour leader – Tony Blair – who brought the grammar school run to an end in 1997, was schooled at Fettes, Scotland's answer to Eton.

In times of bewilderingly rapid change we Brits seem to turn back to the ruling classes of old for reassurance and leadership, and Boris has been a beneficiary of that insecurity. Deference, though not the bended-knee variety, is back in vogue and royalty once again the height of fashion. Boris's calculation appears to be that we want to look up to our leaders as some superior version of ourselves – wealthier, more erudite and undoubtedly better educated. Or perhaps we are convinced that someone who can conjugate Latin verbs or dash off verse in the style of Hilaire Belloc is perfectly suited to preside over a metropolis, though probably not a nation. Boris believes fervently, however, that an Etonian education prepares future rulers for ruling and he can be intensely dismissive of others not similarly steeped in the public school ethos of superiority. As can Cameron, who – according to one Tory insider – treats senior colleagues from similar upmarket backgrounds as 'family', the rest as mere 'staff.'

Both he and David Cameron appear to share the same sense of entitlement to power, a feeling they were born to rule, and with that education and sentiment comes an apparent ease of governing not present in politicians from humbler backgrounds. It works because, despite their social elevation, they also have that modern skill of communication. But it may also make them more vulnerable if they are seen in any way to have abused the trust invested in them. Boris and Cameron have very different styles – with the Mayor more comfortable with his educational CV than the Prime Minister (attending Etonian reunions, for instance, when Cameron declines). Arguably Boris's highly successful stage toff act of the 1990s made it possible for Cameron to thrive in the Noughties in a party that since Thatcher's time has seen poshness as a liability.

The fact that Boris ultimately wants Cameron's job is not in dispute, though, and his chance might come sooner than expected if Livingstone recovers his form and, perhaps aided by external events, lands a mortal blow on his adversary. Of course, whether or not Boris wins in 2012, the political road-map from City Hall to Downing Street is far from clear; whatever his own sense of destiny, he may never make it there. He is dependent on the success – or rather failure – of others to achieve his aim. Arguably, Cameron losing to a resurgent Labour party in 2015 – however unlikely a prospect that might seem – could provide Boris's best chance of leading his party and even his country. What is certain is that if presented with an opportunity, Boris has been endowed with the brains, the emotional intelligence, self-belief and perhaps most of all the good luck to make it. He is blessed with immense charisma, wit, sex appeal and celebrity gold dust; he is also recognised and loved by millions – although less so by many who have had to work closely with him (let alone depend on him). Resourceful, cunning and strategic, he can pull off serious political coups when the greater good happens to coincide with his personal advantage.

Boris inspires sympathy and loyalty but rarely repays it; he's friendly though not often a friend. He cheers people up, is physically brave and apparently tireless but also prone to indulgent attention-seeking and so often seems to favour the frivolous over the serious, the rich and powerful over the humble, the quick-fix publicity stunt over a longer-lasting genuine achievement, a monologue to genuine conversation, a convenient evasion over an awkward truth. He is never boring but still seems to lack vision or moral convictions, although he bears grudges aplenty. Complicated, original, surprising and inspiring, however, he is without doubt the most interesting public figure in Britain today. In short, he has the gifts and the artistry to be the 'break-the mould leader' that the country so desperately needs but he is capable of much, much more than he gives – indeed, he disappoints far more than he offends.

For all his opportunities and abilities, his chief substantive achievement so far has been merely the accumulation of enormous fame. As he approaches 50, it's high time that his formidable energy and talents were put to better use for the benefit of the many voters who adore him, as well as those who don't. Until he shows that he has a real purpose for power beyond power itself, the suspicion will remain that he is in it for only one cause and for only one person: Just Boris.

Sources

Boris Johnson is without doubt one of the most fascinating figures in British public life and few people lack an opinion on him. Nonetheless during the process of researching and writing this book I have been astonished by the number of former and current friends, colleagues, opponents and observers of Boris and his family who have agreed to interviews and to do so on the record. Without their contributions the foregoing text would be considerably shorter and my understanding of this enigmatic and entertaining man all the poorer. Wherever a quote in the book has been included without a note number the material in question has been taken from an original interview. A list of the interviews conducted can be found below, excluding, of course, those individuals who wished to remain anonymous.

Face-to-Face Interviews

Andrew, Jill: 18 June 2010, plus later calls.
Berry, Don: 24 November 2010.
Bienkov, Adam: 10 January 2010.
Binyon, Michael: 23 April 2009.
Black, Guy: 15 June 2010.
Blezard, Paul: 20 April 2011.
Boles, Nick: 1 December 2010 and 4 February 2011, plus calls.
Colman, Dan: 3 December 2010.
Comfort, Nick: 30 June 2010.
Cook, Chris: 13 September 2010.
Crawshay-Williams, Melissa: 16 July 2010.
Crick, Michael: 16 March 2010, plus others.
Crosby, Lynton: 2 July 2009, plus emails.
Elliott, Francis: 13 May 2009.
Evans, Lloyd: 27 May 2010, plus subsequent emails/calls.
Fairbrother, Tom: 24 March 2010 and others.
Field, MP, Mark: 30 March 2010, plus later calls.
Frieze, Anthony: 23 June 2010.
Gardiner, Nigel: 24 April 2009.
Gardner, David: 24 August 2010.
Gilligan, Andrew: 19 May 2010, plus later emails.
Gimson, Andrew: 8 March 2010.
Goodhart, David: 10 March 2010.
Goodman, Anthony: 2 June 2010.
Goodman, Paul: 18 June 2010, plus calls.
Grant, Charles: 20 May 2009.
Griffin, Jasper: 21 May 2010, plus later calls.
Guilford, Peter: 27 March 2009.
Harri, Guto: 6 April 2009, 24 November 2010 and emails.
Helm, Sarah: 24 March 2009.
Helm, Toby: 22 April 2009.
Hillier, Lorraine: 7 May 2010.
Hinsliff, Gaby: 12 March 2009.
Hoscik, Martin: 10 January 2011.
Howard, Anthony: 13 December 2010.
Howard, Lord Michael: 8 September 2010.
Howell, MP, John: 23 June 2010.
Hurd, Lord Douglas: 29 June 2010.
Jenks, Emma: 23 March 2010, plus later calls.
Johnson, Brian: 9 November 2010.
Jones, George: 6 May 2009 and calls.
Jones, Jenny: 15 December 2010.
Kirkbride, Julie: 26 February 2010.
Landale, James: 27 July 2010.
Law, Mark: 2 November 2010.
Lawson, Dominic: 13 October 2010.
Le Fanu, James: 9 November 2010.
Leith, Sam: 20 May 2010.
Letts, Quentin: 18 October 2010.
Livingstone, Ken: 16 March 2011.
Macdonald Milner, Tommy: 16 September 2010.
Mackay, Andrew: 16 March 2010, plus later phone calls.
Marland, Lord Jonathan: 13 April 2011.
Mayer, Anthony: 24 January 2011.
McElvoy, Anne: 17 February 2011.
McLoughlin, Chris: 29 April 2009.
McSmith, Andy: 11 October 2010.
Meade, Geoff: 24 April 2009.
Mitchell, MP, Rt. Hon. Andrew: 14 June 2010, plus later calls.
Mount, Harry: 20 May 2010.
O'Leary, John: 23 March 2010.
Paddick, Brian: 10 January 2011.
Palmer, John: 23 March 2009.
Parris, Matthew: 26 May 2010.

Patrick, Aaron: 13 May 2009.
Pope, Steve: 20 May 2009.
Pullen, Maggie and Richard: 5 June 2010.
Quick, Robert: 11 January 2010, 16 February 2011, plus later calls.
Raphael, Adam: 6 July 2010.
Raynsford, Nick: 20 January 2011.
Reed, Richard: 30 April 2010.
Reid, Stuart: 9 April 2010, plus later calls.
Reissmann, Ian: 6 May 2010.
Robinson, Nick: 13 July 2010.
Robinson, Stephen: 18 November 2010.
Rolin, Pierre: 25 March 2011.
Royce, Rachel: 27 April 2010.
Rudd, Roland: 30 March 2010.
Sands, Sarah: 7 December 2010.
Sapsted, David: 19 November 2010.
Scriven, Marcus: 18 March 2010 and calls, etc.
Shakespeare, Sebastian: 4 May 2010, plus later calls.
Sharman, Tim: 5 February 2011.
Sherlock, Neil: 17 March 2010, 22 March 2010, plus later calls.
Stanway, Mark: 10 July 2009.
Sutherland, Peter: 7 May 2010.
Taylor, Frank: 19 November 2010.
Travers, Tony: 25 November 2010.
Vaz, MP, Keith: 23 November 2010.
Wadley, Veronica: 14 January 2011.
Young, Toby: 19 May 2010.

Interviews by phone, post or email

Anderson, Sir Eric
Baldry, Don
Barnes, Jonathan
Bell, Steve
Black, Conrad
Brand, Charles
Burns, MP, Simon
Carnegie, Mark
Connor, Tim
Davison, Bernice
Delingpole, James
Forbes, Patrick
Fowler, Lord Norman
Guilford, David
Hendy, Peter
Lewis, Roger
Lonsdale, Revd. Andrew
Luntz, Frank
Macmillan Scott, Edward
Minogue, Noonie
Murray, Oswyn
Parker, Tim
Reynolds, Ian
Robinson, Stephen
Robinson, Tony
Seabrook, QC, Robert
Servadio, Gaia
Stagg, Sir Richard
Teodurczuk, Tom
Tickell, Sir Crispin
Tickell, Oliver
Tiptree, Brian
Turner, Derek
Wade, Nigel
Warren, Marcus
Winnick, MP, David

Notes

Introduction

1. Johnson, Rachel (ed). *The Oxford Myth*, Weidenfeld and Nicolson, London, 1988, p. 71.
2. *Evening Standard*, 9 April 2010.
3. *Tatler*, May 2008.
4. *Telegraph*, 15 October 2006.

Chapter One: 'Peter Pan and Wendy'

1. Johnson, Stanley. *Stanley I Presume*, Fourth Estate, London, 2009, p. 186.
2. *Ibid.*
3. Gimson, Andrew. *Boris: The Rise of Boris Johnson*, Simon & Schuster, London, 2006, p. 3.
4. *Independent on Sunday*, 22 March 2009.
5. Johnson, Stanley. *Stanley I Presume*, Fourth Estate, London, 2009, p. 93.
6. *Ibid.*, p. 183.
7. *Ibid.*, p. 172.
8. Gimson, Andrew. *Boris: The Rise of Boris Johnson*, Simon & Schuster, London, 2006, p. 16.
9. Johnson, Stanley. *Stanley I Presume*, Fourth Estate, London, 2009, p. 189.
10. Gimson, Andrew. *Boris: The Rise of Boris Johnson*, Simon & Schuster, London, 2006, p. 11.
11. *Desert Island Discs*, BBC Radio 4, 30 October 2005.
12. Johnson, Stanley. *Stanley I Presume*, Fourth Estate, London, 2009, p. 192.
13. *Daily Telegraph*, 17 May 2008.
14. Johnson, Stanley. *Stanley I Presume*, Fourth Estate, London, 2009, p. 219.
15. *Ibid.*, p. 286.
16. Johnson, Boris. *Lend Me Your Ears*, Harper Perennial, London, 2004, p. 414.
17. *Spectator*, 23 April 2008.
18. Johnson, Stanley. *Stanley I Presume*, Fourth Estate, London, 2009, p. 75.
19. *Who Do You Think You Are?* Wall to Wall productions, 20 August 2008.
20. Johnson, Stanley. *Stanley I Presume*, Fourth Estate, London, 2009, pp. 38–39.
21. *Ibid.*, p. 45.
22. *Ibid.*, p. 41.
23. *Daily Telegraph*, 31 January 2004.
24. Johnson, Stanley. *Stanley I Presume*, Fourth Estate, London, 2009, p. 57.
25. Sunday Times, 11 May 2008.
26. Johnson, Stanley. *Stanley I Presume*, Fourth Estate, London, 2009, p. 112.
27. *Ibid.*, p. 62.
28. *Ibid.*, p. 150.

29. *ES Magazine*, 29 February 2008.
30. Gimson, Andrew. *Boris: The Rise of Boris Johnson*, Simon & Schuster, London, 2006, p. 19.
31. *Tatler*, May 2008.
32. Gimson, Andrew. *Boris: The Rise of Boris Johnson*, Simon & Schuster, London, 2006, p. 17.
33. *Daily Mail*, 10 May 2008.
34. *Ibid.*, 4 May 2008.
35. *Grove* magazine, January 2005.
36. Johnson, Stanley. *Stanley I Presume*, Fourth Estate, London, 2009, p. 234.
37. Gimson, Andrew. *Boris: The Rise of Boris Johnson*, Simon & Schuster, London, 2006, p. 16.
38. *Daily Telegraph*, 20 January 2009.
39. *Ibid.*
40. Gimson, Andrew. *Boris: The Rise of Boris Johnson*, Simon & Schuster, London, 2006, p. 27.
41. *Ibid.*
42. *The Times*, 27 May 2008.
43. *Sunday Times*, 11 May 2008.
44. *Sunday Telegraph*, 18 May 2008.
45. *Sunday Times*, 12 October 2008.
46. Johnson, Stanley. *Stanley I Presume*, Fourth Estate, London, 2009, p. 287.
47. *Ibid.*
48. *Daily Telegraph*, 31 January 2004.
49. *Sunday Times*, 11 May 2008.
50. *Ibid.*
51. *Sunday Times*, 23 November 2008.
52. Gimson, Andrew. *Boris: The Rise of Boris Johnson*, Simon & Schuster, London, 2006, p. xiv.
53. *Ibid.*, p. 25.
54. *Ibid.*, p. 39.
55. Ibid., p. 35.
56. *Sunday Telegraph*, 18 May 2008.
57. Gimson, Andrew. *Boris: The Rise of Boris Johnson*, Simon & Schuster, London, 2006, pp. 35–36.
58. *Daily Telegraph*, 26 October 2009.

Chapter Two: 'Hey, Hey, ABJ'

1. *Sunday Times*, 11 May 2008.
2. *Sunday Times*, 29 January 2009.
3. *Daily Mail*, 24 January 2009.
4. Gimson, Andrew. *Boris: The Rise of Boris Johnson*, Simon & Schuster, London, 2006, p. 41.
5. *Ibid.*
6. *Ibid.*, p. 42.
7. *Ibid.*, p. 43.
8. *Ibid.*, p. 44.
9. *Ibid.*, p. 46.
10. *Chronicle*, 15 May 1982.
11. *Chronicle*, 12 December 1980
12. *Chronicle*, 16 October 1982
13. Sir James Darling, Geelong Grammar Website.
14. Corian, July and August 1985.
15. *The Times*, 18 February 2010.
16. *Marie Claire*, May 2008.
17. *GQ*, July 2007.
18. *Have I Got News For You*, Hat Trick Productions, 25 November 2005.

Chapter Three: Toffs, Tugs and Stains

1. Waugh, Evelyn. *Brideshead Revisited*, Penguin Books Ltd., London.
2. Johnson, Boris. *Have I Got Views For You*, Harper Perennial, London, 2006 and 2008, p. 34.
3. Private information.
4. Waugh, Evelyn. *Brideshead Revisited*, Penguin Books Ltd., London.
5. *Independent*, 26 April 2010.
6. *Independent*, 23 April 2010.
7. *Daily Telegraph*, 10 November 2005.
8. *When Boris Met Dave*, Channel 4/Blink Films, 2009.
9. Johnson, Boris. *Lend Me Your Ears*, Harper Perennial, London, 2004, p. 398.
10. Crick, Michael. *Michael Heseltine: A Biography*, Hamish Hamilton, London, 1997, p. 39.

11. Gimson, Andrew. *Boris: The Rise of Boris Johnson*, Simon & Schuster, London, 2006, p. 78.
12. *Isis*, January 1985.
13. Johnson, Boris. 'Politics' in Rachel Johnson (ed.). *The Oxford Myth*, Weidenfeld & Nicholson, London, 1988, p. 69.
14. *Ibid.*, p. 71.
15. Oxford Union Tapes.
16. Oxford Union Papers.
17. *Daily Telegraph*, 23 September 2004.
18. *Ibid.*
19. Feltz, Vanessa. BBC London Radio, 25 April 2008.

Chapter Four: World on Speed Dial

1. *Sunday Telegraph*, 1986.
2. *Isis*, June 1984
3. *Isis*, June 1984.
4. Gimson, Andrew. *Boris: The Rise of Boris Johnson*, Simon & Schuster, London, 2006, p. 90.
5. Johnson, Boris. *Lend Me Your Ears*, Harper Perennial, London, 2004, p. 6.
6. *Sunday Times*, 10 September 2006.
7. Johnson, Boris. *Lend Me Your Ears*, Harper Perennial, London, 2004, p. 6.
8. Elliott, Francis & Hanning, James. *Cameron: The Rise of the New Conservative*, Harper Perennial, London, 2007 and 2009, p. 334.
9. Hastings, Max. *Editor: An Inside Story of Newspapers*, Macmillan, London 2002, p. 273.
10. *Observer*, 30 March 2008.
11. *Daily Telegraph*, 12 January 2006.
12. *Daily Telegraph*, 5 July 2010.
13. *Daily Telegraph*, 8 June 2000.
14. *Guardian*, 29 July 1999.
15. *Vanity Fair*, April 2010.
16. Johnson, Boris. *Have I Got Views For You*, Harper Perennial, London 2006 and 2008, p. 46.
17. *Ibid.*, p. 19.
18. Johnson, Boris. *Lend Me Your Ears*, Harper Perennial, London, 2004, p. 70.
19. *Ibid.*, p. 66.
20. *Spectator*, 8 June 1991.
21. *Spectator*, 7 December 1991.
22. Johnson, Boris. *Lend Me Your Ears*, Harper Perennial, London, 2004, p. 112.
23. Law, Mark. *The Pyjama Game: A Journey Into Judo*, Aurum Press, London, 2007, p. 255.

Chapter Five: I Fought Delors . . . And I Won

1. *Daily Telegraph*, 8 May 1991.
2. Major, John. *The Autobiography*, HarperCollins, London, 1999, p. 265.
3. Johnson, Boris. *Lend Me Your Ears*, Harper Perennial, London, 2004, pp. 114 and 284.
4. *Daily Telegraph*, 30 March 2010.
5. *Daily Telegraph*, 15 September 2003.
6. *Desert Island Discs*, BBC Radio 4, 30 October 2005.
7. Major, John. *The Autobiography*, HarperCollins, London, 1999, p. 342.
8. Private information.
9. *Daily Telegraph*, 15 September 2003.
10. *Ibid.*
11. Grant, Charles. *Delors: Inside the House That Jacques Built*, Nicholas Brealey, London, 1994, p. 215.
12. Major, John. *The Autobiography*, HarperCollins, London, 1999, p. 348.
13. Gimson, Andrew. *Boris: The Rise of Boris Johnson*, Simon & Schuster, London, 2006, p. 109.
14. *Ibid.*, pp. 109–110.
15. *ES Magazine*, 29 February 2008.
16. *Daily Mail*, 11 May 2008.

17. Johnson, Boris. *Lend Me Your Ears*, Harper Perennial, London, 2004, p. 20.

Chapter Six: M'learned Wife

1. *Vanity Fair*, September 2004.
2. Johnson, Boris. *Friends, Voters, Countrymen*, Publisher?, Place?, Date?, p. 121.
3. *The Times*, 15 March 2008.
4. *Spectator*, 6 January 2001.
5. *Ibid.*, 16 August 2003.
6. *Ibid.*, 23 May 2007.
7. Johnson, Boris. *Lend Me Your Ears*, Harper Perennial, London, 2004, p. 20.
8. *Daily Telegraph*, 8 October 1997.
9. *Spectator*, 22 April 2009.
10. *Daily Telegraph*, 24 February 2009.
11. *Guardian*, 9 November 2007.
12. *Daily Mail*, 3 July 2008.
13. *Daily Telegraph*, 29 December 2006.

Chapter Seven: Untouchable

1. Johnson, Boris. *Lend Me Your Ears*, Harper Perennial, London, 2004, p. 17.
2. Lamont, Norman. *In Office*, Warner Books, London, 1999, p. 408.
3. Hastings, Max. *Editor*, Macmillan, London, 2002, p. 73.
4. Gimson, Andrew. *Boris: The Rise of Boris Johnson*, Simon & Schuster, London, 2006, p. 124.
5. *Scotland on Sunday*, 16 November 2003.
6. *ConservativeHome*, 24 June 2010.
7. *Daily Telegraph*, 16 February 1996.
8. *Ibid.*, 10 January 2002.
9. *Spectator*, 2 February 2002.
10. *Daily Telegraph*, 27 February 1995.
11. *Spectator*, 6 September 2003.
12. *Daily Telegraph*, 5 April 2001.
13. *Spectator*, 4 September 2004.
14. *Daily Telegraph*, 4 November 2004.
15. *Ibid.*, 2 November 1998.
16. *Ibid.*, 8 October 1997.
17. *Ibid.*, 25 May 2002.
18. *Ibid.*, 21 July 1997.
19. *Daily Telegraph*, 3 September 1997.
20. Ibid., 24 December 1998.
21. *Spectator,* 15 April 2000.
22. Johnson, Boris. *Life in the Fast Lane*, Harper Perennial, London, 2007, p. 260.
23. *Ibid.*, p. 26.
24. *Ibid.*, p. 239.
25. *Spectator*, 10 February 2001.
26. *Observer*, 30 March 2008.
27. Johnson, Boris. *Friends, Voters, Countrymen*, HarperCollins, London, 2002, p. 13.
28. *Daily Telegraph*, 8 November 2001.
29. *Sunday Times*, 16 July 2000.
30. *Week in Westminster*, BBC Radio 4, 5 May 2008.
31. Hastings, Max. *Editor*, Macmillan, London, 2002, p. 273.
32. London Focus, 30 April 2009.

Chapter Eight: 'Sack me!'

1. Johnson, Boris. *Friends, Voters, Countrymen*, HarperCollins, London, 2002, p. 4.
2. Audit Bureau of Circulations
3. *Spectator,* 11 January 2003.
4. *Independent*, 1 February 2001.
5. *Spectator*, 16 November 2002.
6. *Ibid.*, 11 January 2003.
7. *Ibid.*, 24 February 2001.
8. Barber, Lynn. 'Charmed, I'm sure', *Observer*, 5 October 2003.
9. *Mail on Sunday*, 2 February 2003.
10. *Spectator*, 17 December 2005.
11. *Evening Standard*, 14 December 2005.
12. *Spectator*, 3 June 2000.
13. *ES Magazine*, 15 July 2005.
14. *Ibid.*, 12 May 2001.

15. *Ibid.*, 16 November 2002.
16. *Ibid.*, 13 April 2002.
17. *Guardian*, 30 January 2006.
18. *Spectator*, 7 October 1999.
19. Johnson, Boris. *Friends, Voters, Countrymen*, HarperCollins, London, 2002, p. 16.
20. *Ibid.*, p. 12.
21. *Ibid.*, p. 13.
22. *Ibid.*
23. Johnson, Boris. *Friends, Voters, Countrymen*, HarperCollins, London, 2002, p. 46.
24. *Ibid.*, p. 32.
25. *Evening Standard*, 14 July 2000.
26. *Sunday Times*, 27 May 2001.
27. Johnson, Boris. *Friends, Voters, Countrymen*, HarperCollins, London, 2002, p. 235.
28. *Evening Standard*, 14 July 2000.
29. Johnson, Boris. *Friends, Voters, Countrymen*, HarperCollins, London, 2002, p. 236.

Chapter Nine: On Yer Bike!

1. Johnson, Boris. *Lend Me Your Ears*, Harper Perennial, London, 2004, p. 377.
2. Aldous, Richard. *The Lion and the Unicorn: Gladstone vs Disraeli*, Pimlico, London, 2007, p. 34.
3. *Daily Telegraph*, 27 May 2004.
4. *Sunday Times*, 15 December 2002.
5. *Ibid.*
6. GQ, May 2003.
7. *Independent*, 7 July 2002.
8. *Daily Telegraph*, 23 February 2002.
9. *Henley Standard*
10. *Henley Standard*, 7 May 2004.
11. *Daily Telegraph*, 11 March 2004.
12. *Henley Standard*
13. Johnson, Boris. *Friends, Voters, Countrymen*, HarperCollins, London, 2002, p. 24.
14. *Spectator*, 28 October 1995.
15. *Guardian*, 7 May 2004.
16. *Daily Mail*, 10 July 2004.
17. *Ibid.*, 20 December 2004.
18. *Vanity Fair*, February 2007.
19. *Spectator*, 24 January 2004.
20. *Ibid.*
21. *Spectator*, 18 September 2004.
22. *Ibid.*
23. Johnson, Boris. *Seventy-Two Virgins*, HarperCollins, London, 2005, p. 139.
24. *Ibid.*, p. 143.
25. *Evening Standard*, 10 September 2004.
26. *Vanity Fair*, September 2004.
27. *Spectator*, 16 October 2004.
28. *Ibid.*
29. *Guardian*, 16 October 2004.

Chapter Ten: 'Busting with spunk'

1. *Mail on Sunday*, 14 November 2004.
2. *Daily Telegraph*, 28 January 1998.
3. *Ibid.*, 2 December 2004.
4. *Independent*, 11 July 2005.
5. *New Statesman*, 22 November 2004.
6. *Sunday Times*, 21 November 2004.
7. *Evening Standard*, 28 February 2005.
8. *Henley Standard*, 23 December 2005.
9. *Evening Standard*, 15 July 2005.
10. *Independent*, 11 July 2005.
11. *Ibid.*
12. *Ibid.*

Chapter Eleven: 'Cynical self-interest', 2005–2007

1. *Daily Telegraph*, 6 October 2005.
2. *New Statesman*, 6 October 2005.
3. *Independent*, 22 November 2004.
4. *Daily Telegraph*, 9 February 2006.
5. Gimson, Andrew. *Boris: The Rise of Boris Johnson*, Simon & Schuster, London, 2006, p. 252.
6. *Evening Standard*, 5 April 2006.
7. *Independent*, 6 July 2006.
8. *Daily Telegraph*, 5 October 2006.

9. *Ibid.*, 15 October 2006.
10. Elliott, Francis & Hanning, James. *Cameron: The Rise of the New Conservative,* Harper Perennial, London, 2009, p. 337.
11. *Henley Standard*, 20 July 2007.

Chapter Twelve: Too Funny to be Mayor, 2007–2008

1. *Daily Telegraph*, 21 April 2007.
2. *Daily Telegraph*, 29 January 2004.
3. Lanson Public Affairs Agency research.

Chapter Thirteen: Sense of Wonderment

1. *Spectator*, 25 January 2003.

Chapter Fourteen: The Politics of Power

1. Blair, Sir Ian. *Policing Controversy*, Profile Books, London, 2009, pp. 270–271.
2. MGLA071008-0856 FOI Request.
3. *Guardian*, 6 October 2008.
4. *Independent*, 27 April 2009.
5. Blair, Sir Ian. *Policing Controversy*, Profile Books, London, 2009, pp. 273.
6. *Guardian*, 2 November 2009.
7. Guardian, 22 December 2008.
8. *Daily Mail*, 28 November 2009.
9. Standards Board Investigation by Jonathan Goolden, 24 February 2009.
10. Mayoral Question Time, 15 September 2010.
11. *Daily Telegraph*, 11 April 2010.
12. BBC Radio 4 *Today* programme, 7 July 2011.
13. *Guardian*, 1 May 2009.
14. *Guardian*, 30 April 2009.
15. *Evening Standard*, 24 February 2009.
16. *Guardian*, 1 May 2009.
17. *Newsweek*, 12 January 2009.
18. Tory Troll, 30 April 2009.
19. *Guardian*, 13 May 2009.
20. *Telegraph*, 3 June 2009.
21. ConservativeHome, 15 July 2009.
22. *Independent on Sunday*, 2 September 2010.
23. *Spectator*, 19 September 2009.
24. *Evening Standard*, 19 January 2010.
25. *Sunday Times*, 29 August 2010.
26. *Telegraph*, 6 September 2010.
27. *Telegraph*, 28 October 2010.

Epilogue:

1. YouGov/*New Statesman*, 21 June 2011.
2. *Independent*, 19 July 2011.
3. Mayor's Question Time, 25 March 2009.
4. *Observer*, Sunday, 4 April 2010.
5. Mayor's Question Time, 15 June 2011.
6. *The Times*, 9 April 2008.

Index